Social Development Models of Gang Involvement

This book—containing contributions from scholars who are well-known for their research on gangs, and selected as experts on the assigned topics—examines youth gangs from a developmental/life-course perspective, exploring a myriad of issues related to gang membership, its causes, its consequences, and various intervention efforts to both prevent gang membership and also reduce the problematic impact of gangs.

Beginning with research exploring the intergenerational continuity in gang membership and examining the causal processes leading to gang membership, the structure of the book reflects the developmental sequence of gang membership. The consequences of gang membership for youth are examined, as are intervention strategies. The book also presents the first conceptual framework on female gang involvement, taking into account the differences in the paths and roles that women and girls may take into the gang. The book concludes by exploring how gang membership affects job possibilities for young adults.

This book was originally published as a special issue of the *Journal of Crime and Justice*.

Marvin D. Krohn is a Professor in the Department of Sociology and Criminology & Law at the University of Florida, Gainesville, USA. He is primarily interested in developmental and life-course approaches to the explanation of delinquency, drug use, and crime. He is a Fellow of the American Society of Criminology.

James C. Howell is a Senior Research Associate with the National Gang Center, Tallahassee, USA. He is author of *The History of Street Gangs in the United States* (2015), and a textbook, *Gangs in America's Communities* (2019). His numerous other works on youth gangs include a developmental theory of gang involvement.

Social Development Models of Gang Involvement

Recent Contributions

Edited by
Marvin D. Krohn and James C. Howell

LONDON AND NEW YORK

First published 2019
by Routledge
2 Park Square, Milton Park, Abingdon, Oxon, OX14 4RN, UK

and by Routledge
52 Vanderbilt Avenue, New York, NY 10017, USA

Routledge is an imprint of the Taylor & Francis Group, an informa business

© 2019 Midwestern Criminal Justice Association

All rights reserved. No part of this book may be reprinted or reproduced or utilised in any form or by any electronic, mechanical, or other means, now known or hereafter invented, including photocopying and recording, or in any information storage or retrieval system, without permission in writing from the publishers.

Trademark notice: Product or corporate names may be trademarks or registered trademarks, and are used only for identification and explanation without intent to infringe.

British Library Cataloguing-in-Publication Data
A catalogue record for this book is available from the British Library

ISBN13: 978-1-138-49388-9

Typeset in Myriad Pro
by codeMantra

Publisher's Note
The publisher accepts responsibility for any inconsistencies that may have arisen during the conversion of this book from journal articles to book chapters, namely the possible inclusion of journal terminology.

Disclaimer
Every effort has been made to contact copyright holders for their permission to reprint material in this book. The publishers would be grateful to hear from any copyright holder who is not here acknowledged and will undertake to rectify any errors or omissions in future editions of this book.

Contents

Citation Information		vii
Notes on Contributors		ix
	Introduction Marvin D. Krohn and James C. Howell	1
1	Exploring intergenerational continuity in gang membership Megan Bears Augustyn, Jeffrey T. Ward and Marvin D. Krohn	7
2	Developmental pathways of youth gang membership: a structural test of the social development model Asia S. Bishop, Karl G. Hill, Amanda B. Gilman, James C. Howell, Richard F. Catalano and J. David Hawkins	30
3	Differentiating between delinquent groups and gangs: moving beyond offending consequences Dena C. Carson, Stephanie A. Wiley and Finn-Aage Esbensen	52
4	School transitions as a turning point for gang status Dena C. Carson, Chris Melde, Stephanie A. Wiley and Finn-Aage Esbensen	71
5	Leveraging the pushes and pulls of gang disengagement to improve gang intervention: findings from three multi-site studies and a review of relevant gang programs Caterina G. Roman, Scott H. Decker and David C. Pyrooz	92
6	Toward a multiracial feminist framework for understanding females' gang involvement Dana Peterson and Vanessa R. Panfil	113
7	The practical utility of a life-course gang theory for intervention James C. Howell, Margaret J. F. Braun and Paul Bellatty	134

CONTENTS

8 The labor market and gang membership in adulthood: is the availability, quality, and nature of legal work associated with adult gang involvement? 152
Adam M. Watkins

Index 171

Citation Information

The chapters in this book were originally published in the *Journal of Crime and Justice*, volume 40 (2017). When citing this material, please use the original page numbering for each article, as follows:

Chapter 1
Exploring intergenerational continuity in gang membership
Megan Bears Augustyn, Jeffrey T. Ward and Marvin D. Krohn
Journal of Crime and Justice, volume 40, issue 3 (September 2017) pp. 252–274

Chapter 2
Developmental pathways of youth gang membership: a structural test of the social development model
Asia S. Bishop, Karl G. Hill, Amanda B. Gilman, James C. Howell, Richard F. Catalano and J. David Hawkins
Journal of Crime and Justice, volume 40, issue 3 (September 2017) pp. 275–296

Chapter 3
Differentiating between delinquent groups and gangs: moving beyond offending consequences
Dena C. Carson, Stephanie A. Wiley and Finn-Aage Esbensen
Journal of Crime and Justice, volume 40, issue 3 (September 2017) pp. 297–315

Chapter 4
School transitions as a turning point for gang status
Dena C. Carson, Chris Melde, Stephanie A. Wiley and Finn-Aage Esbensen
Journal of Crime and Justice, volume 40, issue 4 (December 2017) pp. 396–416

Chapter 5
Leveraging the pushes and pulls of gang disengagement to improve gang intervention: findings from three multi-site studies and a review of relevant gang programs
Caterina G. Roman, Scott H. Decker and David C. Pyrooz
Journal of Crime and Justice, volume 40, issue 3 (September 2017) pp. 316–336

Chapter 6
Toward a multiracial feminist framework for understanding females' gang involvement
Dana Peterson and Vanessa R. Panfil
Journal of Crime and Justice, volume 40, issue 3 (September 2017) pp. 337–357

CITATION INFORMATION

Chapter 7
The practical utility of a life-course gang theory for intervention
James C. (Buddy) Howell, Margaret J. F. Braun and Paul Bellatty
Journal of Crime and Justice, volume 40, issue 3 (September 2017) pp. 358–375

Chapter 8
The labor market and gang membership in adulthood: is the availability, quality, and nature of legal work associated with adult gang involvement?
Adam M. Watkins
Journal of Crime and Justice, volume 40, issue 3 (September 2017) pp. 376–394

For any permission-related enquiries please visit:
http://www.tandfonline.com/page/help/permissions

Notes on Contributors

Megan Bears Augustyn is an Assistant Professor in the Department of Criminal Justice at the University of Texas at San Antonio, USA. Her research focuses on the causes and consequences of crime and victimization across the life course and legal socialization.

Paul Bellatty is the Manager of the Research Unit within the Oregon Youth Authority Director's Office, USA. His interests include juvenile delinquency and gang research, data analytics, machine learning, and matching off ender characteristics with evidence-based programs.

Asia S. Bishop is a Research Analyst Lead in Public Behavioral Health and Justice Policy at the University of Washington, Seattle, USA. Her work and research focus on juvenile justice reform policy and evaluation.

Margaret J. F. Braun is a Research Scientist for Program Design and Evaluation Services, an interagency research and program evaluation unit within Multnomah County Health Department and Oregon Health Authority, USA. Her research interests include linked datasets, social determinants of health and behavior, and pathways to the criminal justice system

Dena C. Carson is an Assistant Professor in the School of Public and Environmental Affairs at Indiana University – Purdue University Indianapolis, USA. Her research interests include youth violence, victimization, gangs, and delinquent peer groups.

Richard F. Catalano is a Professor in the School of Social Work at the University of Washington, Seattle, USA, where he is also the Co-Founder of the Social Development Research Group. His work focuses on discovering risk and protective factors for behavioral health problems, designing and evaluating programs to address these factors, and using this knowledge to understand and improve prevention service systems in states and communities.

Scott H. Decker is a Foundation Professor of Criminology and Criminal Justice at Arizona State University, Tempe, USA. His research interests are in gangs and the relationship among policy, research, and theory.

Finn-Aage Esbensen is a Professor of Youth Crime and Violence in the Department of Criminology and Criminal Justice at the University of Missouri–St. Louis, USA. His research has covered a broad spectrum of methodologies and topics from participant observation in a county jail to conducting longitudinal national surveys of adolescents.

NOTES ON CONTRIBUTORS

Amanda B. Gilman is a Senior Research Associate at the Washington State Center for Court Research, USA. Her research looks at the role of detention and detention alternatives in the juvenile justice system, evidence-based practice, and gang prevention.

J. David Hawkins is the Endowed Professor of Prevention Emeritus, and Founding Director of the Social Development Research Group, at the University of Washington, Seattle, USA. His research focuses on understanding and preventing child and adolescent health and behavior problems.

Karl G. Hill is the Director of the Program on Problem Behavior and Positive Youth Development and a Professor of Psychology and Neuroscience at the University of Colorado Boulder, USA. His work asks what are the optimal family, peer, school, and community environments that encourage healthy youth and adult development; and how do we work with communities to make this happen?

James C. Howell is a Senior Research Associate with the National Gang Center, Tallahassee, USA. He is author of *The History of Street Gangs in the United States* (2015), and a textbook, *Gangs in America's Communities* (2019). His numerous other works on youth gangs include a developmental theory of gang involvement.

Marvin D. Krohn is a Professor in the Department of Sociology and Criminology & Law at the University of Florida, Gainesville, USA. He is primarily interested in developmental and life-course approaches to the explanation of delinquency, drug use, and crime. He is a Fellow of the American Society of Criminology.

Chris Melde is the Director of Graduate Studies and an Associate Professor in the School of Criminal Justice at Michigan State University, East Lansing, USA. His research interests include street gangs, youth violence, adolescent development, individual and community reactions to crime and victimization risk, and program evaluation.

Vanessa R. Panfil is an Assistant Professor of Sociology and Criminal Justice at Old Dominion University, Norfolk, USA. Her work explores how intersections of gender and sexuality structure individuals' experiences with gangs, crime, victimization, and the criminal and juvenile justice systems.

Dana Peterson is an Associate Professor in the School of Criminal Justice at the University at Albany, USA. She is particularly interested in the debate over whether gender-specific or gender-neutral theories of and responses to delinquency and youth gangs are necessary, as well as in the ways that gender structures delinquency and gang involvement.

David C. Pyrooz is an Assistant Professor of Sociology at the University of Colorado Boulder, USA. His research interests include gangs and criminal networks, incarceration and offender reentry, crime trends and life-course criminology, and criminal justice policy and practice.

Caterina G. Roman is an Associate Professor in the Department of Criminal Justice at Temple University, Philadelphia, USA. Her research interests include the social networks of gang members and high-risk youth; the relationship among neighborhood characteristics, fear, violence, and health; and the evaluation of violence reduction programs.

NOTES ON CONTRIBUTORS

Jeffrey T. Ward is an Associate Professor in the Department of Criminal Justice at Temple University, Philadelphia, USA. His areas of research include developmental and life-course criminology, juvenile delinquency, and measurement.

Adam M. Watkins is an Associate Professor of Criminal Justice at Bowling Green State University, USA. His primary research interests include youth gang membership, program evaluation, gun violence, and victim and bystander responses to crime.

Stephanie A. Wiley is an Assistant Professor in the School of Criminology at Simon Fraser University, Burnaby, Canada. Her research interests include the effects of sanctions on delinquent attitudes and behavior, quantitative methods, and developmental criminology.

Introduction

Marvin D. Krohn and James C. Howell

It is increasingly evident that to achieve a comprehensive understanding of the impetus to join gangs, the immediate impact of gangs on criminal and noncriminal attitudes and behaviors, and the longer-term consequences of gang membership, it would be advantageous to apply a developmental life-course lens (Dong, Gibson, and Krohn, 2015; Howell and Griffiths, 2019). Several early risk factors for later gang joining have been identified, suggesting that the process of entering a gang begins in childhood, and progresses through the school entry, childhood, and adolescent developmental stages (Howell and Egley, 2005; Raby and Jones, 2016).

Proximal factors such as school and peer-related variables are important correlates of gang membership. Being in a gang has an immediate impact on criminal behavior, which in turn increases the probability of off-time transitions (in a normative sense) such as dropping out of school, teenage fatherhood and pregnancy, and cohabitation prior to completing one's education (Thornberry et al., 2003). The problematic consequences of gang membership have a cascading effect on youth, decreasing the probability of a successful transition into adulthood, even for youths who desist from gang activities (Krohn et al., 2011; Gilman, Hill, and Hawkins, 2014).

The importance of the developmental life-course perspective is certainly not exclusive to the study of gangs. Indeed, Cullen (2011) identified the perspective as one of the most important theoretical and analytical developments in the study of crime and called for its increasing use. The developmental perspective was introduced to social science through the work of Elder (1994). He created a conceptual vocabulary to describe how intraindividual change through the course of one's life could be examined in terms of trajectories (e.g. education, relationships, employment) representing different aspects of a person's life. The life-course perspective emphasizes how these trajectories are intertwined so that a development in one trajectory will influence another; as one example, the education trajectory influences the employment trajectory (Thornberry and Krohn, 2005). As persons traverse trajectories, they go through transitions, some of which may lead to continuance along a similar advantageous path (high school graduation), and others may well alter their path. The timing of the trajectories may be important, as off-time transitions may have problematic consequences for the life course (e.g. an unexpected pregnancy). Transitions that are particularly significant in terms of their consequences are considered 'turning points' (Sampson and Laub, 1993). Joining a gang can be considered a turning point, and gang involvement can be conceptualized in terms of a trajectory.

Over the past 20 years, scholars have examined gang involvement and its consequences through the lens of the developmental and life-course perspective. Theoretically, Sampson and Laub's age graded theory (1993), Hawkins et al.'s Social Development Theory (Catalano and Hawkins, 1996), and Thornberry and Krohn's Interactional Theory (Thornberry et al., 2003; Thornberry and Krohn, 2005; Dong, Gibson, and Krohn, 2015) have all been used to examine various aspects of gang involvement. Importantly, research has established the salient risk and protective factors involved in gang involvement (Esbensen and Huizinga, 1993; Hill et al., 1999; Thornberry et al., 2003; Howell and Egley, 2005; Esbensen et al., 2010). Howell and Egley (2005) codified risk factors leading to gang involvement that had been substantiated in prospective longitudinal studies, and then used their review to generate a general developmental theory of gang involvement. While each developmental perspective is different on certain aspects of the process, they are in agreement on the importance of focusing on the entire life course as the path to understanding the causes, correlates, and consequences of gang membership.

Recent research on gang participation reflects widespread adoption of a life-course perspective. Early developmental periods have been examined to determine the precursors of gang membership. Of course, the importance of the teenage years has been emphasized as family relationships and parenting strategies, peers and their behavior, and attitudes and behaviors in school figure prominently in gang membership and continuation or desistence from the gang (Craig et al., 2002; Thornberry et al., 2003; Howell and Egley, 2005). The implications for criminal behavior of joining a gang and the subsequent difficulties gang membership and criminal behavior have for transitions to adulthood have been examined (Krohn et al., 2011; Gilman, Hill, and Hawkins, 2014). Recently, significant work on how and why gang members desist from gang involvement has been the focus of both theoretical development and empirical research (Pyrooz and Decker, 2011; Decker, Pyrooz, and Moule, 2014).

Although significant strides have been made in understanding gang involvement and its consequences, there is much that we do not understand about the implications of gang involvement for the life course and, vice versa, the implications of the life-course issues for gang involvement. We asked the authors of the articles that appear in this volume to view gang involvement from a life-course perspective. For the most part, they did so in this collection of articles that address gang involvement from the very early influence of developmental factors that led to joining a gang in childhood onward through desistance. Several of the articles add the ever-important practical implications of their findings suggesting research-supported strategies to either prevent gang involvement, or minimize the impact of it on life-course outcomes. To the extent possible, we have arrayed these articles in a sequence that corresponds with the life-course stage that they address.

The exploration of gangs throughout the life course in this volume begins with an examination of the intergenerational continuity in gang membership (Augustyn, Ward, and Krohn). Augustyn et al. take advantage of the intergenerational prospective research design of the Rochester Youth Development Study data and the Rochester Intergenerational Study to examine how parental membership in a gang affects the probability that their children will also be in a gang. The authors examine 371 parent–child dyads and find that intergenerational continuity in gang membership is gender-specific. Mothers' gang membership directly increases the probability of their daughters' gang membership. For boys and their fathers, continuity is dependent on whether the father and son are in sufficient contact. The authors also examined characteristics of parenting that may mediate the relationship between parental gang membership, and that of their children. None of the parenting variables mediated the relationship between mothers' gang involvement and daughters'. The relationship between fathers' membership and that of their sons was mediated by parental maltreatment. This is a critical first step in establishing the intergenerational relationship of gang membership as it identifies the importance of gender-specific effects and, in the case of fathers and sons, the level of contact they have. The fact that few mediating effects were observed would suggest this is an avenue for future research to explore more thoroughly.

The chapter by Bishop, Hill, Gilman, et al. moves us along the development process by focusing on the factors that may lead to gang membership during the teenage years. Using data from the Seattle Social Development Project, the study examines 808 students when they were 13, 14, and 16 years old. The theoretical framework for the structural equation model estimated was the Social Development Model (SDM), a developmental theory that integrates processes identified in social learning theory, social control theory, and differential association theory, specifying both pro- and antisocial developmental pathways. Although the results are much too complex to review in this brief introduction, the overall conclusion is that the model performs well for the purpose of predicting gang membership. As the authors note, the SDM was developed to guide preventive interventions. Hence, the article concludes with rather specific implications for prevention policy, highlighting the role that prosocial skills, prosocial socialization, and prosocial opportunities play in predicting gang membership.

The question of whether gangs are simply the high end of a continuum of involvement in delinquent youth groups or whether they represent something synergistic, making them qualitatively different from delinquent groups, is addressed in the chapter by Carson, Wiley, and Esbensen. The authors use Bandura's (2002) social cognitive theory to explore potential differences between gangs and delinquent youth groups and 'typical youth groups'. They suggest that because individuals' actions and cognitions cannot be separated from social influences, the impact of gang membership should be seen in attitudes such as guilt, empathy, self-centeredness, and hitting neutralization; interactional dimensions such as negative peer commitment, prosocial peers, and school commitment; and behaviors such as nonviolent and violent delinquent behavior. Their results provide mixed support for the perspective. Importantly, gang members are less committed to school than delinquent group members and participate in more violent behavior.

In the subsequent chapter, Carson, Melde, Wiley, et al. focus on a potentially important turning point in youths' lives—school transitions. Using a mixed-methods approach, they examine both qualitative and quantitative data from the G.R.E.A.T. evaluation to determine how moving from one school to another may affect gang membership status. School transitions included both the move from middle school to high school and the moves from one school to another. Neither the qualitative nor quantitative data analysis demonstrated that moving from one school to another increased the probability of joining a gang. However, interviews with former gang members suggested that moving from one school to another facilitated the 'knifing off' from peers who were also in the gang. In addition, moving to a new school allowed for a period of self-reflection. The quantitative analysis presented more mixed results. Normative school transition increased the probability of gang desistance; however, nonnormative transition did not. In addition, school transition impacted factors associated with a turning point such as prosocial peers' school commitment and anger identity. In brief, Carson et al.'s study highlights the need to be cognizant of significant transitions in a youth's life, even those that are expected such as the move from middle school to high school. Such transitions may afford an opportunity for intervention to enhance youths' opportunity to establish prosocial ties and decrease attitudes conducive to violence.

Given that research has shown that even the most deeply embedded gang members can succeed in disengaging from their gang (Decker, Pyrooz, and Moule, 2014), Roman, Decker, and Pyrooz set out to identify specific times and events in the life course of gang membership and criminal involvement that are most salient for intervention—as revealed in their careful review of three large studies of gang disengagement. Importantly, they find that 'push' factors (those that relate to attractive aspects of gang membership that are internal to the gang) exceed the influence of 'pull' factors that are external to the gang, both in prevalence and frequency. In addition, they suggest that new prosocial roles can be used to leverage desistance from gang membership.

From our viewpoint, desistance-promoting enterprises could benefit from the guidance provided by the very broad Interactional Model (Thornberry and Krohn, 2005) that draws attention to several interacting domains that can account for life-course patterns of gang career onset, course length and shape, and desistance.

> While desistance can occur suddenly, as when an addict quits cold turkey, the more typical pattern is a gradual movement away from off ending as the person's environmental and interactional patterns change. Thus [one should not] anticipate sharp turning points that quickly deflect off ending trajectories from high levels to zero.
> (Thornberry, 2005, 161)

Peterson and Panfil valiantly accept the formidable challenge of laying the groundwork for the first developmental female gang theory in their chapter. Each of the life-course gang theories to date (including each of those published in the present collection) is presumed to apply to both genders;

however, the samples on which they are based are overwhelmingly comprised of males. Peterson and Panfil explicitly draw upon existing gang theories along with research on gendered pathways to construct a unified framework for understanding females' gang involvement. Of course, the benchmark in this enterprise is the development of a conceptual framework that would generate hypotheses distinct from those that we see in theories based on male gang members; and thereby, distinguish a unique explanation for girls' gang joining. The authors have succeeded in this endeavor, although Peterson and Panfil explicitly caution readers that their offering is not an explicit theory; rather, they present a 'unified conceptual framework', one grounded in multiracial feminism that suggests the primary components of an integrated, life-course framework.

Howell, Braun, and Bellatty explore the practical utility of applying an existing developmental life-course gang theory to a statewide juvenile justice system, with the aim in mind of guiding early intervention strategies. Of course, a key finding from longitudinal studies of gang involvement—and numerous other adolescent problem behaviors for that matter—is the presence of risk factors in multiple interactional developmental domains—including individual, family, peer, school, and neighborhood experiences (Hill et al., 1999; Thornberry et al., 2003). Juvenile justice system involvement is a common stage in the life course of adolescent gang members, thus the chosen research setting, the Oregon Youth Authority (OYA), provided an opportunity to explore the practical application of Howell and Egley's (2005) life-course developmental model of gang involvement. Given that Raby and Jones' (2016) systematic review of risk factors for gang joining drawn from longitudinal studies generally substantiates Howell and Egley's four developmental age periods (preschool, school entry, childhood, and adolescence), the research team explored the possibility of tailoring existing rehabilitation programs and services to multiple risk factors and treatment needs of young gang members who were actively involved in juvenile delinquency and court-referred to the OYA. The researchers analyzed data that were recorded of juvenile offenders who either were on probation or confined in the OYA; and, in addition, extracted data on this offender group and their families in 'feeder' systems (i.e. welfare, mental health treatment, alcohol and drug treatment, foster care, Child Protective Services, and education). This research suggests that gang involvement can be routinely addressed within a comprehensive array of treatment and rehabilitation programs aimed at reducing the total volume of serious, violent, and chronic juvenile delinquency.

Adam Watkins' article uniquely focuses on a key developmental opportunity for desisting ex-gang members: employment. He carries out a rigorous analysis of the availability of legal work opportunities in 133 large cities plagued with chronic gang problems as reported in the National Youth Gang Survey. Watkins' research makes a very important contribution to prior studies in this arena by finding support for measuring labor market conditions beyond simply the availability of work (e.g. rate of unemployment), such as measures of the quality (e.g. extent of full-time employment) and the nature of work (e.g. degree of employment in service occupations). The modest gains that Watkins reports should not be dismissed out of hand because successful employment of gang adolescents and adults may help reduce crime and perhaps promote desistance. In Spergel's (2007) evaluation of the effects of the Little Village Project on hardcore gang youth, members of the targeted gangs generally improved their educational and employment status during the program period, and employment was associated with a general reduction in youth's criminal activity, especially with regard to reductions in drug dealing.

However, preparing hardcore gang youth for employment and linking them with conventional jobs is no easy task. The founder of Homeboy Industries in the center of multiple gang territories in East Los Angeles, Father Greg Boyle, publicly expresses regret about the initial mantra he developed in the early years for the purpose of garnishing public support and drawing in financial contributions: 'Nothing stops a bullet like a job'. Father Boyle soon learned that hardcore gang youth who grew up in an area in which several gangs had sheltered youngsters for at least a half century—if they even survived— were by no means ready for job training, much less employment (Boyle, 2011). Thus, he built an incremental job-training program, coupled with mental health and substance abuse treatment, along with a variety of other social development services and supports that first must be provided to prepare youth for the world of work. One program, the Comprehensive Gang Program Model, has hastened gang disengagement, and reductions in youth's level of gang affiliation were associated with lower violence and drug arrests (Spergel, Wa, and Sosa, 2006).

The task of first understanding the developmental processes that lead to membership in a gang and the consequences of taking such a path is a complex one. Applying that understanding to the design of prevention and desistance programs and implementing those programs with a sufficient degree of fidelity to the acquired understanding presents an even greater challenge. The developmental and life-course approach provides the conceptual tools to address these complex issues. As an example, in a controlled study, a gang-adapted version of Functional Family Therapy, outcomes favored the FFT-G cases, and the magnitude of some of the differences was large (Thornberry et al., In Press).

The chapters in this issue continue the exploration of the causes and consequences of gang membership as well as the implications of the research for both the prevention of gang membership and either encouraging desistance from gang activities or, at least, buffering the effects of such activities on the life course. The chapters cover a lot of ground as they examine the intergenerational continuity in gang membership, the impact of anti- and prosocial influences on gang membership, the importance of specific transitions during the life course such as the change in schools and the importance of the quality of employment, and how many of these factors specifically impact those who are female and of color. In addition, the implications of a theoretical understanding of the causes of gang membership, many of which are developmentally specific, that suggest programs to address gang membership have also been examined.

As the editors of this volume, we hope that the compilation of research studies will stimulate a continued interest in the developmental and life-course approach to the study of gang membership. There are, of course, a myriad other issue we need to understand about the causes, consequences, and effective prevention and treatment of gang membership. We trust that the general conceptual approach represented in these articles will serve future explorations into these issues as well.

References

Boyle, G. 2011. *Tattoos on the Heart: The Power of Boundless Compassion*. New York: Free Press.

Catalano, R. F., and J. D. Hawkins. 1996. "The Social Development Model: A Theory of Antisocial Behavior". In *Delinquency and Crime: Current Theories*, edited by J. D. Hawkins, 149–197. New York: Cambridge University Press.

Craig, W. M., F. Vitaro, Laude Gagnon, and R. E. Tremblay. 2002. "The Road to Gang Membership: Characteristics of Male Gang and Nongang Members from Ages 10 to 14" *Social Development* 11: 53–68.

Cullen, F. T. 2011. "Beyond Adolescence-limited Criminology: Choosing Our Future. American Society of Criminology 2010 Sutherland Address" *Criminology* 49: 287–330.

Decker, S. H., D. C. Pyrooz, and R. K. Moule. 2014. "Disengagement From Gangs as Role Transitions" *Journal of Research on Adolescence* 24: 268–283.

Dong, B., C. L. Gibson, and M. D. Krohn. 2015. "Gangs in a Developmental and Life-course Perspective." In *The Handbook of Gangs*, edited by S. H. Decker and D. C. Pyrooz, 78–97. Hoboken, MA: Wiley.

Elder, G. H. 1994. "Time, Human Agency, and Social Change: Perspectives on the Life Course." *Social Psychology Quarterly* 57: 4–15.

Esbensen, F., and D. Huizinga. 1993. "Gangs, Drugs, and Delinquency in a Survey of Urban Youth." *Criminology* 31: 565–589.

Esbensen, F., D. Peterson, T. J. Taylor, and A. Freng. 2010. *Youth Violence: Sex and Race Differences in Offending, Victimization, and Gang Membership*. Philadelphia, PA: Temple University Press.

Gilman, A., K. G. Hill, and J. D. Hawkins. 2014. "Long-term Consequences of Adolescent Gang Membership for Adult Functioning." *Journal of Public Health* 104: 938–945.

Hill, K. G., J. C. Howell, J. D. Hawkins, and S. R. Battin-Pearson. 1999. "Childhood Risk Factors for Adolescent Gang Membership: Results from the Seattle Social Development Project." *Journal of Research in Crime and Delinquency* 36: 300–322.

Howell, J. C., and A. Egley Jr. 2005. "Moving Risk Factors into Developmental Theories of Gang Membership." *Youth Violence and Juvenile Justice* 3: 334–354.

Howell, J. C., and E. Griffiths. Forthcoming. *Gangs in America's Communities*. 3rd ed. Thousand Oaks, CA: Sage.

Krohn, M. D., J. T. Ward, T. P. Thornberry, A. Lizotte, and R. Chu. 2011. "The Cascading Effects of Adolescent Gang Involvement Across the Life Course." *Criminology* 49: 991–1028.

Pyrooz, D. C., and S. H. Decker. 2011. "Motives and Methods for Leaving the Gang: Understanding the Process of Gang Desistance." *Journal of Criminal Justice* 39: 417–425.

Raby, C., and F. Jones. 2016. "Identifying Risks for Male Street Gang Affiliation: A Systematic Review and Narrative Synthesis." *The Journal of Forensic Psychiatry & Psychology* 27: 601–644.

Sampson, R. J., and J. H. Laub. 1993. *Crime in the Making: Pathways and Turning Points Through Life*. Cambridge, MA: Harvard University Press.

Spergel, I. A. 2007. *Reducing Youth Gang Violence: The Little Village Gang Project in Chicago*. Lanham, MD: AltaMira Press.

Spergel, I. A., K. M. Wa, and R. V. Sosa. 2006. "The Comprehensive, Community-wide, Gang Program Model: Success and Failure." In *Studying Youth Gangs*, edited by J. F. Short and L. A. Hughes, 203–224. Lanham, MD: AltaMira Press.

Thornberry, T. P. 2005. "Explaining Multiple Patterns of Offending Across the Life Course and Across Generations." *The ANNALS of the American Academy of Political and Social Science* 602: 156–195.

Thornberry, T. P., Kearley, B., Gottfredson, D. C., Slothower, M., Devlin, D., and Fader, J. J. (In press). "Reducing Crime among Youth at Risk for Gang Involvement: A Randomized Trial". *Criminology and Public Policy*.

Thornberry, T. P., and M. D. Krohn. 2005. "Applying Interactional Theory to the Explanation of Continuity and Change in Antisocial Behavior." In *Integrated Developmental Life-course Theories of Offending*, edited by D. P. Farrington, 183–210. New Brunswick, NJ: Transaction Publishing'.

Thornberry, T. P., M. D. Krohn, A. J. Lizotte, C. A. Smith, and K. Tobin. 2003. *Gangs and Delinquency in Developmental Perspective*. New York: Cambridge University Press.

Exploring intergenerational continuity in gang membership

Megan Bears Augustyn, Jeffrey T. Ward and Marvin D. Krohn

ABSTRACT
Little is known regarding intergenerational continuity in gang membership. Qualitative literature is suggestive of intergenerational parallelism yet no known research examines the causal mechanisms associated with this cycle, if it even exists. Prospective, longitudinal data from the Rochester Youth Development Study (RYDS) and the Rochester Intergenerational Study (RIGS) assess intergenerational continuity in gang membership among 371 parent–child dyads in a series of logistic regressions accounting for moderating influences of parent sex, child sex, parent–child sex combinations, and level of contact. Path analyses reported herein explore whether parenting behaviors mediate the relationship between parent and child gang membership among fathers and mothers, respectively. Three key findings emerge. First, intergenerational continuity in gang membership exists between mothers and daughters and, conditional on contact, between fathers and sons. Second, maltreatment mediates some of this relationship among father–son dyads. Third, no pathways to daughter gang membership were identified among mothers. In sum, this study provides evidence of intergenerational continuity in gang membership and further highlights the importance of parent sex, child sex, and level of contact in intergenerational research. Future research should further explore the causal pathways between parent and child gang membership.

Little is known about intergenerational continuity in gang membership, including whether or not the cycle of gang membership even exists (Dong, Gibson, and Krohn 2015). By in large, qualitative research suggests that intergenerational parallelism in gang membership exists, but these studies are limited to locales with longstanding gang problems resulting from migration/immigration (e.g., Los Angeles and Chicago) and utilize respondent reports of past generation participation (Moore et al. 1978; Horowitz 1983; Vigil 1988). Unfortunately, reliance upon this type of research as evidence for a cycle of gang membership is potentially problematic from validity and generalizeability standpoints.

Recognizing the limitations in extant literature, this research assesses intergenerational continuity in gang membership using data from a jurisdiction with an emergent gang problem at the time of measurement for parental gang membership (i.e., 30 years ago). We believe the focus on this jurisdiction is advantageous from a generalizeability standpoint for two reasons. First, the type of gang classification (i.e., emergent problem) in this city is similar to the majority of locales with gang problems in the United States (Howell, Egley, and Gleason 2002; Howell 2015). Second, gang membership in this location taps into participation in criminal organizations that formed on the street and operate in neighborhoods without known leadership beyond one's community, and it is these types of gangs that pose the most significant threat to communities (National Gang Intelligence Center 2015). As a result, this research speaks to the cycle of gang membership in a broader perspective (i.e., not limited to cities with culturally entrenched gangs). We also determine whether or not the cycle of gang membership exists in accordance with methodological criteria necessary to establish intergenerational continuity (Ertem, Leventhal, and Dobbs 2000; Thornberry, Knight, and Lovegrove 2012). Specifically, prospective, longitudinal data from two generations are used to assess self-reported gang membership in the focal generation (children) and parent generation. Moreover, the data cover overlapping periods of the life course when gang membership is prominent (ages 13–17) in order to more definitively assess continuity in gang participation. Finally, we draw upon extant literature regarding intergenerational continuity, in general, and assess continuity across parent sex, child sex, parent and child sex combinations, and level of contact in order to speak to the scope of intergenerational continuity in gang membership.

The question of whether or not intergenerational continuity in gang membership exists and the scope of that continuity are important because, if this cycle does exist, the results have significant implications for targeted prevention strategies among the children of former gang members. However, equally important is the identification of the mechanisms that account for intergenerational continuity and lead to intergenerational transmission of behavior. This information is particularly useful, as it can provide targeted goals for prevention programs aiming to reduce gang participation. Therefore, this research also takes advantage of the richness of the Rochester Youth Development Study and the Rochester Intergenerational Study data and explores potential indirect mechanisms that may link parental gang membership to subsequent participation in gangs by one's child.

As a starting point, we briefly review what is known about intergenerational continuity in gang membership. Given the limited information, we then draw upon interactional theory which would suggest the cycle of gang membership likely exists. In particular, we adopt a life course perspective and highlight the consequences of gang membership that are likely to link parental gang membership to child gang membership. We then focus on parenting behaviors as an intervening mechanism that may perpetuate the cycle of gang membership given the importance of the family domain to the notion of linked lives and its prominence in developmental theories of gang behavior (Thornberry, Freeman-Gallant, et al. 2003; Howell and Egley 2005).

Intergenerational gang membership

Intergenerational continuity of maladaptive behaviors refers to the basic idea that children will end up like their parents in one or more problematic ways. Thornberry and colleagues (2003) distinguish intergenerational continuity from intergenerational transmission, the latter of which refers to present consequences for children due to current parent behaviors and circumstances. A particularly important distinction is that intergenerational continuity refers to parallelism in behavior during the same period of the life course across generations. Evaluations of intergenerational continuity in maladaptive behaviors span a wide range of antisocial behaviors including substance use (Velleman 1992; Capaldi et al. 2003; Pears, Capaldi, and Owen 2007; Knight, Menard, and Simmons 2014), arrests and convictions (Farrington, Coid, and Murray 2009; Van de Rakt et al. 2010; Miller and Barnes 2013; Besemer, Axelsson, and Sarnecki 2016), and conduct problems and antisocial behavior (Thornberry, Freeman-Gallant, et al. 2003; Junger et al. 2013; Raudino et al. 2013), to name a few. However, literature regarding intergenerational continuity in gang membership is scarce and exclusively qualitative in nature.

In his assessment of Chicano gangs in Los Angeles, Vigil (1988, 2002) notes a tradition of gang membership in Chicano culture and invokes the notion of intergenerational influences on gang participation among Chicano youth. Similarly, Moore and colleagues (1978) underscore the importance of intergenerational influences as current adult gang members passed along the culture of gang membership within Mexican-American neighborhoods in East Los Angeles. Horowitz (1983) also proposed an intergenerational aspect to gangs as membership was a form of honor passed down through Chicano culture in her research examining the Lions gang in Chicago. Taking note of extant research, Huff (2001) argues that intergenerational continuity in gang membership is probably more common in cities with longstanding gang problems that are tied to ethnic and cultural identity resulting from immigration or migration. Nevertheless, given the shortage of research, we are far from being able to make a conclusive statement regarding the existence of a cycle of gang membership.

In contrast to the ethnographic studies of Vigil (1988, 2002), Moore and colleagues (1978), and Horowitz (1983), Decker and van Winkle (1996) found little evidence of an intergenerational character to gang membership in St. Louis ($n = 232$) in their research conducted in the late 1990s. Among interviewed gang members, only nine individuals reported ($n = 13$) reported that one of their parents was previously in a gang, and many parents who participated in gangs did so in a different city (e.g., Chicago versus St. Louis). Over 80% of their sample, on the other hand, indicated that they were unsure as to whether or not a parent was in a gang or they indicated that their parents were not gang members, which suggests a lack of continuity in gang membership predominates. However, this lack of evidence of intergenerational continuity in gang membership may be tied to the emergent nature of gangs in St. Louis in the last two decades of the twentieth century. As we have now eclipsed the third era of gang membership and growth (Howell 2015), the time is ripe to further explore intergenerational continuity in gang membership outside of specific cities with culturally entrenched gangs, as street-based gangs, that make up the third era of gang membership and growth has continued to proliferate over the past 30 years in the majority of cities with gang problems (National Gang Intelligence Center 2015). We now discuss the theoretical foundations regarding why we would expect to see intergenerational continuity in gang membership, particularly in locations where specific gangs are not deeply ingrained in the city's culture and history.

Theoretical foundations for intergenerational continuity

Developmental and life course theories have been extended to explain how what occurred and is occurring in the lives of one generation affect what happens in the lives of the next generation (Capaldi et al. 2003; Conger et al. 2003; Thornberry 2005; Thornberry 2009; Kaplan and Tolle 2006). The current research is premised on the application of interactional theory (Thornberry 1987; Thornberry and Krohn 2001, 2005) to intergenerational continuity (Thornberry 2005; Thornberry, Krohn, and Freeman-Gallant 2006). Interactional theory is particularly appropriate for the examination of intergenerational continuity because one of its key assumptions is the importance of the consequences of delinquent behavior not only in the lives of one generation but also in the lives of the next. Moreover, the theory recognizes the importance of the degree of involvement in delinquent activity so that the more embedded the person is in delinquent behavior, the more problematic the consequences will be and the greater the risk of intergenerational continuity (Thornberry 2005). Gang membership represents a high degree of embeddedness in a delinquent lifestyle (Hagan 1997; Krohn et al. 2011) and therefore the consequences should be problematic both for the one generation and their offspring.

Interactional theory suggests that involvement in serious delinquency will have negative impacts on the ability of individuals to successfully make the transition to adult statuses. In turn, less successful transitions increase the risk of experiencing structural adversity such as difficulty in completing an education and obtaining a career-oriented job. These deficits increase structural adversity, stress, and create the conditions for a greater likelihood of the continuity in deviant behavior among the next generation. Moreover, these problems combine to adversely affect partner relationships. In tandem, the aforementioned consequences arising from involvement in serious delinquency in one generation jeopardize effective parenting of the next generation. Thornberry (2005, 183) asserts that parenting style '…is likely to be the most powerful and proximate influence mediating the effect' of prior antisocial behavior and its consequences on the antisocial behavior of children. While the theory recognizes that some of the effects of parental involvement in delinquent and criminal behavior directly relate to antisocial behavior among children because parents can serve as role models providing the child with both antisocial norms and reinforcements for deviant behavior, it hypothesizes that '…the dominant pathway is indirect, mediated by family processes like family conflict, hostility and especially by the quality of parenting' (Thornberry 2005, 183).[1]

Our examination of the intergenerational continuity in gang membership does not attempt to examine all the potential mediating factors that account for the relationship. Rather, we focus on the hypothesized prominent mediating role of the quality of parenting in the cycle of gang membership. We now review research on the consequences of gang involvement and demonstrate how involvement in gangs has particularly salient consequences that affect the ability of parents to effectively raise their children.

Consequences of gang membership

Gang involvement represents a particularly pernicious form of embeddedness in problematic behavior (Battin-Pearson et al. 1998; Krohn and Thornberry 2008; Snyder and Sickmund 2006; Thornberry et al. 1993; Thornberry et al. 2003). Gang members contribute disproportionately to both violent and non-violent crime (Thornberry, Krohn, et al. 2003; Snyder and Sickmund 2006). Additionally, gang membership amplifies the rate of crime during the time individuals are in the gang and, to a lesser extent, when they leave the gang (Battin-Pearson et al. 1998; DeLisi et al. 2009; Krohn and Thornberry 2008; Thornberry et al. 1993).

Given the impact of gang membership on the prevalence and incidence of crime, it is not surprising that membership in a gang is also related to problematic outcomes for other life course transitions and trajectories. Gang members are less likely to graduate from high school (Moore 1993; Curry and Decker 1998; Hagedorn 1998; Thornberry, Krohn, et al. 2003; Krohn et al. 2011; Melde and Esbensen 2011; Gilman, Hill, and Hawkins 2014; Pyrooz 2014a) and to obtain steady employment (Curry and Decker 1998; Krohn et al. 2011; Melde and Esbensen 2011; Gilman, Hill, and Hawkins 2014). In addition, gang members are also more likely to be teenage parents and cohabit in their late teens and early adulthood (Thornberry, Smith, and Howard 1997; Thornberry, Krohn, et al. 2003; Krohn et al. 2011). The result of these processes is a greater likelihood of economic hardship (Harden et al. 2009; Krohn et al. 2011) and stymied social development.

The difficulties in making a successful transition to adulthood incurred at least partially by having been involved in a gang combined with the higher probability of continued involvement in criminal behavior and drug use create stress and conflict within the family (Thornberry 2009; Krohn et al. 2011) that foster ineffective parenting (Thornberry 2009; Augustyn, Thornberry, and Krohn 2014). As interactional theory suggests, ineffective parenting (e.g., maltreatment, lack of supervision, inconsistent discipline) is the prime reason for involvement in delinquent and criminal behavior and, in turn, gang membership of the next generation (see also Howell and Egley 2005).

Although interactional theory views ineffective parenting as the key mediating variable in the continuity of gang membership, there is actually very little research examining either the impact of gang membership on parenting or the role that parenting has in the continuity of gang membership across generations (for an exception, see Augustyn, Thornberry, and Krohn 2014). However, prior research focuses on the impact of involvement in criminal and drug using behavior on parenting and the potential mediating role of parenting in the continuity of deviant behavior, in general, and these studies provide key insights useful for our investigation of intergenerational continuity in gang membership.

From consequences to risk: the importance of parenting

Research on the intergenerational continuity of antisocial behavior generally confirms an association between the problematic behavior of parents and that of their children (e.g., Besemer, Axelsson, and Sarnecki 2016; Farrington 1977, 2011; Thornberry 2009; van de Weijer, Augustyn, and Besemer 2017; for exceptions see Cohen et al. 1998; Smith and Farrington 2004). While there are several mechanisms that may explain intergenerational continuity such as criminogenic environments, learning, genetic transmission, official bias, and assortive mating (for a review, see Farrington 2011), Auty and colleagues (2015,

4) note that 'parenting practices have attracted the most attention in the empirical research literature and are thought to be important in explaining the intergenerational transmission of criminal behavior.'

Using data from the Rochester Youth Development Study/Rochester Intergenerational Study, Thornberry (2009) and his colleagues (Thornberry, Freeman-Gallant, and Lovegrove 2009) find that ineffective parenting in the form of low levels of attachment between parent and child, a lack of monitoring and supervision, and inconsistent discipline mediate the link between parent and child antisocial behavior, for both mothers and fathers (see also Thornberry, Freeman-Gallant, et al. 2003). Specifically, adolescent drug use and involvement in delinquency were significantly associated with a composite index of ineffective parenting which, in turn, was negatively associated with child externalizing behaviors. Using data from a sample of junior–senior high schools from the Houston Independent School District, Kaplan and Liu (1999) found a strong intergenerational link in antisocial behavior, and ineffective parenting, which included parental surveillance of adolescent behavior, partially mediated this relationship. Similarly, Ehrensaft et al. (2003) found evidence to suggest parenting practices, including family conflict and low parental monitoring, mediated the relationship between parent conduct disorder and child antisocial conduct. More recently, Dong and Krohn (2015) produced developmental trajectories of offending among parents and their children using data from RYDS/RIGS and used these trajectories to examine intergenerational continuity and discontinuity in antisocial behavior. While they found support for both continuity and discontinuity, pertinent to this research is the finding that consistency of discipline by one's parent during childhood was a significant mediator of continuity in offending behavior across generations. Taken together, there is evidence to support the idea that parenting practices are an important, though likely partial, explanation for the relationship between the parent's past antisocial behavior and the child's current antisocial behavior.

In a similar vein, parenting practices may serve as an important mediator of intergenerational continuity in gang membership, should it even exist. The family is one of the several domains of risk for gang membership and cumulative risk across multiple domains (i.e., individual, family, peer, school, and neighborhood/community) is particularly problematic (Hill et al. 1999; Thornberry, Krohn, et al. 2003). Yet, Howell and Egley (2005) emphasize family process and parenting as particularly important in the developmental model of gang membership and there are numerous studies suggesting that various ineffective parenting behaviors are risk factors for gang membership (see Hill et al. 1999; Howell and Egley 2005; Lahey et al. 1999; Thornberry, Krohn, et al. 2003). With respect to the most serious form of ineffective parenting, child maltreatment is associated with gang membership (Thompson and Braaten-Antrim 1998; Thornberry et al. 2003). Moreover, ineffective parenting styles including inconsistent discipline and low levels of attachment are linked to participation in gangs in late childhood and early adolescence (Hill et al. 1999; Lahey et al. 1999; Thornberry et al. 2003; for an exception see Gilman, Hill, and Hawkins 2014). This line of research, in general, leads to the notion that ineffective parenting should, at least partially, explain any intergenerational continuity in gang membership.

Current study

As it stands currently, we know little about the cycle of gang membership including whether or not it exists. Therefore, we draw upon the interactional theory of intergenerational continuity in maladaptive behaviors (Thornberry 2005) and integrate research on the nature and consequences of gang membership with the known predictors of gang membership and examine the following hypotheses regarding intergenerational continuity in gang membership.

(1) G2 gang membership is a predictor of G3 gang membership.
(2) G2 gang membership negatively affects G2 parenting behaviors in the form of ineffective parenting.
(3) Ineffective parenting behaviors by G2 predict G3 gang membership.
(4) Ineffective parenting behaviors by G2 mediate the relationship between G2 gang membership and G3 gang membership.

In any study of IG continuity, it is important to acknowledge the sex of the parent, the sex of the child, and the level of contact between parent and child as complex intergenerational pathways likely exist across these contingencies. It is well documented that parenting behaviors vary for mothers and fathers (e.g., Craig 2006) and for sons and daughters (e.g., Hagan, Gillis, and Simpson 1990). Evidence also indicates that the antisocial behavior of fathers and mothers differentially affects children with evidence of greater continuity in antisocial behavior between fathers and their children compared to mothers and their children (Auty, Farrington, and Coid 2015; see also Henry and Augustyn, 2017). The sources of continuity may also vary, which is in line with research conducted by Thornberry and colleagues (2003a) who found a direct relationship between parent adolescent delinquency and child delinquency among fathers and evidence for partial mediation through parenting behaviors, but this same relationship was entirely mediated by parenting behaviors among mothers. In addition, sex of the child is important to intergenerational research. While in most cases the risk factors for antisocial behavior are the same between sexes, the degree to which individuals are negatively affected by risk factors varies across sex (Smith and Paternoster 1987), and this may affect continuity in behavior. Given these potential differences, it is no surprise, then, that research indicates intergenerational continuity, at times, varies by parent–child sex combinations. Whereas Kim and colleagues (2009) found that father externalizing behaviors exerted a stronger influence on daughters' externalizing behaviors than on sons', Auty and colleagues (2015) found that the strongest evidence of intergenerational continuity was between mothers and daughters with respect to convictions. With respect to the focus of this research – gang membership – some literature suggests that family processes including ineffective parenting are only relevant for male participation in gangs (Thornberry, Krohn, et al. 2003), whereas other work demonstrates comparable relationships across sex (Hill et al. 1999; Bell 2009; Petersen and Howell 2013).

To this end, the sex of parent and child is particularly important to the study of intergenerational continuity in gang membership. Furthermore, prior research has demonstrated that level of contact between a parent and child, especially fathers, is also likely to be important as it can speak to the degree to which a child is subject to the risk presented by the parent (Thornberry, Krohn, and Freeman-Gallant 2006). With these potential contingencies in mind, a full depiction of our proposed theoretical model of intergenerational continuity in gang membership with potential moderators can be seen in Figure 1.

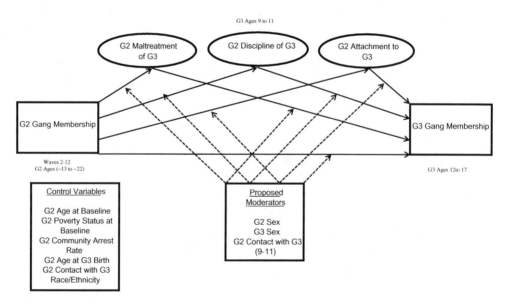

Figure 1. Proposed Theoretical Model Linking Parent Gang Membership to Child Gang Membership.
Note: Solid lines represent proposed theoretical paths. Dashed lines represent moderation.

Data and methods

To explore intergenerational transmission in gang membership, we use data from two longitudinal, companion studies – the Rochester Youth Development Study (RYDS) and its intergenerational extension, the Rochester Intergenerational Study (RIGS). The RYDS data originally consisted of a birth cohort of 1000 adolescents (referred to as G2; their primary caregiver is referred to as G1) and it is representative of the seventh- and eighth-grade public school population of Rochester, NY in 1988, an urban jurisdiction with a high crime rate (Howell et al. 2011). The following sampling strategy was used to account for the fact that the base rates of serious delinquency and drug use are relatively low (Wolfgang, Thornberry, and Figlio 1987; Elliott, Huizinga, and Menard 1989). First, males were oversampled *(75% versus 25%)* because they are more likely than females to engage in serious antisocial behaviors (Blumstein et al. 1986). Second, adolescents who lived in areas of the city with a high proportion of adult offenders were oversampled on the premise that youth residing in these areas were at a greater risk for offending. The resident arrest rate for each census tract in Rochester was calculated using the proportion of the total population living in that tract arrested by the Rochester police in 1986. Adolescents were sampled proportionate to the rate of offenders living in their tract of residence.

Adolescents (G2s) completed face-to-face interviews in school or home every six months from 1988 to 1992 (Phase 1), annually from 1994 to 1996 (Phase 2), and biannually from 2003 to 2006 (Phase 3), spanning the average age of 14 to 31. This information is supplemented with school records (Phase 1), social service records from New York State Office of Child and Family Services (OCFS; Phase 1), and official arrest records collected from the state of New York and the FBI. G1 was also interviewed every six months (up to 8 times) in Phase 1 and annually in Phase 2 (up to 11 times total). The comparison of characteristics of those who were retained at Phase 3 to those who left the study demonstrates that attrition does not bias the sample (Bushway et al. 2013; Thornberry 2016).

Beginning in 1999, RIGS recruited G2's oldest biological child (G3) to participate in the study and added new firstborns to the G3 sample when they turned two in each subsequent year. Both G2 and G3's other primary caregiver completed annual interviews since the inception of RIGS or when G3 turned two years of age. These interviews continue until G3 turns/turned 18. Beginning at the age of eight, G3 completed annual interviews. To date, there are prospective, longitudinal data on 529 parent–child dyads, our unit of analysis. All data collection procedures for RYDS and RIGS were approved by the University at Albany's Institutional Review Board.

Sample

The present analysis utilizes data from 371 parent–child (G2-G3) dyads; this includes all dyads in which G3 was at least 17 by the last available RIGS interview (collected through 2015) in order for us to construct consistent measures of the prevalence of G3 gang membership by the age of 17 across all parent–child dyads. We require G3s to be at least 17 years of age in order to cover a significant period of the life course where youth join gangs and to generate a large enough sample size to perform analyses of IG transmission of gang membership. We selected this cut-off given recent work by Pyrooz (2014b) indicating that close to 90% of gang members first join a gang prior to the age of 18.[2] Notably, we have yearly G3 interview data from each dyad beginning at the age of eight and all of our data taken from G3 interviews are ascertained after the age of eight. The gender representation of G2s is skewed toward G2 males (60% male), which is expected given the initial sampling strategy of RYDS, and are predominantly minorities (77% black and 14% Hispanic). G3s are approximately evenly split by sex (49% male).

Measures

Dependent variable

Our dependent variable is *G3 gang membership*. Prior research suggests that self-nominations of gang membership are a valid indicator of gang membership (Esbensen et al. 2001) and are able to distinguish between gang members and non-gang members with respect to delinquent attitudes and delinquent behaviors (Matsuda et al. 2013). When G3s were 12 years old (and all G3 were part of the study by the age of 12), RIGS asked G3s 'have you ever been a member of a street gang or posse' (0 = no and 1 = yes). This was followed by the questions, 'how old were you when you joined?' and 'since your last interview, were you a member of a street gang or posse?' (0 = no and 1 = yes).[3] Our measure of G3 gang membership is a binary variable indicating if the subject ever self-reported participating in a gang through age 17.

Independent variable
G2 Gang Membership is also measured using the self-report method. In wave 2 of RYDS, G2s were asked, 'were you ever a member of a street gang or posse' (0 = no and 1 = yes). In each additional wave (through wave 12), subjects were asked since the date of the last interview, 'were you a member of a street gang or posse' (0 = no and 1 = yes). Additional analyses with the RYDS data reveal that this self-report measure of gang membership generates a nearly identical list of gang members based on other selection criteria such as the name of the gang (verified), size of the gang, or role in the gang (Thornberry et al. 1993), and it has good predictive validity as it is strongly related to serious, violent delinquency, drug use, drug sales, and weapon carrying (Thornberry, Krohn, et al. 2003). Our measure of G2 gang membership is a binary variable indicating if G2 ever self-reported gang involvement spanning waves 2 to 12 (through average age 23).

Proposed moderators of IG transmission in gang membership
We explore three potential moderators of the relationship between G2 gang membership and G3 gang membership. *G2 sex* or parent sex is measured using a binary variable (0 = female and 1 = male). Similarly, *G3 sex* or child sex is measured with a binary indicator (0 = female and 1 = male). The level of contact between G2 and G3 is measured using RIGS data spanning G3 ages 9 to 11, which is prior to G3 first joining a gang. In each RIGS interview, G2s self-reported whether or not G3 currently lived with them (0 = no and 1 = yes). If G2 reported the child did not live with them, then he or she was queried about the level of contact with the child. This information was combined to construct a scale of G2 contact with G3 (0 = no contact, 1 = visits with G3 or phone contact with G3 but no supervision of G3, 2 = supervisory contact of one hour or more at least once or twice a year, 3 = supervisory contact of at least one hour or more less than once a month, 4 = supervisory contact of at least one hour or more at least one or more times a month, 5 = supervisory contact of at least an hour at least once a week, and 6 = lives with G3. From this information, we created a set of non-mutually exclusive binary variables indicating the level of contact between G2 and G3 in early childhood spanning ages 9 to 11 – *any supervisory contact, monthly supervisory contact, weekly supervisory contact,* and *G2 lives with G3*.

Potential mediators of IG transmission in gang membership
We analyze three potential mediators of the relationship between G2 gang membership and G3 gang membership. Our first mediator is *G2 maltreatment of G3* and it includes any physical abuse, sexual abuse, emotional abuse, and neglect (CAPTA (Child Abuse Prevention & Treatment Act) 1974; IOM (Institute of Medicine) and NRC (National Research Council) 2014) committed by G2 against G3. Information was collected from Child Protective Services (CPS) records at the New York State Office of Children and Family Services (OCFS) through 2010. Information was only collected on substantiated incidents in which G2 was a perpetrator of any type of child maltreatment or where G3 was a victim of maltreatment. This information was then cross-checked and used to create a binary variable indicating whether G2 maltreated G3 (0 = no and 1 = yes).[4,5]

Our other two mediators are measured in late childhood, which is temporally prior to G3 gang membership. G2 consistency of discipline is based on G3 self-reports of G2 disciplinary behaviors. We use G3 self-reports of G2 parenting behavior instead of G2 self-reports of parenting behaviors given that perception of parenting is important to antisocial behavior and prior research examining the relationship between parenting behaviors and gang membership relies upon subject and not parent self-reports (see Thornberry, Krohn, et al. 2003; Howell and Egley 2005). G3 reports of G2 parenting behaviors are also less likely to be subject to social desirability bias. In each year spanning ages 9 to 11, G3s responded to four questions regarding G2s consistency of discipline (e.g., 'Imagine that he/she tells you to stop doing something or you'll get punished. If you don't stop, how often does he/she punish you?'; 0 = never, 1 = almost never, 2 = sometimes, 3 = a lot). All responses were coded so that higher values indicate more consistency and an average was taken. We then averaged the yearly (age 9 to 11) indicators of consistency of discipline to get an average level of G2 consistency of discipline in late childhood. Our other measure of G2 parenting is G2's affective ties to G3. In each yearly interview spanning G3 ages 9 to11, G2s responded to 10 questions regarding G2's affect for G3 based on a Hudson's Index of Parental Attitudes (e.g., 'you wish your child was more like others you know'; 1 = never, 2 = seldom, 3 = sometimes, 4 = often; Hudson 1996). All items were coded so that higher scores indicate more attachment. We then averaged the yearly (ages 9 to 11) scores of G2 attachment to G3 to get an average level of G2 attachment to G3 in late childhood. Notably, questions pertaining to discipline and attachment were only asked of G2s and G3s if G2 supervised them for a minimum of an hour in the month prior to the interview. Therefore, analyses with our mediators require a minimum of monthly supervisory contact in one year between the ages of 9 and 11.

Control variables

We include two sets of control variables. The first set of control variables are causally prior to G2 gang membership: *G2 race/ethnicity* (black, Hispanic, and other is the reference category); *G2 age* at the start of RYDS; *G2 poverty status* at the start of RYDS (a binary indicator of poverty-level income of G2's family of origin); *G2's community arrest rate,* which is the arrest rate per 100 people based on Rochester Police Records; and *G2 delinquency* at baseline, which is the total frequency of involvement in 28 different criminal behaviors ranging from minor property crimes to serious violent and property crimes such as robbery prior to the start of the study. When we are not exploring potential moderating relationships, we also include G2 sex (0 = female and 1 = male) as a control variable. We also control for factors that are not causally prior to G2 gang membership but are important when modeling G3 gang membership. Specifically, we include *G2 age at G3's birth,*[6] and the *average level of contact of G2 with G3* in early childhood, which is based on the scale measure of G2 contact with G3 described above. The final contact score was formed by averaging the scores spanning G3 ages 9 to 11. When not exploring potential moderating relationships, *G3 sex* (0 = female and 1 = male) is also included. Descriptive statistics are presented in Table 1 for the full sample as well as for G2 males, G2 females, G3 males, and G3 females.

Analytic plan

The overarching goals of this study are to determine whether or not there is IG continuity in gang membership and, if so, whether ineffective parenting behaviors mediate this relationship. As such, the analysis will proceed in two steps. First, a series of logistic regressions will be estimated to examine the effect of G2 gang membership on G3 gang membership accounting for potential moderators of this relationship (see Figure 2). In essence, this set of regressions estimates C, which is the total effect of G2 gang membership (X) on G3 gang membership (Y), and the contingent effect of G2 gang membership on G3 gang membership across moderator W_n (n = 1, 2, 3) is calculated as C x C_n. Given that we identified three potential moderators of this IG relationship and we are interested in the individual as well as interactive effect of each moderator, we separate the sample by G2 sex, G3 sex, and G2 and G3 sex combinations and calculate the contingent effect of minimum level of contact.

The second step in our analytic process is to examine *how* G2 gang membership affects G3 gang membership. Mediation analysis allows for the exploration of potential causal mechanisms between an independent variable (i.e., G2 gang membership) and an outcome (i.e., G3 gang membership) by examining how intervening variables (i.e., mediators) transmit the effect of the independent variable on the dependent variable (MacKinnon and Fairchild 2009; Imai, Keele, and Yamamoto 2010). Mediation is examined through the estimation of two effects: (1) the effect of the independent variable on the

Table 1. Descriptive statistics.

	Range	Full Sample (N = 371) Mean (SD)/Proportion	G2 Males (N = 223) Mean (SD)/Proportion	G2 Females (N = 148) Mean (SD)/Proportion	G3 Males (N = 183) Mean (SD)/Proportion	G3 Females (N = 188) Mean (SD)/Proportion
Outcome						
G3 Gang Membership	0,1	.156	.161	.149	.202	.112
Treatment						
G2 Gang Membership	0,1	.374	.404	.331	.344	.404
Mediators						
Maltreatment	0,1	.140	.112	.182	.146	.133
Discipline[a]	0–3	1.828 (.413)	1.789 (.403)	1.886 (.421)	1.864 (.395)	1.792 (.429)
Attachment[a]	0–3	3.868 (.168)	3.887 (.144)	3.842 (.195)	3.852 (.182)	3.886 (.151)
Control Variables						
G2 Age at Baseline	11.8–15.4	14.040 (.731)	14.10 (.734)	13.944 (.720)	14.020 (.763)	14.060 (.700)
G2 Sex	0,1	.601	–	–	.596	.606
G2 Community Arrest Rate	.12–7.87	4.472 (1.985)	4.194 (1.839)	4.892 (2.124)	4.609 (1.933)	4.338 (2.031)
G2 Poverty Level	0,1	.366 (.482)	.358 (.481)	.378 (.487)	.344 (.476)	.388 (.489)
G2 Delinquency at Baseline	0–213	8.583 (22.450)	9.754 (24.757)	6.817 (18.398)	9.400 (26.263)	7.787 (18.017)
G2 Age at G3 Birth	13.2–25.5	19.594 (2.574)	20.257 (2.220)	18.594 (2.751)	19.384 (2.440)	19.798 (2.689)
G2 Contact with G3 Aged 9–11	0–6	5.183 (1.460)	4.672 (1.682)	5.935 (.397)	5.206 (1.372)	5.160 (1.548)
G3 Sex	0,1	.493	.489	.500	–	–
Black	0,1	.768	.700	.872	.754	.781
Hispanic	0,1	.143	.179	.088	.164	.122

[a]Sample size is reduced because this measure is only calculated for G2s who had a minimum of monthly supervisory contact: Full Sample (N = 332); G2 Males (M = 192); G2 Females (N = 140); G3 Males (N = 171); G3 Females (N = 161).

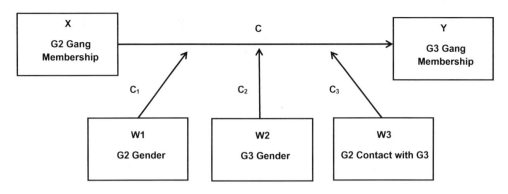

Figure 2. Direct Effect of G2 Gang Membership on G3 Gang Membership.

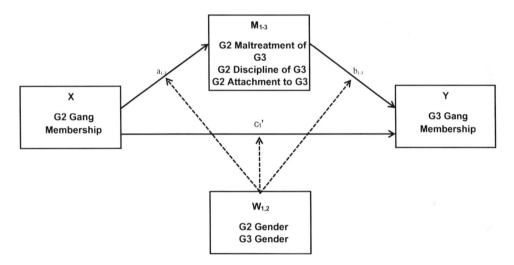

Figure 3. Moderated Mediation (Hayes 2013) with Multiple Mediators Assessing the Effects of G2 Gang Membership on G3 Gang Membership.

mediator (path 'a' in Figure 3) and (2) the effect of the mediator on the dependent variable (path 'b' in Figure 3). The product of these two coefficients (a*b) is the indirect effect.

Specifically, we utilize a procedure established by Kohler, Karlson, and Holm (2011; Karlson and Holm 2011) that compares nested nonlinear probability models and subsequently decomposes the total effect of an independent variable on a dependent variable into direct and indirect effects. This method – the KHB method – was developed specifically for binary outcomes (but can also be used with other nonlinear probability models and linear regression) and can decompose effects when including discrete or continuous mediators (Breen, Karlson, and Holm 2013). Additional advantages of this method include (1) it allows for the simultaneous estimation of mediators which reduces omitted variable bias to assess overall indirect effects, (2) it assesses the combined effect of the mediators to determine whether the sum of the mediators eliminates the direct effect, and (3) it disentangles the contribution of the mediators allowing for the identification of the contribution of each mediator to the total effect (Breen, Karlson, and Holm 2013; see also Preacher and Hayes 2008).

Figure 3 presents our proposed mediation model with multiple mediators where X is the independent variable (i.e., G2 gang membership), Y is the outcome of interest (i.e., G3 gang membership), and M_{1-3} are the proposed mediators (i.e., G2 maltreatment of G3, G2 discipline of G3, and G2 attachment to G3). Figure 3 shows the direct and indirect paths from G2 gang membership to G3 gang membership with c' representing the direct effect, a_{1-3} representing the effect for independent variable on each mediator, and b_{1-3} representing the effect of the mediators on the dependent variable. Since we propose that both G2 sex and G3 sex moderate the relationship between G2 gang membership and G3 gang membership, we estimate all paths (a paths, b paths, c' path) separately for G2 sex–G3 sex dyad subsamples (i.e., G2 males and G3 males, G2 males and G3 females, G2 females and G3 males, and G2 females and G3 females).

When modeling our 'a' paths, we utilized a logistic regression model to estimate the effects of G2 gang membership on G2 maltreatment of G3, which is a binary outcome, and we used Ordinary Least Squares (OLS) regression for our other two mediators. Prior to estimation of the effect of G2 gang membership on G2 attachment to G3, we first log transformed the variable given the extreme left skew of G2 attachment, which violates the assumption of a normally distributed residuals for OLS. We then estimated each 'b' path using logistic regression given the binary nature of our dependent variable, G3 gang membership. Finally, we estimated the direct, indirect, and total effects using logistic regression as well. Specifically, we estimated the direct, indirect, and total effect of G2 gang membership on G3 gang membership for each proposed mediator individually before combining all three proposed mediators in the same model to assess the direct, cumulative indirect effect, and total effect of G2 gang membership on G3 gang membership accounting for our proposed mediators. We then decomposed the indirect effect of each mediator and estimated its contribution to the overall total effect when all of our mediators were included in the same model. All analyses were performed in Stata 14 (StataCorp 2015).

Results

Naïve direct effects

We first explored whether or not G2 gang membership is a risk factor for G3 gang membership. Given the potential for G2 sex, G3 sex, the G2–G3 sex combination, and minimum level of contact between G2 and G3 in late childhood to moderate this relationship, we present the odds ratios from a series of logistic regressions generated across each potential moderator and combination of moderators in Table 2.

The results indicate that when grouping all G2s together, there is no evidence of intergenerational continuity in gang membership as G2 gang membership is not a significant predictor for G3 gang membership across any level of contact. Moreover, once we allowed only G2 sex or G3 sex and level of contact to moderate the relationship between G2 gang membership and G3 gang membership, there is no evidence of continuity as none of the odds ratios reach statistical significance ($p > .05$). However, dividing the sample by the sex combination of the parent–child dyad reveals evidence of

Table 2. Logistic regressions results examining the effect of G2 gang membership on G3 gang membership across G2 levels of contact with G3 from ages 9–11.

	All eligible G2s	G2s with any supervisory contact	G2s with at least monthly supervisory contact	G2s with at least weekly supervisory contact	G2s living with G3s
	OR	OR	OR	OR	OR
Full Sample	1.252	1.420	1.556	1.556	1.374
G2 Males	1.389	1.681	1.962	1.706	1.460
G2 Females	1.317	1.317	1.317	1.317	1.317
G3 Males	1.532	1.890	2.038	1.947	1.926
G3 Females	.974	1.143	1.297	1.121	1.027
G2 Males and G3 Males	2.680†	4.192*	5.606*	5.579*	7.390*
G2 Males and G3 Females	.435	.502	.378	.213	.120
G2 Females and G3 Males	.423	.423	.423	.423	.423
G2 Females and G3 Females	8.159*	8.159*	8.159*	8.159*	8.159*

Notes: All models control for G2 age at baseline, G2 Sex (if necessary), G2 poverty status at baseline, G2 community arrest rate at baseline, G2 delinquency at baseline, G2 age at G3 birth, G2 level of contact with G3, G3 Sex, race/ethnicity. OR = Odds ratio.
†$p < .10$; *$p < .05$

intergenerational continuity in gang membership. Among G2 fathers, gang membership increases the likelihood of gang membership among sons, but this relationship is moderated by level of contact between fathers and sons in late childhood. Specifically, among all eligible G2 fathers, the relationship between G2 gang membership and G3 gang membership is positive, but only marginally significant (OR = 2.680, $p < .10$). However, the relationship between G2 gang membership and G3 gang membership is positive and statistically significant once we limited the sample to those fathers who supervise their sons for at least one hour a year (OR = 4.192, $p < .05$), and the effect of G2 gang membership on G3 gang membership among father–son dyads increases in strength as level of contact increases. In fact, among fathers who supervise their sons for at least an hour a month or at least an hour a week, prior gang membership increases the likelihood of child gang membership over fivefold. Moreover, sons who live with their fathers are over seven times more likely to join a gang if their father was previously in a gang (OR = 7.390, $p < .05$). There is also evidence of intergenerational continuity in gang membership between mothers and daughters, but unlike father–son dyads, this relationship is not moderated by level of contact. This latter finding is a result of all G2 mothers living with their daughters. Among G2–G3 female dyads, daughters were over eight times more likely to join a gang if their mother was in a gang (OR = 8.159, $p < .05$).

Mediation analyses

The next step in our analysis involved analyzing whether the proposed G2 parenting behaviors mediate the relationship between G2 gang membership and G3 gang membership, net of control variables. We remind the reader that the mediational analyses were only conducted among G2s who had a minimum of monthly supervisory contact in one year (G3 ages 9 to 11) with G3s as this requirement was necessary to construct two of our parenting measures (e.g., consistency of discipline and attachment). In addition, we estimated all paths across G2 sex–G3 sex dyads given the importance of the G2–G3 sex dyad. Table 3 displays the effect of G2 gang membership on our proposed mediators ('a' paths). There is a significant relationship between G2 gang membership and G2 maltreatment of G3 among father–son dyads ($b = 2.213$, $p < .05$). In other words, former male gang members are over nine times more likely to maltreat their sons. We also see that G2 gang membership negatively affects discipline among mother–daughter dyads as mothers who were in a gang exhibit less consistent discipline of their daughters ($b = -.284$, $p < .01$). Among opposite sex dyads, G2 gang membership is unrelated to any of the specified parenting behaviors. G2 gang membership is also unrelated to discipline and attachment among father–son dyads and maltreatment and attachment among mother–daughter dyads.

Table 4 shows the relationship between G2 parenting behaviors and G3 gang membership ('b' paths). Among father–son dyads, we see that G2 maltreatment of G3 increases the likelihood that a son will join a gang ($b = 2.205$, $p < .01$). In fact, boys who are abused by one's father are over nine times more likely to join a gang compared to boys who are not abused by one's father. Among father–daughter dyads, attachment to G3 in late childhood is negatively related to G3 joining a gang ($b = -13.376$, $p < .10$), but this relationship is only marginally significant. Consistency of discipline by fathers is unrelated to the likelihood of gang participation among sons or daughters. With respect to G2 female parenting behaviors, more consistent discipline decreases likelihood of one's son joining a gang, but this relationship is only marginally significant as well ($b = -1.839$, $p < .10$). The remaining maternal parenting behaviors are unrelated to the likelihood of gang membership among sons and daughters.

We now turn attention to direct, indirect, and total effects of G2 gang membership on G3 gang membership across G2 sex–G3 sex dyads (see Table 5). We focus on G2 males and G3 males first and examine the effects through each proposed mediator prior to examining the cumulative mediating effect of all three parenting behaviors. Recall, G2 gang membership increased the likelihood of G2 maltreatment of G3 and, in turn, G2 maltreatment of G3 increased the likelihood of G3 gang membership among father–son dyads. Based on the joint significance test of the 'a' path and the 'b' path (Taylor, MacKinnon, and Tein 2008), there appears to be an indirect effect of G2 gang membership on G3 gang membership through G2 maltreatment of G3 among father–son dyads. Table 5 supports this

Table 3. Regression results for 'a' paths of mediation model (mediator regressed on G2 gang membership).

Mediator	Estimate	95% CI
G2 Males and G3 Males (N = 100)		
Maltreatment[a]	2.213*	(.797, 3.488)
Discipline	−.017	(−.154, .120)
Attachment	−.022	(−.034, .008)
G2 Males and G3 Females (N = 92)		
Maltreatment[a]	−.276	(−1.738, 1.185)
Discipline	.069	(−.112, .249)
Attachment	−.004	(−.019, .010)
G2 Females and G3 Males (N = 71)		
Maltreatment[a]	.963	(−.480, 2.407)
Discipline	−.067	(−.309, .175)
Attachment	−.021	(−.051, .009)
G2 Females and G3 Females (N = 69)		
Maltreatment[a]	.017	(−1.476, 1.510)
Discipline	−.284**	(−.475, −.094)
Attachment	−.003	(−.027, .018)

Notes: All models control for G2 age at baseline, G2 poverty status at baseline, G2 community arrest rate at baseline, G2 delinquency at baseline, G2 age at G3 birth, G2 level of contact with G3, G3 sex, race/ethnicity. CI = Confidence interval.
[a]Logistic regression used.
*$p < .05$; **$p < .01$.

Table 4. Logistic regression results for 'b' path of mediation model (G3 gang membership regressed on mediators).

Mediator	Estimate	95% CI
G2 Males and G3 Males (N = 100)		
Maltreatment	2.205**	(.820, 3.590)
Discipline	−.162	(−1.540, 1.216)
Attachment	2.164	(−12.589, 16.917)
G2 Males and G3 Females (N = 92)		
Maltreatment	−.125	(−.205, 1.804)
Discipline	−1.054	(−2.676, .567)
Attachment	−13.376†	(−28.101, 1.349)
G2 Females and G3 Males (N = 71)		
Maltreatment	−.661	(−2.612, 1.290)
Discipline	−1.839†	(−3.684, .006)
Attachment	−3.145	(−14.232, 7.943)
G2 Females and G3 Females (N = 69)		
Maltreatment	.698	(−1.341, 2.738)
Discipline	−1.537	(−3.979, .906)
Attachment	8.365	(−16.731, 33.462)

Notes: All models control for G2 age at baseline, G2 poverty status at baseline, G2 community arrest rate at baseline, G2 delinquency at baseline, G2 age at G3 birth, G2 level of contact with G3, G3 sex, race/ethnicity. OR = Odds ratio; CI = Confidence interval.
†$p < .10$; **$p < .01$.

specific indirect effect ($b = .383, p < .05$), and it accounts for nearly 40% (.383/.978) of the total effect of G2 gang membership on G3 gang membership among father–son dyads. Notably, though, the total effect of G2 gang membership on G3 gang membership among father–son dyads is positive but only marginally significant ($b = .978, p < .10$). For the other two proposed paths between G2 gang membership and G3 gang membership – G2 consistency of discipline and G2 attachment to G3 – we see no evidence of significant indirect effects through these mediators, respectively, and this is expected given the lack of significant 'a' paths and 'b' paths for these mediators. Nevertheless, there is a positive, total effect of G2 gang membership on G3 gang membership. When accounting for all three parenting behaviors in the same model, there is evidence of a marginally significant and positive, direct effect of G2 gang membership on G3 gang membership ($b = 1.248, p < .10$) and a significant and positive, total effect of G2 gang membership on G3 gang membership ($b = 1.335, p < .05$) among father–son dyads. Table 6 shows the individual contribution of each parenting behavior to the total effect of G2 gang

Table 5. Model results of direct, indirect, and total effects of G2 gang membership on G3 gang membership.

	Direct effect		Indirect effect		Total effect	
Mediator	Estimate	95% CI	Estimate	95% CI	Estimate	95% CI
G2 Males and G3 Males (N = 100)						
Maltreatment	.595	(−.524, 1.714)	.383*	(.015, 1.714)	.978[†]	(−.114, 2.071)
Discipline	.972[†]	(−.073, 2.018)	.001	(−.093, .095)	.973[†]	(−.066, 2.013)
Attachment	1.609*	(.341, 2.018)	−.172	(−.536, .191)	1.436*	(.227, 2.645)
All Mediators	1.248[†]	(−.060, 2.556)	.087	(−.472, .647)	1.335*	(.097, 2.574)
G2 Males and G3 Females (N = 92)						
Maltreatment	−.833	(−2.445, .786)	.001	(−.028, .024)	−.832	(−2.452, .787)
Discipline	−1.172	(−2.918, .575)	−.108	(−.365, .148)	−1.280	(−3.047, .486)
Attachment	−.903	(−2.658, .852)	.028	(−.203, .261)	−.874	(−2.626, .878)
All Mediators	−1.291	(−3.226, .643)	−.103	(−.560, .354)	−1.395	(−3.355, .566)
G2 Females and G3 Males (N = 71)						
Maltreatment	−.202	(−1.699, 1.294)	−.003	(−.190, .183)	−.205	(−1.703, 1.291)
Discipline	−1.458	(−3.444, .587)	.154	(−.405, .712)	−1.304	(−3.248, .639)
Attachment	−.964	(−2.719, .791)	.103	(−.183, .389)	−.861	(−2.572, .851)
All Mediators	−1.406	(−3.449, .637)	.131	(−.497, .759)	−1.275	(−3.232, .682)
G2 Females and G3 Females (N = 69)						
Maltreatment	2.166*	(.037, 4.296)	−.030	(−.201, .142)	2.136*	(.012, 4.261)
Discipline	1.946[†]	(−.215, 4.109)	.294	(−.533, 1.120)	2.241*	(.040, 4.441)
Attachment	2.167*	(.048, 4.190)	−.048	(−.316, .219)	2.118*	(.088, 4.246)
All Mediators	2.033[†]	(−.197, 4.264)	.233	(−.691, 1.157)	2.266*	(.045, 4.488)

Notes: All models control for G2 age at baseline, G2 poverty status at baseline, G2 community arrest rate at baseline, G2 delinquency at baseline, G2 age at G3 birth, G2 level of contact with G3, G3 sex, race/ethnicity. OR = Odds ratio; CI = Confidence interval.
[†]$p < .10$; *$p < .05$

Table 6. Contribution of mediators to total effect of G2 gang membership on G3 gang membership when all mediators included in the same model.

Mediator	Indirect effect estimate	SE	% of Total effect
G2 Males and G3 Males ($N = 100$)			
Maltreatment	.390[†]	(.221)	29.2
Discipline	−.043	(.084)	−3.24
Attachment	−.259	(.215)	−19.53
G2 Males and G3 Females ($N = 92$)			
Maltreatment	−.000	(.002)	0.00
Discipline	−.109	(.172)	7.85
Attachment	.155	(.155)	−0.43
G2 Females and G3 Males ($N = 71$)			
Maltreatment	−.024	(.077)	1.88
Discipline	.149	(.277)	−11.65
Attachment	.007	(.151)	−.53
G2 Females and G3 Females ($N = 69$)			
Maltreatment	−.022	(.126)	−.96
Discipline	.243	(.440)	10.74
Attachment	.011	(.011)	.50

Notes: All models control for G2 age at baseline, G2 poverty status at baseline, G2 community arrest rate at baseline, G2 delinquency at baseline, G2 age at G3 birth, G2 level of contact with G3, G3 sex, race/ethnicity. SE = Standard error.
[†]$p < .10$

membership on G3 gang membership. Although the total indirect effect of all three mediators does not achieve statistical significance as indicated in Table 5, the specific indirect effect of G2 maltreatment of G3 is marginally significant ($b = .390, p < .10$), which can be seen in Table 6. Furthermore, this specific indirect effect accounts for a little over 29% of the total effect of G2 gang membership on G3 gang membership among father–son dyads.

Tables 5–6 fail to demonstrate any evidence of a direct, indirect, or total effect of G2 gang membership on G3 gang membership among father–daughter dyads and mother–son dyads. Not only are these results consistent with estimates from our 'a' paths and 'b' paths, but the lack of significant total effects of G2 gang membership on G3 gang membership is also consistent with the results regarding the naïve direct effects of G2 gang membership on G3 gang membership among these two subsamples.

Among mother–daughter dyads, Table 5 shows no evidence that any of the parenting behaviors examined mediate the relationship between G2 gang membership and G3 gang membership since there are no significant indirect effects for any proposed mediator individually or cumulatively. However, we see that in each model estimated, G2 gang membership has a positive, significant direct effect on G3 gang membership. For two of our models, the mediation model including consistency of discipline only and the mediation model including all three parenting behaviors, the direct effect is only marginally significant ($p < .10$). This effect achieves statistical significance ($p < .05$) in the model that includes maltreatment of G3 as the mediator and G2 attachment to G3, individually. Moreover, the direct effect between G2 and G3 gang membership, by in large, accounts for the positive, significant total effect of G2 gang membership on G3 gang membership that is consistent across each model estimated for mother–daughter dyads. In fact, Table 6 demonstrates that when all three mediators are included in the same model, the direct effect of G2 gang membership on G3 gang membership among mother–dyads accounts for nearly 90% of the total effect of G2 gang membership on G3 gang membership ($1-[10.74 + .50 - .96]$).

Discussion

Prior qualitative work on gang involvement is suggestive of continuity in gang membership across successive generations (Horowitz 1983; Moore et al. 1978; Vigil 1988, 2002; cf. Decker and van Winkle 1996), but exacting data requirements has until now resulted in a general lack of quantitative evidence evaluating intergenerational continuity of gang involvement. Drawing on the developmental and life course perspective and intergenerational interactional theory (see Thornberry 2005), the current study employed data from the prospective, longitudinal RYDS/RIGS studies to quantitatively assess intergenerational continuity in gang membership. Informed by research on the intergenerational continuity in various maladaptive behaviors (e.g., Thornberry, Freeman-Gallant, et al. 2003; Auty, Farrington, and Coid 2015), we explored whether parent and child sex and level of contact serve as key moderators of any observed link across generations and, moreover, examined the role of parenting processes as an explanation for the link between parent gang membership and child gang membership.

Overall, results yielded mixed evidence for the intergenerational continuity of gang involvement, with findings supportive of intergenerational continuity depending upon parent–child sex dyads and contact level. Evidence for intergenerational parallelism in gang membership was confined to same-sex parent–child dyads. G3 daughters of G2 gang-involved mothers were markedly more likely to become involved in a gang. Indeed, when mother's (G2) gang involvement status is considered as a risk factor for G3 daughter gang involvement, the odds of G3 joining a gang are over eight times greater when the child's mother participated in a gang as an adolescent herself, as compared to not being gang involved. The connection between mother and daughter gang involvement was not conditional on contact level; in general, supervisory levels were high with G3 daughters in the sample living with G2 mothers. With mothers and daughters in close contact, results of this study strongly suggest that efforts to prevent gang membership among girls should consider the added risk to girls who were born to a mother who was herself involved in a gang as an adolescent. Interestingly, though, the intergenerational continuity between mothers and daughters does not appear to be the result of problematic parenting behaviors during late childhood. Among mothers, G2 gang involvement did adversely impact consistency of discipline for daughters (though, interestingly, there was no such adverse effect of G2 gang involvement on discipline style for sons). While inconsistent discipline may lead to other developmental problems, it was not found to be a significant predictor of gang involvement among G3 females in this analysis. Thus, findings for intergenerational continuity between mothers and daughters remain in moderated mediation models and appear, at least in these analyses, to be direct in nature (which implies either a true direct effect or an alternative mechanism not modeled). We suggest replication of this relationship among larger samples to further confirm the connection between mother and daughters' gang involvement as well as explore other potential mediating pathways from G2 gang membership to G3 gang membership among mother–daughter dyads.

Intergenerational continuity was also found for father–son dyads, but this relationship was conditional on level of contact. Recall, G2 males have considerably less contact with G3s as compared to G2 females (see Table 1). When a gang-involved father's contact level reaches at least monthly supervisory contact, G2 gang involvement becomes a significant risk factor for G3 gang involvement ($p < 0.05$), whereas it was only marginally significant for the minimum level of any contact/no contact ($p < 0.10$). Though not as pronounced as the risk among mother–daughter dyads, fathers' gang membership still substantially increased the odds of G3 gang involvement over fivefold when supervision includes monthly or weekly contact and well over sevenfold when fathers and sons lived under the same roof during late childhood.

While the assessed parenting behaviors failed to explain continuity in gang membership among mothers and daughters, there is evidence to support an indirect effect of father gang membership on son gang membership through child maltreatment, specifically. A father's gang participation during his adolescence increases maltreatment of sons which, in turn, increases a son's likelihood of joining a gang prior to the age of 18. The specific indirect path from G2 gang membership to G3 gang membership through maltreatment among father–son dyads finding is important in many respects. It is informative with respect to the consequences of gang membership and the criminogenic consequences of maltreatment. With regard to the consequences of gang membership, prior work finds a relationship between gang membership and child maltreatment, in general (Augustyn, Thornberry, and Krohn 2014). However, the present research limited the examination of the effects of gang membership to maltreatment of one's own biological children and only found evidence of an increased likelihood of maltreatment among gang-involved fathers and their sons. The present research is also enlightening with respect to the criminogenic effects of victimization (see also Gilman et al. 2016). For instance, prior research indicates that child maltreatment during adolescence, and not childhood, appears to be related to criminal and delinquent behavior (Eckenrode et al. 2001; Thornberry, Ireland, and Smith 2001; Ireland, Smith, and Thornberry 2002), whereas we found that a son's maltreatment by one's father during childhood (prior to the age of 11) increases the likelihood of gang membership, a known correlate of delinquency. Therefore, it appears that there is more variation in the criminogenic effects of maltreatment and the consequences of gang membership on maltreatment than previously suggested.

This identified pathway is also important because it can guide gang prevention programs to focus efforts among father–son dyads where the father is a former gang member. Disrupting intergenerational continuity in gang membership for males necessitates a focus on preventing child maltreatment including physical, sexual, and emotional abuse as well as child neglect. Conflict resolution in the gang environment often involves violence or other maladaptive behaviors (Klein 1995; Miller 2011; Curry, Decker, and Pyrooz 2014). Behaviors or neglect of expected responsibilities which are learned or reinforced in a gang may show up through maltreatment of one's kin. As for the offspring, experiencing physical abuse may teach a son it is okay to address conflict through violence, whereas being neglected may make the social connections that a gang may provide more appealing. In this way, child maltreatment may contribute to direct transmission (e.g., direct modeling of behaviors and attitudes) as well as indirect transmission (e.g., indirect communication that conventional responsibilities are unimportant) (see Giordano 2010). To distinguish between these possibilities, additional research unpacking the type or types of child maltreatment experienced might be usefully pursued.

As it stands, programs for male ex-gang members that encourage effective parenting and prosocial conflict resolution techniques such as the Triple P Positive Parenting Program (Prinz et al. 2009) and Parent-Child Interaction Therapy (Chaffin et al. 2004) are likely to help break the family cycle of gang membership. Perhaps not surprisingly, programmatic efforts would have the most impact when they focus on fathers who have nontrivial levels of contact with their sons. We caution, though, that these results suggest that we should reduce the level of contact between formerly gang-involved fathers and their sons. Because fathers (and mothers) provide many benefits to children, families, and communities even if they were once gang-involved or currently engage in antisocial activities (e.g., Rose and Clear 1998), we of course do not recommend reducing contact as a general strategy to reduce intergenerational continuity in gang membership, though there are, unfortunately, instances where reduced contact may benefit the prosocial development of the child, including lowering the likelihood of gang participation.

The fact that intergenerational continuity occurs in same-sex parent–child dyads underscores the idea that children often more closely identify with parents of the same sex. However, we rightly acknowledge this study did not fully identify how same-sex dyads promote intergenerational continuity in gang membership. Among female dyads, we only found evidence of a direct effect, and among male dyads we only found evidence of partial mediation through maltreatment. Future research on intergenerational continuity in gang membership should further explore how the dynamics of same-sex parent–child dyads promote parallelism in behavior and it should also explore alternative mediating pathways or explanations of intergenerational continuity including learning, criminogenic environments, and genetics (see Farrington 2011).

The current study provides much needed quantitative evidence on the intergenerational continuity of gang involvement, but there are certain limitations of the current research, which provide opportunities for refinement in future research. First, we suggest replication of our analyses with larger sample sizes in order to increase power and confirm the results presented herein. Not all daughters and sons of G2s have reached the age to be included in this analysis; thus, replication with the RYDS/RIGS data several years down the line is also encouraged. In particular, we did not find evidence for intergenerational continuity across opposite-sex dyads, though risk factor analyses revealed negative, albeit not statistically significant, odds ratios. These findings are suggestive of the possibility that intergenerational discontinuity (i.e., a protective effect) might be observed for father–daughter and mother–son dyads with larger samples sizes yielding increased power. Second, we note that these data are from one city in the United States with an emergent gang problem and data collection began when parents were teens in the late 1980s and early 1990s. It is true that most intergenerational research is conducted using a sample from one city and one cohort, but OJJDP's sponsorship of similar studies (i.e., in Denver, Pittsburgh, and Seattle) that generated similar findings on an array of topics related to crime and delinquency suggest generalizeability is enhanced. Furthermore, our sample consists of predominantly minorities. Thus, we encourage replication of this study's findings with alternative data sources to confirm our results. Third, our study examined the role of parenting practices—including maltreatment, attachment, and consistency of discipline—during late childhood only. While this enabled us to preserve appropriate time order between mediating and outcome variables, some research on intergenerational continuity of antisocial behavior suggests that parenting behaviors, specifically maltreatment, are more problematic if they occur in adolescence as opposed to childhood (Eckenrode et al. 2001; Thornberry, Ireland, and Smith 2001; Ireland, Smith, and Thornberry 2002). To achieve sufficient sample sizes for analyses, we defined gang membership as any participation in adolescence (e.g., age 12 when G3s first reported gang membership through the age 17). If we also measured our mediators during adolescence, temporal ordering would certainly be an issue. Therefore, if sample sizes permit, future research to examine more contemporaneous effects of parenting on gang membership as well as test alternative mediating pathways and explanations beyond parenting is encouraged.

Although this study addresses a limited set of factors that might contribute to the intergenerational continuity of gang membership, we found that the sex of the parent and child and relatedly the contact between them were significant moderators of this continuity. Additionally, in some instances, the pathway to gang membership among the second generation operated through the quality of parenting. However, life course and development theories generally, and interactional theory, specifically, suggest that other factors might affect continuity in gang membership as well (e.g., norms or values). We hope that this initial examination of intergenerational continuity in gang membership will stimulate further investigations that explore other mediating and moderating factors and yield useful information for policy-makers seeking to break a family cycle of gang participation.

Notes

1. This is very similar to the arguments of Giordano (2010) who refers to direct transmission (i.e., modeling behaviors and conveying attitudes) and indirect transmission (i.e., providing poor environmental conditions and ineffective coping strategies) of antisocial behavior.
2. We rightfully acknowledge that we do not examine the role of IG transmission among adult onset gang members. In all likelihood, the causes of gang membership among those who join for the first time at age 18 or older are likely different from those who join a gang for the first time as a juvenile.
3. The age of first self-reported gang membership is also used to ensure temporal ordering between our independent variable, mediators, moderators, and G3 gang membership.
4. Additional information was collected indicating the age of G3 at maltreatment. This was used to ensure temporal ordering so that G2 maltreatment of G3 was temporally prior to G3 joining a gang.
5. There is an element of right-censoring in the measurement of maltreatment perpetration and victimization. If a G2–G3 dyad moved out of New York state, we are unable to assess maltreatment perpetration and victimization. However, the implication of this limitation is that we falsely identify G2s as not perpetrating an act of maltreatment against G3. This would mean that our estimates are biased downward and we are presenting a conservative estimate of the relationship between G2 gang membership, G2 perpetration of maltreatment of G3, and G3 gang membership.
6. Prior intergenerational research looking at time-stable information regarding parent–child dyads generated from prospective, longitudinal design originating from one birth cohort accounts for the parent age at birth of the child in two ways: (1) as a control variable or (2) as a mediator of the relationship between parental behavior and child behavior. Therefore, our analyses were run both ways to determine the sensitivity to methodological decisions. In both analyses, the results on our variables of interest in terms of magnitude and significance are the same. Moreover, age at birth of the child was not a significant mediator of the relationship between parent gang membership and child gang membership, but it is significant in some of the individual paths estimated. Thus, we present the models controlling for age at birth only.

Disclosure statement

No potential conflict of interest was reported by the authors.

Funding

Support for the Rochester Youth Development Study has been provided by the Centers for Disease Control and Prevention [grant number R01CE001572]; the Office of Juvenile Justice and Delinquency Prevention [grant number 2006-JW-BX-0074], [grant number 86-JN-CX-0007], [grant number 96-MU-FX-0014], [grant number 2004-MU-FX-0062]; the National Institute on Drug Abuse [grant number R01DA020195], [grant number R01DA005512]; the National Science Foundation [grant number SBR-9123299]; and the National Institute of Mental Health [grant number R01MH56486], [grant number R01MH63386]. Work on this project was also aided by grants to the Center for Social and Demographic Analysis at the University at Albany from NICHD [grant number P30HD32041]; and NSF [grant number SBR-9512290].

References

Augustyn, M. B., T. P. Thornberry, and M. D. Krohn. 2014. "Gang Membership and Pathways to Maladaptive Parenting." *Journal of Research on Adolescence* 24: 252–267.

Auty, K. M., D. P. Farrington, and J. W. Coid. 2015. "Intergenerational Transmission of Psychopathy and Mediation via Psychosocial Risk Factors." *The British Journal of Psychiatry* 206: 26–31.

Battin-Pearson, S. R., T. P. Thornberry, J. D. Hawkins, and M. D. Krohn. 1998. *Gang Membership, Delinquent Peers, and Delinquent Behavior*. Washington, DC: Office of Juvenile Justice and Delinquency Prevention.

Bell, K. E. 2009. "Gender and Gangs a Quantitative Comparison." *Crime & Delinquency* 55: 363–387.

Besemer, S., J. Axelsson, and J. Sarnecki 2016. "Intergenerational Transmission of Trajectories of Offending over Three Generations." *Journal of Developmental and Life-Course Criminology* 2: 417–441. doi: 10.1007/s40865-016-0037-2.

Blumstein, A., J. Cohen, J. A. Roth, and C. Visher 1986. *Criminal Careers and "Career Criminals"* (Vol 1). Washington D.C.: National Academy Press.

Breen, R., K. B. Karlson, and A. Holm. 2013. "Total, Direct, and Indirect Effects in Logit and Probit Models." *Sociological Methods & Research* 42 (2): 164–191.

Bushway, Shawn D., Marvin D. Krohn, Alan J. Lizotte, Matthew D. Phillips, and Nicole M. Schmidt. 2013. "Are Risky Youth Less Protectable as They Age? The Dynamics of Protection during Adolescence and Young Adulthood." *Justice Quarterly* 30: 84–116.

Capaldi, D. M., K. C. Pears, G. R. Patterson, and L. D. Owen. 2003. "Continuity of Parenting Practices across Generations in an at-Risk Sample: A Prospective Comparison of Direct and Mediated Associations." *Journal of Abnormal Child Psychology* 31: 127–142.

Chaffin, M., J. F. Silovsky, B. Funderburk, L. A. Valle, E. V. Brestan, T. Balachova, S. Jackson, et al 2004. "Parent-Child Interaction Therapy with Physically Abusive Parents: Efficacy for Reducing Future Abuse Reports." *Journal of Consulting and Clinical Psychology* 72: 500.

Child Abuse Prevention and Treatment Act. 1974. *Public Law 93–247*.

Cohen, P., S. Kasen, J. S. Brook, and C. Hartmark. 1998. "Behavior Patterns of Young Children and Their Offspring: A Two-Generation Study." *Developmental Psychology* 341: 202–1208.

Conger, R. D., T. Neppl, K. J. Kim, and L. V. Scaramella. 2003. "Angry and Aggressive Behavior across Three Generations: A Prospective, Longitudinal Study of Parents and Children." *Journal of Abnormal Child Psychology* 31: 143–160.

Craig, L. 2006. "Does Father Care Mean Fathers Share? A Comparison of How Mothers and Fathers in Intact Families Spend Time with Children." *Gender & Society* 20: 259–281.

Curry, G. D., and S. H. Decker. 1998. *Confronting Gangs: Crime and Community*. Los Angeles, CA: Roxbury Press.

Curry, G. D., S. H. Decker, and D. Pyrooz. 2014. *Confronting Gangs: Crime and Community*. New York: Oxford University Press.

Decker, S. H., and B. van Winkle. 1996. *Life in the Gang: Family, Friends, and Violence*. Cambridge: Cambridge University Press.

DeLisi, M., J. C. Barnes, K. M. Beaver, and C. L. Gibson. 2009. "Delinquent Gangs and Adolescent Victimization Revisited: A Propensity Score Matching Approach." *Criminal Justice and Behavior* 36: 808–823.

Dong, B., C. L. Gibson, & M. D. Krohn. 2015. Gang Membership in a Developmental and Life Course Perspective. In *The Handbook of Gangs*, edited by S. H. Decker and D. C. Pyrooz, 78–97. New York: Wiley & Sons, Inc.

Dong, B., and M. D. Krohn. 2015. "Exploring Intergenerational Discontinuity in Problem Behavior Bad Parents with Good Children." *Youth Violence and Juvenile Justice* 13: 99–122.

Eckenrode, J., D. Zielinski, E. Smith, L. A. Marcynyszyn, C. R. Henderson Jr, H. Kitzman, R. Cole, et al. 2001. "Child Maltreatment and the Early Onset of Problem Behaviors: Can a Program of Nurse Home Visitation Break the Link?" *Development and Psychopathology* 13: 873–890.

Ehrensaft, M. K., P. Cohen, J. Brown, E. Smailes, H. Chen, and J. G. Johnson. 2003. "Intergenerational Transmission of Partner Violence: A 20-Year Prospective Study." *Journal of Consulting and Clinical Psychology* 71: 741.

Elliott, D. S., D. Huizinga, and S. Menard. 1989. *Multiple Problem Youth: Delinquency, Substance Use, and Mental Health Problems*. New York: Springer-Verlag.

Ertem, I. O., J. M. Leventhal, and S. Dobbs. 2000. "Intergenerational Continuity of Child Physical Abuse: How Good is the Evidence?" *The Lancet* 356 (9232): 814–819.

Esbensen, F. A., L. T. Winfree Jr, N. He, and T. J. Taylor. 2001. "Youth Gangs and Definitional Issues: When is a Gang a Gang, and Why Does it Matter?" *NCCD News* 47 (1): 105–130.

Farrington, D. P. 1977. "The Family Backgrounds of Aggressive Youths." Book Supplement to the *Journal of Child Psychology and Psychiatry* 1: 73–93.

Farrington, D. P. 2011. *Integrated Developmental and Life-Course Theories of Offending* (Vol. 1). New Brunswick, NJ: Transaction Publishers.

Farrington, D. P., J. W. Coid, and J. Murray. 2009. "Family Factors in the Intergenerational Transmission of Offending." *Criminal Behaviour and Mental Health* 19: 109–124.

Gilman, A., K. G. Hill, and J. D. Hawkins. 2014. "Long-Term Consequences of Adolescent Gang Membership for Adult Functioning." *American Journal of Public Health* 104: 938–945.

Gilman, A. B., J. C. Howell, A. E. Hipwell, and S. D. Stepp. 2016. "The Reciprocal Relationship Between Gang Involvement and Victimization by Peers: Findings from the Pittsburgh Girls Study." *Journal of Developmental and Life-Course Criminology*: 1–17.

Giordano, P. C. 2010. *Legacies of Crime: A Follow-up of the Children of Highly Delinquent Girls and Boys*. New York: Cambridge University Press.

Hagan, J. 1997. "Crime and Capitalization: Toward a Developmental Theory of Street Crime in America." In *Developmental Theories of Crime and Delinquency*, edited by T. P. Thornberry, 287–308. New Brunswick, NJ: Transaction.

Hagan, J., A. R. Gillis, and J. Simpson. 1990. "Clarifying and Extending Power-Control Theory." *American Journal of Sociology* 95: 1024–1037.

Hagedorn, J. M. 1998. *People and Folks: Gangs, Crime and the Underclass in a Rustbelt City*. Chicago, IL: Lake View Press.

Harden, A., G. Brunton, A. Fletcher, and A. Oakley. 2009. "Teenage Pregnancy and Social Disadvantage: Systematic Review Integrating Controlled Trials and Qualitative Studies." *BMJ* 339: b4254.

Hayes, A. F. 2013. *Introduction to Mediation, Moderation, and Conditional Process Analysis: A Regression-Based Approach*. New York: Guilford Press.

Henry, K. L., and M. B. Augustyn. 2017. "Intergenerational Continuity in Cannabis Use: The Role of Parent's Early Onset and Lifetime Disorder on Child's Early Onset." *Journal of Adolescent Health* 60 (1): 87–92.

Hill, K. G., J. D. Hawkins, R. F. Catalano, R. Kosterman, R. D. Abbott, and T. Edwards 1996. "The Longitudinal Dynamics of Gang Membership and Problem Behavior: A Replication and Extension of the Denver and Rochester Gang Studies in Seattle." Paper presented at the annual meeting of the American Society of Criminology, Chicago, IL.

Hill, K. G., J. C. Howell, J. D. Hawkins, and S. R. Battin-Pearson. 1999. "Childhood Risk Factors for Adolescent Gang Membership: Results from the Seattle Social Development Project." *Journal of Research in Crime and Delinquency* 36 (3): 300–322.

Horowitz, R. 1983. *Honor and the American Dream: Culture and Identity in a Chicano Community*. New Brunswick, NJ: Rutgers University Press.

Howell, J. C. 2015. *The History of Street Gangs in the United States: Their Origins and Transformations*. Lanham, MD: Lexington Books.

Howell, J. C., and A. Egley. 2005. "Moving Risk Factors into Developmental Theories of Gang Membership." *Youth Violence and Juvenile Justice* 3: 334–354.

Howell, J. C., Egley, A., and Gleason, D. K. 2002. *Modern Day Youth Gangs*. Washington D.C.: Office of Juvenile Justice and Delinquency Prevention, National Institute of Justice. http://citeseerx.ist.psu.edu/viewdoc/download;jsessionid=83A75A87E007DF345E53030282D07399?doi=10.1.1.523.1584&rep=rep1&type=pdf.

Howell, J. C., A. Egley Jr., G. Tita, and E. Griffiths 2011. *U.S. Gang Problem Trends and Seriousness, 1996–2009*. Tallahassee, FL: Institute for Intergovernmental Research, National Gang Center.

Hudson, W. H. 1996. *WALMYR Assessment Scales Scoring Manual*. Tempe, AZ: WALMYR.

Ireland, T. O., C. A. Smith, and T. P. Thornberry. 2002. "Developmental Issues in the Impact of Child Maltreatment on Later Delinquency and Drug Use." *Criminology* 40: 359–400.

Imai, K., L. Keele, and T. Yamamoto. 2010. "Identification, Inference and Sensitivity Analysis for Causal Mediation Effects." *Statistical Science* 25: 51–71.

IOM (Institute of Medicine) and NRC (National Research Council). 2014. *New Directions in Child Abuse and Neglect Research*. Washington, DC: The National Academies Press.

Huff, C. R. 2001. *Gangs in America III*. Thousand Oaks, CA: Sage publications.

Junger, M., J. Greene, R. Schipper, F. Hesper, and V. Estourgie. 2013. "Parental Criminality, Family Violence and Intergenerational Transmission of Crime Within a Birth Cohort." *European Journal on Criminal Policy and Research* 19 (2): 117–133.

Kaplan, H. B., and X. Liu. 1999. "Explaining Transgenerational Continuity in Antisocial Behavior during Early Adolescence." In *Historical and Geographical Influences on Psychopathology*, edited by P. Cohen, C. Slomkowski and L. N. Robins, 163–191. Mahway, NJ: Erlbaum.

Kaplan, H., and G. C. Tolle. 2006. *The Cycle of Deviant Behavior*. New York: Springer-Verlag.

Karlson, K. B., and A. Holm. 2011. "Decomposing Primary and Secondary Effects: A New Decomposition Method." *Research in Social Stratification and Mobility* 29: 221–237.

Kohler, U., K. B. Karlson, and A. Holm. 2011. "Comparing Coefficients of Nested Nonlinear Probability Models." *Stata Journal* 11 (3): 420–438.

Kim, H. K., D. M. Capaldi, K. C. Pears, D. C. Kerr, and L. D. Owen. 2009. "Intergenerational Transmission of Internalising and Externalising Behaviours across Three Generations: Gender-Specific Pathways." *Criminal Behaviour and Mental Health* 19: 125–141.

Klein, M. W. 1995. *The American Street Gang: Its Nature, Prevalence, and Control*. New York: Oxford University Press.

Knight, K. E., S. Menard, and S. B. Simmons. 2014. "Intergenerational Continuity of Substance Use." *Substance Use and Misuse* 49: 221–233.

Krohn, M. D., and T. P. Thornberry. 2008. "Longitudinal Perspectives on Adolescent Street Gangs." In *The Long View of Crime: A Synthesis of Longitudinal Research*, edited by A. M. Liberman, 128–160. New York: Springer.

Krohn, M. D., J. T. Ward, T. P. Thornberry, A. J. Lizotte, and R. Chu. 2011. "The Cascading Effects of Adolescent Gang Involvement across the Life Course." *Criminology* 49: 991–1028.

Lahey, B. B., R. A. Gordon, R. Loeber, M. Stouthamer-Loeber, and D. P. Farrington. 1999. "Boys Who Join Gangs: A Prospective Study of Predictors of First Gang Entry." *Journal of Abnormal Child Psychology* 27: 261–276.

MacKinnon, D. P., and A. J. Fairchild. 2009. "Current Directions in Mediation Analysis." *Current Directions in Psychological Science* 18: 16–20.

Matsuda, K. N., C. Melde, T. J. Taylor, A. Freng, and F. A. Esbensen. 2013. "Gang Membership and Adherence to the "Code of the Street"." *Justice Quarterly* 30: 440–468.

Melde, C., and F. Esbensen. 2011. "Gang Membership as a Turning Point in the Life Course." *Criminology* 49: 513–552.

Miller, H. V., and J. C. Barnes. 2013. "Genetic Transmission Effects and Intergenerational Contact with the Criminal Justice System: A Consideration of Three Dopamine Polymorphisms." *Criminal Justice and Behavior* 40: 671–689.

Miller, W. B. 2011. *City Gangs*. https://live-crim.ws.asu.edu/sites/default/files/%5Bterm%3Aname%5D/%5Bnode%3Acreate%3Acustom%3AYm%5D/city-gangs-book.pdf.

Moore, J. 1993. *Going Down To The Barrio*. Philadelphia, PA: Temple University Press.

Moore, J. W., R. Garcia, J. W. Moore, and C. Garcia. 1978. *Homeboys: Gangs, Drugs, and Prison in the Barrios of Los Angeles*. Philadelphia, PA: Temple University Press.

National Gang Intelligence Center. 2015. *National Gang Report 2015*. Washington, DC: Federal Bureau of Investigation.

Pears, K. C., D. M. Capaldi, and L. D. Owen. 2007. "Substance Use Risk across Three Generations: The Roles of Parent Discipline Practices and Inhibitory Control." *Psychology of Addictive Behaviors* 21: 373–386.

Petersen, R. D., and J. C. Howell. 2013. "Program Approaches for Girls in Gangs: Female Specific or Gender Neutral?" *Criminal Justice Review* 38: 491–509.

Preacher, K. J., and A. F. Hayes. 2008. "Asymptotic and Resampling Strategies for Assessing and Comparing Indirect Effects in Multiple Mediator Models." *Behavior Research Methods* 40: 879–891.

Prinz, R. J., M. R. Sanders, C. J. Shapiro, D. J. Whitaker, and J. R. Lutzker. 2009. "Population-Based Prevention of Child Maltreatment: The U.S. Triple P System Population Trial." *Prevention Science* 10: 1–12.

Pyrooz, D. C. 2014. "'From Your First Cigarette to Your Last Dyin' Day': the Patterning of Gang Membership in the Life-Course." *Journal of Quantitative Criminology* 30 (2): 349–372.

Pyrooz, D. C. 2014. "From Colors and Guns to Caps and Gowns? The Effects of Gang Membership on Educational Attainment." *Journal of Research in Crime and Delinquency* 51 (1): 56–87.

Raudino, A., D. M. Fergusson, L. J. Woodward, and L. J. Horwood. 2013. "The Intergenerational Transmission of Conduct Problems." *Social Psychiatry and Psychiatric Epidemiology* 48: 465–476.

Rose, D. R., and T. R. Clear. 1998. "Incarceration, Social Capital, and Crime: Implications for Social Disorganization Theory." *Criminology* 36: 441–480.

Smith, C. A., and D. P. Farrington. 2004. "Continuities in Antisocial Behavior and Parenting across Three Generations." *Journal of Child Psychology and Psychiatry* 45: 230–247.

Smith, D. A., and R. Paternoster. 1987. "The Gender Gap in Theories of Deviance: Issues and Evidence." *Journal of Research in Crime and Delinquency* 24 (2): 140–172.

Snyder, H.N., and Sickmund, M. 2006. *Juvenile Offenders and Victims: 2006 National Report*. Washington, DC: US Department of Justice, Office of Justice Programs, Office of Juvenile Justice and Delinquency Prevention.

StataCorp. 2015. *Stata Statistical Software: Release 14*. College Station, TX: StataCorp LP.

Taylor, A. B., D. P. MacKinnon, and J. Y. Tein. 2008. "Tests of the Three-path Mediated Effect." *Organizational Research Methods* 11 (2): 241–269.

Thompson, K. M., and R. Braaten-Antrim. 1998. "Youth Maltreatment and Gang Involvement." *Journal of Interpersonal Violence* 13 (3): 328–345.

Thornberry, T. P. 1987. "Toward an Interactional Theory of Delinquency." *Criminology* 25: 863–892.

Thornberry, T. P. 2005. "Explaining Multiple Patterns of Offending across the Life Course and across Generations." *The ANNALS of the American Academy of Political and Social Science* 602: 156–195.

Thornberry, T. P. 2009. "The Apple Doesn't Fall Far from the Tree (or Does It?): Intergenerational Patterns of Antisocial Behavior-the American Society of Criminology 2008 Sutherland Address." *Criminology* 47: 297–325.

Thornberry, T. P. 2016. "Three Generation Studies: Methodological Challenges and Promise." In *Handbook of the Life Course*, edited by M. J. Shanahan, J. T. Mortimer and M. K. Johnson, 571–596. New York: Springer International Publishing.

Thornberry, T. P., C. S. Smith, and G. J. Howard. 1997. "Risk Factors for Teenage Fatherhood." *Journal of Marriage and the Family* 59: 505–522.

Thornberry, T. P., A. Freeman-Gallant, and P. J. Lovegrove. 2009. "Intergenerational Linkages in Antisocial Behaviour." *Criminal Behaviour and Mental Health* 19: 80–93.

Thornberry, T. P., A. Freeman-Gallant, A. J. Lizotte, M. D. Krohn, and C. A. Smith. 2003. "Linked Lives: The Intergenerational Transmission of Antisocial Behavior." *Journal of Abnormal Child Psychology* 31: 171–184.

Thornberry, T. P., T. O. Ireland, and C. A. Smith. 2001. "The Importance of Timing: The Varying Impact of Childhood and Adolescent Maltreatment on Multiple Problem Outcomes." *Development and Psychopathology* 13: 957–979.

Thornberry, T. P., K. E. Knight, and P. J. Lovegrove. 2012. "Does Maltreatment Beget Maltreatment? A Systematic Review of the Intergenerational Literature." *Trauma, Violence, & Abuse* 13: 135–152.

Thornberry, T. P., and M. D. Krohn. 2001. "The Development of Delinquency: An Interactional Perspective." In *Handbook of Youth and Justice*, edited by S. O. White, 289–305. New York: Plenum. NCJ 187115.

Thornberry, T. P., and M. D. Krohn. 2005. "Applying Interactional Theory to the Explanation of Continuity and Change in Antisocial Behavior." In *Integrated Developmental and Life-Course Theories of Offending*, edited by D. P. Farrington, 183–209. New Brunswick, NJ: Transaction Publishers.

Thornberry, T. P., M. D. Krohn, and A. Freeman-Gallant. 2006. "Intergenerational Roots of Early Onset Substance Use." *Journal of Drug Issues* 36: 1–28.

Thornberry, T. P., M. D. Krohn, A. J. Lizotte, and D. Chard-Wierschem. 1993. "The Role of Juvenile Gangs in Facilitating Delinquent Behavior." *Journal of Research in Crime and Delinquency* 30 (1): 55–87.

Thornberry, T. P., M. Krohn, A. J. Lizotte, C. A. Smith, and K. Tobin. 2003. *Gangs and Delinquency in the Developmental Perspective*. New York: Cambridge University Press.

Van de Rakt, M., S. Ruiter, N. De Graaf, and P. Nieuwbeerta. 2010. "When Does the Apple Fall from the Tree? Static versus Dynamic Theories Predicting Intergenerational Transmission of Convictions." *Journal of Quantitative Criminology* 26: 371–389.

Velleman, R. 1992. "Intergenerational Effects—A Review of Environmentally Oriented Studies concerning the Relationship between Parental Alcohol Problems and Family Disharmony in the Genesis of Alcohol and Other Problems. II: The Intergenerational Effects of Family Disharmony." *International Journal of the Addictions* 27: 367–389.

Vigil, J. D. 1988. "Group Processes and Street Identity: Adolescent Chicano Gang Members." *Ethos* 16: 421–445.

Vigil, J. D. 2002. *A Rainbow of Gangs: Street Life and Identity in the Mega-City*. Austin: University of Texas Press.

van de Weijer, S., M. B. Augustyn, and S. Besemer. 2017. "Intergenerational Transmission of Crime." In *The Routledge International Handbook of Life-Course Criminology*, edited by A. Blokland and V. van der Geest, 279–297.

Wolfgang, M. E., T. P. Thornberry, and R. M. Figlio. 1987. *From Boy to Man, from Delinquency to Crime*. Chicago, IL: University of Chicago Press.

Developmental pathways of youth gang membership: a structural test of the social development model

Asia S. Bishop, Karl G. Hill, Amanda B. Gilman, James C. Howell, Richard F. Catalano and J. David Hawkins

ABSTRACT
As a result of nearly 40 years of research using a risk and protective factor approach, much is known about the predictors of gang onset. Little theoretical work, however, has been done to situate this approach to studying gang membership within a more comprehensive developmental model. Using structural equation modeling techniques, the current study is the first to test the capacity of the social development model (SDM) to predict the developmental pathways that increase and decrease the likelihood of gang membership. Results suggest that the SDM provides a good accounting of the social developmental processes at age 13 that are predictive of later gang membership. These findings support the promotion of a theoretical understanding of gang membership that specifies both pro- and antisocial developmental pathways. Additionally, as the SDM is intended as a model that can guide preventive intervention, results also hold practical utility for designing strategies that can be implemented in early adolescence to address the likelihood of later gang involvement. Three key preventive intervention points to address gang membership are discussed, including promoting efforts to enhance social skills, increasing the availability of prosocial opportunities and rewarding engagement in these opportunities, and reducing antisocial socialization experiences throughout the middle- and high school years.

Introduction

Scholarly inquiries of youth gang membership since the early 1980s have largely focused on identifying the risk and protective factors associated with youth gang membership and related delinquency and criminal offending. This is not surprising given the surge in media and public attention, statistical advances, and increased governmental funding during that time which promoted a risk and protective factors approach to gang research (Howell 2003; Miller 2001). Despite the rapid growth of research examining why youth join gangs, the translation of this research into effective gang prevention programs has been significantly slower (for a notable exception, see Esbensen et al. 2011, 2013). Consequently, prevention efforts are increasingly emphasizing the need for more research that can have direct implications for programming to help youth who are gang-involved or at-risk of involvement (Boxer, Kubik et al. 2015; Howell and Griffiths 2016).

To date, little theoretical work has been done to situate the risk and protective factors approach to studying gang membership within a more comprehensive developmental model. However, for this knowledge to have utility, it is important to also understand the mechanisms by which the development of antisocial behavior (such as gang membership) is cultivated or inhibited. The social development model (Catalano and Hawkins 1996; Hawkins and Weis 1985) has been used to study several antisocial adolescent behaviors, including delinquency (Catalano et al. 2005; Deng and Roosa 2007; Sullivan and Hirschfield 2011) and violence (Catalano et al. 2005; Herrenkohl et al. 2001; Huang et al. 2001; Kim 2009), and could be a useful framework for understanding gang membership as well. The current study uses longitudinal data to test the capacity of the social development model to predict the developmental pathways that increase and decrease the likelihood of gang membership using relevant social development constructs. Understanding the pathways that reduce risks and enhance protective influences to mitigate gang involvement has the potential to inform the development of targeted preventive intervention strategies.

Risk and protective factors approach to gang involvement

It is imperative to understand why youth join gangs in order to develop successful prevention strategies. Fortunately, much work has been done to determine the risk and protective factors experienced in childhood that are predictive of gang membership in adolescence and early adulthood (Howell, Braun, & Bellatty, this journal issue). Risk factors are individual or environmental hazards that increase an individual's vulnerability to negative developmental outcomes (Shader 2001). Initially, researchers used the risk factors approach to determine the factors predictive of adolescent drug use, general delinquency, and violence (e.g., Hawkins, Catalano, and Miller 1992; Herrenkohl et al. 2000; Thornberry et al. 2003). Several longitudinal studies using large community samples have also examined the risk factors predictive of gang membership, including studies conducted in Seattle, Washington (e.g., Hill et al. 1999), Rochester, New York (e.g., Thornberry et al. 2003), Pittsburgh, Pennsylvania (e.g., Lahey et al. 1999), and Denver, Colorado (e.g., Huizinga et al. 2003). Each study includes a subsample of gang-involved youth from whom data were collected at various points across time. Analyses from these studies, as well as other gang research efforts, have produced three major findings with respect to the impact of risk factors on the likelihood of gang membership. First, gang involvement can be grouped into five developmental domains: individual characteristics, family, school, peer, and community (neighborhood) conditions (Howell and Egley 2005). Second, risk factors have an additive effect; that is, the more risk factors a youth is exposed to, the more likely he or she is to join a gang (e.g., Esbensen et al. 2010; Hill et al. 1999). Finally, the accumulation of risk factors interacting across multiple domains over time appears to further enhance the likelihood of gang membership (Thornberry et al. 2003) – a key premise of Thornberry and Krohn's interactional theory of gang membership (Thornberry 2005; Thornberry and Krohn 2001, 2005; Thornberry et al. 2003).

While the utility of the risk factors approach in identifying targets for gang prevention strategies in specific domains of risk is unarguable, a limitation of the risk factors framework is that it is relatively atheoretical; namely, the risk factors approach itself does not integrate the various components across risk domains into a single, testable causal model. The social development model (Catalano and Hawkins 1996), however, allows for the causal integration of various risk and protective factors into a coherent, testable model that can be applied to more holistically understand the developmental pathways resulting in various youth behaviors, including, we hypothesize, gang membership.

The social development model

The social development model (SDM) organizes a broad range of risk and protective factors into a model specifying causal hypotheses to capture key elements of socialization. To do this, the SDM integrates features of three criminological theories that, individually, only partially account for observed processes in the etiology of delinquency: social learning theory, social control theory, and differential association theory.

Social learning theory (Akers 1973; Bandura 1977; Bandura and Walters 1963) specifies the general social, emotional and cognitive learning mechanisms by which the rationalizations, norms, rules, and motivations of behavior are learned and perpetuated. Children learn patterns of behavior from socializing units of family, school, religious and other community institutions, and peers. The underlying socialization follows the same processes of social learning whether it produces prosocial or problem behavior. Children are socialized through processes involving four constructs: (1) opportunities for involvement in activities and interactions with others, (2) the degree of involvement and interaction, (3) the social, emotional and cognitive skills that are derived from social learning, which are necessary to participate in these involvements and interactions and to access rewards from these interactions, and (4) the reinforcement resulting from performance in activities and interactions. When opportunities and skills are adequate and performance is rewarded, a social bond develops between the individual and the socializing agent, group or institution. Social learning theory informs the social development model by identifying which patterns of behavior are adopted, reinforced, and discouraged and the mechanisms by which these patterns occur. Specifically, the SDM hypothesizes that if prosocial interactions and involvement are experienced as rewarding, they reinforce the development of bonds to prosocial others and commitment to prosocial lines of action. Alternatively, if involvement and interactions with those engaged in antisocial behaviors are experienced as rewarding, they reinforce the development of bonds to antisocial others and perceptions that antisocial behavior will be rewarded.

Social control theory broadly refers to the regulation of behavior as a function of formal or informal social controls (Hirshi 1969), and has been used to identify causal elements in the etiology of problem and positive behaviors. Controls are embedded within institutions that vary across people's lives, and may account for stability or change in antisocial behavior. Formal social controls are legally institutionalized, whereas informal social controls emerge from role relationships across key social institutions such as families, schools, peer networks, and community-based associations. Informal social controls emphasize the structure of interpersonal bonds linking individuals to each other and to other social institutions. Among youth, for example, weak ties to informal social control entities such as parents, school, and conventional peers increases the probability of the initiation and continuation of delinquent behaviors (Thornberry et al. 2003). The social development model incorporates a key perspective from social control theory by suggesting that, once strongly established, social bonds have the power to affect behavior by creating an informal control on future behavior (Catalano and Hawkins 1996). Social bonds, as suggested by control theory, consist of attachment to others in the social unit and a commitment to, or investment in, the actions and beliefs of the socializing unit. The SDM hypothesizes that an individual's behavior will be pro- or antisocial depending on the predominant behaviors, norms, and values held by those to whom the individual is bonded (Catalano and Hawkins 1996). SDM hypotheses depart from social control theory in two primary ways, suggesting (1) that bonds among typically prosocial entities (e.g., family) may in fact contribute to antisocial behavior if the beliefs and actions of that group are antisocial; and (2) that involvement, while playing a role in the theory, does not contribute to the social bond itself unless this involvement is recognized or rewarded.

Differential association theory (Cressey 1953; Matsueda 1982, 1988; Sutherland 1973; Sutherland and Cressey 1970) posits that delinquency is learned through interactions with others in a process of communication within intimate social groups. Under differential association theory, delinquency results from the cumulative exposure to individuals who engage in violations of the law relative to those who do not. Differential association theory is incorporated into the SDM as a driver for parallel, but separate, causal paths for prosocial and antisocial processes. While similar to social learning theory in that individuals learn non-normative behavior socially, differential association further hypothesizes that deviance results from an accrual of antisocial associations at a sufficient quantity and quality. For example, an individual's antisocial bonds may override their prosocial bonds, pushing them toward a higher likelihood of engaging in antisocial behavior (Catalano and Hawkins 1996). Each social path operates concurrently within the SDM, with antisocial bonds increasing the likelihood of antisocial behavior and prosocial bonds increasing the likelihood of prosocial behavior. The SDM includes pathways from antisocial rewards or antisocial beliefs to antisocial behaviors, which are distinct from the influences of deviant peers as postulated by differential association.

To summarize, the SDM is an integrated developmental theory that combines propositions of social learning, social control, and differential association theories to describe causal and mediating processes hypothesized to predict behavior over the course of development (Catalano and Hawkins 1996; Hawkins and Weis 1985). Children learn patterns of behavior, whether prosocial or antisocial, from socializing institutions (family, peers, school, community agencies, etc.). Socialization follows the same processes of social learning whether it produces prosocial or antisocial behavior. Specifically, children are socialized through processes involving four constructs: (1) opportunities for involvement in activities and interactions with others, (2) the degree of involvement and interaction, (3) skills to participate in these involvements and interactions, and (4) the reinforcement resulting from performance in activities and interactions. When opportunities and skills are adequate and performance is rewarded, a social bond develops between the individual and the socializing agent, group or institution. Once established, this social bond has the power to influence behavior by creating an informal control on future behavior. This control hinders or promotes deviant behaviors based on the individual's conformity to the norms and values of the socializing unit. Finally, an individual's behavior will be prosocial or antisocial depending on the predominant behaviors, norms, and values held by those to whom the individual is bonded.

Recognizing that many individuals experience both prosocial and antisocial influences, the SDM hypothesizes that an individual's behavior will be prosocial and/or antisocial depending on the degree of association with and bonding to prosocial and antisocial individuals and the adoption of associated beliefs. Thus, as illustrated in Figure 1, the SDM hypothesizes two parallel development pathways leading to prosocial and antisocial outcomes (Catalano and Hawkins 1996; Hawkins and Weis 1985). The prosocial path specifies how protective processes of opportunities, involvement, skill development, and recognition for prosocial behavior build prosocial bonds and beliefs or norms that are protective against antisocial behavior. The antisocial path specifies how risk factors interact in processes similar to those operating on the prosocial path to produce antisocial behavior. The constructs that form these paths are the same except those on the prosocial path are operationally protective factors and those on the antisocial path are risk factors. Opportunities, involvement, skills, and rewards are the fundamental building blocks of the model. From here, the SDM hypothesizes that the interplay of specific factors during development influence the degree to which children develop bonds to social institutions. Bonding subsequently affects the individual's beliefs in the moral order, which in turn, affects behavior. On the antisocial path, the model also hypothesizes direct paths from (1) antisocial rewards to antisocial behavior, and (2) antisocial bonding to antisocial behavior.

It is also important to note that the SDM hypothesizes a sequence of processes in each of a series of sub-models specific to stages of development ranging from early childhood through adolescence

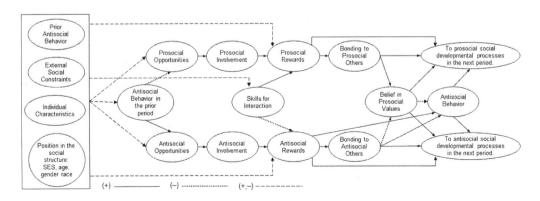

Figure 1. The social development model of antisocial behavior: a general model.

that lead to behavioral outcomes through the cumulative effects of prosocial and antisocial influences. The model also allows for the examination of exogenous factors including position in the social structure (including age, race, gender, and socioeconomic status), individual characteristics (e.g., cognitive ability, poor concentration, early aggressiveness), and external constraints (e.g., formal and informal parent, school, and legal constraints on behavior). The SDM hypothesizes that these exogenous factors are mediated by the processes of socialization or social development that occur along the two major pathways of the model (Catalano and Hawkins 1996).

Prior tests of the SDM

Full model tests using structural equation or latent modeling techniques have provided empirical support for the SDM's ability to predict a number of delinquent behaviors in adolescence and early adulthood. These include substance use, misuse, and dependence (Brown et al. 2005; Catalano et al. 1996, 2005; Fleming et al. 1997; Kosterman et al. 2014; Lonczak et al. 2001; O'Donnell, Hawkins, and Abbott 1995; Sullivan and Hirschfield 2011); delinquency and antisocial behavior (Brown et al. 2005; Catalano et al. 2005; Kosterman et al. 2004; Sullivan and Hirschfield 2011); violence (Catalano et al. 2005; Herrenkohl et al. 2001; Huang et al. 2001; Kim 2009); school problems (Catalano et al. 2005); and other child problem behavior (Catalano et al. 1999; Fleming et al. 2002; Sullivan and Hirschfield 2011). Partial tests of the SDM have also provided empirical support for the model's predictive ability to identify causes of school problems (Kim 2000); substance use (Choi et al. 2005; Kim 2000); delinquency and antisocial behavior (Deng and Roosa 2007; Kim 2000); aggression (Deng and Roosa 2007; Kim 2000); externalizing behavior (Roosa et al. 2011); and violence (Choi et al. 2005) in diverse samples.

While the SDM as an integrated model has yet to be applied to the study of gang membership, key tenets of social control, social learning, and differential association theories have independently been supported in explaining onset, or other aspects, of youth gang membership. For instance, social control theory has been used to predict the onset of gang membership (Thornberry 2006), determine the correlates of gang membership (Brownfield 2003, 2010; Brownfield, Thompson, and Sorenson 1997), and assess the relationship between youth gang involvement and criminal and delinquent behaviors (Cepeda et al. 2016). In a similar fashion, social learning theory has also been used to understand the correlates of gang membership (Brownfield, Thompson, and Sorenson 1997), while also distinguishing gang from non-gang youth, particularly in relation to higher rates of group-based offending (Winfree, Backstrom, and Mays 1994; Winfree, Mays, and Vigil-Bäckström 1994) and substantial increases in violent delinquency (Thornberry et al. 1993). Researchers have also used measured constructs of differential association independently to determine the correlates of gang membership (Brownfield 2003; Winfree, Backstrom, and Mays 1994; Winfree, Mays, and Vigil-Bäckström 1994). The synthesis of these theories within the SDM framework has the potential to contribute further to understanding of why youth join gangs.

Current study

Various studies have demonstrated empirical links between SDM constructs and youth behavioral outcomes. Studies have also shown the practicality of applying the SDM's three underlying theories to studying gang membership in youth samples. Taken together, the theoretical and empirical literature supports the application of the SDM to examine the precursory paths leading to gang membership. The SDM is an appropriate theoretical model to examine gang membership because it incorporates relationships among a set of empirically derived risk and protective factors, most of which have been shown to predict gang membership (e.g., Hill et al. 1999). Consequently, the current study is a test of the SDM to assess the degree to which the model is able to explain the developmental paths leading to gang membership, taking into account the degree to which violence earlier in childhood (an indicator of prior antisocial behavior) affects these processes.

Methods

Sample

Data for the current study are drawn from the Seattle Social Development Project (SSDP). SSDP is a longitudinal study following respondents prospectively from age 10 into adulthood. Participants were from 18 Seattle elementary schools that served students from high-crime neighborhoods, as indicated by statistics obtained from the Seattle Police Department. The schools represented approximately 25% of the total number of elementary schools in Seattle at the time, and the study population included all fifth-grade students in these schools ($N = 1053$). From this population, 808 students and their families consented to participate in the study. During elementary school the Seattle School District used mandatory busing to achieve racial equality in schools. As a result, the sample also included students from other neighborhoods in the city. This sample represented 77% of the population of fifth graders targeted for participation.

Of the 808 students, 396 (49%) were female, 381 (47%) were Caucasian-American, 207 (26%) were African-American, 177 (22%) were Asian-American, 43 (5%) were Native American, and the remaining 26 students were of other ethnic backgrounds. Of these, approximately 5% also self-identified as Hispanic. A majority of the participants were from low-income households. More than half of the student sample (52%) had participated in national free or reduced school breakfast/lunch program at some point in the fifth, sixth, or seventh grade. Alongside this, a significant majority of participants were from low-income households – 46% of parents reported a maximum family income of less than $20,000 per year in 1985.

The SSDP panel was interviewed annually from the fifth grade (in 1985) through tenth grade, in the 12th grade, and every three years until the present. Retention rates for the sample have averaged 90% since the onset of the study. In addition to interviews of panel members, SSDP also interviewed parents and teachers, and collected information regarding respondents from school records. All data collection procedures were approved by the University of Washington Human Subjects Review Committee.

With the exception of the gang measure (described below), the analyses of social developmental processes presented here examine data collected in the spring of 1988, 1989, and 1991, when participants were aged 13, 14, and 16 years, respectively. One respondent was identified as an outlier in preliminary analyses, uniformly answering '110 times' across a number of measures of major delinquency at age 18. Consequently, the respondent was dropped from further analysis. This decision aligns with other SDM tests using the SSDP sample (e.g., Huang et al. 2001; Lonczak et al. 2001). The final sample size for the current analysis is 807.

Measures

Gang membership

The use of self-report measures for determining gang involvement has been widely supported in the field of youth gang research (e.g., Boxer, Veysey et al. 2015; Bjerregaard and Smith 1993; Dishion, Nelson, and Yasui 2005; Esbensen et al. 2001; Fox, Lane, and Akers 2010; Klein 1995; Tapia 2011; Thornberry et al. 2003). In the current study, self-reported gang membership was measured prospectively from 7th to 10th grade, in 12th grade, and subsequently every three years in adulthood. Participants were asked, 'Do you belong to a gang?' followed by 'What is the name of the gang?' The latter question was used to distinguish gangs from informal peer groups – a common surveying tactic that is used to obtain the most reliable self-report data on gang involvement possible (Esbensen et al. 2001). The most commonly named gangs in the sample were the Bloods, the Crips, and the Black Gangster Disciples. Gang names were vetted in conjunction with the King County Gang Task Force, and only names deemed credible were used. Initially, youth who reported that they were a member of a gang and could provide a credible name were coded as belonging to a gang. Slight inconsistencies in reporting occurred over time, particularly when respondents were at ages 21 and 24 years, and were asked if they had ever belonged to a gang and the age when they first joined. Sensitivity analyses conducted on the sample revealed (1) no significant differences on an index of childhood risk for those who reported ever joining a gang and later changed their response from those who consistently reported membership, and (2) significant differences for all those who ever reported membership compared with those who had never reported membership (for results of these analyses, see Gilman et al. 2014). As a result, respondents were coded as having joined a gang (1 = yes) if they ever reported having done so, either prospectively or retrospectively. Within the analysis sample, 21% ($n = 172$) of respondents ever reported joining a gang.

Prior violent behavior

Three indicators of self-reported violent behavior in the past year at age 13 were used in the current analyses. These items include picking a fight with someone, hitting someone with the intention of hurting, and beating someone so badly that a doctor's help was needed. Taken together, these indicators have been conceptually considered to be progressively more severe forms of 'street' violence (Huang et al. 2001). To address skewness, the violence items were log-transformed prior to standardization. One latent variable –prior violent behavior – comprised of the three indicators was specified by the model.

SDM constructs

The SDM is a theory of general prosocial and antisocial processes which posits that socialization manifests as opportunities, involvement, rewards and bonding (Catalano and Hawkins 1996). Following the theory and methodology from prior SDM tests (e.g., Huang et al. 2001), a reflective measurement approach was taken to identify latent variables specified by the model. Reflective measurement – where causality flows from the latent construct to the indicators – assumes that a change in the indicator(s) reflects a change in the latent construct (Coltman et al. 2008). All model constructs related to the SDM were measured during the middle school and early high school periods when respondents were between the ages of 14 and 16. Latent variables specified by the model on the prosocial and antisocial paths include opportunities, involvement, rewards, and bonding. Each of these latent variables includes indicators spread across four domains of influence: community, school, family, and peer. Latent variables representing antisocial opportunities, involvement, rewards, and bonding were created in a similar fashion. The rationale for this approach was to create indicators that represented a cross-domain composite of a youth's perceptions, attitudes, beliefs, and socialization experiences. This methodology emphasizes multidomain indicators of a single (latent) concept, and has been used in prior tests of the SDM (e.g., Huang et al. 2001; Lonczak et al. 2001). Additionally, latent variables representing skills for interaction and beliefs in prosocial values were created and included in the analysis models. All items were coded so that higher scores reflect more of the indicated construct, then standardized to account for variation in item scaling prior to scale creation. If a participant had complete data on at least half of the items composing the indicator, the mean of the standardized scores was computed as the value of the indicator. Ultimately, the model constructs used in the current analyses were indicated by three scales. Model constructs and sample items are provided in Table 1 (all items are available from the first author).

Gender, ethnicity and socioeconomic status

As indicated in Figure 1, the SDM permits examination of exogenous factors, such as position in the social structure, that are hypothesized to influence the socialization process (Catalano and Hawkins 1996). The current model test accounts for position in the social structure by controlling for gender, ethnicity and socioeconomic status in the identified paths. This decision is further supported by the fact that being male, non-white, and from a low socioeconomic background have been shown to be significantly correlated with gang membership in the SSDP sample (e.g., Gilman et al. 2014). Gender is coded as a dichotomous variable, where 1 = male and 0 = female. Ethnicity is included in the models as three dummy variables (1 = yes) for African-American, Asian-American, and Native American, with Caucasian set as the referent group. Socioeconomic status is a composite of standardized measures of parental education (mother's and father's) and per capita household income in the 5th and 6th grades, as well as the child's eligibility for participation in the national free or reduced school breakfast/lunch program in the 5th, 6th, and 7th grades.

Table 1. Measurement of SDM constructs.

Construct	N of items	Data sources	Example items
Prior violent behavior (age 13)	7	youth, parent, teacher	Physically attacks people
Opportunities for prosocial involvement	11	youth, parent	My parents give me lots of chances to do things with them
Opportunities for antisocial involvement	18	youth	Have you ever been invited to join a gang?
Involvement in prosocial activities	17	youth, parent	In how many school clubs or activities outside class did you participate this year?
Involvement with those involved in problem behaviors	11	youth, parent, teacher	Hangs around with others who get in trouble
Skills for interaction	9	youth	If one of your friends asked you to skip school, what would you do? [scaled towards peer resistance]
Rewards for prosocial involvement	24	youth	My parents notice when I am doing a good job and let me know about it
Rewards for antisocial involvement	12	youth	What are the chances you would be seen as cool if you beat up somebody?
Bonding to prosocial others and activities (attachment and commitment)	19	youth, parent	Would you like to be the kind of person your mother is? [if mother is not antisocial]
Bonding to antisocial others	9	youth	Do you want to be the kind of person your best friend is? [if friend is antisocial]
Belief in the prosocial values [developed as a single construct scaled towards prosocial beliefs]	12	youth	Is it okay to take something without asking if you can get away with it?

Analytic procedures

Model analyses were conducted in Mplus version 7 (Muthen and Muthen 2012). Structural equation modeling (SEM) typically includes two analytic components: a measurement model (confirmatory factor analysis, CFA) and a structural model (structural equation model, SEM) (Buhi, Goodson, and Neilands 2007). The initial model test is modeled after a prior test of the SDM (Huang et al. 2001) with two notable exceptions: (1) gang membership is the primary outcome of interest and (2) gender and ethnicity are included as control variables not only in the direct path to gang membership, but also in the direct paths in the front of the model as hypothesized by the SDM (for example, gender and ethnicity are included in the direct paths to violent behavior, skills, prosocial socialization, and gang membership in the final second-order model). Because the primary model constructs are the same, CFA results are not provided for the structural models here, except to note that the model fit statistics for the CFA analyses conducted by Huang and colleagues (2001) suggest the measurement models fit the data well (first-order CFA model: $\chi^2 = 1168.32$ (df = 559, n = 807), CFI = 0.96, RMSEA = 0.04; second-order CFA model: $\chi^2 = 1376.80$ (df = 588, n = 807), CFI = 0.95, RMSEA = 0.04).

Structural models

Modeling proceeded in three steps. First, a model was examined that reflected the SDM as specified in Figure 1. Next, following examination of modification indices, and discussion, a revised model was examined that included some additional paths and factor intercorrelations. Finally, the revised SDM was also examined as a second-order model due to the high correlations among opportunities, involvement and rewards which were included in a single socialization factor for each of the two paths (antisocial and prosocial). Since gang membership was assessed cumulatively, to test the time-ordering of the model, sensitivity analyses were run excluding youth who joined a gang prior to age 14. Model fit and path estimates resulting from this analysis were similar to the model results using the full sample. As a result, the final models presented here include all 807 cases.

In the first- and second-order structural models, factor loadings were allowed to freely vary with one referent indicator on each factor set to 1.00 to identify the metric of the latent variables. In the revised model, four pairs of indicator error terms were allowed to correlate to account for parallel items contained in the corresponding indicators (the four pairs were the error terms for V10 and V13, V25 and V28, V26 and V29, and V27 and V30 – these correspond to factors listed in Table 3 in the results section). Additionally, the four pairs of error terms for the corresponding prosocial and antisocial factors (e.g., prosocial opportunities with antisocial opportunities) were also allowed to freely correlate. These correlations were added to account for the conceptual correspondence between the constructs, a technique used in prior SDM tests using SSDP data (e.g., Huang et al. 2001; Lonczak et al. 2001). In line with the above procedures, the residuals for the two higher-order socialization constructs (prosocial socialization and antisocial socialization) were also allowed to freely correlate in the second-order model. All theory-based path coefficients between factors were freely estimated.

As specified by the SDM, gender (one dichotomous variable), ethnicity (three dummy variables), and socioeconomic status were included as control variables in the direct paths to (1) prosocial opportunities, prosocial rewards, antisocial opportunities, and antisocial rewards in the first-order model, and (2) prior violence, skills, and prosocial socialization in the revised and second-order model. Additionally, gender, ethnicity, and socioeconomic status were also included in the model as control variables in the direct path to gang membership. Consequently, all direct effects on gang membership control for gender, ethnicity, and socioeconomic status.

Based on recommendations in the field, overall model fit was assessed using the chi-square model fit, Comparative Fit Index (CFI), Tucker-Lewis Index (TLI), and the Root Mean Square Error of Approximation (RMSEA) (Bentler 1990; Bollen 1989; Bollen and Lennox 1991; Buhi, Goodson, and Neilands 2007; Browne and Cudeck 1993; Hu and Bentler 1999). Chi-square ratios (χ^2/df) between 2 and 5 have been employed in health behavior research to determine a good fitting model (Buhi, Goodson, and Neilands 2007). Values of 0.95 or greater for the CFI/TLI (Hu and Bentler 1999) and 0.05 and lower for the RMSEA (Bollen 1989; Browne and Cudeck 1993) indicate a good model fit and have been recommended by scholars employing SEM techniques. Others have suggested that a cutoff value of 0.90 or greater for the CFI indicates an adequate fit (Newcomb 1990). While little consensus exists with regard to viable cutoff values for determining good model fit, the aforementioned standards have been routinely applied in the social and health sciences (Buhi, Goodson, and Neilands 2007).

Missing data

Little sample attrition occurred over the course of the study. Of the 808 who began the study at age 10, 778 (96%) were interviewed at age 14, 770 (95%) were interviewed at age 16, and 757 (94%) were interviewed at age 18. To avoid any potential bias associated with deletion or mean substitution procedures, missing data were addressed in Mplus using maximum likelihood estimation with robust standard errors (MLR). Maximum likelihood estimation was chosen to address missing data in order to obtain the best estimates of the relationships between variables using all available data without deleting cases. Utilizing this method preserves the natural variability in the data so that the presented estimates are not biased (Graham 2009), and is a substantial improvement over traditional approaches (i.e., listwise or pairwise deletion, mean or regression substitution) when missingness cannot be avoided (Acock 2005).

Results

Factor intercorrelations are presented in Table 2 (correlations, means and standard deviations for measured variables are available from the first author). Measures indicating the same factor were highly correlated in each case. With three exceptions – prosocial opportunities with violence; antisocial bonding with prosocial opportunities; and antisocial bonding with prosocial socialization – the majority of coefficients were in the expected direction, with positive correlations among prosocial constructs and negative correlations between prosocial constructs and antisocial constructs. Results suggest that, in general, the scales indicating each factor share substantial common variance, and that relationships

Table 2. Factor intercorrelations for the first- and second-order factor models.

Factor	1	2	3	4	5	6	7	8	9	10	11	12	13
First-order constructs													
1. Prior violent behavior (age 13)	−.30***												
2. Skills for interaction	.01	.40***											
3. Prosocial opportunities	.47***	−.57***	−.25***										
4. Antisocial opportunities	−.14*	.52***	.65***	−.35***									
5. Prosocial involvement	.54***	−.64***	−.12*	.77***	−.40***								
6. Antisocial involvement	−.12*	.54***	.73***	−.51***	.72***	−.48***							
7. Prosocial rewards	.27***	−.71***	−.42***	.59***	−.47***	.55***	−.59***						
8. Antisocial rewards	−.24***	.37***	.32***	−.44***	.36***	−.37***	.44***	−.33***					
9. Prosocial bonding	.12**	−.29***	−.04	.37***	−.15**	.39***	−.26***	.26***	−.57***				
10. Antisocial bonding	−.23***	.48***	.29***	−.33***	.29***	−.32***	.39***	−.46***	.58***	−.39***			
11. Belief in prosocial values													
Second-order constructs													
12. Prosocial socialization	−.02*	.09***	—	—	—	—	—	—	.09***	.01***	.08***		
13. Antisocial socialization	.13***	−.15***	—	—	—	—	—	—	−.11***	.16***	−.11***	−.08***	
14. Gang membership (1 = yes)[a]	7.00***	0.17***	0.74	2.57***	1.52	3.39***	0.38*	6.19***	0.60*	1.21	0.33***	0.81	14.31***

[a]Presented as odds ratios from bivariate logistic regressions examining the relationships between gang membership and the latent factors. Blanks (−) are listed for first-order factors that serve as indicators of the second-order factors.
*Significant at $p < .05$; **$p < .01$; ***$p < .001$.

Table 3. Standardized factor loadings for the first- and second-order factor structures.

Construct	Indicator variable	First-order factor model	Second-order factor model
Prior violent behavior	V1	.68***	.69***
	V2	.56***	.57***
	V3	.68r	.68r
Skills for interaction	V4	.66r	.71r
	V5	.57***	.63***
	V6	.57***	.59***
Prosocial opportunities	V7	.73r	.73r
	V8	.63***	.65***
	V9	.43***	.44***
Antisocial opportunities	V10	.78***	.79***
	V11	.75***	.75***
	V12	.76r	.76r
Prosocial involvement	V13	.74r	.84r
	V14	.50***	.46***
	V15	.53***	.53***
Antisocial involvement	V16	.74***	.73***
	V17	.45***	.45***
	V18	.71r	.73r
Prosocial rewards	V19	.85r	.85r
	V20	.86***	.87***
	V21	.73***	.73***
Antisocial rewards	V22	.65r	.66r
	V23	.65***	.67***
	V24	.80***	.80***
Prosocial bonding	V25	.86***	.86***
	V26	.87r	.87r
	V27	.83***	.83***
Antisocial bonding	V28	.93r	.93r
	V29	.98***	.98***
	V30	.98***	.98***
Belief in prosocial values	V31	.84***	.84***
	V32	.78***	.78***
	V33	.89r	.89r

Notes: r = reference indicator with unstandardized loadings fixed at 1.00 to identify the metric of the latent variable. All factor loadings are standardized estimates.
***significant at $p < .001$.

among factors are consistent with hypothesized distinctions between prosocial and antisocial constructs within the model.

As indicated in Table 3, all factor loadings for the first- and second-order model factors were significant and in the expected direction.

First-order factor model

The initial first-order model was tested by including structural paths hypothesized by the SDM a priori. Taken together, results from this initial test suggest a poor-to-modest fit of the data; $\chi^2 = 2128.80$ (df = 650, $n = 807$), CFI = 0.88, TLI = 0.86, RMSEA = 0.05 (95% CI: 0.051 – 0.056). While the SDM specifies that antisocial behavior in prior developmental periods affects later behavior only as it is mediated by opportunities in the subsequent period, we revised the first-order model to include an alternative hypothesis (e.g., Loeber 1996; Huang et al. 2001) of an unmediated path from violent behavior at age 13 to later gang membership. We also tested a direct path from violence at age 13 to skills, and from skills to pro- and antisocial opportunities as supported by findings from dynamic transactional theories of delinquency (e.g., Dishion et al. 1991; Granic and Patterson 2006; Lytton 1990; Patterson, DeBaryshe, and Ramsey 1989; Sameroff 2009). The revised model fit the data better than the traditional model tested a priori, with model fit statistics reaching acceptable values; $\chi^2 = 1651.68$ (df = 609, $n = 807$), CFI = 0.91, TLI = 0.90, RMSEA = 0.05 (95% CI: 0.043 – 0.049). Additionally, results from a chi-square difference test

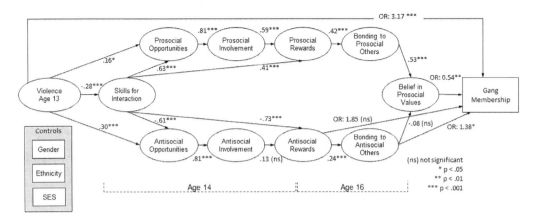

Figure 2. Structural path estimates for the final first-order factor model.

between the a priori (original theory) and revised models suggest that the inclusion of three alternative paths significantly improved the fit of the model ($\chi^2 = 788.64$, df = 4, p-value < .001).

Figure 2 presents the estimated path coefficients for the revised first-order model including the alternative hypothesized paths directly from violence to gang membership, violence to skills, and skills to opportunities. All but three paths specified by SDM were significant and in the expected direction. With the exception of the paths from violence at age 13 to prosocial opportunities (significant, positive effect), from antisocial involvement to antisocial rewards (non-significant), and antisocial bonding to prosocial beliefs (non-significant), all SDM hypotheses were supported. Although the factor intercorrelation between violence at age 13 and prosocial opportunities was near zero and non-significant ($r = .01$, nonsig), the association between violence at age 13 and prosocial opportunities became positive in the context of other variables in the model (control variables for this path include skills, gender, race, and socioeconomic status), suggesting a suppressor effect (MacKinnon, Krull, and Lockwood 2000; Pandey and Elliott 2010). Additionally, results provide evidence for the alternative hypotheses suggesting prior violent behavior predicts lower skills at age 14 ($b = -.28$, $p < .001$), and that, in turn, higher skills predicted significantly more prosocial opportunities ($b = .63$, $p < .001$), fewer antisocial opportunities ($b = -.61$, $p < .001$), and a 3.17 increase in the odds of later gang membership as a result of early delinquency (i.e., violent behavior).

In the interest of parsimony, the effects of gender, ethnicity, and socioeconomic status are not presented in Figure 2. However, results suggest that being male (compared to female) is significantly related to reductions in skills and antisocial opportunities, as well as increases in violent behavior, prosocial rewards, and the odds of joining a gang (OR = 4.57, $p < .001$). Being African-American (compared to Caucasian) is significantly associated with an increase in antisocial opportunities, antisocial rewards, skills, prior violence, and gang membership (OR = 2.54, $p < .001$); being Asian-American is associated with increased skills and gang membership (OR = 1.99, $p < .05$) compared to Caucasian; and being Native American is associated with increased odds of gang membership (OR = 4.78, $p < .01$). Higher socioeconomic status is significantly associated with increased prosocial opportunities and prosocial rewards, and reductions in antisocial opportunities, prior violence, and gang membership (OR = 0.61, $p < .001$). Path estimates for the effects of gender, ethnicity, and socioeconomic status on model constructs for the first-order model are available from the first author.

Second-order factor model

Results from prior tests of the SDM suggest that model fit may be improved if the opportunities, involvement, and rewards constructs are modeled as second-order factors representing more general

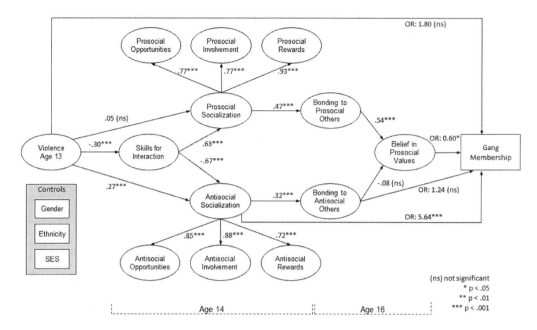

Figure 3. Structural path estimates for the final second-order factor model.

socialization processes – prosocial socialization and antisocial socialization (e.g., Catalano et al. 1996; Huang et al. 2001; Lonczak et al. 2001). While distinguishing between the distinct prosocial and antisocial socialization constructs (opportunities, involvement, and rewards) allows for conceptual and practical applications of the theory, these constructs have also been shown to be highly correlated in the SSDP data (Huang et al. 2001; Lonczak et al. 2001). As a result, modeling second-order factors is advantageous in the current analysis because (1) it allows us to capture the substantial common variance in opportunities, involvement, and rewards, and (2) test direct links to gang membership from the socialization experience in general rather than requiring it to be mediated through rewards and bonding exclusively. Although the SDM hypothesizes that rewards mediate the effects of opportunities and involvement in specific situations (Catalano and Hawkins 1996), the data for these analyses are based on annual assessments and do not allow for a robust test of this aspect of the theory. As a result, the use of second-order socialization factors has been considered a more appropriate fit for the current data (e.g., Huang et al. 2001).

The overall fit of the model improved with the addition of the second-order socialization factors; $\chi^2 = 1594.79$ (df = 616, n = 807), CFI = 0.92, TLI = 0.91, RMSEA = 0.04 (95% CI: 0.042 – 0.047). Results from a chi-square difference test between the first- and second-order models suggest that the inclusion of second-order socialization factors significantly improves the model fit ($\chi^2 = 41.95$, df = 9, p-value < .001). As indicated in Figure 3, all theory-based path coefficients were significant and in the expected direction, with two exceptions: the path from violence at age 13 to prosocial socialization, and the path from bonding to antisocial others to gang membership. Neither of these paths reached statistical significance. Additionally, while in the expected direction, the path from antisocial bonding to prosocial beliefs was also not statistically significant. For clarity, the effects of gender, ethnicity, and socioeconomic status are not presented in Figure 3, but are provided in Table 4. In this model, being male is significantly associated with increased prior violence and gang membership (OR = 5.01, p < .001), as well as decreased skills. When compared with Caucasian, being African-American is significantly associated with increased prior violence, skills, and gang membership (OR = 2.33, p < .01); being Asian-American is associated with increased skills and gang membership (OR = 2.44, p < .01), and decreased prior violence; and being Native American is associated with gang membership (OR = 3.72, p < .01). Higher socioeconomic

Table 4. Standardized betas, standard errors, and p-values for the final second-order structural paths.

Structural paths	β	s.e.	p-value
Prior Violent Behavior			
Gender (1 = male)	.12	.04	.006
African American (1 = yes)	.16	.06	.007
Asian American (1 = yes)	−.15	.04	.001
Native American (1 = yes)	.01	.04	.857
Socioeconomic status	−.18	.05	.001
Skills for Interaction			
Prior violent behavior	−.30	.07	.001
Gender (1 = male)	−.17	.04	.001
African American (1 = yes)	.11	.05	.024
Asian American (1 = yes)	.13	.05	.006
Native American (1 = yes)	−.09	.05	.063
Socioeconomic status	.03	.05	.568
Prosocial Socialization			
Prior violent behavior	.05	.06	.407
Skills for interaction	.63	.05	.001
Gender (1 = male)	.08	.04	.052
African American (1 = yes)	.02	.05	.735
Asian American (1 = yes)	.01	.04	.807
Native American (1 = yes)	.04	.03	.230
Socioeconomic status	.09	.04	.024
Antisocial Socialization			
Prior violent behavior	.27	.06	.001
Skills for interaction	−.67	.05	.001
Prosocial Bonding			
Prosocial socialization	.47	.04	.001
Antisocial Bonding			
Antisocial socialization	.32	.04	.001
Belief in Prosocial Values			
Prosocial bonding	.54	.04	.001
Antisocial bonding	−.08	.04	.062
Ever Joined a Gang (1 = yes)[a]			
Antisocial socialization	.29 (5.64)	.08	.001
Antisocial bonding	.08 (1.24)	.05	.137
Belief in prosocial values	−.13 (0.60)	.06	.019
Prior violent behavior	.14 (1.80)	.07	.052
Gender (1 = male)	.33 (5.01)	.04	.001
African American (1 = yes)	.15 (2.33)	.05	.002
Asian American (1 = yes)	.15 (2.44)	.05	.006
Native American (1 = yes)	.12 (3.72)	.05	.010
Socioeconomic status	−.15 (0.64)	.05	.002

[a]Estimates are presented as point biserial correlations with odds ratios in parentheses.

status is associated with decreased prior violence and gang membership (OR = 0.64, $p < .01$), as well as increased prosocial socialization.

Overall, results from the final second-order model indicate that both prosocial socialization and antisocial socialization (as specified by the SDM) are predictive of gang membership. The prosocial path aligns with the hypotheses specified by the SDM, as we see a significant and negative path from prosocial socialization to gang membership through bonding to prosocial others and beliefs in prosocial values. Antisocial socialization is also predictive of gang membership, but had a direct positive effect, rather than an indirect effect through bonding to prosocial others. Both the prosocial and antisocial path are significantly affected by prior violent behavior through skills. Prior violent behavior, however, does not remain predictive of gang membership after controlling for gender, ethnicity, and socioeconomic status. An effect decomposition identified two statistically significant indirect pathways from violence at 13 to gang membership: violence at 13 → antisocial socialization → gang ($p < .01$) and violence at 13 → skills → antisocial socialization → gang ($p < .01$). These results suggest that the most salient pathways to gang membership in the second-order model were the antisocial socialization pathway and the pathway through skills and antisocial socialization.

Discussion

The current test of the SDM to predict gang membership is an important contribution to the available theoretical and empirical literature on youth gang membership. Various studies have demonstrated empirical links between SDM constructs and youth behavioral outcomes (e.g., Brown et al. 2005; Catalano et al. 1996, 2005; Herrenkohl et al. 2001; Huang et al. 2001; Fleming et al. 1997; Lonczak et al. 2001), and while the SDM's three underlying theories have been applied to study gang membership independently, the current study is the first to apply the SDM as an integrated theory to examine the developmental pathways beginning at age 13 that are predictive of gang membership. Results from the structural model tests presented here suggest that the SDM provides a good accounting of the social developmental processes that predict gang membership, despite the potential temporal constraints of study constructs (detailed further below). Taken together, study findings support the promotion of a theoretical understanding of gang membership that specifies social development pathways, while holding practical utility for designing preventive intervention strategies in early adolescence to address the likelihood of later gang involvement in high risk samples.

Potential model modifications

A test of the fit of the structural paths as originally hypothesized by the social development model using multiple indicators of latent constructs demonstrated a moderate fit for the data. Subsequently, we revised the model to include three alternative hypotheses: (1) a direct path from violent behavior at age 13 to gang membership, (2) a direct path from violent behavior to skills for interaction, and (3) direct paths from skills for interaction to pro- and antisocial opportunities. The revised model fit the data better, and provided empirical support for the addition of the alternative hypotheses. The addition of these paths is also theoretically supported in the literature on child-driven processes. Specifically, prior theory and research have supported the inclusion of child-driven processes such that more socially skilled children, for example, are also likely to have more prosocial opportunities and fewer antisocial opportunities (Granic and Patterson 2006; Lytton 1990; Patterson, DeBaryshe, and Ramsey 1989; Sameroff 2009). Future applications of the model to study the developmental pathways of gang membership should consider including the child-driven paths proposed here.

Further, although ethnicity and gender were included as control variables, we did not examine whether the SDM processes varied by ethnic and gender groups. Despite increasing rates of female gang involvement, research on girls and gangs is still in its infancy, and little theoretical developments have been made to explain the unique processes by which girls join gangs (Howell and Griffiths 2016). Results from the second-order model suggest that boys are five times more likely to join gangs compared to girls within the social development framework. It is possible that alternative mechanisms than those specified by the SDM will better explain the developmental pathways that result in gang membership for girls specifically. Future theory development and research efforts for exploring how and why girls join gangs is needed to advance our knowledge around gangs and girls more generally. While some theoretical work has been done to help explain the processes resulting in gang membership for youth in ethnically marginalized communities (see Vigil's work on multiple marginality, 1988, 2002; Vigil and Yun 2002), the literature is still rather unclear on whether the developmental pathways resulting in gang membership differ across various ethnic groups. Given this observation, it would be important for future SDM tests to assess whether the SDM pathways predicting gang membership are moderated by ethnicity specifically. This is particularly salient given the significant relationships between all three ethnic groups (African-American, Asian-American, and Native American) in predicting higher odds of gang membership compared to white youth after controlling for other model constructs. In the final second-order model, we found significant, positive relationships between being African-American and Asian-American (compared to whites) and skills for interaction as well as gang membership (for reference, see Table 4). This is an interesting finding that also warrants further examination, and highlights the importance of determining whether different mechanisms of socialization result in gang membership for different groups. Overall, additional efforts are needed to clarify the mechanisms of socialization that result in gang membership for girls specifically, as well as those pathways that result in gang membership for ethnically diverse groups.

Informing preventive-intervention efforts

The SDM is intended as a model to guide the development of preventive interventions. While each of the SDM constructs is a potential focus for prevention to reduce the likelihood of gang membership, results from these analyses suggest a number of points for preventive intervention worth noting. First, in the final second-order model, skills for interaction at age 14 was significantly and positively related to prosocial socialization and negatively related to antisocial socialization, which, in turn, both significantly affected youths' risk of joining a gang in the expected directions. Additionally, we found a significant, negative relationship between prior violence and skills and between skills and subsequent pro- and antisocial opportunities. These results suggest the importance of addressing early violence onset as well as enhancing subsequent skills for interaction with others to promote greater prosocial socialization while simultaneously reducing antisocial socialization, particularly for youth already engaged in antisocial behavior in the periods of late childhood and early adolescence. This finding is encouraging because skills are modifiable characteristics. Because skills are malleable, promoting skills development is a promising point for intervention efforts. In fact, this aligns with a more general push in the field of juvenile justice to promote therapeutic interventions that aim to enhance socio-emotional and behavioral skills to reduce problem behaviors such as recidivism (Howell, Lipsey, and Wilson 2014; Walker and Bishop 2016).

These conclusions also align with those made by evaluators of the Gang Resistance Education and Training (G.R.E.A.T.) program. After a rigorous longitudinal evaluation showed no effects of G.R.E.A.T. on violence, delinquency, or gang involvement, the program curriculum was revised to more directly focus on youth skill-building through interactive teaching techniques (Esbensen et al. 2011). An updated evaluation of the G.R.E.A.T. program, which utilized a randomized experimental design, found a significant reduction in gang involvement for the treatment versus the control group for four years post-treatment (Esbensen et al. 2011, 2013). Thus, it appears that skill-building, such as teaching refusal skills and conflict resolution skills, is a valuable component to gang prevention efforts. The results of our study strongly suggest that the importance of these skills could be in their ability to facilitate prosocial socialization and avoid antisocial socialization to mitigate gang involvement.

The second practical conclusion that can be drawn from the current study is the importance of prosocial socialization processes. While much of the gang literature focuses on risk factors, results from the current study suggest significant, positive relationships among factors across the prosocial pathway (prosocial opportunities → bonding → beliefs in prosocial values), which culminate in a reduction of the odds of gang membership. Not surprisingly, we also see positive relationships among the prosocial socialization factors, with higher beliefs in prosocial values resulting in reduced odds of gang membership in the second-order model. This suggests that prevention efforts aimed at reducing the likelihood of gang membership should find viable ways to increase the availability of prosocial opportunities for involvement in family and friend groups, schools, and neighborhood activities. Further, rewards for engaging in these prosocial opportunities should be enhanced, in addition to encouraging the development of prosocial beliefs that align with the values associated with prosocial environments. Results also suggest that beliefs can be influenced by increasing the availability of prosocial opportunities in youth's lives. This is particularly salient because beliefs are often thought of as difficult to change, yet our findings suggest that youth's values can be influenced by providing them with prosocial opportunities and rewards that encourage them to continue on the prosocial pathway.

While results suggest that the likelihood of gang membership can be mitigated by prosocial socialization experiences, model results also suggests that antisocial socialization processes increase the odds of gang membership. It is noteworthy that no relationship was found between antisocial involvement and antisocial rewards in the first-order model. However, a strong, direct effect of antisocial socialization processes on gang membership in the second-order model suggests that the combination of multiple antisocial socialization experiences (opportunities, involvement, and rewards) across an array of domains (family, school, neighborhood, peer) is more highly predictive of gang membership than any one factor independently. These results align with other studies suggesting that the interaction of risk factors in multiple domains produces the greatest risk of gang membership (Thornberry et al. 2003). Aiming to reduce antisocial socialization experiences may prove fruitful in interrupting the trajectory toward gang membership for youth who experience antisocial socialization in late childhood and early adolescence.

While bonding to antisocial others was directly related to gang membership in the first-order model, no significant relationship was found between antisocial bonding and gang membership in the second-order model. Although bonding to antisocial others has been shown to be a predictor of delinquent behavior in this sample (e.g., substance use, Catalano et al. 1996), it only had a slight indirect effect (through beliefs) on gang membership in the final model. On the antisocial path, only antisocial socialization and violent behavior had direct effects on gang membership. Attachment and commitment to peers involved in antisocial behaviors appears to reduce one's belief in prosocial values, whereas gang membership may stem more directly from prior delinquent behavior, engagement with antisocial environments, and the perception that antisocial behavior is rewarding. In the current analyses, gang membership appears to be affected by the strength or weakness of the bonds one has with others engaged in antisocial behavior only to the extent to which these bonds diminish beliefs in prosocial values. This suggests that even youth who are bonded to antisocial others can be positively influenced to avoid gang membership by efforts to enhance their beliefs in prosocial values – a youth can have antisocial bonds and not actively join the gang if their prosocial beliefs are fostered. Further exploration of this relationship is warranted, particularly given what we know about the effects of antisocial peers (Esbensen et al. 2009; Gilman et al. 2014; Huizinga et al. 2003; Lahey et al. 1999) and long-term embeddedness within antisocial networks on sustaining gang membership over time (Pyrooz, Sweeten, and Piquero 2013).

Study limitations

The current study had constraints worth noting. First, data used for these analyses come from a community sample located in Seattle, WA, with participants who were in their adolescent years in the 1980s and 1990s. Consequently, subsequent model tests in samples from other geographic areas or time periods are needed. Second, while self-reported gang membership is commonly used (Boxer, Veysey et al., 2015; Bjerregaard and Smith 1993; Dishion, Nelson, and Yasui 2005; Esbensen et al. 2001; Fox, Lane, and Akers 2010; Klein 1995; Tapia 2011; Thornberry et al. 2003) and empirically supported as a valid measure (Esbensen et al. 2010), there are risks with self-reported data including the possibility or over- or under-reporting. Finally, because gang membership in the sample was measured, in part, during the same time period (7th through 10th grades, when the respondents were 12–15 years old) as the items that comprised the SDM constructs, questions regarding temporal ordering cannot be definitively resolved. This has been a commonly discussed issue in the field of gang research, particularly related to the use of cross-sectional data to determine risk factors for gang onset (e.g., Howell 2012). If risk factors and outcomes are measured at the same time, causal ordering cannot be determined with certainty, which raises the question of whether predictive factors for gang membership might also be outcomes of the membership itself. However, sensitivity analyses exploring the issue of temporality in the current analyses suggested little to no differences in model fit and path estimates as a result of excluding youth who joined a gang during the SDM construct measurement period. Furthermore, prior SDM tests where model constructs (predictor variables) explicitly temporally preceded outcomes related to gang membership (e.g., violence, alcohol use, substance use) yielded results highly consistent with the present study (see for example, Catalano et al. 1996; Huang et al. 2001; Kosterman et al. 2014; and Lonczak et al. 2001). Additional tests of the SDM's prediction of gang membership with clear temporal ordering are warranted to support the present findings.

Conclusions

The current study is the first to test the capacity of the social development model (SDM) to predict the developmental pathways that increase and decrease the likelihood of gang membership using relevant social development constructs. Understanding the pathways that reduce risks and enhance protective influences to mitigate gang involvement has the potential to inform the development of targeted preventive intervention strategies. Results suggest that the SDM provides a good accounting of the developmental pathways that contribute to gang membership, particularly when including additional child-driven paths from social skills to opportunities. While each of the constructs in the SDM is a potential focus for preventive intervention to reduce the likelihood of gang membership, results from these analyses suggest three key intervention points worth considering. First, enhancing skills for interaction with others has the potential to increase prosocial socialization and reduce antisocial socialization processes. Second, increasing the availability of prosocial opportunities, while reducing antisocial opportunities, and rewarding engagement in these opportunities will influence positive beliefs and values which in turn reduce the likelihood of gang membership. Finally, efforts to reduce antisocial socialization experiences throughout the middle- and high school years are promising targets for gang preventive intervention efforts.

Disclosure statement

No potential conflict of interest was reported by the authors.

Funding

This work was supported by the National Institute of Drug Abuse [R01DA003721, R01DA009679, R01DA024411] and the Robert Wood Johnson Foundation [21548].

References

Acock, A. C. 2005. "Working with Missing Values." *Journal of Marriage and Family* 67: 1012–1028.
Akers, R. L. 1973. *Deviant Behavior: A Social Learning Approach*. 1st ed. Belmont, CA: Wadsworth.
Bandura, A. 1977. *Social Learning Theory*. Englewood Cliffs, NJ: Prentice-Hall.
Bandura, A., and R. H. Walters. 1963. *Social Learning and Personality Development*. New York: Holt Rinehart and Winston.
Bentler, P. M. 1990. "Comparative Fit Indexes in Structural Models." *Psychological Bulletin* 107: 238–246.
Bjerregaard, B., and C. Smith. 1993. "Gender Differences in Gang Participation, Delinquency, and Substance Use." *Journal of Quantitative Criminology* 9 (4): 329–355.
Bollen, K. A. 1989. *Structural Equations with Latent Variables*. New York: John Wiley & Sons.
Bollen, K., and R. Lennox. 1991. "Conventional Wisdom on Measurement: A Structural Equation Perspective." *Psychological Bulletin* 110: 305–314.
Boxer, P., J. Kubik, M. Ostermann, and B. Veysey. 2015. "Gang Involvement Moderates the Effectiveness of Evidence-based Intervention for Justice-involved Youth." *Children and Youth Services Review* 52: 26–33.
Boxer, P., B. Veysey, M. Ostermann, and J. Kubik. 2015. "Measuring Gang Involvement in a Justice-referred Sample of Youth in Treatment." *Youth Violence and Juvenile Justice* 13 (1): 41–59.
Brown, E. C., R. F. Catalano, C. B. Fleming, K. P. Haggerty, and R. D. Abbott. 2005. "Adolescent Substance Use Outcomes in the Raising Healthy Children Project: A Two-part Latent Growth Curve Analysis." *Journal of Consulting and Clinical Psychology* 73 (4): 699–710.
Brown, E. C., R. F. Catalano, C. B. Fleming, K. P. Haggerty, R. D. Abbott, R. R. Cortes, and J. Park. 2005. "Mediator Effects in the Social Development Model: An Examination of Constituent Theories." *Criminal Behaviour and Mental Health* 15 (4): 221–235.
Browne, M. W., and R. Cudeck. 1993. "Alternative Ways of Assessing Model Fit." In *Testing Structural Models*, edited by K. A. Bollen and J. S. Long, 136–162. Newbury Park, CA: Sage.
Brownfield, D. 2003. "Differential Association and Gang Membership." *Journal of Gang Research* 11 (1): 1–12.
Brownfield, D. 2010. "Social Control, Self-control, & Gang Membership." *Journal of Gang Research* 17 (4): 1–12.
Brownfield, D., K. M. Thompson, and A. M. Sorenson. 1997. "Correlates of Gang Membership: A Test of Strain, Social Learning, and Social Control Theories." *Journal of Gang Research* 4 (4): 11–22.
Buhi, E. R., P. Goodson, and T. B. Neilands. 2007. "Structural Equation Modeling: A Primer for Health Behavior Researchers." *American Journal of Health Behavior* 31 (1): 74–85.
Catalano, R. F., and J. D. Hawkins. 1996. "The Social Development Model: A Theory of Antisocial Behavior." In *Delinquency and Crime: Current Theories*, edited by J. David Hawkins, 149–197. New York: Cambridge University Press.
Catalano, R. F., R. Kosterman, J. D. Hawkins, M. D. Newcomb, and R. D. Abbott. 1996. "Modeling the Etiology of Adolescent Substance Use: A Test of the Social Development Model." *Journal of Drug Issues* 26: 429–455.
Catalano, R. F., M. L. Oxford, T. W. Harachi, R. D. Abbott, and K. P. Haggerty. 1999. "A Test of the Social Development Model to Predict Problem Behaviour during the Elementary School Period." *Criminal Behaviour and Mental Health* 9: 39–56.
Catalano, R. F., J. Park, T. W. Harachi, K. P. Haggerty, R. D. Abbott, and J. D. Hawkins. 2005. "Mediating the Effects of Poverty, Gender, Individual Characteristics, and External Constraints on Antisocial Behavior: A Test of the Social Development Model and Implications for Developmental Life-course Theory." *Advances in Criminological Theory* 14: 93–123.
Cepeda, A., J. M. S. Onge, K. M. Nowotny, and A. Valdez. 2016. "Associations between Long-term Gang Membership and Informal Social Control Processes, Drug Use, and Delinquent Behavior among Mexican American Youth." *International Journal of Offender Therapy and Comparative Criminology* 60 (13): 1532–1548.

Choi, Y., T. W. Harachi, M. R. Gillmore, and R. F. Catalano. 2005. "Applicability of the Social Development Model to Urban Ethnic Minority Youth: Examining the Relationship between External Constraints, Family Socialization, and Problem Behaviors." *Journal of Research on Adolescence* 15 (4): 505–534.

Coltman, T., T. M. Devinney, D. F. Midgley, and S. Venaik. 2008. "Formative versus Reflective Measurement Models: Two Applications of Formative Measurement." *Journal of Business Research* 61: 1250–1262.

Cressey, D. R. 1953. *Other People's Money: A Study of the Social Psychology of Embezzlement*. New York: The Press.

Deng, S., and M. W. Roosa. 2007. "Family Influences on Adolescent Delinquent Behaviors: Applying the Social Development Model to a Chinese Sample." *American Journal of Community Psychology* 40 (3–4): 333–344.

Dishion, T. J., S. E. Nelson, and M. Yasui. 2005. "Predicting Early Adolescent Gang Involvement from Middle School Adaptation." *Journal of Clinical Child & Adolescent Psychology* 34 (1): 62–73.

Dishion, T. J., G. R. Patterson, M. Stoolmiller, and M. L. Skinner. 1991. "Family, School, and Behavioral Antecedents to Early Adolescent Involvement with Antisocial Peers." *Developmental Psychology* 27 (1): 172–180.

Esbensen, F.-A., D. W. Osgood, D. Peterson, T. J. Taylor, and D. C. Carson. 2013. "Short- and Long-Term Outcome Results from a Multisite Evaluation of the G.R.E.A.T. Program." *Criminology & Public Policy* 12 (3): 375–411.

Esbensen, F.-A., D. Peterson, T. J. Taylor, and A. Freng. 2010. *Youth Violence: Sex and Race Differences in Offending, Victimization, and Gang Membership*. Philadelphia, PA: Temple University Press.

Esbensen, F.-A., D. Peterson, T. J. Taylor, and A. Freng. 2009. "Similarities and Differences in Risk Factors for Violent Offending and Gang Membership." *Australian and New Zealand Journal of Criminology* 42 (3): 310–335.

Esbensen, F.-A., D. Peterson, T. J. Taylor, and D. W. Osgood. 2011. "Results from a Multi-Site Evaluation of the G.R.E.A.T Program." *Justice Quarterly* 29 (1): 125–151.

Esbensen, F.-A., L. T. Winfree, N. He, and T. J. Taylor. 2001. "Youth Gangs and Definitional Issues: When is a Gang a Gang, and Why Does It Matter?" *Crime and Delinquency* 47 (1): 105–130.

Fleming, C. B., D. D. Brewer, R. R. Gainey, K. P. Haggerty, and R. F. Catalano. 1997. "Parent Drug Use and Bonding to Parents as Predictors of Substance Use in Children of Substance Abusers." *Journal of Child and Adolescent Substance Abuse* 6: 75–86.

Fleming, C. B., R. F. Catalano, M. L. Oxford, and T. W. Harachi. 2002. "A Test of Generalizability of the Social Development Model across Gender and Income Groups with Longitudinal Data from the Elementary School Developmental Period." *Journal of Quantitative Criminology* 18 (4): 423–439.

Fox, K., J. Lane, and R. Akers. 2010. "Do Perceptions of Neighborhood Disorganization Predict Crime or Victimization? An Examination of Gang Member versus Non-gang Member Jail Inmates." *Journal of Criminal Justice* 38: 720–729.

Gilman, A. B., K. G. Hill, J. D. Hawkins, J. C. Howell, and R. Kosterman. 2014. "The Developmental Dynamics of Joining a Gang in Adolescence: Patterns and Predictors of Gang Membership." *Journal of Research on Adolescence* 24 (2): 204–219.

Graham, J. W. 2009. "Missing Data Analysis: Making It Work in the Real World." *Annual Review of Psychology* 60: 549–576.

Granic, I., and G. R. Patterson. 2006. "Toward a Comprehensive Model of Antisocial Development: A Dynamic Systems Approach." *Psychological Review* 113 (1): 101–131.

Hawkins, J. D., R. F. Catalano, and J. Y. Miller. 1992. "Risk and Protective Factors for Alcohol and Other Drug Problems in Adolescence and Early Adulthood: Implications for Substance-Abuse Prevention." *Psychological Bulletin* 112: 64–105.

Hawkins, J. D., and J. G. Weis. 1985. "The Social Development Model: An Integrated Approach to Delinquency Prevention." *The Journal of Primary Prevention* 6: 73–97.

Herrenkohl, T. I., B. Huang, R. Kosterman, J. D. Hawkins, R. F. Catalano, and B. H. Smith. 2001. "A Comparison of Social Development Processes Leading to Violent Behavior in Late Adolescence for Childhood Initiators and Adolescent Initiators of Violence." *Journal of Research in Crime and Delinquency* 38 (1): 45–63.

Herrenkohl, T. I., E. Maguin, K. G. Hill, J. D. Hawkins, R. D. Abbott, and R. F. Catalano. 2000. "Developmental Risk Factors for Youth Violence." *Journal of Adolescent Health* 26: 176–186.

Hill, K. G., J. C. Howell, J. D. Hawkins, and S. Battin-Pearson. 1999. "Childhood Risk Factors for Adolescent Gang Membership: Results from the Seattle Social Development Project." *Journal of Research in Crime and Delinquency* 36: 300–322.

Hirshi, T. 1969. *Causes of Delinquency*. Berkeley, CA: University of California Press.

Howell, J. C. 2003. *Preventing and Reducing Juvenile Delinquency: A Comprehensive Framework*. Thousand Oaks, CA: Sage.

Howell, J. C. 2012. *Gangs in America's Communities*. Thousand Oaks, CA: SAGE.

Howell, J. C., and E. Griffiths. 2016. *Gangs in America's Communities*. 2nd ed. Thousand Oaks, CA: SAGE.

Howell, J. C., and A. Egley. 2005. "Moving Risk Factors into Developmental Theories of Gang Membership." *Youth Violence and Juvenile Justice* 3: 334–354.

Howell, J. C., M. W. Lipsey, and J. J. Wilson. 2014. *A Handbook for Evidence-based Juvenile Justice Systems*. Lanham, MD: Lexington Books.

Hu, L., and P. M. Bentler. 1999. "Cutoff Criteria for Fit Indexes in Covariance Structure Analysis: Conventional Criteria versus New Alternatives." *Structural Equation Modeling: A Multidisciplinary Journal* 6: 1–55.

Huang, B., R. Kosterman, R. F. Catalano, J. D. Hawkins, and R. D. Abbott. 2001. "Modeling Mediation in the Etiology of Violent Behavior in Adolescence: A Test of the Social Development Model*." *Criminology* 39: 75–108.

Huizinga, D., A. W. Weiher, R. Espiritu, and F.-A. Esbensen. 2003. "Delinquency and Crime: Some Highlights from the Denver Youth Survey." In *Taking Stock of Delinquency*, edited by T. P. Thornberry and M. D. Krohn, 47–91. New York: Kluwer Academic/Plenum Publishers.

Kim, M. J. 2009. "Youth Violence Prevention: Social Development Model Approaches to Predicting and Preventing the Progression of Childhood Aggression into Youth Violence." Doctoral diss., Retrieved from *Dissertation Abstracts International, A: The Humanities and Social Sciences, 59*(08).

Kim, S. 2000. "The Effects of Parent Bonding, School Bonding, Belief on the Structure of Problem Behaviors in Elementary School-age Children." *Dissertation Abstracts International, a: The Humanities and Social Sciences* 61(6): 1–113.

Klein, M. 1995. *The American Street Gang: Its Nature, Prevalence, and Control*. New York: Oxford University Press.

Kosterman, R., K. P. Haggerty, R. Spoth, and C. Redmond. 2004. "Unique Influence of Mothers and Fathers on Their Children's Antisocial Behavior." *Journal of Marriage and Family* 66 (3): 762–778.

Kosterman, R., K. G. Hill, J. O. Lee, M. C. Meacham, R. D. Abbott, R. F. Catalano, and J. D. Hawkins. 2014. "Young Adult Social Development as a Mediator of Alcohol Use Disorder Symptoms from Age 21 to 30." *Psychology of Addictive Behaviors* 28 (2): 348–358.

Lahey, B. B., R. A. Gordon, R. Loeber, M. Stouthamer-Loeber, and D. P. Farrington. 1999. "Boys Who Join Gangs: A Prospective Study of Predictors of First Gang Entry." *Journal of Abnormal Child Psychology* 27: 261–276.

Loeber, R. 1996. "Developmental Continuity, Change, and Pathways in Male Juvenile Problem Behaviors and Delinquency." In *Delinquency and Crime: Current Theories*, edited by J. David Hawkins, 1–27. New York: Cambridge University Press.

Lonczak, H. S., B. Huang, R. F. Catalano, J. D. Hawkins, K. G. Hill, R. D. Abbott, J. A. M. Ryan, and R. Kosterman. 2001. "The Social Predictors of Adolescent Alcohol Misuse: A Test of the Social Development Model." *Journal of Studies on Alcohol* 62 (2): 179–189.

Lytton, H. 1990. "Child and Parent Effects in Boys' Conduct Disorder: A Reinterpretation." *Developmental Psychology* 26 (5): 683–697.

Pandey, S., and W. Elliott. 2010. "Suppressor Variables in Social Work Research: Ways to Identify in Multiple Regression Models." *Journal of the Society for Social Work Research* 1 (1): 28–40.

MacKinnon, D. P., J. L. Krull, and C. M. Lockwood. 2000. "Equivalence of the Mediation, Confounding and Suppression Effect." *Prevention Science* 1 (4): 173–181.

Matsueda, R. L. 1982. "Testing Control Theory and Differential Association: A Causal Modeling Approach." *American Sociological Review* 47: 489–504.

Matsueda, R. L. 1988. "The Current State of Differential Association Theory." *Crime and Delinquency* 34: 277–306.

Miller, W. B. 2001. *The Growth of Youth Gang Problems in the United States: 1970–98*. Washington, DC: U.S. Department of Justice. Report from the *Office of Juvenile Justice and Delinquency Prevention*.

Muthen, L. K., and B. O. Muthen. 2012. *Mplus User's Guide*. 7th ed. Los Angeles, CA: Muthen & Muthen.

Newcomb, M. D. 1990. "What Structural Modeling Techniques Can Tell Us about Social Support." In Irwin G. Sarason, Barbara R. Sarason, and Gregory R. Pierce (Eds.), *Social Support: An Interactional View*, 26–63. New York: Wiley.

O'Donnell, J., J. D. Hawkins, and R. D. Abbott. 1995. "Predicting Serious Delinquency and Substance Use among Aggressive Boys." *Journal of Consulting and Clinical Psychology* 63 (4): 529–537.

Patterson, G. R., B. D. DeBaryshe, and E. Ramsey. 1989. "A Developmental Perspective on Antisocial-Behavior." *American Psychologist* 44 (2): 329–335.

Pyrooz, D. C., G. Sweeten, and A. R. Piquero. 2013. "Continuity and Change in Gang Membership and Gang Embeddedness." *Journal of Research in Crime and Delinquency* 50 (2): 239–271.

Roosa, M. W., K. H. Zeiders, G. P. Knight, N. A. Gonzales, J.-Y. Tein, D. Saenz, M. O'Donnell, and C. Berkel. 2011. "A Test of the Social Development Model during the Transition to Junior High with Mexican American Adolescents." *Developmental Psychology* 47 (2): 527–537.

Sameroff, A. 2009. *The Transactional Model of Development: How Children and Contexts Shape Each Other*. Washington, DC: American Psychological Association.

Shader, M. 2001. *Risk Factors for Delinquency: An Overview*. Washington, DC: U.S. Department of Justice, Office of Juvenile Justice and Delinquency Prevention.

Sullivan, C. J., and P. Hirschfield. 2011. "Problem Behavior in the Middle School Years: An Assessment of the Social Development Model." *Journal of Research in Crime and Delinquency* 48 (4): 566–593.

Sutherland, E. H. 1973. "Development of the Theory [Private Paper Published Posthumously]." In *Edwin Sutherland on Analyzing Crime*, edited by Karl F. Schuessler, 13–29. Chicago, IL: University of Chicago Press.

Sutherland, E. H., and D. R. Cressey. 1970. *Criminology*. 9th ed. New York: Lippincott.

Tapia, M. 2011. "Gang Membership and Race as Risk Factors for Juvenile Arrest." *Journal of Research in Crime and Delinquency* 48 (3): 364–395.

Thornberry, T. P. 2005. "Explaining Multiple Patterns of Offending across the Life Course and across Generations." *The ANNALS of the American Academy of Political and Social Science* 602: 156–195.

Thornberry, T. P. 2006. "Membership in Youth Gangs and Involvement in Serious and Violent Offending." In *The Modern Gang Reader*, edited by A. J. Egley, C. L. Maxson, J. Miller and M. W. Klein, 224–232. Lost Angeles, CA: Roxbury Publishing.

Thornberry, T. P., and M. D. Krohn. 2001. "The Development of Delinquency: An Interactional Perspective." In *Handbook of Youth and Justice*, edited by S. O. White, 289–305. New York: Plenum.

Thornberry, T. P., and M. D. Krohn. 2005. "Applying Interactional Theory to the Explanation of Continuity and Change in Antisocial Behavior." In *Integrated Developmental and Life-course Theories of Offending*, edited by D. P. Farrington, 183–210. New Brunswick, NJ: Transaction Publishing.

Thornberry, T. P., M. D. Krohn, A. J. Lizotte, and D. Chard-Wierschem. 1993. "The Role of Juvenile Gangs in Facilitating Delinquent Behavior." *Journal of Research in Crime and Delinquency* 30: 55–87.

Thornberry, T. P., M. D. Krohn, A. J. Lizotte, C. Smith, and K. Tobin. 2003. *Gangs and Delinquency in Developmental Perspective*. New York: Cambridge University Press.

Thornberry, T. P., A. J. Lizotte, M. D. Krohn, C. A. Smith, and P. K. Porter. 2003. "Causes and Consequences of Delinquency: Findings from the Rochester Youth Development Study." In *Taking Stock of Delinquency: An Overview of Findings from Contemporary Longitudinal Studies*, edited by T. P. Thornberry and M. D. Krohn, 11–46. New York: Kluwer Academic/Plenum Publishers.

Vigil, J. D. 1988. *Barrio Gangs*. Austin, TX: University of Texas Press.

Vigil, J. D. 2002. *A Rainbow of Gangs: Street Cultures in the Mega-City*. Austin, TX: University of Texas Press.

Vigil, J. D., and S. C. Yun. 2002. "A Cross-cultural Framework for Understanding Gangs: Multiple Marginality and Los Angeles." In *Gangs in America*. 3rd ed, edited by C. R. Huff, 161–174. Thousand Oaks, CA: Sage.

Walker, S. C., and A. S. Bishop. 2016. "Length of Stay, Therapeutic Change, and Recidivism for Incarcerated Juvenile Offenders." *Journal of Offender Rehabilitation* 55 (6): 355–376.

Winfree, L. T., T. V. Backstrom, and G. L. Mays. 1994. "Social Learning Theory, Self-reported Delinquency, and Youth Gangs: A New Twist on a General Theory of Crime and Delinquency." *Youth and Society* 26 (2): 147–177.

Winfree, L. T., G. L. Mays, and T. Vigil-Bäckström. 1994. "Youth Gangs and Incarcerated Delinquents: Exploring the Ties between Gang Membership, Delinquency, and Social Learning Theory." *Justice Quarterly* 11 (2): 229–256.

Differentiating between delinquent groups and gangs: moving beyond offending consequences

Dena C. Carson, Stephanie A. Wiley and Finn-Aage Esbensen

ABSTRACT
Even when controlling for high levels of delinquent peers, gang youth differ from their nongang counterparts on a variety of attitudinal and behavioral measures. Researchers have argued that differences can be attributed to the group processes present in the gang setting. This study explores the extent to which differences between youth in a gang and those in a delinquent group can be explained by Bandura's social cognitive theory. Much of the prior research in this arena has relied on cross-sectional data; in this study, we expand on this prior research using fixed-effects modeling strategies with a multi-site panel of youth. The results comparing time periods when youth were in a gang versus a delinquent peer group indicate that gang-involved youth are more violent and have fewer conventional bonds. This work is able to advance our knowledge on attitudinal and behavioral differences between gangs and other types of peer groups.

Introduction

One of the more widely documented findings of criminological research is the enhanced effect of youth gang membership on violent offending and victimization (Battin et al. 1998; Esbensen and Carson 2012; Esbensen and Huizinga 1993; Hill et al. 1999; Melde and Esbensen 2013; Thornberry et al. 1993). Moreover, research has documented that gang members are characterized by more risk factors within more domains than youth who are not gang involved (Esbensen et al. 2010; Thornberry et al. 2003). However, these findings may simply be an artifact of belonging to a highly delinquent peer group. That is, gangs are simply at the extreme end of the delinquent peer group continuum and the 'gang effect' is nothing more than a heightened 'peer effect' (Miller 1982). Still, while most comparisons in prior research are limited to gang/nongang status, when controls for other types of delinquent peer groups are introduced, researchers continue to find that gang youth have more risk factors (Battin et al. 1998; Dong and Krohn 2016; Esbensen, Huizinga, and Weiher 1993; Gatti et al. 2005; Gordon et al. 2004; Thornberry et al. 2003). These and similar findings have led gang researchers to argue that gangs are 'qualitatively different' from other delinquent peer groups (Decker, Melde, and Pyrooz 2013; Klein 1995; Klein and Crawford 1967; Klein and Maxson 2006; Moore 1991; Short and Strodtbeck 1965; Thornberry et al. 2003). Moore (1991), for example, maintained that gangs are outside the continuum of 'rowdy' groups and that the effect of gang membership on behavior extends beyond the effect of delinquent peer group membership. These 'qualitative differences' are largely attributed to group processes within the gang, which can create an environment conducive to delinquency and violence (Decker, Melde, and Pyrooz 2013; Esbensen and Maxson 2012; Klein and Maxson 2006; Short and Strodtbeck 1965).

While group processes may influence gang members, individuals are not solely the product of their environment and action is also a result of self-regulatory mechanisms (Bandura 2002). Social cognitive theory (SCT), for example, argues that individuals are driven by the reciprocal relationship between behavior, cognitive factors/affect and environmental agents (Bandura 1986). A mission to understand what makes gangs different from delinquent peer groups has led a number of scholars to compare gang youth to those who report belonging to a delinquent peer group (or having a certain proportion of delinquent friends) on several individual-level factors, including levels of street and violent offending and risk factors for gang membership. In general, this work consistently finds evidence of unique differences between gang youth and those who associate with delinquent peers on violent offending, delinquency, number of delinquent peers, motivations for group joining, as well as arrest (Battin et al. 1998; Bouchard and Spindler 2010; Dong and Krohn 2016; Esbensen, Huizinga, and Weiher 1993; Lachman, Roman, and Cahill 2013; Thornberry et al. 2003).

These works, however, are limited by their reliance on cross-sectional analyses (although see Battin et al. 1998; Dong and Krohn 2016). Self-report panel studies of youth commonly find that gang membership typically only lasts one to two years (Esbensen and Huizinga 1993; Pyrooz, Sweeten, and Piquero 2013; Thornberry et al. 2003) and the use of cross-sectional data limits the ability to account for the transient nature of gang membership. Additionally, much of the prior research in this area is unable to adjust for selection effects due to a reliance on cross-sectional data (Bouchard and Spindler 2010; Esbensen, Huizinga, and Weiher 1993; Lachman, Roman, and Cahill 2013). Controlling for pre-existing differences is important as youth who join a gang differ from those who do not (Thornberry et al. 1993). In this study, we build upon prior research by drawing on a multi-site panel study of youth to examine within-individual change associated with involvement in a gang, a delinquent peer group, or a typical adolescent peer group (i.e., nongang, nondelinquent peer group).[1] In order to account for selection bias, we rely on a fixed-effects modeling strategy, which controls for time-stable individual characteristics that may be correlated with the independent and dependent variables. In addition, we make use of SCT to parse out differences across group membership in not only offending, but also individual-level attitudes and values. The use of psychological perspectives to explain gang phenomena has been limited and mostly relies upon attempts to explain in- and out-group differences (Alleyne, Fernandes, and Pritchard 2014). Gang researchers have called for more research into this arena stating that it would provide a more complete understanding of gangs and gang members (see Alleyne and Wood 2012 and Wood and Alleyne 2010).

Our results are especially relevant to gang prevention and intervention efforts. Policy-makers consistently treat gangs as if they are unique from delinquent peer groups through the use of gang-specific intervention policies and programs (e.g., civil gang injunctions, the G.R.E.A.T. program, Project CeaseFire). The inability of police officers to accurately identify gang members as well as the transiency of gang membership have led some researchers to argue that research and policy should focus on youth violence in general, rather than gangs specifically (Sullivan 2006). If youth's behaviors and attitudes are, in fact, similar regardless of whether they are in a gang or delinquent peer group then gang-specific interventions should have an equally deterrent impact on all delinquent youth and indicate that policies could be more generalized and less specific to gangs and their members. Conversely, if our research demonstrates that gang and nongang delinquent members are unique across a wide range of factors, then understanding the differences between gang youth and those involved in a delinquent peer group will aid practitioners in the identification of high-risk youth for gang prevention programming (Hennigan et al. 2014).

SCT and gang membership

Social psychologists emphasize that the social nature of our lives and the groups in which we are embedded can shape us as individuals. While the idea that gangs have certain properties that affect the behavior of their members is not a new concept for gang researchers (Klein and Crawford 1967; Short and Strodtbeck 1965), it is usually studied through the lens of social identity theory (Goldman, Giles, and Hogg 2014; Hennigan and Spanovic 2012; Vigil 1988). This perspective, however, is limited in its ability to help us understand how attitudes and behaviors are impacted by both the group as well as individual cognitions. Therefore, we draw on social cognitive theory (SCT) to understand how gang involvement impacts individual-level outcomes above and beyond what we may see for delinquent or typical adolescent peer groups. SCT argues that individuals are not 'autonomous moral agents,' but are influenced by social and environmental contexts (Bandura 2002, 02). Bandura (1986) argues that individual behaviors are the result of the reciprocal interaction between cognitive, affective, and social/environmental influences. In other words, our actions and cognitions cannot be separated from social influences. When individuals are in an environment of shared moral standards, the decision to participate in a behavior is based on whether or not that action is socially acceptable. The individual, then, has a cognitive understanding of what behaviors are not socially approved and will refrain from participation (Bandura 1986). When the shared moral standards are prosocial in nature, then this process will produce prosocial attitudes and behaviors. Conversely, when individuals are in an environment that promotes delinquent attitudes and behaviors, such as a gang, then those attitudes and behaviors will be rewarded and individuals may feel free to deviate from the moral standards of the larger society. Furthermore, Bandura (1986) argues that behavior is especially susceptible to outside influences when the individual does not have strong opposing internal standards. This statement is especially relevant to our study because prior research has argued that the high levels of real or perceived cohesiveness within gangs is particularly attractive to individuals who are uncertain about their identity (Goldman, Giles, and Hogg 2014; Vigil 1988; Woo et al. 2015).

Bandura (1991) argues that social influences can have an effect on an individual's attitudes and behaviors because they impact the one's ability to self-regulate. Individuals regulate their moral actions based on their perception of anticipated rewards or punishments associated with that action. Specifically, individuals act morally because of the intrinsic benefits (i.e., altruism) and restrict themselves from immoral behavior to avoid negative consequences (i.e., feelings of guilt). The gang, however, can alter self-regulatory processes because benefits are gained from immoral actions. Immoral behaviors such as participation in crime and violence are met with social approval from the gang, increased status, and, in some cases, monetary gain. Within the gang context, the perceived benefits of increased status and respect from gang peers can alter the ability of gang youth to make moral decisions (McGloin and Collins 2015). In fact, research demonstrates that gang youth exhibit lower levels of guilt and increased self-centeredness (Matsuda et al. 2013; Melde and Esbensen 2011, 2014; Peterson and Morgan 2014), which is unsurprising given that guilt and shame are reduced in group settings (McGloin and Collins 2015). Additionally, empathy is related to an individual's capacity for self-regulation in social situations and, therefore, may be altered during times of active gang membership (Findlay, Girardi, and Coplan 2006). Furthermore, empathy, or lack thereof, is commonly associated with offending (Jolliffe and Farrington 2004) as well as gang involvement (Valdez, Kaplan, and Codina 2000).

Due to their ability to alter self-regulation, social influences are also able to provide 'collective support for adherence to moral standards' (Bandura 1991, 70). Gang youth tend to place more emphasis on the standards and beliefs of their gang peers than individuals or institutions outside the gang (Anderson 1999; Vigil 1988). Thus, if social influences are based on immoral standards, as they are in a gang, then the individual will foster these beliefs rather than prosocial ones. This process was discussed by Vigil (1988), who argued that the attitudes and behaviors held by the gang shape the way a youth 'thinks about himself and others and provides models for how to look and act' (421). Gang youth, therefore, may modify or discard their existing values and attitudes in favor of those consistent with the positive attributes of gang life (Wood and Alleyne 2010). These modifications may be particularly abrupt for gang youth because the gang tends to isolate its members from conventional groups. In fact, a number of studies show that gang youth, as opposed to their nongang counterparts, report stronger commitment to negative peers (Esbensen et al. 2010; Matsuda et al. 2013; Melde and Esbensen 2011, 2014; Peterson and Morgan 2014) and lower levels of involvement with prosocial peers (Esbensen et al. 2010;

Melde and Esbensen 2011, 2014; Peterson and Morgan 2014). The gang's ability to isolate its members also impacts the involvement of gang members in other social institutions, like schools. Cohen (1955) discusses how gangs are frequently in opposition to the culture set up by schools (see also Horowitz 1983). Performing well in school and being the model student does not garner the same amount of respect from the gang as physicality, street smarts and wit (Decker and Van Winkle 1996; Pyrooz 2014; Short and Strodtbeck 1965). Therefore, it is no surprise that gang members demonstrate lower commitment to school than their nongang counterparts (Esbensen et al. 2010; Hill et al. 1999; Melde and Esbensen 2011, 2014; Peterson and Morgan 2014; Thornberry et al. 2003; Weerman, Lovegrove, and Thornberry 2015).

Social influences can also facilitate the 'activation and disengagement' of self-regulation (Bandura 1991, 70). Being in a gang creates moral conflict (i.e., cognitive dissonance) because it presents individuals with benefits that can be the result of inhuman or immoral behaviors (Bandura 1990). In order to reduce this conflict, gang youth commonly use moral disengagement strategies, such as moral justification, euphemistic language, advantageous comparisons, displacement and diffusion of responsibility, distortion of consequences, victim blaming, and dehumanization (see Bandura 2002 for a detailed description of these strategies). Neutralizations for violence, for example, can alleviate dissonance that results from participating in violent behaviors as part of the gang. In fact, gang youth, when compared to nongang youth, report greater agreement with neutralization techniques (Alleyne, Fernandes, and Pritchard 2014; Alleyne and Wood 2010; Esbensen and Weerman 2005; Esbensen et al. 2010; Melde and Esbensen 2011, 2014; Peterson and Morgan 2014). Additionally, Bandura (2002) stated that moral disengagement can impact other aspects of individual cognition and affect, arguing that individuals with high levels of moral disengagement are less prosocial, in general, and experience lower levels of guilt. Overall, then, gangs as social influences can modify the attitudes and behaviors of their members by altering self-regulation processes, providing collective immoral standards, and facilitating moral disengagement.

Comparing gangs and delinquent peer groups

Given the proposed differences between gangs and delinquent peer groups, it is not surprising that researchers have attempted to differentiate these two groups for decades, which has resulted in a small, but important body of literature. This research commonly operationalizes involvement in a delinquent peer group as the presence of a high proportion of delinquent peers. This work often examines the effect of gang membership on offending outcomes above and beyond that of delinquent peers and has identified a unique impact of gang involvement on individual-level delinquency (Battin et al. 1998; Gatti et al. 2005; Gordon et al. 2004), violence, drug sales, and substance use (Thornberry et al. 2003) as well as a long-term impact on violence and arrest (Dong and Krohn 2016). This is important evidence for the unique impact of gang membership on offending when *controlling* for the proportion of delinquent peers. The use of the proportion of delinquent peers as a proxy, however, is unable to account for involvement in a peer group and, therefore, excludes the underlying impact of group processes. Members of both gangs and delinquent peer groups are likely to report association with delinquent peers, which no doubt increases opportunities to offend as well as co-offending behavior. Simply having delinquent peers, however, does not imply the presence of group processes. Youth must identify with a group in order for group processes to be present (Tajfel 1978). Overall, the presence or absence of group involvement is an important distinction given the previously discussed processes that are unique to a group setting.

Research that is able to account for group involvement is comparatively rare. When making comparisons to gang youth, Bouchard and Spindler (2010), for example, asked youth to report on their involvement in a delinquent peer group (i.e., were you a member of a group involved in deviance of any sort?). This work demonstrated differences between gang involved youth and those in a delinquent peer group on individual-level delinquency, property offending, drug sales, and drug use as well as on organizational characteristics and group processes. Youth who reported gang involvement were more likely than youth in a delinquent peer group to report that their group had a name, leader, rules, signs or codes, a hierarchy, an initiation process, and also indicated that their group was territorial and defended its honor or reputation. While these findings are similar to those identified when controlling for delinquent peer associations, it is arguably more accurate to compare youth in a gang to those in a delinquent group. Furthermore, Bouchard and Spindler's (2010) work, despite relying on cross-sectional data, has built on previous research by looking at more than just offending outcomes.

Additional work has attempted to parse out differences between gang youth and delinquent group members in other ways. Esbensen and colleagues (1993) investigated similarities and differences between gang members, youth involved in street offending, and nonoffenders on a variety of behavioral and theoretical variables. Their behavioral results indicated a unique gang effect on street offending, minor and serious offending, and alcohol use. In terms of theoretical variables, the authors identified only one significant difference among 18 attitudinal and perceptual variables: being labeled as bad or disturbed by a teacher was significantly higher for gang members.

In an effort to understand how gangs are unique from delinquent peer groups, prior work has attempted to differentiate these youth on a number of individual-level attitudes and behaviors. While this body of work finds support for a unique impact of being gang involved on levels of offending and violence (i.e., qualitative differences), it is subject to three main limitations. First, much of this work has relied primarily on cross-sectional data, which does not account for the transient nature of gang membership. We address this limitation in the current study by making use of longitudinal data to control for within-person changes associated with involvement in a gang, a delinquent peer group, or typical adolescent group. Second, because previous longitudinal examinations of these differences use a proportion of delinquent peers measure as a proxy for delinquent peer group involvement (Battin et al. 1998; Dong and Krohn 2016; Thornberry et al. 2003), previous work has not accounted for involvement in a peer group and, therefore, excludes the underlying impact of group processes. This is an important omission because, as Bandura's social cognitive theory suggests, gangs can act as social influences in the lives of their members and, thus, modify their attitudes and behaviors by altering their self-regulation processes, providing collective immoral standards, and facilitating moral disengagement among its members. The current study adds to this knowledge base by including a group involvement measure rather than relying on the proportion of delinquent peers. Finally, prior research comparing gang youth with those in a delinquent peer group has relied heavily on behavioral comparisons. It remains unclear the extent to which these youth, who are both impacted by group processes in some way, differ on other outcomes. To address this issue, we examine whether movement through different types of peer groups (i.e., gang, delinquent peer group, typical adolescent group) is associated with changes in offending behavior as well as individual-level attitudes and values. We hypothesize that during periods of active gang membership, youth participate in higher levels of violence and hold more antisocial values than when they are involved in a delinquent peer group. Conversely, when youth belong to a typical adolescent group they should hold fewer delinquent attitudes and participate in less delinquency than periods when they are delinquent peer group members. Understanding the unique differences between these disparate groups of youth will help inform gang-specific prevention and intervention programs.

Methods

In order to examine how changes in peer group status affect attitudinal and behavioral outcomes, this study uses data from the National Evaluation of the G.R.E.A.T. (Gang Resistance Education and Training) program. The G.R.E.A.T. program is a gang prevention program taught by law enforcement officers and targeted at middle school youth. The evaluation consisted of a longitudinal panel study (2006–2011) that took place in seven cities across the US (see Esbensen et al. 2013, for more detail about the evaluation design). Cities were chosen to participate in the evaluation based on the existence of an established G.R.E.A.T. program, geographic and demographic diversity, and presence of gang activity. The final seven sites represent a wide range of cities from the east to the west coast and include the following: Albuquerque, New Mexico; Chicago, Illinois; Greeley, Colorado; Nashville, Tennessee; Philadelphia, Pennsylvania; Portland, Oregon; and a city in the Dallas/Fort Worth, Texas area.

All students in the selected classrooms were eligible to participate in the evaluation. A total of 4,905 students were enrolled in 195 participating classrooms in 31 middle schools at the beginning of the data collection process. After a thorough active parental consent process, 89% (N = 4,372) of youth returned consent forms, and 78% were given permission by a parent or guardian to participate in the evaluation (11% of parents declined) (see Esbensen et al. 2008 for an in-depth description of the active consent procedures). This consent process resulted in a final sample size of 3,820 youth. In 2006, students completed pre-test and post-test (Waves 1 and 2) self-report surveys with completion rates of 98.3 and 94.6%, respectively.[2] Youth also completed four annual follow-up surveys (Waves 3, 4, 5, and 6), with completion rates of 87, 83, 75, and 73%, respectively.

Because we are interested in individual-level change over time, youth with fewer than two waves of complete data were excluded from the analysis sample (n = 434). We also excluded 67 youth who were considered social isolates (i.e., youth who did not identify as being in any of the three specified peer groups across five or more waves of data) because we are interested in the effect of group membership on outcomes and these youth cannot contribute to our analyses. This purposeful exclusion of cases leaves 13,464 time points nested within 3319 youth to contribute to the final analyses.[3] This sample is nearly evenly split by sex (48.7% of the sample is male). The racial makeup of the analysis sample reflects the complete G.R.E.A.T. sample, with 28% white, 17.8% black, 39.7% Hispanic, and 14.5% reporting another or mixed race.

Measures

Independent variable: group status

Three mutually exclusive groups were created to capture (1) involvement in a gang, (2) involvement in a nongang delinquent peer group (also referred to as 'delinquent group'), or (3) involvement in a typical adolescent group. At each wave, youth were coded as belonging to a gang if they responded 'yes' to the question, 'Are you now in a gang?' or 'Do you consider your group of friends to be a gang?'[4] If youth reported that they were not currently in a gang, but responded affirmatively to the question, 'Do people in your group actually do illegal things together,' they were coded as being in a delinquent group for that wave. Finally, if youth reported neither gang involvement nor group participation in illegal activities, but reported that they had a group of friends with whom 'they spend time with, doing things together or just hanging out,' they were categorized as typical adolescent group members at the respective wave.

Dichotomous indicators for each type of group were created for the analyses (e.g., a dichotomous indicator with youth defined as gang members coded '1' and all others coded '0'). We rotated the reference groups depending on the comparisons under consideration. That is, our interest in the changes that occur during delinquent group membership or gang membership as opposed to being in a typical adolescent group requires using the typical peer group as the reference category. Alternatively, when the delinquent peer group serves as the reference category, we can examine the impact of gang membership as opposed to delinquent peer group membership.

Dependent variables: consequences of gang membership

As SCT suggests, social influences may impact the individual's ability to self-regulate. To capture these internal standards, we rely on three measures. First, we include a seven-item scale of *anticipated guilt*, which captures how guilty youth would feel if they participated in various delinquent activities (e.g., 'How guilty or badly would you feel if you sold marijuana or other illegal drugs?') (α = .92).[5] Response categories include '1. Not very guilty/badly,' '2. Somewhat guilty/badly,' and '3. Very guilty/badly.' *Empathy* is a five-item scale that captures youth's agreement with statements such as, 'I would feel sorry for a lonely stranger in a group,' and responses are on a five-point Likert scale with higher scores representing greater empathy (α = .70). Finally, *self-centeredness* is a four-item scale which measures the extent to which youth agree with putting themselves before others (e.g., 'I try to look out for myself first, even if it means making things difficult for other people.') (α = .76). Response categories are on a five-point Likert scale with higher scores representing more self-centeredness.

The gang also shapes youth's prosocial and antisocial beliefs by providing a model and support for moral standards. Gang-involved youth may become isolated from out-groups and more enmeshed with the gang as they begin to drift away from conventional activities and institutions, thereby fostering antisocial rather than prosocial beliefs. We address consequences associated with conventional and delinquent bonding with the inclusion of three variables. First, we include *negative peer commitment*, which consists of a three-item scale asking youth how likely it is that they would go along with friends if they were getting into trouble at home, at school, or with the police (α = .85). This measure was scored on a five-point scale ranging from '1. Not at all likely' to '5. Very likely.' In addition to measuring youth's attachment to deviant peers, we include a four-item scale, *prosocial peers*, which captures youth's associations with prosocial peers (e.g., 'How many of your current friends have gotten along well with teachers and adults at school?'). Response categories are on a five-point scale ranging from '1. None of them' to '5. All of them' (α = .86). *School commitment* is also included as a measure of conventional bonding (α = .81). This seven-item scale captures how much youth agree or disagree with statements such as, 'Homework is a waste of time,' and response categories are based on a five-point Likert scale with higher scores indicating greater commitment to school.

In addition to changing youth's moral standards and collective support for antisocial behavior, gang membership should affect youth's moral conflicts. To capture moral disengagement strategies, we include a mean scale measure of *violent neutralizations*, whereby youth indicate how much they agree or disagree with three statements regarding hitting (e.g., 'It's okay to beat up someone if they hit you first.') (α = .85). Responses are on a five-point Likert scale ranging from '1. Strongly disagree,' to '5. Strongly agree.'

One of the primary proposed differences between gang youth and delinquent peer group members is that gang youth participate in more violent crime. We measure involvement in violent crime within the last six months with five self-reported offending items: 'Carried a hidden weapon for protection,' 'Hit someone with the idea of hurting him or her,' 'Attacked someone with a weapon,' 'Used a weapon or force to get money or things from people,' and 'Been involved in gang fights.'[6] Response categories range from 0 to more than 10 times, resulting in a summed *violent delinquency frequency index* ranging between 0 and 55. In addition to violent delinquency, we are interested in whether youth participate in more overall delinquency when they are gang-involved. Therefore, we include a measure of nonviolent delinquency frequency, which includes nine additional delinquent activities ranging in seriousness from 'Skipped classes without an excuse,' to 'Sold marijuana or other illegal drugs.' The range for the *nonviolent delinquency frequency index* is 0–99. A large number of respondents indicated that they did not participate in any delinquency, therefore, due to the skewed nature of both the violent and nonviolent delinquency variables, we added one and took the natural log prior to data analysis.[7]

Time-varying control variables

We control for a number of time-varying variables associated with the outcomes of interest. These include age, parental monitoring, impulsivity, risk-seeking, anger, stealing neutralizations, proportion of delinquent peers, substance use frequency, victimization frequency, and perceived neighborhood and school disorder. In addition to these variables, we control for violent neutralizations, guilt, empathy, self-centeredness, prosocial peers, negative peer commitment, school commitment, violent delinquency, and nonviolent delinquency when they are not included as outcomes in the models. For example, when assessing the effect of group membership on violent delinquency, all of these variables, with the exception of violent delinquency, are included as controls.

Analytic plan

To isolate the consequences of gang membership and account for selection bias, which is a primary concern in prior research examining differences between gang and nongang youth, we estimate within-individual change for continuous outcomes using fixed-effects models (Allison 2009). Fixed-effects models use the individual as his or her own control, which controls for any time-stable individual characteristics that are correlated with group status and the outcomes of interest. This adjustment for selection bias is particularly important because youth who join gangs are distinct from their nongang peers and may be more easily influenced by the gang due to uncertainty with their own identity. Because our outcomes are continuous or continuous-like, we estimate our fixed-effects models using ordinary least squares regression. The longitudinal data-set was restructured such that a single wave for each individual represents a unique observation. Using the xtreg command with the fixed-effects option in Stata 14.1 (StataCorp 1985–2015), we specify separate models for each outcome of interest to estimate within-individual changes associated with involvement in a typical adolescent group, nongang delinquent group, and gang. These models incorporate cluster-robust standard errors to account for dependence of observations, potential heteroscedasticity, and serial correlation (Cameron and Miller 2015). To determine the effects of delinquent group membership and gang membership relative to typical group membership, we first rely on the typical adolescent group as the reference category. Next, the nongang delinquent group serves as the reference category to allow for examination of the influence of gang membership, relative to delinquent group membership, on our outcomes. Fixed-effects methods estimate parameters only for those individuals who change over time, thus youth who do not change on the outcome do not contribute to estimates of within-individual change.

Disadvantages to fixed-effects analysis include the inability to account for time-stable characteristics (e.g., race, sex) and dynamic selection bias. This first point is of little concern in the current study because we are primarily interested in within-person differences and any individual time-stable variables are accounted for in the person-specific error term. Dynamic selection bias is described by Bjerk (2009) as the bias that arises when the characteristics related to an individual's decision to make a particular choice (in this case, the decision to belong to a certain group) are also related to his or her criminal propensity. If the dynamic characteristics that drive such decisions are not controlled for, then the relationship between the independent variable and outcome is overestimated. By controlling for additional time-varying variables (e.g., age, parental monitoring, impulsivity) we are able to address some of the concern associated with dynamic selection bias; however, the potential for dynamic selection bias to influence our results remains. One alternative to fixed-effects is random-effects analysis, which allows for the inclusion of time-invariant variables but assumes that there are no omitted variables in the model (or if variables are omitted, they are the uncorrelated with the predictors) (see Allison 2009). We chose to analyze our data using fixed-effects analysis because we are concerned with the role that selection and omitted variable bias could play in the interpretation of our results. Furthermore, Hausman test results indicate that fixed-effects models are preferred over random-effects models for our data.

Findings

Descriptive results

Descriptive information regarding group membership is presented in Figures 1 and 2. The values displayed in Figure 1 represent the prevalence of group membership: nearly 96% of youth were ever in a typical adolescent group, while almost 28% were ever in a nongang delinquent group and 24% were ever gang-involved. The within-person percentages reported in Figure 2 represent the percentage of time points in a particular group, contingent on having ever been involved in that group. That is, among youth who had ever been in a typical peer group, nearly 84% of their remaining observed time points were also during typical peer group membership. Stability in group membership decreases for youth in a delinquent peer group: conditional on an individual being in a delinquent peer group at any given time point, only 35% of his or her remaining time points are spent in a delinquent peer group. Within-person

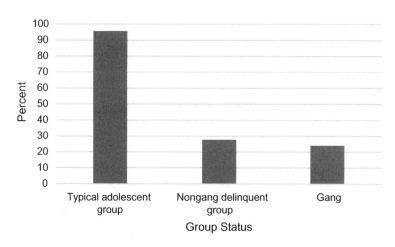

Figure 1. Prevalence of group membership.

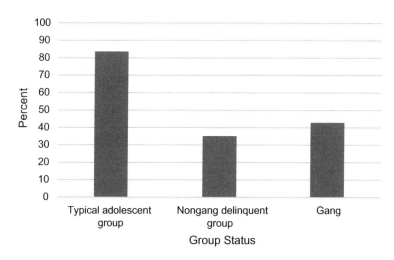

Figure 2. Within-person variability in group membership.

stability is slightly higher for gang membership, albeit much lower than for typical group membership: among youth who have ever been in a gang, approximately 43% of their remaining observations are during periods of gang membership.[8] In other words, fewer than half of these respondents' observations are during periods of gang membership. These descriptive results indicate that within individuals, group membership is most stable among youth who belong to a typical adolescent group; that is, youth who have ever been in a typical adolescent group remain in a typical group for most of their observed time points. More variability is seen for youth who belong to delinquent peer groups or gangs, who spend less than half of their observed time in at least one of the two groups.

Table 1 provides the overall means and standard deviations for the full sample, as well as the standard deviations between and within individuals. The 'Overall Sample' columns refer to each unique observation. Across all observations, the average number of violent delinquent acts committed was 2.28 with a standard deviation of 6.03 and range of 0–55. The standard deviations in the 'Between-person' column are calculated for individuals, rather than time points, and reveal the average deviation from the sample mean. For example, youth deviated from the average number of violent delinquent acts by 4.47. Meanwhile, the within-person data provides information on the deviation from each person's average.

Table 1. Sample descriptives for overall, between-person, and within-person observations.

	Overall sample				Between-person	Within-person
Variable	Mean	SD	Min	Max	SD	SD
Age	13.25	1.60	10	19	.66	1.46
Parental monitoring	4.07	.76	1	5	.56	.52
Impulsivity	2.75	.81	1	5	.58	.57
Risk-seeking	2.70	.96	1	5	.74	.62
Anger	3.01	.99	1	5	.78	.62
Stealing neutralizations	1.87	.90	1	5	.67	.60
Delinquent peers	1.47	.66	1	5	.50	.46
Substance use frequency	.80	1.98	0	16	1.39	1.46
Victimization frequency	9.33	14.28	0	121	10.66	9.89
Perceived disorder	1.69	.52	1	3	.41	.32
Guilt	2.49	.60	1	3	.42	.44
Empathy	3.61	.67	1	5	.51	.45
Self-centeredness	2.41	.83	1	5	.63	.54
Negative peer commitment	1.92	.99	1	5	.71	.70
Prosocial peers	3.45	.95	1	5	.71	.63
School commitment	3.73	.74	1	5	.57	.47
Hitting neutralizations	3.39	1.17	1	5	.90	.75
Nonviolent delinquency frequency	4.79	10.93	0	99	8.07	7.67
Nonviolent delinquency frequency (logged)	.93	1.14	0	4.61	.86	.76
Violent delinquency frequency	2.28	6.03	0	55	4.47	4.26
Violent delinquency frequency (logged)	.55	.92	0	4.03	.70	.62

Notes: Number of youth = 3319.
Abbreviations: SD = standard deviation, Min = minimum, Max = maximum.

For example, over time, youth deviated from their individual mean of violent delinquency by 4.26, on average. Interestingly, comparison of the between- and within-person standard deviations reveal that differences between any two randomly selected individuals are roughly equal to individual differences over time (e.g., the between-person standard deviation for guilt is .42 while the within-person deviation for guilt is .44). These descriptive statistics highlight that there is sufficient within-individual change across the outcomes of interest to assess within-individual change over time.

Fixed-effects analysis results

Turning to the first set of results in Table 2, our fixed-effects analyses reveal that a number of changes occur when youth are involved in a nongang delinquent peer group or gang relative to periods when they are in a typical adolescent group. The row labeled 'Nongang Delinquent Group' indicates that when youth are delinquent group members, relative to times when they are involved in typical adolescent groups, they anticipate less guilt for participating in delinquent acts ($b = -.09, p < .001$), are more committed to their delinquent peers ($b = .11, p < .01$), and report greater agreement with neutralization statements ($b = .08, p < .05$). In addition, the frequency of nonviolent delinquency increases during periods in which youth belong to delinquent peer groups: belonging to a nonviolent delinquent peer group is associated with a 22% increase in nonviolent delinquency frequency ($b = .20, p < .001$).[9] We do not find evidence that empathy, self-centeredness, prosocial peers, school commitment, or violent delinquency change when youth belong to a delinquent versus typical group.

Turning to the row labeled 'Gang,' our results indicate that several differences emerge during periods during periods of gang-involvement relative to periods when these same youth are involved in typical adolescent groups. Specifically, gang involvement is associated with less anticipated guilt ($b = -.07$, $p < .01$), greater negative peer commitment ($b = .17, p < .001$), and fewer prosocial peers ($b = -.09$, $p < .05$). Being gang involved is also associated with increases in both violent and nonviolent delinquency, with youth indicating a 38% increase in violent delinquency ($b = .32, p < .001$) and a 17% increase in nonviolent delinquency ($b = .16, p < .001$).[10] Similar to our delinquent group results, we find that moving from a typical group to a gang has no effect on changes in empathy, self-centeredness,

Table 2. OLS regression: fixed-effects analysis of nongang delinquent group and gang membership (vs. typical group) on outcomes.

	\multicolumn{14}{c}{Outcomes}													
	Guilt		Empathy		Self-centeredness		Negative peer commitment		Prosocial peers		School commitment		Hitting neutralizations		Nonviolent delinquency (logged)		Violent delinquency (logged)	
	b	SE	b	SE	b	SE	b	SE	b	SE	b	SE	b	SE	b	SE	b	SE
Nongang delinquent group	-.09***	.02	.04	.02	-.02	.02	.11**	.03	-.05	.03	.03	.02	.08*	.03	.20***	.03	-.02	.03
Gang	-.07**	.02	-.01	.02	-.02	.03	.17***	.04	-.09*	.03	-.03	.02	-.02	.04	.16***	.04	.32***	.03
Intercept	2.96***	.10	2.46***	.11	2.23***	.13	1.71***	.17	1.78***	.16	3.31***	.11	2.07***	.20	-.27	.15	.51***	.14

Notes: Number of youth = 3319, number of time points = 13,454. Time-invariant control variables omitted from table.
Abbreviations: OLS = Ordinary Least Squares, SE = standard error.
*$p < .05$; **$p < .01$; ***$p < .001$.

Table 3. OLS regression: fixed-effects analysis of typical group and gang membership (vs. delinquent group) on outcomes.

	Outcomes																
	Guilt		Empathy		Self-centeredness		Negative peer commitment		Prosocial peers		School commitment		Hitting neutralizations		Nonviolent delinquency (logged)		Violent delinquency (logged)
	b	SE	b	SE	b	SE	b	SE	b	SE	b	SE	b	SE	b	SE	b	SE
Typical group	.09***	.02	−.04	.02	.02	.02	−.11**	.03	.05	.03	−.03	.02	−.08*	.03	−.20***	.03	.02	.03
Gang	.03	.02	−.04	.03	−.01	.03	.06	.04	−.04	.04	−.06*	.03	−.10*	.04	−.04	.04	.33***	.04
Intercept	2.87***	.10	2.50***	.12	2.21***	.13	1.82***	.17	1.73***	.16	3.34***	.11	2.15***	.20	−.07	.16	.50**	.15

Notes: Number of youth = 3319, number of time points = 13,454. Time-invariant control variables omitted from table.
Abbreviations: OLS = Ordinary Least Squares, SE = standard error.
*p < .05; **p < .01; ***p < .001.

or school commitment. Unlike the effect of delinquent group involvement on hitting neutralizations, we find that gang membership does not increase agreement with hitting neutralization statements.

Rotating the reference group allows us to compare the effect of being in a gang relative to being in a delinquent peer group. That is, the results in Table 3 include the delinquent peer group as the reference category in order to examine whether gang involvement is associated with changes beyond involvement with a delinquent group. Turning to the row labeled 'Gang' in Table 3, our results indicate that few changes occur during periods of gang membership versus delinquent group involvement. Consistent with our hypothesis, however, youth experience less commitment to school during periods of gang membership ($b = -.06, p < .05$). However, contrary to our expectations, agreement with hitting neutralizations decreases while youth are gang-involved ($b = -.10, p < .05$). In line with the notion that gang members are more violent than other delinquent groups, our findings reveal that gang membership is associated with a 39% increase in violent delinquency frequency ($b = .33, p < .001$).[11] We do not find that gang membership influences guilt, empathy, self-centeredness, negative peer commitment, proportion of prosocial peers, or nonviolent delinquency when compared with periods of adolescent group involvement.

Discussion and conclusion

Prior research consistently finds that youth are more violent and hold more deviant attitudes during periods of active gang involvement compared to when they are not in a gang (Esbensen and Carson 2012; Esbensen and Huizinga 1993; Melde and Esbensen 2013). Furthermore, these findings hold even when controlling for the presence of delinquent peers or belonging to a delinquent peer group (Battin et al. 1998; Dong and Krohn 2016; Gatti et al. 2005; Gordon et al. 2004; Thornberry et al. 2003). Some researchers argue that gangs are simply on the extreme end of a delinquent peer group continuum (Miller 1982), while others state that gang youth are somehow qualitatively different from youth in a delinquent peer group (Klein 1995; Klein and Maxson 2006; Moore 1991). Researchers have primarily used group processes to explain the central difference between gang members and youth in delinquent groups – increased violence. The current study builds on prior research by examining these qualitative differences through the lens of social cognitive theory, which argues that individuals are driven by the interaction between behaviors, cognition/affect, and environmental influences (Bandura 1986).

In social cognitive theory, Bandura (1986, 1991) argues that social influences impact self-regulation and adherence to moral standards as well as facilitate activation and disengagement. Gangs and delinquent groups act as social influences in the lives of their members, which impacts their attitudes and behaviors by changing their self-regulation processes, providing collective immoral standards, and facilitating moral disengagement strategies. We find evidence that delinquent group involvement affects self-regulation to some degree. Gang and delinquent group membership are associated with decreased guilt, but guilt is not further altered during periods of active gang involvement. Contrary to our findings regarding anticipated guilt, our results provide no evidence that changes in group status affect self-regulation with regard to empathy and self-centeredness. One likely explanation for this unexpected finding is the fact that the measurement of these variables differs with respect to their frame of reference. Within the G.R.E.A.T. survey, guilt is a measured response to situations (e.g., 'How guilty or badly would you feel if you attacked someone with a weapon?'). Meanwhile, empathy and self-centeredness include more global measures (e.g., 'I worry about how other people feel,' If things I do upset people, it's their problem not mine.'). As such, the measurement of these variables is reflective of two different types of personality concepts: state (guilt) versus trait (empathy and self-centeredness). Trait mechanisms are not only relatively resistant to change (Allport and Odbert 1936), but prior research indicates that global attitudes and situational attitudes do not necessarily correspond to one another (Thomas 2017).

Upon joining a gang, members may become more isolated from out-groups and experience reinforced commitment to the gang. Our findings suggest that periods of delinquent group involvement and gang membership are associated with increased commitment to delinquent peers; yet there is no significant change in negative peer commitment as youth fluctuate between periods of gang membership and delinquent group involvement. We also find that youth report significantly fewer prosocial peers only when moving from typical groups to gangs. Our findings regarding school commitment provide some evidence that gang membership uniquely attenuates youth's conventional bonds, but this relationship appears to be more complex: as youth shift from delinquent groups to gangs, they report decreased commitment to school, but a similar effect is not seen in the transition from typical to delinquent groups or from typical groups to gangs. The fact that we find a decrease in school commitment for the transition from delinquent groups to gangs but not from typical groups to gangs is curious and we can only speculate that this finding is due to idiosyncrasies in the fixed-effects model. Specifically, the transition from typical group to delinquent group is associated with a nonsignificant increase in school commitment, thus indicating that the coefficient difference between delinquent group and gang membership is slightly larger than the difference between the typical group and gang member. Together, these findings regarding conventional and unconventional bonds suggest that the processes that reinforce commitment to delinquent peers are similar for gang youth and those involved in delinquent peer groups, but isolation from prosocial peers and attenuation of prosocial bonds appear to be unique to gang membership.

Our results also provide some support for the idea that social influences facilitate activation and disengagement of self-regulation by creating cognitive dissonance. We find that agreement with hitting neutralizations increases when youth move from a typical to delinquent group, but not when youth move from a typical group to a gang. Surprisingly, we find reduced agreement with hitting neutralizations as youth move from delinquent groups to periods of active gang involvement. This unanticipated finding may reflect differences in-group processes related to gang versus delinquent group membership. We speculate that if violence is considered normative within gangs and gang norms and beliefs supersede those held by groups outside of the gang, then gang-involved youth do not have a need to rationalize violent behavior. In other words, cognitive dissonance does not exist or is less prominent for gang members because violent resolutions are morally acceptable.

Finally, consistent with prior research, we find the most substantial differences in offending. Compared with typical group membership, periods of delinquent group involvement are marked with increases in nonviolent offending, but not violent offending. Meanwhile, gang membership is associated with increases in violent, but not nonviolent, delinquency. This finding is consistent with prior work, which indicates that the unique effect of gang membership does not extend to property offending (Alleyne and Wood 2010; Battin et al. 1998; Melde and Esbensen 2013; Melde, Esbensen, and Carson 2016; Tita and Ridgeway 2007). Some researchers have argued that violence is a central and normative feature in the lives of gang youth (Decker 1996; Hughes and Short 2005). While our findings cannot explain the causes of increased violence during active gang membership, we know from prior research that increased violence throughout the tenure of gang membership may be related to initiation and desistance processes as well as inter- and intra-gang violence (Carson, Peterson, and Esbensen 2013; Carson and Vecchio 2015; Decker and Van Winkle 1996; Pyrooz and Decker 2011). As SCT suggests, individual beliefs, behavioral patterns, and environmental influences interact to shape one another. Thus, to understand why gang members are more violent than their nongang peers, it is necessary to examine the interconnectedness of these systems. Overall, our results suggest that while general delinquent group processes drive changes in negative peer commitment, guilt and nonviolent delinquency, something unique about the gang results in changes in school commitment and violent offending. While our research examines only the direct relationships between various types of group membership and our outcomes, this work provides an important piece of the puzzle. Further work is needed to determine what explains increases in violence during periods of active gang involvement, but according to the principles of SCT, delinquent peer group membership may serve as the gateway to changes in youth's attitudes and offending.

This research, along with similar work, is concerned with the effects of group membership on individual-level behaviors and attitudes. While our study highlights differences in the individual-level consequences of gang versus delinquent group membership, additional work is needed to understand how group processes shape individual-level outcomes. Further research at the group level is needed to continue to identify how gangs differ from delinquent groups (for similar calls for group-level research, see McGloin and Decker 2010; Decker, Melde, and Pyrooz 2013; Hughes 2013; Pyrooz, Sweeten, and Piquero 2013; McGloin and Collins 2015), particularly with regard to group processes and other variables that are commonly associated with violence (e.g., subculture of violence, routine activities).

It is worthwhile to note that our work also highlights the transient nature of gang membership as well as involvement in delinquent groups. When examining within-person change in-group status, youth belonging to a gang or delinquent group spent less than half of their observed time in one of these two groups. This finding is not only in line with prior research that states that youth only remain in a gang for two years or less (Esbensen and Huizinga 1993; Thornberry et al. 1993) but extends it to youth in a delinquent peer group as well. This finding, however, is not consistent with Warr's (1993) work, which argues that delinquent peers are 'sticky friends' that youth become entrenched with over multiple years. These disparate findings may be due to measurement differences in delinquent group membership (i.e., belonging to a delinquent group versus involvement with delinquent friends) or to the relatively minor offenses studied by Warr (1993).

By estimating fixed-effects models, our results provide strong evidence that within-individual changes occur when youth move between different groups even when controlling for time-stable covariates, but interpretation of our findings requires some context. This approach differs from much of the literature reviewed in this paper because it examines within-individual change rather than between-person differences. Thus, while prior research that has focused on group-level variation between gang and nongang members has found differences in self-centeredness, for instance (Matsuda et al. 2013; Melde and Esbensen 2011, 2014; Peterson and Morgan 2014), we do not report similar findings at the individual level. It may be the case that while self-centeredness, among other variables, are risk factors for gang membership, they are typically stable within-person characteristics across group membership status. It is also important to note that our models assume that youth's decisions to become involved in different types of peer groups are time-invariant. Prior research, however, has concluded that self-report data may change over time due to maturation or changes in respondents' interpretations of the survey questions (see Lauritsen 1998). These issues are of concern for our results regarding gang membership, in particular, because self-nominated gang membership may capture changing definitions of what it means to be a gang member. While self-nomination strategies have been shown to be reliable and valid measures for decades (Decker et al. 2014; Esbensen et al. 2001; Thornberry et al. 2003), we are cognizant of the fact that youth who consider themselves gang members at one point may fit the criteria for delinquent group membership at a different time point despite few, if any, changes in their peer group.

Given the unique 'gang effect,' our findings are supportive of programs that target gang youth. In particular, our work highlights the unique impact of gang membership on school commitment and violent delinquency. We caution practitioners and policy-makers, then, against interventions (i.e., suppression tactics, civil gang injunctions, zero-tolerance policies) that may drive gang youth closer to their peers and deepen the divide between conventional institutions and antisocial groups (Klein and Maxson 2006; Wiley, Carson, and Esbensen 2016). Alternatively, efforts should be made to enhance prevention and intervention programs that address the social isolation and marginality of gang youth such as engaging them with prosocial peer groups or school groups (Goldman, Giles, and Hogg 2014; Katz et al. 2011). That said, the work presented here also highlights the detrimental impact of spending time with a delinquent group on moral beliefs, commitment to delinquent peers, and nonviolent offending. It is important, therefore, that practitioners and policy-makers take note of youth who simply spend time with deviant peers, a sentiment that has been echoed elsewhere (Dong and Krohn 2016).

Notes

1. It is important to note that youth who belong to a typical adolescent group may participate in delinquency with some of their friends, but they did not indicate that they participated in illegal activities as a group.

2. Due to an under-representation of African American youth in Chicago schools obtained in the 2006 sampling effort, two additional schools were included in the evaluation, beginning during the 2007–2008 school year (Esbensen et al. 2012).
3. We examined differences between the excluded sample and our analysis sample. Demographically, the excluded sample includes a slightly greater proportion of males as well as youth categorized as black or other race and a smaller percentage of white youth. In terms of group involvement, the excluded sample represents more observations during gang involvement (excluded = 14.2%, final analysis = 9.8%) and less delinquent group membership (excluded sample = 7.3%, final analysis = 9.7%). The excluded sample has lower agreement with hitting neutralizations, less empathy, more self-centeredness, less negative peer commitment, fewer prosocial peers, greater commitment to school, and are less delinquent in terms of both violent and nonviolent offenses. Thus, while these differences indicate that excluded youth are more likely to be gang involved, display reduced tendencies for delinquent attitudes and norms, less delinquency, and less delinquent group involvement.
4. It is important to note that the use of multiple measures of gang involvement is common in prior literature (Alleyne et al. 2016; Lachman, Roman, and Cahill 2013).
5. For this and all other mean scale variables, scales were created if at least half of the included items had nonmissing values.
6. We recognize that this last item, involvement in gang fights, could potentially drive differences when comparing periods of gang membership and delinquent group membership because youth are more likely to be involved in gang fights during periods of active gang membership. We compared the findings reported in this paper to results using only the first four items and the results do not change substantively.
7. Although variety scales are preferable over logged frequency outcomes because they are not driven by less serious high-frequency items and have been found to possess high reliability and validity (Sweeten 2012), negative binomial regression analysis cannot be used for true fixed-effects modeling because it cannot control for time-stable variables (see Allison and Waterman 2002). We examined the robustness of our results using a negative binomial fixed/random-effects hybrid model with a count nonviolent delinquency outcome. These supplemental analyses are discussed in subsequent endnotes.
8. These percentages are based on time points for which we have available data. For example, youth who were in a gang at two waves, but only have available data for two waves, are in a gang for 100% of their time points. While this may overinflate the percentage of time youth appear to be gang involved, the alternative is to drop any youth who have fewer than six waves of data, which limits our sample substantially.
9. Because the delinquency outcomes are log-transformed, the results are interpreted as a percent change in delinquency based on the following equation: $(\exp(b) - 1) \times 100\%$.
10. Because a logged frequency measure of delinquency is not ideal (see footnote 7), and negative binomial fixed-effects for a count outcome cannot control for time-stable variables, we examined the results using a negative binomial hybrid model. While this model could not be examined for violent delinquency due to convergence issues related to variability in the count outcome, we present the fixed- and random-effect results for the nonviolent delinquency outcome here, interpreted as incident rate ratios. As compared with periods of typical group membership, periods of delinquent group membership are associated with a 1.26 times greater delinquency variety ($b = .23$, SE = .03, $p < .001$). Meanwhile, periods of gang membership are associated with a 1.27 times greater variety of nonviolent offenses ($b = .24$, SE = .03, $p < .001$). The coefficients that represent the random effects in the hybrid model indicate that the between-person differences are also significant: delinquent group members report nonviolent delinquency variety at a rate 1.56 times greater than youth in a typical peer group ($b = .44$, SE = .08, $p < .001$), while gang members report 1.34 times more nonviolent acts ($b = .29$, SE = .07, $p < .001$). The complete results are available from the corresponding author.
11. Again, hybrid model results are available only for the nonviolent delinquency variety outcome, but consistent with our OLS fixed effects model, the within-person effect of gang membership, as compared with delinquent group involvement, is not significant ($b = -.002$, SE = .03, $p = .962$). Meanwhile, the random-effects or between-person coefficient indicates that youth in a gang offend at a rate of .86 times that of delinquent group members ($b = -.16$, SE = .08, $p = .05$).

Acknowledgment

The opinions, findings, and conclusions or recommendations expressed in this paper are those of the authors and do not necessarily reflect the views of the Department of Justice. This research was made possible by seven cities including the School District of Philadelphia. Opinions contained in this manuscript reflect those of the author and do not necessarily reflect those of the seven cities.

Disclosure statement

No potential conflict of interest was reported by the authors.

Funding

This work was supported by National Institute of Justice, Office of Justice Programs, U.S. Department of Justice [grant number 2006-JV-FX-0011].

References

Alleyne, E., I. Fernandes, and E. Pritchard. 2014. "Denying Humanness to Victims: How Gang Members Justify Violent Behavior." *Group Processes & Intergroup Relations* 17: 750–762.
Alleyne, E., and J. L. Wood. 2010. "Gang Involvement: Psychological and Behavioral Characteristics of Gang Members, Peripheral Youth, and Nongang Youth." *Aggressive Behavior* 36: 423–436.
Alleyne, E., and J. L. Wood. 2012. "Gang Membership: The Psychological Evidence." In *Youth Gangs in International Perspective: Results from the Eurogang Program of Research*, edited by F.-A. Esbensen and C. Maxson, 151–168. New York: Springer.
Alleyne, E., J. L. Wood, K. Mozova, and M. James. 2016. "Psychological and Behavioural Characteristics That Distinguish Street Gang Members in Custody." *Legal and Criminological Psychology* 21: 266–285.
Allison, P. D. 2009. *Fixed Effects Regression Models*. Thousand Oaks, CA: Sage.
Allison, P. D., and R. P. Waterman. 2002. "Fixed-effects Negative Binomial Regression Models." *Sociological Methodology* 32: 247–265.
Allport, G. W., and H. S. Odbert. 1936. "Trait Names: A Psycho-lexical Study." *Psychological Monographs* 47: 1–171.
Anderson, E. 1999. *Code of the Streets: Decency, Violence, and the Moral Life of the Inner City*. New York: W. W. Norton.
Bandura, A. 1986. *Social Foundations of Thought and Action*. Englewood Cliffs, NJ: Prentice-Hall.
Bandura, A. 1990. "Selective Activation and Disengagement of Moral Control." *Journal of Social Issues* 46: 27–46.
Bandura, A. 1991. "Social Cognition Theory of Moral Thought and Action." In *Handbook of Moral Behavior and Development*, edited by W. M. Kurtines and J. L. Gewirtz, 45–103. Hillsdale, NJ: Lawrence Erlbaum Associates.
Bandura, A. 2002. "Selective Moral Disengagement in the Exercise of Moral Agency." *Journal of Moral Education* 31: 101–119.
Battin, S. R., K. G. Hill, R. D. Abbott, R. F. Catalano, and J. D. Hawkins. 1998. "The Contribution of Gang Membership to Delinquency beyond Delinquent Friends." *Criminology* 36: 93–115.
Bjerk, D. 2009. "How Much Can We Trust Causal Interpretations of Fixed-effects Estimators in the Context of Criminality?" *Journal of Quantitative Criminology* 25: 391–417.
Bouchard, M., and A. Spindler. 2010. "Groups, Gangs, and Delinquency: Does Organization Matter?" *Journal of Criminal Justice* 38: 921–933.
Cameron, A. C., and D. L. Miller. 2015. "A Practitioner's Guide to Cluster-robust Inference." *Journal of Human Resources* 50: 317–372.
Carson, D. C., D. Peterson, and F.-A. Esbensen. 2013. "Youth Gang Desistance: An Examination of the Effect of Different Operational Definitions of Desistance on the Motivations, Methods, and Consequences Associated with Leaving the Gang." *Criminal Justice Review* 38: 510–534.
Carson, D. C., and J. M. Vecchio. 2015. "Leaving the Gang: A Review and Thoughts on Future Research." In *The Handbook of Gangs*, edited by S. H. Decker and D. C. Pyrooz, 257–275. New York: Wiley.
Cohen, A. K. 1955. *Delinquent Boys: The Culture of the Gang*. Glencoe, IL: The Free Press.
Decker, S. H. 1996. "Collective and Normative Features of Gang Violence." *Justice Quarterly* 13: 245–264.
Decker, S. H., C. Melde, and D. C. Pyrooz. 2013. "What Do We Know about Gangs and Gang Members and Where Do We Go from Here." *Justice Quarterly* 30: 369–402.
Decker, S. H., D. C. Pyrooz, G. Sweeten, and R. K. Moule Jr. 2014. "Validating Self-nomination in Gang Research: Assessing Differences in Gang Embeddedness across Non-, Current, and Former Gang Members." *Journal of Quantitative Criminology* 30: 577–598.
Decker, S. H., and B. Van Winkle. 1996. *Life in the Gang: Family, Friends, and Violence*. New York: Cambridge University Press.
Dong, B., and M. D. Krohn. 2016. "Dual Trajectories of Gang Affiliation and Delinquent Peer Association during Adolescence: An Examination of Long-term Offending Outcomes." *Journal of Youth and Adolescence* 45: 746–762.

Esbensen, F.-A., and D. C. Carson. 2012. "Who Are the Gangsters? An Examination of the Age, Race/Ethnicity, Sex, and Immigration Status of Self-reported Gang Members in a Seven-City Study of American Youth." *Journal of Contemporary Criminal Justice* 28: 462–478.

Esbensen, F.-A., and D. Huizinga. 1993. "Gangs, Drugs, and Delinquency in a Survey of Urban Youth." *Criminology* 31: 565–589.

Esbensen, F.-A., D. Huizinga, and A. W. Weiher. 1993. "Gang and Non-gang Youth: Differences in Explanatory Factors." *Journal of Contemporary Criminal Justice* 9: 94–116.

Esbensen, F.-A., and C. L. Maxson. 2012. "The Eurogang Program of Research and Multimethod Comparative Gang Research: Introduction." In *Youth Gangs in International Perspective*, edited by F.-A. Esbensen and C. L. Maxson, 1–14. New York: Springer.

Esbensen, F.-A., C. Melde, T. J. Taylor, and D. Peterson. 2008. "Active Parental Consent in School-based Research: How Much is Enough and How Do We Get It?" *Evaluation Review* 32: 335–362.

Esbensen, F.-A., D. W. Osgood, D. Peterson, T. J. Taylor, and D. C. Carson. 2013. "Short- and Long-term Outcome Results from a Multisite Evaluation of the G.R.E.A.T. Program." *Criminology & Public Policy* 12: 375–411.

Esbensen, F.-A., D. Peterson, T. J. Taylor, and A. Freng. 2010. *Youth Violence: Sex and Race Differences in Offending, Victimization, and Gang Membership*. Philadelphia, PA: Temple University Press.

Esbensen, F.-A., D. Peterson, T. J. Taylor, and D. W. Osgood. 2012. "Results from a Multi-site Evaluation of the G.R.E.A.T. Program." *Justice Quarterly* 29: 125–151.

Esbensen, F.-A., and F. M. Weerman. 2005. "Youth Gangs and Troublesome Youth Groups in the United States and the Netherlands: A Cross-national Comparison." *European Journal of Criminology* 2: 5–37.

Esbensen, F.-A., J. Winfree, L. Thomas, N. He, and T. J. Taylor. 2001. "Youth Gangs and Definitional Issues: When is a Gang a Gang, and Why Does It Matter?" *Crime & Delinquency* 47: 105–130.

Findlay, L., A. Girardi, and R. J. Coplan. 2006. "Links Between Empathy, Social Behavior, and Social Understanding in Early Childhood." *Early Childhood Research Quarterly* 21: 347–359.

Gatti, U., R. E. Tremblay, F. Vitaro, and P. McDuff. 2005. "Youth Gangs, Delinquency and Drug Use: A Test of the Selection, Facilitation, and Enhancement Hypotheses." *Journal of Child Psychology and Psychiatry* 46: 1178–1190.

Goldman, L., H. Giles, and M. A. Hogg. 2014. "Going to Extremes: Social Identity and Communication Processes Associated with Gang Membership." *Group Processes & Intergroup Relations* 17: 813–832.

Gordon, R. A., B. B. Lahey, E. Kawai, R. Loeber, M. Stouthamer-Loeber, and D. P. Farrington. 2004. "Antisocial Behavior and Youth Gang Membership: Selection and Socialization." *Criminology* 42: 55–87.

Hennigan, K. M., C. L. Maxson, D. C. Sloane, K. A. Kolnick, and F. Vindel. 2014. "Identifying High-risk Youth for Secondary Gang Prevention." *Journal of Crime and Justice* 37: 104–128.

Hennigan, K. M., and M. Spanovic. 2012. "Gang Dynamics through the Lens of Social Identity Theory." In *Youth Gangs in International Perspective: Results from the Eurogang Program of Research*, edited by F.-A. Esbensen and C. Maxson, 127–149. New York: Springer.

Hill, K. G., J. C. Howell, J. D. Hawkins, and S. R. Battin-Pearson. 1999. "Childhood Risk Factors for Adolescent Gang Membership: Results from the Seattle Social Development Project." *Journal of Research in Crime and Delinquency* 36: 300–322.

Horowitz, R. 1983. *Honor and the American Dream*. New Brunswick, NJ: Rutgers University Press.

Hughes, L. A. 2013. "Group Cohesiveness, Gang Member Prestige, and Delinquency and Violence in Chicago, 1959–1962." *Criminology* 51: 795–832.

Hughes, L. A., and J. F. Short. 2005. "Disputes Involving Youth Street Gang Members: Micro-social Contexts." *Criminology* 43: 43–76.

Jolliffe, D., and D. P. Farrington. 2004. "Empathy and Offending: A Systematic Review and Meta-analysis." *Aggression and Violent Behavior* 9: 441–476.

Katz, C. M., V. J. Webb, K. Fox, and J. N. Shaffer. 2011. "Understanding the Relationship between Violent Victimization and Gang Membership." *Journal of Criminal Justice* 39: 48–59.

Klein, M. 1995. *The American Street Gang: Its Nature, Prevalence, and Control*. Oxford: Oxford University Press.

Klein, M., and L. Y. Crawford. 1967. "Groups, Gangs, and Cohesiveness." *Journal of Research in Crime and Delinquency* 4: 63–75.

Klein, M., and C. L. Maxson. 2006. *Street Gang Patterns and Policies*. New York: Oxford University Press.

Lachman, P., C. G. Roman, and M. Cahill. 2013. "Assessing Youth Motivations for Joining a Peer Group as Risk Factors for Delinquent and Gang Behavior." *Youth Violence and Juvenile Justice* 11: 212–229.

Lauritsen, J. L. 1998. "The Age-crime Debate: Assessing the Limits of Longitudinal Self-report Data." *Social Forces* 77: 127–155.

Matsuda, K. N., C. Melde, T. J. Taylor, A. Freng, and F.-A. Esbensen. 2013. "Gang Membership and Adherence to the "Code of the Street."" *Justice Quarterly* 30: 440–468.

McGloin, J. M., and M. E. Collins. 2015. "Micro-level Processes of the Gang." In *The Handbook of Gangs*, edited by S. H. Decker and D. C. Pyrooz, 276–293. New York: Wiley.

McGloin, J. M., and S. H. Decker. 2010. "Theories of Gang Behavior and Public Policy." In *Criminology and Public Policy: Putting Theory to Work*, edited by H. D. Barlow and S. H. Decker, 150–165. Philadelphia, PA: Temple University Press.

Melde, C., and F.-A. Esbensen. 2011. "Gang Membership as a Turning Point in the Life Course." *Criminology* 49: 513–552.

Melde, C., and F.-A. Esbensen. 2013. "Gangs and Violence: Disentangling the Impact of Gang Membership on the Level and Nature of Offending." *Journal of Quantitative Criminology* 29: 143–166.

Melde, C., and F.-A. Esbensen. 2014. "The Relative Impact of Gang Status Transitions: Identifying the Mechanisms of Change in Delinquency." *Journal of Research in Crime and Delinquency* 51: 349–376.

Melde, C., F.-A. Esbensen, and D. C. Carson. 2016. "Gang Membership and Involvement in Violence among U.S. Adolescents: A Test of Construct Validity." In *Gang Transitions and Transformations in an International Context*, edited by C. L. Maxson and F.-A. Esbensen, 33–50. New York: Springer.

Miller, W. B. 1982. *Crime by Youth Gangs and Groups in the United States*. Washington, DC: Office of Juvenile Justice and Delinquency Prevention.

Moore, J. W. 1991. *Going down to the Barrio: Homeboys and Homegirls in Change*. Philadelphia, PA: Temple University Press.

Peterson, D., and K. A. Morgan. 2014. "Sex Differences and the Overlap in Youths' Risk Factors for Onset of Violence and Gang Involvement." *Journal of Crime and Justice* 37: 129–154.

Pyrooz, D. C. 2014. "From Colors and Guns to Caps and Gowns? The Effects of Gang Membership on Educational Attainment." *Journal of Research in Crime and Delinquency* 51: 56–87.

Pyrooz, D. C., and S. H. Decker. 2011. "Motives and Methods for Leaving the Gang: Understanding the Process of Gang Desistance." *Journal of Criminal Justice* 39: 417–425.

Pyrooz, D. C., G. Sweeten, and A. R. Piquero. 2013. "Continuity and Change in Gang Membership and Gang Embeddedness." *Journal of Research in Crime and Delinquency* 50: 239–271.

Short, J. F., and F. L. Strodtbeck. 1965. *Group Processes and Gang Delinquency*. Chicago, IL: University of Chicago Press.

Sullivan, M. L. 2006. "Are 'Gang' Studies Dangerous? Youth Violence, Local Context, and the Problem of Reification." In *Studying Youth Gangs*, edited by J. F. Short Jr and L. A. Hughes, 15–35. Oxford: Altamira.

Sweeten, G. 2012. "Scaling Criminal Offending." *Journal of Quantitative Criminology* 28: 533–557.

Tajfel, H. 1978. *An Integrative Theory of Intergroup Conflict*. London: Academic.

Thomas, K. J. 2017. "Revisiting Delinquent Attitudes: Measurement, Dimensionality and Behavioral Effects." *Journal of Quantitative Criminology*. doi:10.1007/s10940-016-9336-3.

Thornberry, T. P., M. D. Krohn, A. J. Lizotte, and D. Chad-Wiershem. 1993. "The Role of Juvenile Gangs in Facilitating Delinquent Behavior." *Journal of Research in Crime and Delinquency* 30: 55–87.

Thornberry, T. P., M. D. Krohn, A. J. Lizotte, C. A. Smith, and K. Tobin. 2003. *Gangs and Delinquency in Developmental Perspective*. New York: Cambridge.

Tita, G., and G. Ridgeway. 2007. "The Impact of Gang Formation on Local Patterns of Crime." *Journal of Research in Crime and Delinquency* 44: 208–237.

Valdez, A., C. D. Kaplan, and E. Codina. 2000. "Psychopathy among Mexican American Gang Members: A Comparative Study." *International Journal of Offender Therapy and Comparative Criminology* 44: 46–58.

Vigil, J. D. 1988. "Group Processes and Street Identity: Adolescent Chicano Gang Members." *Ethos* 16: 421–445.

Warr, M. 1993. "Age, Peers, and Delinquency." *Criminology* 31: 17–40.

Weerman, F. M., P. J. Lovegrove, and T. Thornberry. 2015. "Gang Membership Transitions and Its Consequences: Exploring Changes Related to Joining and Leaving Gangs in Two Countries." *European Journal of Criminology* 12: 70–91.

Wiley, S. A., D. C. Carson, and F.-A. Esbensen. 2016. "Arrest and the Amplification of Deviance: Does Gang Membership Moderate the Relationship?" *Justice Quarterly*: 1–30. doi:10.1080/07418825.2016.1226936.

Woo, D., H. Giles, M. A. Hogg, and L. Goldman. 2015. "Social Pyschology of Gangs: An Intergroup Communication Perspective." In *The Handbook of Gangs*, edited by S. H. Decker and D. C. Pyrooz, 136–156. New York: Wiley.

Wood, J., and E. Alleyne. 2010. "Street Gang Theory and Research: Where Are We Now and Where Do We Go from Here?" *Aggression and Violent Behavior* 15: 100–111.

School transitions as a turning point for gang status

Dena C. Carson, Chris Melde, Stephanie A. Wiley and Finn-Aage Esbensen

ABSTRACT
The study of gangs corresponds well with life course perspectives of crime as the onset, persistence, and desistance from crime parallel the stages of gang membership. This literature commonly draws on turning points to explain the onset and desistance from criminal behavior, which are often synonymous with life transitions such as marriage, military duty, employment –even gang membership itself. In this study we draw on life course perspectives to examine the impact of a specific life transition that is common during adolescence, school transitions, on a youth's gang status as well as variables associated with a turning point in the life course. Specifically, we focus on two competing relationships that school mobility can serve as the impetus for joining a gang, or alternatively, act as a 'hook for change' and facilitate gang leaving. We use a mixed-methods approach by first drawing on qualitative data that examined desisted gang members and their interpretation of their school transition experiences. Second, consistent with a grounded theory approach, we examined these relationships quantitatively using a panel study of youth followed over a five-year period.

Introduction

Gang researchers have often drawn upon life course perspectives to understand the trajectories of gang careers. This is a natural application as the joining, duration, and exit from gang life correspond with the onset, persistence, and desistance stages of the criminal career trajectory. Similarly, those who join a gang do so at varying ages, remain involved for different lengths of time, and have unique exit processes. These trajectories can be impacted or altered by turning points, which according to Sampson and Laub (2005), include life events such as marriage, military duty, and employment. The effect of other life events, such as school mobility, is less clear. Changing schools, either through the normative transition to high school or otherwise, may be salient transition points for youth because they occur during a period when youth are cultivating friendships and shaping their sense of self (Hagan, MacMillan, and Wheaton 1996; Langenkamp 2016; Meeus 2011).

School transitions vary in the impact that they have on youth. Transitioning or transferring to a new school causes disruption as youth must familiarize themselves with a new – and at times, very different – social and physical environment. This disruption can cause uncertainty, confusion, and insecurity. At the same time, enrollment in a new school provides youth with opportunities for changes in peer groups, new social and extracurricular activities, and alteration of social identity. Research that has examined the consequences of school transitions has been mixed, regardless of the type of transition (i.e., normative or non-normative). The normative transition from middle to high school has been found to have both negative and positive impacts including decreased self-esteem (Blyth, Simmons, and Carlton-Ford 1983) and lower test scores (Roeser, Eccles, and Freedman-Doan 1999), but also improved attendance (Isakson and Jarvis 1999). The impact of non-normative school transitions (i.e., changes due to residential moves or mid-year transfers) has also been mixed, with research demonstrating improved school outcomes such as test scores and greater commitment to school (Leventhal and Brooks-Gunn 2004; Ludwig, Ladd, and Duncan 2001) as well as negative impacts such as increased criminal offending (Gasper, DeLuca, and Estacion 2010), reduced commitment to school (Pribesh and Downey 1999), and increased risk for drop out (Rumberger and Larson 1998). Additionally, school transfers are associated with a reduction in the size of a youth's peer network (Siennick, Widdowson, and Ragan 2016; South and Haynie 2004). The current study examines the impact of school mobility on joining or leaving a youth gang, a particular type of peer network.

We draw on the life course perspective as well as previous research on the impact of school mobility to examine whether school transitions impact gang membership status in a manner consistent with a turning point framework. School transitions are a point of concern for practitioners as nearly all school age youth experience at least one change in school context, and approximately 20–25% of youth experience a non-normative school change outside the transition from, for example, middle to high school (Gasper, DeLuca, and Estacion 2010; Rumberger and Larson 1998). Given their regularity, it is important to understand how these transitions impact a youth's life course in order to help school officials reduce potential negative consequences associated with changing schools. To this end, we draw on works from Melde and Esbensen (2011, 2014) and explore the ability of school transitions to act as a turning point in the life course. The variables used by Melde and Esbensen (2011, 2014) represent the processes associated with a turning point in the life course, as described by Sampson and Laub (2005). Sampson and Laub (2005) suggested that changes in these mechanisms are particularly responsible for shaping criminal trajectories across the life course, and can be impacted by salient life events, such as changes in romantic relationships, employment status, and military service in early adulthood. Melde and Esbsensen (2011, 2014) demonstrated that joining a gang, and to a lesser extent leaving a gang, produced substantial changes in these factors, and helped to explain concomitant changes in involvement in delinquent and criminal behavior. There is reason to believe that transitioning schools is also capable of impacting these mechanisms, as well as resulting in changes to gang membership status. Research on school transitions, however, has not yet suggested this event is a systematic turning point in the life course, as there is evidence that changes in schools can be either a positive or negative event for youth, depending upon how youth respond to the change, and thus is not necessarily criminogenic.

Our first goal in this paper is to examine the extent to which school transitions have a direct impact on gang status. Given that school transitions can produce positive and negative effects on youth, depending on how they respond to the move, our second goal is to examine the impact of school transitions on the correlates of gang membership that have been associated with a turning point in the life course. By examining the direct impact of school transitions on these variables, we advance the literature on school transitions as well as determine how changing schools can impact the relationship between gang joining/leaving and the variables outlined by Melde and Esbensen (2011, 2014). Our final goal, then, is to assess the extent to which the interaction between school transitions and gang joining or leaving affect these correlates of gang membership. In other words, school transitions, when coupled with gang joining or leaving, may accelerate or slow changes in these correlates of gang membership. We examine these research questions through a mixed-methods lens by first examining qualitative data on the ways in which desisted gang members interpret their school transition experiences. Consistent with a grounded theory approach, we then look at the more general quantitative relationships found in a panel study of youth.

The potential impact of school transitions on gang status

Gang research has drawn extensively on a life course framework to understand the impact of gang joining (i.e., gang membership as a turning point) as well as to understand leaving the gang (i.e., the desistance process). Research on the age-graded nature of gang membership finds that onset occurs in the early teens, peaks at the age of 14–15, and declines thereafter (Craig et al. 2002; Esbensen and Huizinga 1993; Huff 1996, 1998; Pyrooz 2014). As Thornberry et al. (2003) argued, gang membership can be thought of as a trajectory and as with any life course trajectory, onset and desistance can be altered by turning points in the life course. According to Sampson and Laub (2005), turning points typically change the life course by (1) allowing for 'knifing off' from the past; (2) creating new relationships and altering social supports; (3) changing routine activities; and (4) providing opportunities for identity transformation.

Turning points are often understood in the gang literature in terms of push and pull factors associated with gang leaving and gang joining. In terms of leaving the gang, pull factors away from the gang are most commonly associated with turning points in a life course because they present options that are more attractive than gang membership. Pulls away from the gang can come in the form of life transitions such as employment, entering into a romantic relationship, parenthood and, specific to our interests, school mobility (Carson and Esbensen 2016; Carson, Peterson, and Esbensen 2013; Decker and Lauritsen 2002; Decker and Pyrooz 2011). Push factors are internal to the gang member and may result in making the gang environment seem less appealing such as disillusionment with gang life or maturation (Carson and Esbensen 2016; Carson, Peterson, and Esbensen 2013; Decker and Lauritsen 2002; Decker, Pyrooz, and Moule 2014; Pyrooz and Decker 2011). These push motivations are commonly associated with developmental theories because of an associated identity transformation. While school mobility may be classified as a turning point for gang youth, it can also act as a hook for change that facilitates the process through which youth pull themselves out of a gang as part of a process of identity transformation (Giordano, Schroeder, and Cernkovich 2007). In the case of gang joining, pull factors make the gang look attractive to an outsider and may include access to money or members of the opposite sex, ability to gain respect or status, or simply to fit in better (Decker and Curry 2000; Decker and Van Winkle 1996; Esbensen and Winfree 2013; Thornberry et al. 2003). Pushes into the gang are those mechanisms that compel a youth to join, which is commonly the case when youth seek protection from victimization (Decker and Van Winkle 1996; Esbensen and Winfree 2013; Thornberry et al. 2003). It is possible that school transitions generate the push and pull factors that increase the likelihood of gang joining.

School transitions, even when youth are forewarned, may abruptly 'knife off' youth from their previous relationships. This effect is even more likely if individuals find themselves in a small cohort of youth transitioning to the new school or if youth experience a school transfer outside of the normative school transition. School mobility may immediately lead to gang desistance by cutting off communication with the gang, especially if the move represents upward mobility to a better neighborhood or school. By abruptly knifing off from former gang ties, the school transition also offers a fresh start and opportunity for identity transformation. That is, the school transition can serve as a mechanism to shed the 'gang member' label, which may have been applied by community members, classmates, and/or teachers (Decker and Van Winkle 1996). In particular, the process of identity transformation and changes in peer groups and activities are likely reciprocal: as youth become more self-reflective and aware of their individuality, the social structure of their peer groups change, and youth in turn develop more positive self-conceptions, further altering identity (Kinney 1993). In addition to these processes, the development of social skills such as peer resistance or refusal skills either over time or via prevention programming can aid in gang desistance and keep youth from joining new gangs at their new schools (i.e., Esbensen et al. 2013). These developments are consistent with Giordano and colleagues' (2007, 1607) discussion of desistance processes more generally: 'offenders have much to learn from others whose behavior presents a strong contrast to their own criminal lifestyles, and this contrast poses a distinct developmental challenge that maximizes opportunities for further growth and development.'

Therefore, if youth are successful at breaking away from their gang and antisocial peers more generally and surround themselves with more prosocial others it should affect cognitive and emotional (e.g., anger identity) processes associated with reduced deviant behavior.

Social capital, or the social ties that provide information and resources, can increase the status of youth (Coleman 1990; Hagan, MacMillan, and Wheaton 1996). Peers are a particularly salient form of social capital during adolescence, as youth begin to spend increasingly more time with peers and tend to rely on them as a source of social standing, personal identity, and values (Fuligni et al. 2001; Smetana, Campione-Barr, and Metzger 2006). School mobility (whether normative or non-normative) affects social capital because it can rupture these established friendships (Siennick, Widdowson, and Ragan 2016; Weller 2007). Because the gang is a source of social capital (Moule, Decker, and Pyrooz 2013), school transitions may facilitate the desistance process by removing that source of social capital. But along with removing former sources of social capital, youth typically have a larger pool of peers and wider variety of extracurricular activities when they move to larger schools, such as during the transition from middle to high school. This increased variety provides youth with the opportunity to find friends who are more compatible or have similar interests (Weller 2007). By presenting gang youth with the ability to foster new relationships, moving to a new school can promote disengagement from the gang (Carson and Esbensen 2016) as well as desistance from crime (Warr 1998, 2002).[1] In fact, several studies point to a positive impact of school transitions, whether normative or otherwise, on peer relations, finding that school transitions are associated with increased social support and fewer negative peer relations (Barber and Olsen 2004; Roeser, Eccles, and Freedman-Doan 1999; Weiss and Bearman 2007).

Until this point, we have discussed the ways in which school transitions may facilitate a change in gang status by cutting off ties from the gang, introducing youth to prosocial activities and peers, and generating identity transformations that facilitate gang desistance. Alternatively, school transitions have the potential to introduce youth to a social milieu that encourages gang membership. One of the greatest concerns when transitioning to a new school is the attenuation of bonds with peers, schools, counselors, administrators, and even parents. Because these forms of social capital serve as key sources of supervision as well as social control in the lives of mobile youth (Pribesh and Downey 1999; Siennick, Widdowson, and Ragan 2016), disruptions in social capital could lead to gang joining through several processes. Vigil (1993) observed that the lack of social control is especially problematic during the transition from elementary to middle school and, in turn, facilitated gang joining in his sample. Vigil's (1993) findings are corroborated both by work that finds that gang membership increases from 6th to 7th grade (Gottfredson and Gottfredson 2001) and research on the age-graded incidence of gang status (Craig et al. 2002; Esbensen and Huizinga 1993; Pyrooz 2014).

Gangs can serve as a source of social capital and afford youth with a sense of belonging as well as status and respect (Alleyne and Wood 2010; McGloin and Collins 2015; Woo et al. 2015). In this way, the need to gain respect or increase status acts as a pull mechanism into the gang because it makes the gang an attractive option for quickly building social capital, particularly if youth experience difficulty gaining entrée into prosocial groups (South and Haynie 2004). This notion is upheld in the gang joining literature, as 18–60% of gang members report they joined the gang to attain status or respect (Decker and Curry 2000; Decker and Van Winkle 1996; Esbensen and Winfree 2013). Along with changes in peer groups, some research suggests that participation in extracurricular activities declines following school transitions, particularly in the transition from middle to high school (Barber and Olsen 2004; Blyth, Simmons, and Carlton-Ford 1983; Seidman et al. 1994). These changes in routine activities, combined with the increased autonomy and decreased parental involvement that comes with normative developmental progression as youth transition between levels of school, could result in youth spending more time with or becoming more committed to delinquent peers and deviant groups, such as gangs.

In addition to decreased parental guardianship, the loss of relationships with teachers and peers that come with school transitions can also result in decreased social capital that negatively affects school-related outcomes (Pribesh and Downey 1999). Research on normative school transitions, for instance, indicates that academic achievement, school engagement, and support from teachers decrease after youth transition to a new school (for review, see Benner 2011 or Symonds and Galton 2014). One common explanation for these declines is that the academic rigor and expectations for students increase along the elementary to high school continuum (Eccles, Lord, and Midgley 1991; Eccles and Midgley 1988). Students are often expected to perform at higher levels, but when they fail they tend to withdraw from and become less committed to school. Moreover, school transitions – regardless of timing – involve unfamiliar environments, which can cause anxiety and uncertainty and account for declines in youth's school involvement and academic achievement (Benner and Graham 2009; Isakson and Jarvis 1999).

The unfamiliar school environment, coupled with the lack of guardianship that former classmates and teachers offered, can create a sense of insecurity among youth who change schools. Indeed, bullying is a common student concern when transitioning to middle or high school and is often realized after youth transition to a new school (see Symonds and Galton 2014; for review). Moreover, when mobile youth are classified as 'easy targets' and feel they are vulnerable to victimization (Carson, Esbensen, and Taylor 2013), they may see a gang as their best option for garnering protection (Decker and Van Winkle 1996; Esbensen and Peterson Lynskey 2001; Esbensen and Winfree 2013; Thornberry et al. 2003).[2] Approximately, 54% of gang youth in an 11 city study reported that the gang's ability to provide protection served as a central motivation for joining (Esbensen and Peterson Lynskey 2001). Other research supports the idea that youth who transition schools feel the need for increased protection: those who transitioned to a new school between 8th and 9th grade were more likely than those who did not transition to bring a weapon to school (Weiss and Bearman 2007).

With respect to gang joining, however, all of these potential processes must be tempered by the realization that gangs are active in the selection process (Pyrooz and Densley 2016). That is, even if youth who transition to a new school desire the social and personal benefits (e.g., protection, social capital) afforded through gang membership, gangs in the new school environment may be leery of accepting a new student into their group given the risks this may have for their 'brand.' If gangs were simply to allow any and all willing individuals into their ranks, they run the risk of including individuals that do not personify the attributes and messages their gang wishes to convey in their environment, which routinely includes the ability to intimidate outside groups and persons, and back up this message through violence when necessary (Decker 1996). In this way, school transitions may lead to a reduction in the probability of gang membership whether or not the individual seeks to desist from gang membership or purposively change their social identity. If this is the case, one might find the likelihood of gang membership diminishes, but the associated effect on social-psychological processes is null; only the opportunity for gang membership has changed.

The transition to a new school, therefore, appears to come with both challenges and opportunities for positive youth development. Changes in both the social and physical environment can be stressful for youth, and have been shown to increase anxiety levels while at the same time disrupting ties with potential sources of social support, such as teachers, parents, and friends. On the other hand, transitioning to a new school can be conceptualized as a 'hook for change,' whereby youth can use this opportunity to structure their social lives in a way that allows for and facilitates identity transformations, consistent with Giordano and colleagues (2007) neo-Meadian perspective on changes in the life course. Importantly, this perspective suggests school transitions may be particularly beneficial for gang involved youth who wish to shed their deviant identity in so much as it produces a 'contrast effect in connection with role-taking and social influence processes' (Giordano, Schroeder, and Cernkovich 2007, 1607).

The current study draws on life course perspectives (Giordano, Schroeder, and Cernkovich 2007; Sampson and Laub 2005), as well as research on the impact of both normative and non-normative school transitions to examine the utility of school mobility as a turning point for gang trajectories. Our research goals are threefold: (1) explore the direct impact of school mobility on gang status; (2) examine the impact of school mobility on correlates of gang membership considered to be consistent with a turning points framework (see Figure 1) (see Melde and Esbensen 2011, 2014); and (3) assess whether changes in gang status that are simultaneous to school transitions produce differential effects on these variables, consistent with Giordano, Schroeder, and Cernkovich (2007) discussion of contrast effects.

Methods

The current study uses a mixed-methods approach to examine the link between school mobility and gang status. In the following section, we outline our qualitative and quantitative methods and analysis plans. The quantitative data are drawn from the National Evaluation of the G.R.E.A.T. (Gang Resistance Education and Training) Program. The G.R.E.A.T. program is a school-based gang prevention program taught by law enforcement officers targeting middle school youth (i.e., 11 and 12 year olds). Data collection took place between 2006 and 2012 in seven cities: Albuquerque, New Mexico; Chicago, Illinois; Greeley, Colorado; Nashville, Tennessee; Philadelphia, Pennsylvania; Portland, Oregon; and a city in the Dallas/Fort Worth, Texas area. These cities were selected for the evaluation based on the existence of an established G.R.E.A.T. program, geographic and demographic diversity, and presence of gang activity (see Esbensen et al. 2013; for more detail about the evaluation design). While all students ($n = 4905$) in these classrooms could participate in the evaluation, a thorough active parental consent process resulted in 78% of students being given permission by a parent or guardian to participate in the evaluation ($n = 3820$). This active parental consent rate is exceptional as 89% ($n = 4372$) returned consent forms (see Esbensen et al. 2008 for a detailed description of procedures and factors related to active consent). In 2006, students completed pre-test and post-test (waves 1 and 2) self-report surveys with completion rates of 98.3 and 94.6%, respectively.[3] The sample also completed four annual follow-up surveys (Waves 3, 4, 5, and 6), with participation rates of 87, 83, 75, and 73%, respectively.

The qualitative data come from a subsample of the G.R.E.A.T. evaluation. Those youth who self-reported gang membership (i.e., 'Are you now in a gang?') ($n = 512$) or who met the Eurogang definition[4] ($n = 697$) in one or more waves of the G.R.E.A.T. evaluation were eligible to participate in the second study. The study design called for a comparison of stable (self-nominated involvement in two or more consecutive waves – $n = 156$) and transient (self-reported involvement in at least one, non-consecutive, wave – $n = 356$) gang youth. The sampling strategy relied upon a purposive over-sampling of stable youth ($n = 131$) and a random sampling of both transient gang youth ($n = 198$) and youth who fit the Eurogang definition ($n = 97$).[5] This strategy resulted in a sampling frame of 426 youth who either self-nominated as a gang member or met the Eurogang definition. While few parents and/or youth declined to participate (5.3%), a number of selected youth were not interviewed because they had moved (27.7%), because researchers failed to find the youth at home in spite of repeated visits to the address (20.2%), and for other reasons such as being non-responsive to the inquires to participate (4.2%). The final sample size consisted of 180 youth. It is important to note that given the retrospective nature of the interviews, in some instances, gang membership was reported as far back as 2006 (the qualitative interviews were conducted in the summer of 2012). Given this timeframe, some youth did not acknowledge their gang status during the interviews ($n = 53$).[6] The project staff reviewed, discussed, and confirmed the status of the remaining 127 youth.[7] The focus of the study was on gang desistance and, therefore, a number of the youth were no longer gang involved ($n = 107$). In-depth semi-structured qualitative interviews were conducted face-to-face, in confidential settings, by trained interviewers with these youth in all seven cities included in the G.R.E.A.T. evaluation.

Quantitative variables and measurement

The quantitative variables are consistent with what Sampson and Laub describe as the mechanisms of a turning point, as highlighted by Melde and Esbensen (2011, 2014) and are also relevant outcomes of interest within the school transitions literature (see Figure 1).

Control variables

Demographic (i.e., sex, race/ethnicity, age), school, and programmatic controls were included in all multivariate analyses. Biological sex was coded dichotomously, with male equal to one, and females serving as the reference group. The sample had slightly more female (52%) than male respondents (see Table 1), although 56% of the self-reported gang youth were male, which is comparable to other

Factors Associated with a Turning Point	Measures	Hypothesized Direction of Impact School Transition
(1) new situations that "knife off" the past from the present	Prosocial Peers	-
	School Commitment	-
	Guilt	-
	Violence Neutralizations	+
	Gang Membership	+/-
(2) new situations that provide both supervision and monitoring as well as new opportunities of social support and growth	Parental Monitoring	-
	Negative Peer Commitment	+
(3) new situations that change and structure routine activities	Unstructured Socializing	+
	Peer Delinquency	+
(4) new situations that provide the opportunity for identity transformation	Anger Identity	+

note: The factors associated with a turning point were drawn directly from Sampson and Laub (2005: 17-18). The measures are not necessarily mutually exclusive across factors, but were assigned above for illustrative purposes only. For example, peer delinquency could also be an indicator of factor 2, and parental monitoring is also associated with factor 3. The hypothesized direction of the effects, however, is consistent no matter where they are placed.

Figure 1. Operationalizing a turning point.

school-based studies (e.g., Esbensen et al. 2001; Melde and Esbensen 2011; Pedersen and Lindstad 2012; Weerman 2012). Race/ethnicity was controlled through a series of dummy variables, including black/African American, Hispanic/Latino, and a variable for 'other' race/ethnicity, with non-Hispanic/white respondents serving as the reference group. Hispanic/Latino (38%) respondents were the largest ethnic group in the study, followed by 25% of the sample who reported being non-Hispanic/white, 21% who reported being black/African-American, and 16% of respondents who reported another race/ethnicity.

Controlling for age was particularly important given the aforementioned age and grade-level differences in gang status (Craig et al. 2002; Esbensen and Huizinga 1993; Gottfredson and Gottfredson 2001; Huff 1996, 1998; Pyrooz 2014). Age and age squared, measured at baseline, were included in all multivariate models examining the factors associated with a turning point. Over the study period students ranged in age from 9 to 18 although the majority of the students, who began the study in sixth grade at age 11 (60%) or 12 (29%), were between 11 and 15 years of age over the course of the study. Age was centered at 12 in the multivariate models. The school-level socioeconomic status for students' original school of enrollment was controlled through the inclusion of a variable measuring the percent of students eligible for free or reduced lunch in the school, which ranged from 23 to 96% of students across schools (mean = .64, standard deviation = .23). This variable was standardized through a z-score transformation before it was included in all multivariate models. Finally, a control for involvement in the G.R.E.A.T. program was included in all models (G.R.E.A.T. participant = 1; Control = 0), as was a variable indicating whether or not respondents transitioned to high school at wave 4 or wave 5 of survey administration (wave 4 = 1, wave 5 = 0).

Gang membership

Gang membership was measured via self-nomination by asking respondents 'Are you now in a gang?,' at each wave of data collection, with non-gang members coded '0' and gang members coded '1.' While there remains a debate on the best way to measure gang membership, prior work has found that self-report is a valid indicator of involvement in a gang (Decker et al. 2014; Esbensen et al. 2001; Thornberry et al. 2003). With respect to gang membership, a total of 512 respondents reported being a gang member on at least one occasion during the study. Of those 512 gang members, 288 individuals provided uninterrupted data between the time they had not yet reported gang membership and when they self-identified as a gang member, or what we refer to as gang joining. On the other hand, 325 respondents provided uninterrupted data between the time of their self-reported gang membership and when they ceased to identify as a gang member, or what we label gang desistance. Together, these measures were used to determine whether there was a significant association between school transitions and changes in gang membership status to determine if school transitions were systematically associated with gang membership.

School transitions

School transitions data were documented through logs maintained by program evaluators from the original project. Three dichotomous variables were created to account for school transitions, each coded 0 for no, and 1 for yes. An *overall school transition* variable was created to identify a school transition of any kind, whether normative or non-normative. Alternatively, a variable that identified normative school transitions was created (i.e., *normative school transition*), which identified the transition from middle school to high school in each of the participating sites. Finally, a variable was created to identify school transitions that occurred when they were not an expected part of the normative school progression through grades (i.e., middle school/junior high to high school), labeled *Non-normative Transition*. That is, these school transitions were from one middle school to another middle school, or from one high school to another high school.

Peer group size

Peer group size was measured through an ordinal indicator of the number of friends the respondent reported having. In particular, after respondents were asked whether or not they have a group of friends, they were asked 'about how many people, other than you, belong to this group?' Responses ranged from 1 to 7, with 1 equal to 1, 2 equal to 2–5, 3 equal to 6–10, 4 equal to 11–20, 5 equal to 21–50, 6 equal to 51–100, and 7 equal to more than 100. Those who reported not having a peer group were coded as 0.

Prosocial peers

Our measure of prosocial peers represents the proportion of the respondent's peer group that was considered prosocial based on their responses to a four-item scale. To introduce these items, students were asked 'During the last year, how many of your current friends have done the following?' Then each of the following items were read to the students: 'Have been thought of as good students,' 'Have gotten along well with teachers and adults at school,' 'Have been generally honest and told the truth,' and 'Almost always obeyed school rules.' Responses were based on a five-point scale ranging from 'None of them' to 'All of them' ($\alpha = .83$).[8]

Peer delinquency

Peer delinquency was measured by a construct that identified the proportion of the respondent's peers who engaged in seven different delinquent behaviors, including acts that ranged in severity from skipping school without an excuse to attacking someone with a weapon. Responses were coded on a five-point scale with one equal to 'none of them' and five equal to 'all of them' ($\alpha = .89$).

School commitment

School commitment was measured through student responses to seven statements about school activities, including 'I try hard in school,' 'In general, I like school,' and 'Grades are very important to me.' Responses were based on a five-point Likert scale ranging from 'strongly disagree' to 'strongly agree' ($\alpha = .77$).

Violence neutralization

Consistent with Sykes and Matza's (1957) techniques of neutralization, three statements concerning the appropriateness of violence in certain situations were presented to respondents, including: 'It's okay to beat up someone if they hit you first,' 'It's okay to beat up someone if you have to stand up for or protect your rights,' and 'It's okay to beat up someone if they are threatening to hurt your friends or family.' Answers were recorded using a five-point Likert scale ($\alpha = .88$).

Parental monitoring

Four items were presented to respondents concerning how closely their parents monitored their behavior. Statements included items such as 'My parents know who I am with if I am not at home,' and 'My parents know where I am when I am not at home or at school.' These items were measured on a five-point Likert scale ($\alpha = .81$).

Negative peer commitment

Commitment to deviant peers was assessed using three items measured on a five-point scale ranging from 'not at all likely' to 'very likely.' The three questions included in the scale ($\alpha = .86$) asked respondents 'If your group of friends was getting you into trouble (at home/ at school/ with the police), how likely is it that you would still hang out with them?'

Unstructured socializing

To measure unstructured socializing, we created a three-item additive index based on whether youth engaged in particular activities. Respondents indicated whether or not they 'spend a lot of time together in public places like the park, the street, shopping area, or the neighborhood,' 'ever spend time hanging around with your current friends not doing anything in particular where no adults are present,' or 'ever spend time getting together with your current friends where drugs and alcohol are available.' The index ranges from zero to three.

Guilt

To measure respondents' anticipated feelings of guilt related to participation in delinquent activities, respondents were asked, 'How guilty or how badly would you feel if you...,' engaged in seven different acts that ranged in severity from 'stole something worth less than $50' to 'attacked someone with a weapon.' Responses were based on a three-point scale ranging from 'not very guilty/badly' to 'very guilty/badly' ($\alpha = .93$).

Anger identity

We utilized the four-item scale developed by Grasmick et al. (1993) to measure the anger/temper component of the self-control construct as our indicator of anger identity. This is consistent with Giordano, Schroeder, and Cernkovich (2007) concept, which has been found to be a robust correlate of violent behavior across the life course. Items included statements such as 'I lose my temper pretty easily,' and 'When I'm really angry, other people better stay away from me.' Responses were coded on a five-point Likert scale ($\alpha = .83$).

Qualitative and quantitative analytic plan

In keeping with a grounded theory approach, we began our analyses with examination of the qualitative data and then moved on to a larger, more general, quantitative sample. The qualitative portion of these analyses utilized in-depth interviews with desisted gang youth to identify themes surrounding the desistance motivation associated with mobility. The narratives were examined using line-by-line open and focused coding, which allowed for the identification of themes using a modified grounded theory approach (Charmaz 2006; Glaser and Strauss 1967). The results presented below represent the most common patterns that emerged around mobility as a motivation for gang disengagement and, consistent with grounded theory, serve as the basis for our quantitative analyses. While the qualitative results are not generalizable to the population or completely representative of our sample, they provide insight into the experiences of these desisted youth as well as the meanings they assigned to their unique desistance processes.

Using the quantitative data, we assess the impact of school transitions on gang membership status and the cognitive, affective, and behavioral components characteristic of a turning point in the life course (Graber and Brooks-Dunn 1996; Rutter 1996; Sampson and Laub 2005), using two strategies. First, we use panel fixed effects logit regression to estimate the impact of school transitions (both normative transitions and non-normative transitions) on the probability of gang onset, persistence, and desistance. We restricted these models to only those cases where respondents reported going through these stages of gang membership at some point during the study (n = 288, 512, 325) given the absence of variation in this outcome across schools.[9] An advantage in panel fixed effects models is that they control for all time-stable characteristics of the persons under study, and thus help to isolate the effect of a school transition on gang status transitions (Allison 2009).

Second, we use three-level discontinuous regression models (Singer and Willett 2003) to assess the impact of school transitions on factors associated with a turning point in the life course to account for the nested structure of our data, with multiple observations (i.e., Level 1-within person effects) nested within persons (i.e., Level 2-between person effects), who are nested in schools (i.e., Level 3-between school effects). Discontinuous regression models are well-suited for this analysis because they allow for both the examination of immediate changes in the outcome (e.g., peer delinquency, school commitment) that accompany school transitions, as well as ongoing changes in the outcome the longer respondents remained in a particular school. This strategy also allows for the examination of potential interaction effects associated with gang desistance when it occurs at the same time as a school transition. That is, these models can detect whether or not the gang desistance process is particularly impactful when it is accompanied by a change in schools.[10]

School transitions as a turning point for gang desistance

In the qualitative interviews youth were asked to expound upon the various reasons why they began to disengage from their gang. Of the 107 youth who reported desisting from a gang, approximately 59% discussed how school transitions impacted their disengagement process. A major theme that emerged centered on the ability of school transitions to facilitate changes in peer groups via either a knifing off of gang ties or a gradual process (see Decker and Lauritsen 2002). The knifing off of gang ties was illustrated through discussions of an abrupt change in the peer group. Curtis, for example, stated, 'As we hit new schools we never talked to each other again' and Jasmin echoes, 'Yeah…everybody like split up.' Other youth discussed a more gradual disengagement process. Harry, for instance, explained how his gang broke apart 'I mean, ever since 9th grade when we separated, little by little we just stopped hanging out, we got into high school [and] we hang out with different people now.' Similarly, Maria described how her gang maintained contact at first, '…after I moved schools, like, they talked to me for, like, the first month or two and then after that they stopped talking to me.'

The process of breaking away from gang peers following a school transition is commonly associated with building new friendships, akin to Sergio's statement '…I met new people and I hang out with different people.' Mariah discussed that after her school transition her peers were more prosocial in nature: 'I just went to a different high school and I met better, like, other people.' While less common than discussions of new peer connections, youth also described their school transition in ways that are consistent with a hook for change. Brandon illustrates this point when asked by the interviewer if his school transition was beneficial:

> Yeah definitely…'cause I mean … I was talking to my friend the other day, he's like 'Man, if you woulda kept going to [Previous School]' he's like 'Who knows where you woulda been right now' and I was like 'Yeah that's pretty crazy' I could be, my life could be, you know, [in a] totally different direction, but yeah goin' over to [Current School] and settling down, focusing on school and college.

Still other youth discussed their cognitive decision to change schools, which indicates they began a self-reflection process and, therefore, viewed school transitions as a way to facilitate the gang desistance process. For example, Jeremey reveals that 'Yeah, I changed schools. Mostly [to] get away from people at that school.' Additionally, Jose discusses the fact that he chose to distance himself from his former gang:

It was just kinda my decision ... I stopped hanging out with them kind of towards the end of 10th grade, but then what made it better for me [was] to be, like, just stick completely away from 'em that's when I switched to [Current School] going into Junior year. So like I had like no contact with them I had no reason to be around 'em or anything.

These narratives illustrate how school transitions can help to facilitate the relationship between gang desistance and correlates of gang membership such as changes in peer groups as well as by providing opportunities for self-reflection, which could lead to changes in self-identity. In the next section, we examine the direct relationship between school transitions and gang status using the quantitative data.

A quantitative look at school transitions and gang status

Before describing our multivariate analyses, we begin by describing the univariate descriptive statistics and bivariate measures of association related to school transitions and gang membership. As seen in Table 1, we observed at least one school transition for the majority of our sample (74.3%), while just over 11% of respondents experienced more than one school move.[11] The majority of these cases (59.3%) represent the normative transition to high school. Fifteen percent of the sample experienced a non-normative transition. Results suggest that school transitions are not associated with gang joining, as only 13.2% of cases of gang joining ($n = 38$) occurred at the time of a normative school transition ($\chi^2 = .171$, df = 1, $p > .05$), and only 3.5% of the total number of observations of gang joining ($n = 10$) occurred during the same wave as a non-normative school transition ($\chi^2 = .012$, df = 1, $p > .05$). There was also no association between being in a gang and school transitions overall ($\chi^2 = .184$, df = 1, $p > .05$), given roughly 16.9% of the total number of observations of gang membership occurred at the same wave as a school transition (i.e., 136 of 804). There was also no association between gang membership and school transitions when the type of transition (i.e., normative or non-normative) was accounted for. School transitions were, however, significantly and positively associated with observations of gang desistance ($\chi^2 = 21.48$, df = 1, $p < .05$), with 27.2% of all instances of leaving a gang observed at the same wave of a school transition (i.e., 88 of 324 observed cases[12]). With respect to the type of school transition, results suggest that gang desistance was significantly associated with normative school transitions ($\chi^2 = 14.42$, df = 1, $p < .05$), as well as non-normative school transitions ($\chi^2 = 7.67$, df = 1, $p < .05$) at the bivariate level. In sum, school transitions do not appear to be a catalyst for gang joining, but they are associated with gang desistance.[13]

We next move on to our multivariate analyses, where we assess the association between school transitions and changes in gang status using panel fixed effects models. Importantly, these models control for time, which takes into account any systematic change in the probability of gang status transitions over time, as well as all time stable characteristics of respondents. In all, models 1, 2, and 3 examine the probability of joining a gang for the first time (i.e., gang joining), being in a gang regardless of prior gang membership status (i.e., gang membership), or leaving a gang (i.e., gang desistance) at the time of either a normative school transition or a non-normative transition. After controlling for these myriad factors, model 1 suggests that changing schools is unassociated with gang joining. With respect to being in a gang after a school transition, regardless of whether or not they had previously reported being in a gang, model two suggests there is also no association between school transitions and gang membership, regardless of the type of school transition experienced. Finally, with respect to our fixed effects regression analysis for those youth who reported leaving a gang at some point in our study, results suggest that their probability of desisting from gang activity increased as they experienced a normative transition to a new school ($b = .30, p < .05$), but was unassociated with non-normative school transitions ($b = .16, p > .05$).

Given the results, which suggest the probability of joining a gang diminishes after a school transition, while the probability of leaving a gang increases systematically, we turn our attention to our second research question: What is the influence of school transitions on correlates of gang membership considered to be consistent with a turning points framework in prior research? The odd numbered models in Table 3 provide information on the association between school transitions and time after a school transition on these factors, while controlling for a number of demographic characteristics, including

Table 1. Descriptive statistics.

Variables	n	Percent (%)	Mean	SD
School level	(n = 31)			
% Free and reduced lunch			0.64[a]	0.23
Person level	(n = 3820)			
White	1041	27.3		
Black	687	18.0		
Hispanic	1517	39.7		
Other	575	15.1		
Age			11.47	0.71
Age[b]			132.13	16.73
Male	1839	48.2		
Ever gang	512	13.5		
School transitions				
0 school transitions	983	25.7		
1 school transition	2408	63.0		
2 school transitions	374	9.8		
3 school transitions	53	1.4		
4 school transitions	2	.1		
Overall school transition	2837	74.30		
Normative school transition	2264	59.3		
Non-normative school transition	573	15.0		
Within person/across time	(n = 20,340)			
Peer group size			2.84	1.48
Prosocial peers			3.43	0.95
Peer delinquency			1.48	0.67
School commitment			3.72	0.74
Violence neutralization			3.40	1.17
Parental monitoring			4.07	0.76
Negative peer commit			1.93	1.00
Unstructured socializing			1.35	0.93
Guilt			2.48	0.61
Anger identity			3.03	0.99

[a]The range in percent free and reduced lunch is from a minimum of 23% to a maximum of 96% of students.
[b]Age reflects age at wave one. Age and age squared were based on age centered at 12 in all regression models. The range in ages of youth across the survey period was from 9 to 18 years, although roughly 90% of youth were 11 or 12 at baseline and thus 15 or 16 at the final wave of data collection.

Table 2. The effect of school transitions on gang member status.

	Model 1 Gang joining (obs. = 1468) (n = 288)		Model 2 Gang membership (obs. = 2302) (n = 462)		Model 3 Gang desistance (obs. = 1636) (n = 305)	
Time	0.05	0.04	−0.13	0.04*	0.17	0.04*
Normative school transition	−0.03	0.19	0.08	0.13	0.30	0.15*
Non-normative transition	−0.39	0.39	−0.21	0.19	0.16	0.33
Log likelihood	−457.34		−819.07		−507.59	
Wald χ^2(df)	2.06 (3)		11.44*(3)		29.97*(3)	

Notes: All models are based upon panel fixed effects logit models using Stata 14.0 (i.e., xtlogit). Standard errors were produced using bootstrap methods (100 replications), with bias corrected and accelerated confidence intervals, and the seed was set at 100 for replication purposes.
*$p < .05$; obs. = total number of observations; n = total number of respondents.

gang membership status as well as the linear time trend. Due to space constraints, however, we limit our tables to only those variables related to our research questions under consideration, although all models control for all of the characteristics described in our measures section, and included in Table 2 (full model results available upon request).

Table 3. The effect of school transitions on factors associated with a turning point.

	Model 1		Model 2		Model 3		Model 4	
	Peer Group Size		Peer Group Size		Prosocial Peers		Prosocial Peers	
	B	s.e.	B	s.e.	B	s.e.	B	s.e.
Intercept	2.85	0.06*	2.84	0.07*	3.46	0.06*	3.45	0.06*
Time	0.03	0.01*	0.03	0.01*	−0.02	0.01*	−0.02	0.01*
School Transition	−0.15	0.04*	−0.13	0.04*	0.10	0.02*	0.09	0.02*
Time in New School	−0.05	0.04	0.01	0.13	0.14	0.02*	0.15	0.08*
Self-reported gang member	1.39	0.07*	1.39	0.07*	−0.70	0.04*	−0.70	0.04*
Desisted from gang membership	0.36	0.07*	0.54	0.10*	−0.22	0.04*	−0.34	0.06*
Desisted x School Transition	–	–	−0.27	0.14*	–	–	0.20	0.08*
Desisted x Time in New School	–	–	−0.03	0.06	–	–	−0.01	0.03
BIC	−18,998.32		−18,978.83		−13,804.32		−13,784.35	
Δ BIC	492.04		511.53		467.22		487.19	
	Model 5		Model 6		Model 7		Model 8	
	Peer Delinquency		Peer Delinquency		School Commitment		School Commitment	
	B	s.e.	B	s.e.	B	s.e.	B	s.e.
Intercept	1.28	0.03*	1.26	0.03*	3.92	0.04*	3.91	0.04*
Time	0.10	0.00*	0.09	0.00*	−0.09	0.00*	−0.09	0.00*
School Transition	0.02	0.01	0.02	0.02	0.09	0.02*	0.07	0.02*
Time in New School	−0.06	0.01*	0.02	0.05	0.08	0.02*	0.09	0.06
Self-reported gang member	1.02	0.03*	1.02	0.03*	−0.53	0.03*	−0.54	0.03*
Desisted from gang membership	0.41	0.03*	0.44	0.04*	−0.10	0.03*	−0.27	0.05*
Desisted x School Transition	–	–	−0.02	0.05	–	–	0.28	0.06*
Desisted x Time in New School	–	–	−0.04	0.02	–	–	−0.01	0.02
BIC	−8,958.13		−8,939.98		−10,517.05		−10,486.17	
Δ BIC	926.10		944.25		446.68		477.56	
	Model 9		Model 10		Model 11		Model 12	
	Violence Neut.		Violence Neut.		Parental Monitoring		Parental Monitoring	
	B	s.e.	B	s.e.	B	s.e.	B	s.e.
Intercept	3.16	0.08*	3.15	0.08*	4.13	0.04*	4.14	0.04*
Time	0.07	0.01*	0.07	0.01*	−0.02	0.00*	−0.02	0.00*
School Transition	−0.17	0.03*	−0.15	0.03*	−0.05	0.02*	−0.05	0.02*
Time in New School	−0.09	0.02*	−0.04	0.09	0.06	0.02*	0.00	0.06
Self-reported gang member	0.68	0.05*	0.68	0.05*	−0.52	0.03*	−0.52	0.03*
Desisted from gang membership	0.21	0.05*	0.35	0.07*	−0.28	0.04*	−0.33	0.05*
Desisted x School Transition	–	–	−0.20	0.09*	–	–	0.04	0.06
Desisted x Time in New School	–	–	−0.02	0.04	–	–	0.03	0.03
BIC	−15,797.87		−15,777.54		−11,458.59		−11,441.21	
Δ BIC	486.66		506.99		405.99		423.37	
	Model 13		Model 14		Model 15		Model 16	
	Neg. Peer Commit.		Neg. Peer Commit.		Unstructured Socializing		Unstructured Socializing	
	B	s.e.	B	s.e.	B	s.e.	B	s.e.
Intercept	1.65	0.05*	1.63	0.05*	0.02	0.04	0.01	0.04
Time	0.12	0.01*	0.12	0.01*	0.11	0.01*	0.11	0.01*
School Transition	−0.03	0.02	−0.02	0.02	−0.01	0.02	0.00	0.02

(Continued)

Table 3. (*Continued*).

	B	s.e.	B	s.e.	B	s.e.	B	s.e.
Time in New School	−0.11	0.02*	0.04	0.08	−0.05	0.02*	0.02	0.06
Self-reported gang member	0.94	0.05*	0.94	0.05*	0.46	0.03*	0.46	0.03*
Desisted from gang membership	0.36	0.05*	0.48	0.07*	0.19	0.04*	0.26	0.05*
Desisted x School Transition	–	–	−0.12	0.08	–	–	−0.08	0.06
Desisted x Time in New School	–	–	−0.07	0.04	–	–	−0.03	0.03
BIC	−14,713.85		−14,692.50		−11,712.44		−11,694.30	
Δ BIC	514.05		535.40		304.28		322.42	

	Model 17 Guilt		Model 18 Guilt		Model 19 Anger Identity		Model 20 Anger Identity	
	B	s.e.	B	s.e.	B	s.e.	B	s.e.
Intercept	2.69	0.03*	2.69	0.03*	3.07	0.06*	3.06	0.06*
Time	−0.09	0.00*	−0.09	0.00*	−0.02	0.01*	−0.02	0.01*
School Transition	0.01	0.01	0.00	0.01	−0.10	0.02*	−0.09	0.02*
Time in New School	0.05	0.01*	0.00	0.05	−0.09	0.02*	−0.02	0.08
Self-reported gang member	−0.54	0.03*	−0.54	0.03*	0.49	0.04*	0.49	0.04*
Desisted from gang membership	−0.35	0.03*	−0.43	0.04*	0.32	0.05*	0.40	0.06*
Desisted x School Transition	–	–	0.10	0.05*	–	–	−0.10	0.08
Desisted x Time in New School	–	–	0.02	0.02	–	–	−0.03	0.03
BIC	−8402.63		−8381.68		−13974.75		−13956.39	
Δ BIC	474.75		495.70		319.14		337.50	

Notes: All analyses are derived from three-level HLM models estimated in HLM 7.0, including controls for percent of students on free and reduced lunch at level 3 (school level) and demographic characteristics at level two (person level). The BIC was calculated based on the level 2 sample size (BIC = -2LL + [ln(n)*p]). Change in Bayesian Information Criterion (i.e., ΔBIC) is relative to a model with only time included.
*$p < .05$.

With respect to peer group size, results suggest that, on average, the size of a peer group increases slightly across time ($b = .03$). As youth change schools, the size of their peer group diminishes abruptly ($b = −.15$), although it does not change significantly more than expected the longer the respondent stays in school.[14] The impact of school transitions on the proportion of respondents' peers who are prosocial suggests that youth are surrounded by a systematically more prosocial peer group than prior to their school transition ($b = .10$) and that this proportion increases the longer they remain in that school ($b = .12$). The proportion of delinquent friends, however, does not change systematically during a school transition, although the longer youth spend in their new school their rate of growth in delinquent peers is slowed ($b = [−.06 + .10] = .04$) relative to the average growth across time ($b = .10$). Commitment to school increases abruptly ($b = .09$) as youth transition schools, and then appears to level off the longer youth remain in their new school ($b = [.08 = −.09] = −.01$). Neutralizations for violent behavior diminish during a school transition ($b = −.17$), as well as the longer youth remain in a new school ($b = −.09$), effectively canceling out the upward trend in this variable found in the data ($b = [−.09 + .07] = −.02$). Parental monitoring appears to decrease slightly immediately following a school transition ($b = −.05$), although it increases thereafter ($b = .04$). While commitment to deviant peers increased slightly, on average, across time, and school transitions did not produce an immediate impact on these attitudes, the intensity of these attitudes remained stable the longer youth spent in the new school ($b = [−.11 + .12] = .01$). Similarly, while unstructured socializing increased systematically across time, and was not immediately impacted by a school transition, this rate of increase slowed significantly the longer youth remained in a new school ($b = [.11 + −.05] = .06$). From an emotional standpoint, while anticipated guilt for participating in deviant acts diminished across time for the sample, and was not impacted immediately upon transition into a new school, this downward trend was not as steep the longer youth remained in their new school ($b = [−.09 + .05] = −.04$). Anger identity, however, diminished significantly as youth transitioned to a new school ($b = −.10$) and continued this downward trend the longer they remained in a new school ($b = −.11$). In sum, current results suggest that school transitions do not produce systematic negative consequences on youth, and actually appear to produce a positive impact on factors associated with crime, deviance, and gang membership. The magnitude of the impact of school transitions on these variables, however, is rather small in absolute terms.

Lastly, the even numbered models in Table 3 provide results pertinent to our third research question, which addresses whether changes in gang status that occur at the same time as a school transition[15] produce a differential impact on these associated correlates of gang membership. Given results in Table 2, these models focus solely on gang desistance, as there is no evidence that school transitions lead to gang joining in a systematic fashion. With respect to peer group size, while self-reported gang members ($b = 1.39$) and those who desisted from gang membership ($b = .54$) report significantly larger peer groups than those youths who never reported gang membership, when youth report leaving a gang at the same time they transitioned to a new school, findings indicate that the size of their peer group diminishes to a greater extent than youth who desisted from gang membership but remained in the same school ($b = −.27$). While school transitions were found to lead to an increase in the proportion of prosocial peers more generally ($b = 09$), the impact was especially pronounced for youth who reported leaving a gang during the transition to a new school ($b = .20$). Similarly, while school commitment improved, on average, as youth transitioned to a new school, this effect was stronger for youth who also reported desisting from a gang ($b = .28$). There was also a significant decline in the acceptance of neutralizations for violence for youth who reported leaving a gang during a school transition ($b = −.20$). While school transitions did not produce an immediate impact on anticipated guilt for youth more generally, youth who reported leaving a gang at the transition point reported higher levels of guilt ($b = .10$) than would have been expected had they desisted from gang membership but remained in the same school. Finally, desistance from gang membership during a school transition did not produce systematically different results than gang desistance at other points in time for peer delinquency, parental monitoring, negative peer commitment, unstructured socializing, and anger identity. It should be noted, however, that those who reported having left a gang reported lower levels of these variables than was reported by gang involved youth.

Discussion and conclusion

Our study expands research on the intersection between gang status and life course criminology by examining the impact of school transitions as a potential facilitator to change gang status. Both qualitative and quantitative studies on gang desistance point toward the utility of life events, such as school moves, in facilitating these processes. Moreover, prior work demonstrates that school transitions (whether normative or otherwise) impact several correlates of gang membership such as academic outcomes, peer relations, extracurricular activities, and individual attributes. The relationship of school transitions to these variables – which are also associated with a turning points framework – suggest that school transitions may provide opportunities for change in gang membership status. Informed by this prior research we pursued three main goals: (1) explore the direct impact of school transitions on gang status; (2) examine the impact of school transitions on correlates of gang membership considered to be consistent with the turning points framework in prior research (Melde and Esbensen 2011, 2014); and (3) examine the interaction between two potential turning points, changes in gang status and school transitions, on changes in these correlates of gang membership. Our findings add to the life course literature as well as research on gang desistance by considering an underexplored event, school transition, as a potential turning point. This research adds another piece to the gang desistance puzzle by identifying the positive impact that school change has on gang desistance and correlates of gang membership (see Figure 1). Interestingly, though, we did not find any evidence to suggest that school mobility facilitated gang joining.

Results from prior work on motivations for gang desistance have suggested that life events such as changing residences and/or transitioning to a new school can facilitate gang desistance. Both our qualitative and quantitative results confirmed this relationship. Youth who experienced a school transition were significantly more likely to be gang desisters. While this study is the first, at least to our knowledge, to examine the direct impact of school transitions on gang status, it also confirms both qualitative and quantitative research on motivations for gang desistance, which typically find school or residential mobility play a role in this process (Carson and Esbensen 2016; Carson, Peterson, and Esbensen 2013; Decker and Lauritsen 2002; Decker and Pyrooz 2011). Moreover, our qualitative analysis identified some of the underlying processes associated with this relationship. During the in-depth interviews, youth discussed how the transition to a new school changed their associations with their gang peers. The connections were broken gradually in some cases and more abruptly in others, but the school transition allowed youth to build new, oftentimes prosocial, friendships. Consistent with a turning point framework and prior research (Melde and Esbensen 2014), the 'knifing off' of gang attachments (i.e., gang desistance) is associated with increases in commitment to school as well as prosocial peers. The quantitative findings presented here indicate that youth who desist from their gang in conjunction with a school transition experience greater increases in their commitment to school and more attachments to prosocial peers.

In addition to examining the impact of school transitions on peer associations, we explored the impact on guilt associated with delinquent acts and neutralizations for violence in order to capture changes in conventional beliefs associated with a severing of gang membership. While themes related to this did not appear in the qualitative analysis, our quantitative results demonstrated that youth who simultaneously disengaged from the gang and changed schools reported more feelings of guilt as well as fewer rationalizations for violent behavior than those who desisted without a change in schools. It appears then that the impact of gang desistance on variables associated with the knifing off of gang attachments is amplified in the presence of a school transition.

Neither the qualitative nor quantitative analyses were able to identify changes in other variables consistent with the turning point framework, indicating that school transitions do not amplify the relationship between gang desistance and patterns of supervision (e.g., parental monitoring) and investments in new or old relationships (e.g., negative peer commitment). These results, especially in the quantitative analysis, are not surprising as Melde and Esbensen (2014) found that these variables did not change upon leaving a gang. Our qualitative and quantitative analyses were unable to identify an amplification effect of school transitions on the relationship between gang desistance and unstructured socializing and associations with delinquent peers.

School transitions, however, can act as hooks for change by providing gang youth an opportunity for self-reflection, which was a noticeable theme in the qualitative interviews. In these narratives, youth expressed a conscious decision to leave the gang through self-reflection at the time of the school transition and also discussed how they and their goals changed after moving to a new school. This suggests that youth may have already begun to shed the label of gang member and initiated the process of taking on a new role. We attempted to capture these changes in the quantitative analysis by examining changes in anger identity. Results, however, showed no amplification effect of school transitions on the relationship between gang desistance and anger identity. It is unlikely that the null findings indicate that youth have not had time to formulate a change in identity, as there was also no effect for time in the new school. It is possible, however, that changes in identity came in other forms not captured in our quantitative data.

Overall, our findings indicate that school transitions have some utility in facilitating gang desistance and for amplifying factors associated with knifing off from the gang. However, the results with regards to identity transformation were not as conclusive. While the qualitative results indicate that school transitions can act as hooks for change, this was not supported by our quantitative analyses. Despite this finding, the results presented here will be helpful to practitioners working in a school setting and indicate that focus should be placed on helping youth who are making school transitions build prosocial attachments. School transitions are an important opportunity for youth, especially gang youth, to get a fresh start and shed the label of gang member. However, given the omnipresence of gangs in many communities, youth will most likely be exposed to gangs in their new school; therefore, it is especially important to use this opportunity to build ties with nondelinquent peers and to work to increase their involvement in school and commitment to their grades and their future.

Prior research also indicated that school transitions could increase the likelihood of gang joining as a way to quickly garner social capital, which the gang can provide (Alleyne and Wood 2010; McGloin and Collins 2015; Woo et al. 2015). Moreover, youth who move to a new school are at risk for victimization (Carson, Esbensen, and Taylor 2013), which may result in joining a gang for the perceived protection they can provide. We did not find support for these propositions. This null finding may be attributable to the fact that joining a gang simultaneous with transitioning schools is an extremely rare event in our data. In the over 20,000 observations in the sample, we only observed 48 instances where youth reported joining a gang at the same time that s/he experienced a school transition. The low probability of simultaneously experiencing gang joining and school transition is consistent with prior literature that finds that school mobility is not predictive of association with delinquent peers (Siennick, Widdowson, and Ragan 2016). However, we are hesitant to completely reject this hypothesis and suggest that future research should continue to explore this link with gang or nongang high-risk youth, as some prior research suggests that school transitions are particularly difficult for a small group of students who were previously considered high-risk (Roderick 1993). Additionally, future research should examine the impact of moving to schools with higher levels of disorder on gang joining. Students report higher levels of fear and victimization in schools with high levels of disorder (Gottfredson 2001; Randa and Wilcox 2010; Schreck and Miller 2003); therefore, a lack of social capital may be especially impactful for youth transitioning to these schools.

Additionally, it is important to note that our findings with regards to gang joining could be seen as being inconsistent with observations from Vigil (1993). He found evidence of an increase in gang joining during the early school transition from elementary to middle school, while we find the opposite for later school transitions. One possible explanation for the dissident findings is that later transitions more closely approximate the time in a youth's life course when they are beginning to transition out of the gang (Craig et al. 2002; Esbensen and Huizinga 1993; Huff 1996, 1998; Pyrooz 2014). Fortunately, we were able to control for the relationship between age and gang status in our analysis, which helps to isolate the role of school transitions from age- and grade-level effects, unlike Vigil (1993) and others who have examined the age- and grade-level correlates of the gang career.

Our discussion has focused on the impact of school transitions on gang status as well as its ability to amplify the relationship between gang desistance and factors associated with the turning point framework. Our results, however, are also able to inform the school transitions literature through examination of the direct impact of school transitions on academic outcomes, peer relationships, extracurricular activities, and individual attributes. Our results demonstrate that school transitions have an immediate positive impact on many of these measures including commitment to school, improved associations with prosocial peers, decreased rationalizations for violent behavior, and reduced anger identity. Additionally, as youth spent time in their new school they continued to see improvement in these variables and experienced a lagged reduction in delinquent friends, commitment to delinquent youth, and a decrease in unstructured socializing. The findings are mostly consistent with prior literature (Barber and Olsen 2004; Kinney 1993; Roeser, Eccles, and Freedman-Doan 1999; Weiss and Bearman 2007) and indicate that breaking away from peers and the subsequent loss of social capital can act as a turning point for youth, allowing them to build more prosocial bonds to peers and school as well as help transform their self-identity.

This work adds to the understanding of the impact of school transitions on gang status and correlates of gang membership, but also suffers from some limitations. The nature of these data limits the ability to generalize to the entire population. While the G.R.E.A.T. data offer a sample that is geographically broad, it is not nationally representative of the United States. Additionally, the reliance on a school-based sample to study gang membership limits our ability to examine the most highly delinquent members of the gang as well as older gang youth. However, the focus on a young population is important as younger offenders are more likely to occupy groups, are less entrenched in their delinquent ways (Pyrooz and Decker 2011), and are, therefore, more susceptible to change.

Notes

1. We note that dropping out of school can also facilitate the desistance process (Brunson and Miller 2009; Pyrooz, Decker, and Webb 2014; Pyrooz, Fox, and Decker 2010). However, because our quantitative sample does not include youth who dropped out of school, we cannot empirically examine this effect.
2. Joining a gang for protection frequently leads to the opposite effect, as gang youth are more likely to be victimized than nongang youth (Melde, Taylor, and Esbensen 2009; Taylor et al. 2008, 2007).
3. Due to an under-representation of African American youth in Chicago schools obtained in a 2006 sampling effort, two additional schools were included in the evaluation, beginning during the 2007–2008 school year (Esbensen et al. 2013).
4. The Eurogang Program of Research defines a street gang as 'any durable, street-oriented youth group whose involvement in illegal activity is part of its group identity.' For more information on the Eurogang and this definition please see Maxson and Esbensen (2016).
5. It is important to note that the sampling strategy of the original study design stipulated that youth were not included in the pool of Eurogang youth if they self-nominated as a gang member at any wave of the G.R.E.A.T. evaluation.
6. While reasons for reinterpretation vary, statistical analysis reveals no differences across youth who retrospectively reported gang membership and those who did not on a variety of variables ranging from demographics to attitudes and behaviors.
7. Three to four project members read the interview transcripts and formed consensus opinions on the gang status of each youth.
8. All alpha scores are calculated at wave 1.
9. There was non-significant variation at level 3 (i.e., the school level) in three level HLM models when the outcome was restricted to those experiencing some variation in gang status.
10. Analyses were conducted in HLM 7.0. Missing data were handled through listwise deletion. The final sample size for all models was 3233 respondents.
11. It is important to note that everyone in our sample experienced the normal transition to high school. The 25.7% of youth who did not transition in our sample simply did not transition during the times for which we have survey data for them.
12. We did not have valid transition data from one respondent for which we observed gang desistance.
13. With the exception of the post-test, which was conducted in the spring of the initial school year of data collection, survey data were collected in the fall of each school year.
14. Calculation of the effect of time in a new school is equal to the sum of the effect of time and time in new school.
15. Given the relatively small number of non-normative school transitions, and the fact that the effect was in the same direction as normal school transitions in the fixed effects models, we use the overall school transition variable in all models in Table 3.

Disclosure statement

No potential conflict of interest was reported by the authors.

Funding

This work was supported by seven school districts, including the School District of Philadelphia [grant number 2006-JV-FX-0011] and [grant number 2011-JP-FX-0101] from the National Institute of Justice, Office of Justice Programs, U.S. Department of Justice. The opinions, findings, and conclusions or recommendations expressed in this manuscript are those of the authors and do not necessarily reflect the views of the Department of Justice or of the seven participating school districts.

References

Alleyne, E., and J. L. Wood. 2010. "Gang Involvement: Psychological and Behavioral Characteristics of Gang Members, Peripheral Youth, and Nongang Youth." *Aggressive Behavior* 36: 423–436.
Allison, P. D. 2009. *Fixed Effects Regression Models*. Thousand Oaks, CA: Sage.
Barber, B. K., and J. A. Olsen. 2004. "Assessing the Transitions to Middle and High School." *Journal of Adolescent Research* 19: 3–30.
Benner, A. D. 2011. "The Transition to High School: Current Knowledge, Future Directions." *Educational Psychology Review* 23: 299–328.
Benner, A. D., and S. Graham. 2009. "The Transition to High School as a Developmental Process among Multiethnic Urban Youth." *Child Development* 80: 356–376.
Blyth, D. A., R. G. Simmons, and S. Carlton-Ford. 1983. "The Adjustment of Early Adolescents to School Transition." *Journal of Early Adolescence* 3: 105–120.
Brunson, R. K., and J. Miller. 2009. "Schools, Neighborhoods, and Adolescent Conflicts: A Situational Examiniation of Reciprocal Dynamics." *Justice Quarterly* 26: 183–210.
Carson, D. C., and F.-A. Esbensen. 2016. "Motivations for Leaving: A Qualitative Comparison of Leaving Processes across Gang Definition." In *Gang Transitions and Transformations in an International Context*, edited by C. L. Maxson and F.-A. Esbensen, 139–155. New York: Springer.
Carson, D. C., F.-A. Esbensen, and T. J. Taylor. 2013. "A Longitudinal Analysis of the Relationship between School Victimization and Student Mobility." *Youth Violence and Juvenile Justice* 11: 275–294.
Carson, D. C., D. Peterson, and F.-A. Esbensen. 2013. "Youth Gang Desistance: An Examination of the Effect of Different Operational Definitions of Desistance on the Motivations, Methods, and Consequences Associated with Leaving the Gang." *Criminal Justice Review* 38: 510–534.
Charmaz, K. 2006. *Constructing Grounded Theory: A Practical Guide through Qualitative Analysis*. Thousand Oaks, CA: Sage.
Coleman, J. S. 1990. *Foundations of Social Theory*. Cambridge, MA: Belknap Press of Harvard University Press.
Craig, W. M., F. Vitaro, C. Gagnon, and R. E. Tremblay. 2002. "The Road to Gang Membership: Characteristics of Male Gang and Nongang Members from Ages 10 to 14." *Social Development* 11: 53–68.
Decker, S. H. 1996. "Collective and Normative Features of Gang Violence." *Justice Quarterly* 13: 245–264.
Decker, S. H., and G. D. Curry. 2000. "Addressing Key Features of Gang Membership: Measuring the Involvement of Young Members." *Journal of Criminal Justice* 28: 473–482.
Decker, S. H., and J. L. Lauritsen. 2002. "Leaving the Gang." In *Gangs in America*, edited by C. R. Huff, 51–67. Thousand Oaks, CA: Sage.
Decker, S. H., and D. C. Pyrooz. 2011. Leaving the Gang: Logging off and Moving on. *Council on Foreign Affairs*, http://www.cfr.org/counterradicalization/save-supportingdocument-leaving-gang/p26590.
Decker, S. H., D. C. Pyrooz, and R. K. Moule Jr. 2014. "Disengagement from Gangs as Role Transitions." *Journal of Research on Adolescence* 24: 268–283.
Decker, S. H., D. C. Pyrooz, G. Sweeten, and R. K. Moule Jr. 2014. "Validating Self-nomination in Gang Research: Assessing Differences in Gang Embeddedness across Non-, Current, and Former Gang Members." *Journal of Quantitative Criminology* 30: 577–598.
Decker, S. H., and B. Van Winkle. 1996. *Life in the Gang: Family, Friends, and Violence*. New York: Cambridge University Press.
Eccles, J. S., S. Lord, and C. Midgley. 1991. "What Are We Doing to Early Adolescents? The Impact of Educational Contexts on Early Adolescents." *American Journal of Education* 99: 521–542.

Eccles, J. S., and C. Midgley. 1988. "Stage/Environment Fit: Developmentally Appropriate Classrooms for Early Adolescents." In *Research on Motivation in Education, vol. 3*, edited by R. E. Ames and C. Ames, 136–186. New York: Academic Press.

Esbensen, F.-A., and D. Huizinga. 1993. "Gangs, Drugs, and Delinquency in a Survey of Urban Youth." *Criminology* 31: 565–589.

Esbensen, F.-A., C. Melde, T. J. Taylor, and D. Peterson. 2008. "Active Parental Consent in School-based Research: How Much is Enough and How Do We Get It?" *Evaluation Review* 32: 335–362.

Esbensen, F.-A., D. W. Osgood, D. Peterson, T. J. Taylor, and D. C. Carson. 2013. "Short- and Long-Term Outcome Results from a Multisite Evaluation of the G.R.E.A.T. Program." *Criminology & Public Policy* 12: 375–411.

Esbensen, F.-A., D. W. Osgood, T. J. Taylor, D. Peterson, and A. Freng. 2001. "How Great is G.R.E.A.T.?: Results from a Quasi-experimental Design." *Criminology & Public Policy* 1: 87–118.

Esbensen, F.-A., and D. Peterson Lynskey. 2001. "Young Gang Members in a School Survey." In *The Eurogang Paradox: Street Gangs and Youth Groups in the U.S. and Europe*, edited by M. W. Klein, H.-J. Kerner, C. L. Maxson, and E. G. M. Weitekamp, 93–114. Dordrecht: Kluwer Academic Publishers.

Esbensen, F.-A., and L. T. Winfree Jr. 2013. "Motivations for Gang Joining: Does Context Matter?" In *Festscrift for Hans Kerner*, edited by K. Boers, T. Feltes, J. Kinzig, L. W. Sherman, and F. Streng, 77–90. Tuebingen: Mohr Publishing.

Esbensen, F.-A., L. T. Winfree Jr, N. He, and T. J. Taylor. 2001. "Youth Gangs and Definitional Issues: When is a Gang a Gang, and Why Does It Matter?" *Crime & Delinquency* 47: 105–130.

Fuligni, A. J., J. S. Eccles, B. L. Barber, and P. Clements. 2001. "Early Adolescent Peer Orientation and Adjustment during High School." *Developmental Psychology* 37: 28–36.

Gasper, J., S. DeLuca, and A. Estacion. 2010. "Coming and Going: Explaining the Effects of Residential and School Mobility on Adolescent Delinquency." *Social Science Research* 39: 459–476.

Giordano, P. C., R. D. Schroeder, and S. A. Cernkovich. 2007. "Emotions and Crime over the Life Course: A Neo-median Perspective on Criminal Continuity and Change." *American Journal of Sociology* 112: 1603–1661.

Glaser, B. G., and A. Strauss. 1967. *The Discovery of Grounded Theory*. New York: Aldine.

Gottfredson, D. C. 2001. *Schools and Delinquency*. New York: Cambridge University Press.

Gottfredson, G. D., and D. C. Gottfredson. 2001. *Gang Problems and Gang Programs in a National Sample of Schools*. Ellicot City, MD: Gottfredson Associates.

Graber, J. A., and J. Brooks-Dunn. 1996. "Transitions and Turning Points: Navigating the Passage from Childhood through Adolescence." *Developmental Psychology* 32: 768–776.

Grasmick, H. G., C. R. Tittle, R. J. Bursik, and B. J. Arneklev. 1993. "Testing the Core Empirical Implications of Gottfredson and Hirschi's General Theory of Crime." *Journal of Research in Crime and Delinquency* 30: 5–29.

Hagan, J., R. MacMillan, and B. Wheaton. 1996. "New Kid in Town: Social Capital and the Life Course Effects of Family Migration on Children." *American Sociological Review* 61: 368–385.

Huff, C. R. 1996. "The Criminal Behavior of Gang Members and Non-Gang At-risk Youth." In *Gangs in America (2nd ed)*, edited by C. R. Huff, 75–102. Thousand Oaks, CA: Sage.

Huff, C. R. 1998. *Comparing the Criminal Behavior of Youth Gangs and At-risk Youths*. Washington, DC: National Institute of Justice: Research in Brief.

Isakson, K., and P. Jarvis. 1999. "The Adjustment of Adolescents during the Transition into High School: A Short-term Longitudinal Study." *Journal of Youth and Adolescence* 28: 1–26.

Kinney, D. A. 1993. "From Nerds to Normals: The Recovery of Identity among Adoelscents from Middle School to High School." *Sociology of Education* 66: 21–40.

Langenkamp, A. G. 2016. "Effects of School Mobility on Adolescent Social Ties and Academic Adjustment." *Youth & Society* 48: 810–833.

Leventhal, T., and J. Brooks-Gunn. 2004. "A Randomized Study of Neighborhood Effects on Low-income Children's Educational Outcomes." *Developmental Psychology* 40: 488–507.

Ludwig, J., H. F. Ladd, and G. J. Duncan. 2001. "Urban Poverty and Educational Outcomes." In *Brookings-Wharton Papers on Urban Affairs*, edited by W. Gale and J. Rothenberg Pack, 147–201. Washington, DC: Brookings Institution.

McGloin, J. M., and M. E. Collins. 2015. "Micro-level Processes of the Gang." In *The Handbook of Gangs*, edited by S. H. Decker and D. C. Pyrooz, 276–293. New York: Wiley.

Meeus, W. 2011. "The Study of Adolescent Identity Formation 2000-2010: A Review of Longitudinal Research." *Journal of Research on Adolescence* 2: 75–94.

Melde, C., and F.-A. Esbensen. 2011. "Gang Membership as a Turning Point in the Life Course." *Criminology* 49: 513–552.

Melde, C., and F.-A. Esbensen. 2014. "The Relative Impact of Gang Status Transitions: Identifying the Mechanisms of Change in Delinquency." *Journal of Research in Crime and Delinquency* 51: 349–376.

Melde, C., T. J. Taylor, and F.-A. Esbensen. 2009. "'I Got Your Back': An Examination of the Protective Function of Gang Membership in Adolescence." *Criminology* 47: 565–594.

Moule Jr, R. K., S. H. Decker, and D. C. Pyrooz. 2013. "Social Capital, the Life-course, and Gangs." In *Handbook of Life-course Criminology: Emerging Trends and Directions for Future Research*, edited by C. Gibson and M. D. Krohn, 143–158. New York: Springer.

Pedersen, M. L., and J. M. Lindstad. 2012. "The Danish Gang-joining Project: Methodological Issues and Preliminary Results." In *Youth Gangs in International Perspective: Results from the Eurogang Program of Research*, edited by F.-A. Esbensen and C. L. Maxson, 239–250. New York: Springer.

Pribesh, S., and D. B. Downey. 1999. "Why Are Residental and School Moves Associated with Poor School Performance?" *Demography* 36: 521–534.

Pyrooz, D. C. 2014. "'From Your First Cigarette to Your Last Dyin' Day': The Patterning of Gang Membership in the Life-course." *Journal of Quantitative Criminology* 30: 349–372.

Pyrooz, D. C., and S. H. Decker. 2011. "Motives and Methods for Leaving the Gang: Understanding the Process of Gang Desistance." *Journal of Criminal Justice* 39: 417–425.

Pyrooz, D. C., S. H. Decker, and V. J. Webb. 2014. "The Ties That Bind: Desistance from Gangs." *Crime & Delinquency* 60: 491–516.

Pyrooz, D. C., and J. A. Densley. 2016. "Selection into Street Gangs: Signaling Theory, Gang Membership, and Criminal Offending." *Journal of Research in Crime and Delinquency* 53: 447–481.

Pyrooz, D. C., A. M. Fox, and S. H. Decker. 2010. "Racial and Ethnic Heterogeneity, Economic Disadvantage, and Gangs: A Macro-level Study of Gang Membership in Urban America." *Justice Quarterly* 27: 867–892.

Randa, R., and P. Wilcox. 2010. "School Disorder, Victimization, and General V. Place-specific Student Avoidance." *Journal of Criminal Justice* 38: 854–861.

Roderick, M. R. 1993. *The Path to Dropping Out*. Westport, CT: Auburn House.

Roeser, R. W., J. S. Eccles, and C. Freedman-Doan. 1999. "Academic Functioning and Mental Health in Adolescence: Patterns, Progressions, and Routes from Childhood." *Journal of Adolescent Research* 14: 135–174.

Rumberger, R. W., and K. A. Larson. 1998. "Student Mobility and the Increased Risk of High School Dropout." *American Journal of Education* 107: 1–35.

Rutter, M. 1996. "Transitions and Turning Points in Developmental Psychology: As Applied to the Age Span between Childhood and Mid-adulthood." *International Journal of Behavioral Development* 19: 603–626.

Sampson, R. J., and J. H. Laub. 2005. "A Life-course View of the Development of Crime." *ANNALS of the American Academy of Political and Social Sciences* 602: 12–45.

Schreck, C. J., and J. M. Miller. 2003. "Sources of Fear of Crime at School: What is the Relative Contribution of Disorder, Individual Characteristics, and School Security?" *Journal of School Violence* 2: 57–79.

Seidman, E., L. Allen, J. L. Aber, C. Mitchell, and J. Feinman. 1994. "The Impact of School Transitions in Early Adolescence on the Self-system and Perceived Socail Context of Poor Urban Youth." *Child Development* 65: 507–522.

Siennick, S. E., A. O. Widdowson, and D. T. Ragan. 2016. "New Students' Peer Integration and Exposure to Deviant Peers: Spurious Effects of School Moves?" *Journal of Early Adolescence*. doi:10.1177/0272431616659563.

Singer, J. D., and J. B. Willett. 2003. *Applied Longitudinal Data Analysis*. New York: Oxford University Press.

Smetana, J. G., N. Campione-Barr, and A. Metzger. 2006. "Adolescent Development in Interpersonal and Societal Contexts." *Annual Review of Psychology* 57: 255–284.

South, S. J., and D. L. Haynie. 2004. "Friendship Networks of Mobile Adolescents." *Social Forces* 83: 315–350.

Sykes, G. M., and D. Matza. 1957. "Techniques of Neutralization: A Theory of Delinquency." *American Sociological Review* 22: 664–670.

Symonds, J. E., and M. Galton. 2014. "Moving to the Next School at Age 10–14 Years: An International Review of Psychological Development at School Transition." *Review of Education* 2: 1–27.

Taylor, T. J., A. Freng, F.-A. Esbensen, and D. Peterson. 2008. "Youth Gang Membership and Serious Violent Victimization: The Importance of Lifestyles and Routine Activities." *Journal of Interpersonal Violence* 23: 1441–1464.

Taylor, T. J., D. Peterson, F.-A. Esbensen, and A. Freng. 2007. "Gang Membership as a Risk Factor for Adolescent Violent Victimization." *Journal of Research in Crime and Delinquency* 44: 351–380.

Thornberry, T. P., M. D. Krohn, A. J. Lizotte, C. A. Smith, and K. Tobin. 2003. *Gangs and Delinquency in Developmental Perspective*. New York: Cambridge University Press.

Vigil, J. D. 1993. "The Established Gang." In *Gangs: The Origins and Impact of Contemporary Youth Gangs in the United States*, edited by S. Cummings and D. J. Monti, 95–112. Albany, NY: State University of New York Press.

Warr, M. 1998. "Life-course Transitions and Desistance from Crime." *Criminology* 26: 183–216.

Warr, M. 2002. *Companions in Crime: The Social Aspects of Criminal Conduct*. Cambridge: Cambridge University Press.

Weerman, F. M. 2012. "Are Correlates and Effects of Gang Membership Sex-specific? Troublesome Youth Groups and Delinquency in Dutch Girls." In *Youth Gangs in International Perspective: Results from the Eurogang Program of Research*, edited by F.-A. Esbensen and C. L. Maxson, 271–287. New York: Springer.

Weiss, C. C., and P. S. Bearman. 2007. "Fresh Starts: Reinvestigating the Effects of the Transition to High School on Student Outcomes." *American Journal of Education* 113: 395–421.

Weller, S. 2007. "'Sticking with Your Mates?' Children's Friendship Trajectories during the Transition from Primary to Secondary School." *Children & Society* 21: 339–351.

Woo, D., H. Giles, M. A. Hogg, and L. Goldman. 2015. "Social Pyschology of Gangs: An Intergroup Communication Perspective." In *The Handbook of Gangs*, edited by S. H. Decker and D. C. Pyrooz, 136–156. New York: Wiley.

Leveraging the pushes and pulls of gang disengagement to improve gang intervention: findings from three multi-site studies and a review of relevant gang programs

Caterina G. Roman, Scott H. Decker and David C. Pyrooz

ABSTRACT
The purpose of this article is to situate knowledge on the pushes and pulls of disengagement from gangs within the inventory of gang intervention programs. Drawing on developmental and life course criminological theory and three major, multi-site studies on gang disengagement, we examined the self-reported pushes and pulls that led gang members to reduce their gang embeddedness and move toward disengagement more effectively. We found that (1) multiple rather than single factors for leaving gangs were most common, (2) push factors exceeded pull factors in prevalence and frequency, and (3) motivations for disengagement may be age-graded, and appear to increase in complexity with age. We complemented the multi-site findings by examining prominent programmatic efforts to reduce or prevent gang involvement that have the most explicit theory of change related to the pushes and pulls in gang disengagement: focused deterrence, hospital-based interventions, jobs programs, and relationship-based interventions that have street-outreach, therapeutic, family, and fatherhood areas of focus. Programs that address individuals disillusioned with their gang and simultaneously offer sustained opportunities to develop and engage in prosocial networks are most likely to enjoy success. The success of such interventions, however, may be dependent on developmental stages in the life course.

Introduction

While a large body of research addresses why youth and young adults join gangs, there have been fewer studies of why individuals leave gangs. Examining the reasons for disengaging from gangs and the processes of doing so is important because gang disengagement greatly reduces one's involvement in crime (Gordon et al. 2004; Melde and Esbensen 2013; Sweeten, Pyrooz, and Piquero 2013). Victimization also is greatly reduced after leaving a gang (Peterson, Taylor, and Esbensen 2004; Sweeten, Pyrooz, and Piquero 2013), although individuals who retain some ties to their former gang are likely to have higher victimization levels than those who have cut all ties (Pyrooz, Decker, and Webb 2014). Within the nascent research on gang disengagement and gang crime desistance, researchers have begun to examine the process of disengagement, including the factors that hasten or hinder separation from the gang. The goal of this paper is to identify specific times and events in the life course of gang membership and criminal involvement that are most salient for intervention. Leveraging the motivations for leaving a gang has become all the more important as research has shown that even the most deeply embedded gang members can, indeed, disengage from their gang (Decker, Pyrooz, and Moule 2014).

Understanding pivotal moments of life in the gang or specific factors related to gang leaving can pay dividends by helping to strengthen existing gang intervention strategies and developing new and innovative strategies designed to motivate gang leaving. A review of the gang disengagement literature suggests that the practical implications of research on the reasons for gang exit have been underutilized in the development of policy and programs. This observation also appears to be relevant in criminal justice interventions concerned with desistance from crime more generally (Barlow 1995; Maruna, Immarigeon, and LeBel 2004; Weaver 2016). Interventions seldom use theory as an explicit guide in development of the intervention (Barlow and Decker 2010; Sherman 2003).

To bring together research and practice on gang disengagement, this paper has four goals: (1) to systematically review what is known about the reasons for leaving gangs; (2) to identify how this research can best be integrated into the crime desistance literature; (3) to situate the reasons for leaving gangs within the current inventory of gang prevention and intervention programs; and (4) to suggest where programmatic innovation and change might effectively promote, support, and hasten gang exit processes. We draw on the gang disengagement literature, including recent comprehensive reviews (see Carson and Vecchio 2015; Pyrooz and Decker 2014), data the authors and colleagues have collected in recent years (Carson, Peterson, and Esbensen 2013; Decker and Pyrooz 2011; Roman, Cahill, and Eidson 2016), and the current state of knowledge on interventions that are relevant to gangs and disengagement.

Background

Applying developmental and life course approaches to gang disengagement

Research on disengagement from gangs has grown in recent years (see Bolden 2013; Carson, Peterson, and Esbensen 2013; Decker, Pyrooz, and Moule 2014; Flores 2013; Moloney et al. 2009; O'Neal et al. 2016; Pyrooz and Decker 2011, 2014; Roman, Cahill, and Eidson 2016; Sharkey, Stifel, and Mayworm 2015). The application of developmental and life course frameworks (Krohn et al. 2011; Melde and Esbensen 2011; Pyrooz, Decker, and Webb 2014; Sweeten, Pyrooz, and Piquero 2013) has facilitated an understanding of the dynamic processes related to gang disengagement. Such frameworks provide a context for situating gang membership along dimensions of continuity and change as individuals age and experience potential turning points. Within these frameworks, life events are unpredictable, yet salient, features that modify or influence criminal careers. The timing of these events in the life course and their relationship to other events or contexts also play a crucial role in behavior.

A developmental framework emphasizes non-random change in individuals' offending behavior across stages of development (Loeber and Le Blanc 1990). It is relevant for understanding gang membership and disengagement because the transitional periods during adolescent development can be associated with the periods in which youth and young adults transition in and out of their gang identities (Giordano, Cernkovich, and Rudolph 2002). Indeed, gang membership itself can be viewed as a trajectory – a pathway of development over the life span – as identified in longitudinal research (Pyrooz 2014a; Thornberry et al. 2003). A developmental framework is also relevant to gangs because the influence of specific risk factors varies by developmental stage. Howell and Egley (2005) have outlined these parallel processes, pairing risk domains (e.g., community, family, school, peer, and individual) across life stages (e.g., preschool, school entry, late childhood, early adolescent, and mid-adolescence).

The developmental and life course framework, particularly the parameters of criminal careers (Piquero, Farrington, and Blumstein 2003), is especially relevant for examining disengagement from gangs because gang membership follows patterns comparable to crime in the life course. Specifically, an individual first joins a gang (onset), then either continues in gang life (persists), or leaves the gang (desists) (Pyrooz, Decker, and Webb 2014). Though gang membership constitutes a life state while criminal offending constitutes life events, there is the potential for developmental and life course theories of crime desistance to be applied to gang disengagement, much like scholars have drawn on general theories of crime to explain entry processes into gangs (see, e.g., Curry, Decker, and Pyrooz 2014; Densley 2015). In this framework, the reasons for disengaging from a gang can be internal (i.e., consistent with human agency) or external (i.e., consistent with structures or events) to the individual, or provide influence through a complex interplay. Depending on one's specific theoretical lens regarding crime desistance, agency and structure can take on more or less dominant roles.

Turning points within a life course framework

Sampson and Laub's (1990, 1993) age-graded theory of crime states that crime occurs when bonds to society are weakened or broken, and emphasizes one's interaction with age-graded institutions. Significant life events or socialization experiences in adulthood – called turning points – can modify trajectories of crime in significant ways. Turning points are external – the result of macro-level institutional processes and the resultant roles (Laub and Sampson 2001, 2003) – and hence are largely contextual or situation based. Turning points are the product of situations that change rapidly, provide supervision or new opportunities for social support, or structure routine activities. Sampson and Laub (2003) also note that these situations provide prospects for identity transformation. For crime desistance, new opportunities, supervision, and social support (e.g., new relationships or existing relationships that take on new meaning alongside new opportunities) are the dominant mechanisms that provide implications for policy and practice. Human agency and personal choice play a role, but occur subsequent to turning points. The role of identity transformations has been discussed in more detail by Sampson and Laub in earlier writings (2005; Laub and Sampson 2003), where they conclude from analyses of the Glueck data that the source of change was 'below the surface of active consciousness and did not involve purposeful identity change' (Sampson and Laub 2016, 328). In their recent essay (2016, 329), they move further away from an emphasis on human agency:

> Although we have gone down this analytic road [theorizing about human agency and identity] in considerable depth, as have several others, we now worry that this move may have been a distraction rather than a theoretical advance.

With regard to gangs, age-graded theory suggests that leaving a gang can be viewed as a transitional life event that may also function as a turning point (Pyrooz and Decker 2014; Thornberry et al. 2003), redirecting the life course and changing one's likelihood of engaging in criminal activities (see Laub, Sampson, and Sweeten 2006). Similarly, and particularly relevant to reasons for leaving a gang, policy responses to crime, such as macro-level shifts in incarceration and the emergence of targeted policing policies, can create turning points that shape criminal behavior and group participation (Sampson and Laub 2016).

Historically, however, the focus of life course literature has been mostly on prosocial events – marriage, military, employment, birth of a child – that alter crime trajectories (Elder 1985; Sampson and Laub 1993). As the idea of turning points was being empirically tested, gang research began showing that some of the key turning points were not readily generalizable to gangs because gang youth are younger than marital age, tend not to marry even in their twenties, and do not secure the same prosocial opportunities (e.g., post-secondary education, jobs, military service, etc.) as the average youth, let alone delinquent youth (Carson and Vecchio 2015). Recent work by others (Soyer 2014; Teruya and Hser 2010) and the articulation by Sampson and Laub (2016) of additional turning points have sought to broaden the concept to include adverse life events and experiences, such as incarceration and violent victimization. These events have more relevance to gang member life experiences, and, consistent with Melde and Esbensen (2011) and others (Gilman, Hill, and Hawkins 2014; Pyrooz 2014b), identify gang membership as a negative turning point in the life course.

Age-graded theory and social contexts that promote opportunities suggest that prescriptions for desistance policy may be based on formal or informal social control. Under formal social control, aspects of incarceration – specifically those that are rehabilitative and/or offer productive, formal supervision – are opportunities to regain lost human and social capital that assist in moving offenders toward desistance (Farrall et al. 2014). Age-graded theory would generally suggest that opportunities for bonding and increasing social capital come from the community (Bursik and Grasmick 1993; Laub and Allen 1999). Opportunities need to be directed toward the social and personal contexts in which people are situated – at the community level where informal social control is generated and maintained. Community-based policy prescriptions are relevant for both gang disengagement and gang-related crime desistance, as many of the well-known programmatic interventions have focused on community-based opportunities provision as provided by jobs programs, mentoring programs, fatherhood support, and parenting support programs. More of these details are reviewed in the discussion of interventions.

Human agency and identity reformation

A large body of work has emerged that stands in contrast to the idea that desistance is mostly influenced by outside forces. This research posits that human agency plays a dominant role in desistance from offending (Bushway and Paternoster 2013; Maruna 2001; Paternoster and Bushway 2009). With regard to gangs, some researchers (Decker, Pyrooz, and Moule 2014) suggest that disengagement occurs through a process that begins with first doubts, in which cognitive shifts take place and the individual desires an alternative future that does not involve being in a gang (or offending). These cognitive shifts are internal reevaluations that give voice to dissatisfaction with some aspects of a current lifestyle or the prospects for an improved life. These reevaluations induce motivation to change (or, with gang disengagement, motivation to leave a gang). Such cognitive shifts can be related to maturational processes and/or conscious decisions based on a reappraisal of the costs and benefits of crime (see Clarke and Cornish 1985). Cognitive shifts can lead to changes in the external environment or contexts that support or weaken bonds. Gang members may take on more prosocial roles and relationships or be open to participation in conventional institutions *after* initial cognitive shifts. Work by Giordano and colleagues (2002, 2007) gives particular voice to an individual's own role in selectively appropriating elements in the environment that act as 'hooks for change.' The focus is first on agentic moves because the emphasis is on how individuals respond to the structural obstacles they encounter, not the objective social circumstances. The role of agency in this view of change is important for the consideration of programs because it is within the immediate control of individuals.

Some desistance theorists view changes in offending as more of a balanced interaction between structural forces and human agency, and do not necessarily impose a causal ordering on the factors that create change (see for instance, Bottoms 2004; Farrall 2002; Weaver 2012). Weaver (2012), drawing on relational sociology, suggests that individuals seek meaningful and consistent ways to refer to themselves (the creation of an identity) and that this reflexive nature cannot be disentangled from the social context. Weaver and other desistance theorists who fall into the interactionist camp often emphasize social roles. Social roles are particularly relevant for gang disengagement because gangs, by definition, are social groups with roles and identities, and aspects of group belonging are highly relevant for understanding disengagement. Within interactionist theories of desistance, the delinquent peer group or gang can condition the impact of social structures. It can be the peer group itself that creates unique barriers for transitioning to prosocial identities (Barber, Eccles, and Stone 2001; McLean, Breen, and Fournier 2010).

Regardless of the weight placed on social structure or human agency, these articulations of theory, which draw on social roles and identity within the group, are important given that articulated reasons for leaving a group may have to do with the group itself rather than external forces. Policy and programming prescriptions that have an emphasis on identity change include individual-focused cognitive behavioral therapies and therapeutic interventions that focus on prosocial role development. Providing access to such programming for individuals who articulate changes in identity or whose behavior foreshadows such changes may pay dividends in hastening disengagement from gangs.

Where motivations fit in the gang disengagement process

Disengaging from gangs is most often a process, not an event (Pyrooz and Decker 2011). Decker and colleagues (2014) developed a four stage-based model of gang disengagement to capture this process, drawing on role exit theory (Ebaugh 1988; Merton 1957). This model of gang disengagement affords weight to both agency and social structure. Decker and colleagues (2014) presented empirical evidence from a mixed-methods study of 260 former gang members, finding that the exit process generally moves through stages: (1) first doubts, where gang members contemplate the symbolic and instrumental value of their current role; (2) weighing alternative roles, where gang members engage in anticipatory socialization of new or different roles; (3) turning points, which function as crystallization of discontent to act on the aforementioned considerations; and (4) post exit certification, which works to validate new roles while inoculating gang members from old ones. These stages need not be passed linearly, nor are they free from relapse to old expectations and roles. Indeed, disengagement from gangs was described by the authors as an 'ongoing contest between gang life and conformity' (280), which occurs in the context of numerous other identities and roles, both conventional and deviant.

Whereas some theories of gang exit afford considerable (e.g., Bubolz and Simi 2015) or negligible (e.g., Flores 2013) power to identity-based motivations for leaving the gang, the Decker, Pyrooz, and Moule (2014) model contends that such reasons – and, by extension, agency – are continually orbiting throughout the disengagement process. The fact that 'first doubts' operates as the launch point for the role exit model is evidence of such prominence. 'First doubts' can occur before or after the occurrence of push and pull factors. But, put simply, if the seeds of first doubts are not sown, according to Decker and colleagues, gang members will not engage in anticipatory socialization nor will they interpret turning points as triggers that lead to alternative roles. Hence, this can aid in understanding why risk and protective factors are rarely deterministic – for some gang members, a first gunshot victimization or birth of their first child is enough to call it quits, while for others, it requires repeated personal or vicarious victimization or a second or even third child. Therefore, while identity-based motivations are not the single source underlying disengagement from gangs, they are indeed an important early part of the exit process. The next section of the paper provides a review of research on the reasons gang members offer for leaving their gang.

The pushes and pulls of disengagement from gangs

The lack of a concrete theoretical focus for gang disengagement has left researchers to focus more on general conceptualizations that offer systematic examinations of the reasons for leaving a gang. The frequently used 'push-pull' framework, originally conceptualized by Decker and Van Winkle (1996) with regard to gang entry, divides the reasons into those that relate to aspects of gang membership that are internal to the gang (pushes) and those that are external to the gang (pulls). Behind most pushes and pulls is a 'factor' that creates a motive to leave. However, as we have described above, these factors are rarely uniform. Reasons for leaving a gang are self-attributed or cognitive motives that are largely conscious and linked to aspects of the self (different from implicit motives, which are largely unconscious) (McClelland, Koestner, and Weinberger 1992). The pushes and pulls of gang disengagement are a subjective component of the exit process – the studies describing pushes and pulls generally ask respondents to reflect on their *reasons* for leaving the gang or peer group. The reasons for leaving include both concrete factors (e.g., had a child, got a job) and subjective assessments of changes in the self (e.g., got tired of the lifestyle, it wasn't what I thought). Understanding these pushes and pulls helps organize thinking about positive and negative aspects of gang processes and disengagement. Push factors make membership undesirable, while pull factors offer new opportunities external to the gang. This framework has been employed to explain gang membership cross-culturally (Bjorgo 1999) as well as to account for the movement of terrorists in and out of terrorist groups (Bjorgo 2013).

Push factors generally have been described as negative influences or occurrences that bring to light the adverse consequences of gang lifestyle. These factors directly or indirectly create a cognitive shift that reorients an individual toward the idea of conformity or having an identity that is less gang-involved and by nature more prosocial. Push factors can be experiences like incarceration, personal victimization, or vicarious victimization – victimization that occurs to loved ones or fellow gang members. They can also include arrests or simply pressure from police or other law enforcement agencies (e.g., probation officers). Push factors have been described by Carson and Vecchio (2015, 261) as largely consistent with developmental theories and theories of cognitive shift 'because they typically occur within the individual.' While we agree with this statement, it is important to note that factors or events such as vicarious victimization incidents are pushes external to the individual, but the underlying mechanism attributed to the change is the cognitive shift in the gang-involved individual, likely attributable to the violent street culture. Furthermore, a push can involve leaving the gang simply because it fell apart, possibly due to gang members moving or getting jobs because it is endogenous to the gang itself.

Pull factors, on the other hand, are generally external to gang dynamics and serve to attract gang members to states or new life opportunities that may include such things as the birth of a child, a job opportunity, or a move to a different city. Pull factors have turning point-like qualities, and can act as hooks for change in that these reasons often have to do with new prosocial opportunities or roles that support or facilitate the development of bonds to conventional society. Pull factors can include familial responsibilities, such as wanting to or getting pressure to spend more time with a significant other or family member, or simply that a sibling or family member left the gang. By their very nature, pulls introduce separation between the individual and their gang, to the point where the gang is no longer prioritized by the individual.

The mechanisms by which pushes and pulls operate to separate a gang member from the gang are not well understood. It is important to distinguish between identity-based motives and push/pull factors, because when they operate in concert, individuals are most likely amenable to messages of disengagement – hence the emphasis on stages in the Decker, Pyrooz, and Moule (2014) model. For example, the birth of a child is not always an effective mechanism for promoting gang disengagement. Only when the birth of that child creates a motive – perhaps in the desire to see the child grow up or create a better life for the child – is it effective as a pull factor in promoting disengagement. The intersection of push factors and motives illustrates this point as well. Gang members experience and create violence on a regular basis, and some have argued (Decker and Lauritsen 1996; Melde and Esbensen 2013) that violence is a defining hallmark of life in the gang. But not all violence produces a push to disengage from the gang because it is not accompanied by a complementary motive that leads to steps toward disengagement. Such a factor must be sufficiently salient to produce a motive for disengagement.

Drawing on the conversations and empirical evidence in the broader crime desistance literature surrounding the debate between human agency and structure, articulated motives for leaving a gang may not necessarily be attached to a factor. A gang member may simply state that he or she wanted something different or more from life, or it was time to grow up, and as such, maturation or disillusionment are the active agents (at least as voiced by the gang member) for discontinuing in the gang or in criminal behavior. Even then, motives on their own may not be sufficient to lead directly to gang exit, as we observe that many gang members waver between staying and leaving.

Current focus

Given these complexities in understanding the motives and factors in gang disengagement, as well as the nascent state of this literature generally, we examine data on the motivations for leaving gangs from the three most prominent multi-site studies of disengagement from gangs: the Google Ideas study of gangs, disengagement, and technology (Decker and Pyrooz 2011), the second evaluation of the Gang Resistance Education and Training program (Carson, Peterson, and Esbensen 2013; Esbensen et al. 2013); and the Connect Survey of gangs, networks, and desistance from gangs (Roman, Cahill, and Eidson 2016). We take an inventory of the articulated motivations for leaving gangs by analyzing published findings as well as producing new findings.

Our overarching goal is to move the dialog about motivations for leaving more closely into the realm of theories on crime desistance in order to connect the research on interventions to the empirical study of gang disengagement. Even in the last few years, the literature on this topic has matured in significant ways since last taking stock of knowledge with regard to policy and practice (Pyrooz and Decker 2014). Part of the way we accomplish this important task is by working to fill the void in the exchange between research on one end, and policy and practice on the other, to develop programming that directly taps the reasons for leaving. Indeed, we summarize findings on reasons for leaving to examine their utility in supporting gang programs' theories of change. Drawing tangible connections among theory, research, and interventions provides links that can not only help policy-makers and practitioners devise solutions, but also can assist in a deeper theoretical examination of disengagement from gangs. Given the strong facilitation effect of gang membership on violence and victimization and the resultant harm to communities, it is imperative to devise programs that not only have face validity but also have a strong theory of change – one that is rooted in empirical findings from disengagement studies.

Reasons for leaving gangs

Data sources

We focus on three recent studies of youth or young adults who were queried about their reasons for leaving a gang. The three data sources have differences with regard to study focus and sample, and all three studies include gang members from multiple cities. We chose these studies because they were the three most recent multi-site studies from the United States that had been developed with a focus on gangs and disengagement and the study protocols included similar items specifically about motivations for leaving gangs. The Google Ideas study set out to interview three groups: active gang members, non-gang members, and former gang members. Of the 629 interviewed across the 3 groups, 268 were former gang members. The Connect Survey set out to only recruit gang members. Individuals were recruited into the study if they were between the ages of 14 and 25 and loosely met the Eurogang criteria[1] of street gang member, but were validated as gang members by street outreach workers knowledgeable about the respondents (see Eidson, Roman, and Cahill 2016 for more details on recruitment and sampling). Of the 229 gang-involved respondents in the Connect Survey sample, 51 left the gang during the three-wave study period. The G.R.E.A.T. II study (Esbensen et al. 2013) was designed as a longitudinal evaluation study of middle school students in classrooms that were randomly assigned to an educational curriculum. There were 473 person-pooled instances of gang leaving in the multi-wave study.

Differences in samples and methods of data collection in each study present an opportunity to speculate on the association of variables such as age, criminal involvement, and method of administration. The G.R.E.A.T. II data allow us to learn about motivations for gang leaving among adolescents, while the Connect Survey and Google Ideas studies were conducted with older, criminal justice-involved samples. Together, we view the methodological differences across the samples as a strength that will offer new insights about gang processes and disengagement. In the discussion section, we highlight a number of areas where sample differences may have resulted in differences found across study samples.

Descriptive information on the pushes and pulls across the three data sources is provided in Table 1. This table also provides relevant information on how the studies were conducted and indicates the elapsed time between being in a gang and reporting reasons for leaving. Questionnaires often borrow or build on items used in past research, which is why the content of the questions are largely similar across the three studies. But, there were differences in the administration of the survey. In the Google Ideas survey, trained interviewers administered a questionnaire with both fixed and open-ended items. Thirteen questions were asked regarding motives for leaving the gang, and eight questions were asked about institutions or individuals who may have assisted in that process. In the Connect Survey, respondents were provided 16 reasons for leaving the gang and asked to select all that applied. Three reasons that related to the main idea of adult encouragement or intervention ('an adult encouraged

Table 1. Three studies examining the motivating pushes and pulls[a] for leaving the gang.

Study investigators	Decker and Pyrooz	Roman et al.	Carson et al.
Study name	Google ideas	Connect survey	G.R.E.A.T
Study characteristics	• Fresno, Los Angeles, Phoenix, and St. Louis • N = 260 former gang members[b] • Purposive, high-risk criminal justice sample, cross-sectional • Face-to-face interview	• Philadelphia and Washington DC • N = 51 former gang members • Purposive, gang-involved prospective • Self-administered survey in small groups	• Albuquerque, Chicago, Greeley, Nashville, Portland, Philadelphia, and Dallas-Fort Worth • N = 473 person-pooled former gang members[c] • School-based, prospective • Self-administered survey
Operationalization of former gang membership	Self-reported ever gang, but no longer active	Self-reported leaving criminal 'peer group' from Wave 1 at Wave 2 or 3	Prior self-reported active and no longer active
Mean age of sample	30 years (interview)	19.3 years (baseline)	12.5 years (baseline)
Time elapsed between survey and gang exit	6.4 years	Variable, <2 years	Variable, 1–4 years
Push reasons for leaving[b]			
Disillusionment (all forms)	85%	88.9%	55.4%
Grew out of the lifestyle	85%	75.6%	–
Just felt like it	–	–	42.3%
It wasn't what I thought	–	42.2%	21.8%
Bored	–	51.1%	–
Something happened that I didn't like	–	40.0%	–
Criminal justice involvement	49%	22.2%	–
Police harassment/pressure	38%	26.7%	23.9%
Victimization (all forms)	42%	31.1%	40.6%
Personal	–	22.2%	18.0%
Vicarious	–	26.7%	31.1% friend 16.7% family
Forced out by gang	–	11.1%	–
Gang fell apart	24%	–	–
Pull reasons for leaving[b]			
Familial responsibilities	57%	37.8%	–
Family left gang	17%	–	–
Job responsibilities	49%	42.2%	–
Made new friends	–	57.8%	30.2%
Moved (home or school)	34%	28.9%	13.5%
Significant other or adult	34%	40.0%	34.8%
Summary			
Total pushes (mean)	2.33	3.18	0.83
Total pulls (mean)	1.86	2.10	0.64
Total pushes/pulls (mean)	4.20	5.24	1.47
% pushes only	14%	4.4%	15.9%
% pulls only	5.0%	8.9%	33.2%
% pushes and pulls	78%	84.4%	43.8%

[a]Pushes and pulls are not mutually exclusive; respondents could choose all that apply.
[b]Percentages in rows are based on valid responses.
[c]Person-pooled refers to multiple instances of gang leaving among individual respondents.

you,' 'significant other wanted you to get out,' and 'parents made you leave') were collapsed into a single category (significant other/adult encouragement). In the G.R.E.A.T II evaluation (Esbensen et al. 2013), respondents were provided a list of 11 possible reasons for leaving a gang. Like the Connect Survey, they were instructed to select all that apply. 'Other' responses were recoded into existing reasons, and 'the gang fell apart,' was placed into its own category they called 'gang dissolution.' This response was not frequent and was not analyzed in the original study. Also, the G.R.E.A.T. II survey of middle school youth did not ask about jobs or children, a likely artifact of the sample's age. To populate Table 1 with findings from the G.R.E.A.T. II study, we draw on a recent paper by Carson and colleagues (2013) as well as personal correspondence with the lead author to provide summary information.[2]

Findings

Table 1 shows that across the Google Ideas, Connect Survey, and G.R.E.A.T. II studies, the most frequent reason cited for disengagement was related to disillusionment (85, 89, and 55%, respectively). In the Google Ideas study, the next most frequent reasons provided were familial responsibilities (57%), followed equally by both job responsibilities (49%) and criminal justice involvement (49%). Familial responsibilities (38%) and job responsibilities (42%) ranked high for the Connect Survey, but were outranked by 'made new friends' (58%), which was not offered as a response category in the Google Ideas study.

Comparing across studies also shows that victimization falls somewhere in the middle in terms of frequency of response, but remains a salient factor, with 42% from Google Ideas study and 31% from Connect Survey reporting either victimization of self or to a friend or family member as a reason for leaving. In the G.R.E.A.T. II sample, victimization was the second most frequently reported reason for leaving (41%). Given the average age of the G.R.E.A.T. II sample (12.5 years), this seems surprisingly high, particularly the finding that 18% reported violence against self as a reason for leaving. Overall, for the G.R.E.A.T. II sample, negative experiences – those related to the gang lifestyle – seem to hold more weight with regard to reasons for leaving, than factors related to prosocial opportunities or positive relationships. Comparing just the Google Ideas and the Connect Survey samples, where the average age falls into the emerging adulthood and/or adulthood developmental stages, the pull factors that represent life changes (i.e., family responsibilities, jobs, moving) are more salient in the Google Ideas sample. This is likely because the respondents in Google Ideas are at least 10 years older on average, and hence, are likely to have greater exposure to job and family responsibilities. Similar reasoning can be applied to citing criminal justice involvement as a push factor in leaving when comparing these two samples.

Our summary findings reveal that there may be differences between juveniles and adults in the motivations for exiting gangs. In general, few respondents reported only push or pull factors. For the most part, respondents report a mix of both push and pull factors in their reasons for leaving, although most gang members in the G.R.E.A.T. II study reported only one or the other. As mentioned above, this also may be an artifact of the young age of the sample – these youth simply have not had as many life experiences as the older individuals from the two other samples. Regardless, the average number of reasons for leaving across samples suggests that one single source is rarely the driving factor in the disengagement process, which may become more prominent with age. Multiple pushes and pulls appear to be working simultaneously to motivate gang members to leave their gang. This is important to keep in mind as we transition to our focus on gang intervention.

Gang interventions

In this section, we focus specifically on programs designed to decrease crime by gang members or disengage youth from gangs. We also focus on programs that theoretically could help youth and young adults disengage from gangs because they directly address the push or pull factors, but may not be targeted expressly to gang members. Rarely do interventions directly attempt to disengage youth from gangs; for the most part, targeted gang interventions articulate and measure outcomes related to violence reduction. As such, we cast a slightly wider net and include programs that theoretically could affect gang processes and motivate gang members to leave behind their gangs and the attendant violence. We do not discuss gang *prevention* programs unless their theory of change places emphasis on the pushes and pulls of leaving gang life. Instead, we ask: what are the possible disengagement-enabling features of these programs? To be included, the programs must have shown some significant impact or promising results in achieving their overarching goal. Table 2 provides a summary of the relevant push–pull aspects of the programs discussed in the sections below.[3]

Table 2. Summary of programs relevant to pushes and pulls of gang disengagement.

Program	Push factor	Pull factor	Eligibility/targets	Evaluation results
Focused deterrence	Police pressure; CJ involvement	Some opportunities provision through social services	Group-based individuals	Successful in reducing aggregate levels of violence
Hospital interventions	Victimization	Can link to long-term opportunities provision through community-based street outreach.	Victims of violent injury; mostly group-based individuals	Potentially promising results
Jobs-based programs- Operation Build, JobCorps, YouthBuild	None	New opportunities through job training, placement and related services	Does not necessarily target gang members	Promising with regard to job-related outcomes; Evaluation results examine crime and delinquency outcomes forthcoming
Relationship-based programs- Cure Violence	None	New relationships to model behavioral expectations and values; also opportunities provision	Targets street culture; by default often gang members	Promising with regard to aggregate reductions in gun violence
Relationship-based - Fatherhood programs	None	Bonding with family and child	Does not target gang members; has been used with success with reentry population	Successful in increasing family related outcomes; No evaluations related to violence or gang disengagement
Relationship-based- Therapeutic (MST)	Disillusionment	Bonding with family, strengthen parenting (bonds of youth to parent)	At risk youth; currently being evaluated with gang members	Successful with at-risk youth and considered evidence-based; Evaluation results forthcoming with gang members
Relationship-based- mentoring/counseling with cognitive behavioral-like components (B.A.M.)	Disillusionment	Bonding with prosocial adults; develops prosocial values	At risk, school-based youth	RCT: Successful in reducing arrests for violent and non-violent crimes

Programs and policies that leverage 'pushes'

Deterrence-based law enforcement programs

In this category of programs, deterrence is the mainstay underlying the forces that reduce the likelihood of offending. The principle of deterrence is based on the idea that humans are rational actors and will weigh the costs and benefits of engaging in crime. Deterrence-based programs naturally fit into the 'push' side of gang disengagement. Law enforcement strategies have evolved over the years to utilize the certainty, severity, and celerity of punishment in innovative ways to specifically target certain types of offenders and places (Decker 2003). These interventions, known as focused deterrence strategies, were developed partly on the successes of Boston's Operation CeaseFire (Kennedy 2011). Operation CeaseFire was a collaborative problem-solving approach that utilized a strategic research-based problem-solving policing model (Eck and Spelman 1987; Goldstein 1990) aimed at reducing firearms violence through enforcement and deterrence efforts that are focused on the most violent active gangs/groups in a targeted geographic area (Braga and Weisburd 2012). The approach used theoretical knowledge about how small, cohesive gangs operate; the intervention was predicated on the idea of collective accountability where gang members who received the deterrence message would spread the message as means to foster internal social pressure that would deter others. Though the theory of change is directed at offender groups (i.e., crews and gangs) and reducing area-levels of gun violence, the components of theory are not directed specifically at getting individuals out of gangs.

Aspects of prevention are present in such models and include using social services to recruit individuals who have been targeted for intervention. Social services are not a required component of these strategies, and the use or emphasis on social services varies widely across jurisdictions that have utilized the strategy. A recent meta-analyses (Braga and Weisburd 2012) found that these strategies have been largely successful in reducing gun violence. Kennedy's (2011) articulated theory of change stresses individual deterrence, normative change in offender behavior, and increasing views on legitimacy and procedural justice, but these components have not been directly tested using rigorous evaluation methods. In addition, evaluations have not specifically tested how varying levels of social services relate to program successes, thus not directly measuring the component, but assumed to be part of the change mechanism. In general, a key weakness of models that rely on deterrence is sustainability – if the mechanism of change involves incapacitation or the threat of incarceration, then the pressure or threat must be consistent over time. These efforts may be successful in the short run, but are rarely effective in the long run (Butts and Roman 2010).

Hospital-based and trauma-focused interventions

Another type of intervention that is relevant for gang members and addresses the push motives are community-focused, hospital-based, or trauma-based programs designed to reduce (re)injury and retaliation of those that have been violently injured or killed. Programs that operate through hospitals are often termed 'hospital-responder' programs; these programs employ a trauma-informed approach or public health model. Such programs consider the adversity that clients have experienced over their life course and recognize that addressing this trauma is critical to breaking the cycle of violence. Key programmatic components include: assessment, intensive case management, navigation/mentoring psycho-educational groups, and multidisciplinary case review. Clients are usually recruited through emergency departments after they have been admitted to the hospital for a violent injury. These programs have become part of the National Network of Hospital-based Violence Intervention Programs, an organization designed to support best practices across programs and assist in developing new programs (for more information, see Trotti, Dougherty, and Klofas 2014).

Some programs employ 'violence interrupters,' who are culturally appropriate messengers who interact with patients and loved ones in hospitals and for a brief period after violent events to attempt to defuse retaliation or further violence. In some programs, the client is also connected to another community-based staff person, who takes on the role of case manager and helps the client remain free from violence and street conflict through promoting alternatives to violence and referring participants to services. Case managers work with individuals for up to two years and will be further discussed in the section on pulls, below. An evaluation of the first year of a program implemented in New Orleans (only involving the hospital response component) found that although the program did not significantly reduce the rate of injury compared to comparison zip codes, there was a discernable declining trend in injury in the target zip code that was not evident in the other zip codes (McVey et al. 2014). Programs like Syracuse's Trauma Response Team operate similarly but are triggered after a gang-related homicide, hence it does not fall neatly under the umbrella of hospital response. Syracuse's program has similar strategies targeted at reducing victimization and vicarious victimization and the harms associated with homicides. Preliminary evaluation results are promising (Jennings-Bey et al. 2015). In addition to reducing re-injury and preventing retaliatory violence, an Oakland hospital-based program also sought to reduce reentry into the criminal justice system. An evaluation found that participants were 70% less likely to be arrested for any offense and 60% less likely to have any criminal involvement, compared to controls (Becker et al. 2004).

Programs and policies that leverage pulls

Bonding to prosocial institutions and opportunities provision

Because 'pulls' represent forces that provide opportunities to bond individuals to prosocial institutions, or actually entail new or expanded prosocial relationships, relevant interventions are programs that provide opportunities for bonding or building prosocial relationships. Following age-graded social control theory, opportunities would be found largely within nongovernmental institutions such as families, schools, workplaces, and neighborhoods (Laub et al. 1995). A review of the literature on these types of programs reveals that there are very few opportunity provision programs explicitly designed to help youth leave gangs; most programs in this area target outcomes related to crime and violence reduction, or are designed to increase attachment to school or jobs, or support parenthood.

Chicago's BUILD (Broader Urban Involvement and Leadership Development; now the BUILD Violence Intervention Curriculum) program is targeted to gang members, and is designed to meet both the immediate problem of preventing at-risk youth from joining gangs as well as working with gang-involved youth to encourage them to leave gangs. The program includes a set of strategies that provide various prosocial alternatives for youths, such as deploying trained street workers, organizing afterschool sports programs, providing career training, and implementing the BUILD Violence Intervention Curriculum. The curriculum focuses on self-esteem enhancement, communication skills, problem-solving techniques, goal-setting, and decision-making. An evaluation of the curriculum-based program for youth detained from 1998 to 1999 found that participating youth had significantly lower rates of recidivism compared to non-Project BUILD youth (Lurigio et al. 2000).

There is also a large number of job provision programs around the country that offer services to at-risk youth but do not necessarily target gang youth. These high-intensity skills-provision programs include the well-known YouthBuild and JobCorps programs. YouthBuild, a program administered by the U.S. Department of Labor, is a community-based alternative education program that targets youth ages 16–24 and teaches them construction skills while they build affordable housing in their own neighborhoods. The program is currently being evaluated (recruitment consisted of 72 sites) to determine if the program has an impact on educational attainment, postsecondary planning, employment, earnings, delinquency, and involvement with the criminal justice system, with findings expected in 2018. JobCorps is a similar program, focused on career technical training and education program for young people ages 16–24. Addressing an additional pull, JobCorps programs usually involve moving a youth out of his/her home neighborhood, and some have cited the benefits of the residential requirement as providing new opportunities, not simply for skills and job placements services, but via new experiences and positive role models (Schochet, Burghardt, and McConnell 2006).

One of the most well-known job-related programs that attempt to provide a number of pull factors specifically to gang members is Homeboy Industries (Leap et al. 2011). Homeboy Industries provides a range of social services, including counseling, curriculum and training (e.g., life skills, education, 12-step, and art programs), and tattoo removal, but is mostly known for operating several social enterprises that serve as job-training sites. At this time, neither the program nor a subset of its strategies (e.g., entrepreneurship services) have been rigorously evaluated. We list Homeboy Industries solely as a relevant and unique program given its theory of change emphasizing some of the important pull factors highlighted in our findings – job responsibilities and new prosocial networks – but we simultaneously recognize that there is currently no evidence to support its impact.

Bonding to prosocial individuals as a means of norm change

This category includes fatherhood and parenting programs, which may or may not expressly target gang youth, and programs that, through street outreach, seek to work with those that have a constellation of high-risk street-oriented behavior, such as Cure Violence. Responsible fatherhood programs are programs designed to promote and sustain marriage, support responsible parenting, and support economic stability through job training, employment services, and career-advancing education. The Office of the Administration for Children and Families (ACF), a division of the U.S. Health and Human Services, has funded dozens of sites around the country to support fathers. Although none of these programs target gang members, some fatherhood programs are specifically for men returning from prison or jail. An impact evaluation of National Fatherhood Initiative's InsideOut Dad® program found statistically significant improvements in parenting self-efficacy, knowledge, attitudes, and contact with children, compared to the control group. The evaluation did not measure recidivism or desistance from crime (Block et al. 2014).

The Cure Violence model, which originated in Chicago, is a public health-based gun violence reduction program that seeks to reduce community-levels of gun violence through direct work with individuals and street groups (Butts et al. 2015). The model does not directly target gangs as groups, but instead targets the street culture of violence that emanates from these groups. Although the theory of change operates at the community level (i.e., outcomes are measured at the aggregate level), the program components involve direct intervention with individuals and groups. Cure Violence programs employ street-based outreach workers from within the targeted communities, many of whom were once gang members themselves, some having served lengthy prison sentences for serious violent crimes, to recruit high-risk youth and young adults. Outreach workers are trained to develop relationships with participants using cognitive behavior techniques, alert them to the dangers of gun violence, and provide them with alternative means of conflict resolution. Outreach workers also attempt to connect participants with resources to help them in a variety of areas, as needed, such as job readiness and education, and also refer them to other services including assistance with mental health issues. Program staff also include violence interrupters, who do not carry a caseload, but are specifically tasked with mediating violent conflicts and retaliations in the neighborhood. The careful selection of 'credible messengers' (both the outreach workers and the violence interrupters) targeting the most high-risk youth is intended to aid acceptance of the message that violence harms the community and that there are alternative means of conflict resolution that do not involve violence. The staff members act as de facto mentors, providing real life, day-to-day examples of how one can turn his/her life away from street violence. They operate, in essence, as hooks for change. Although the program focuses much of its efforts on preventing violence among the most high-risk individuals, it works simultaneously to instill anti-conflict and antiviolence norms throughout the community through media campaigns, signs and billboards, and public events such as antiviolence marches and post-shooting vigils. In the longer term, program processes involve strengthening informal social controls that should result in long-term changes in norms. As described earlier, in recent years, the Cure Violence model has been developing complementary hospital-based interventions that recruit participants through hospitals, in hopes of leveraging the push of victimization.

There have been roughly a half dozen published evaluations of the Cure Violence model and the evaluation evidence in support of the model is mixed. A recent quasi-experimental evaluation of Philadelphia's Cure Violence program showed positive results (Roman et al. 2017), but the effects were small. Evaluations in Chicago and Baltimore found that the intervention worked in some neighborhoods, but not others (see Butts et al. 2015 for details on evaluation findings). However, in the Baltimore and Chicago evaluations there were more neighborhoods with positive results than null results and the neighborhoods with null results were the ones linked to serious implementation obstacles. Similar to the issues with evaluation methods used to measure focused deterrence initiative outcomes, to date, there have been no evaluations of Cure Violence models that assess the relationship of particular program components (e.g., conflict mediations, participant outreach and services, community engagement) to outcomes achieved, making it difficult to determine the particular mechanisms of change that are operating. Despite the limited evidence, we suggest that the theory of change behind Cure Violence – at least the dedicated street outreach and case management component – has promise given the model's stated ability to leverage a variety of the most salient reasons for leaving.

Bonding to individuals – therapeutic/counseling interventions
In the area of relationship building and counseling, we discuss two evidence-based programs designed to reduce delinquency: Multisystemic Therapy (MST) and Becoming a Man. MST is an intensive family focused community-based treatment designed to simultaneously improve parenting skills and youth coping mechanisms as a means to reduce antisocial behavior in youth (Henggeler, Schoenwald, and Pickrel 1995). MST support goes beyond the immediate family and into consideration that court-involved families are isolated and cut off from extended family and community networks. Through a home-based model usually lasting four months, the counselors help families and youth rebuild these networks. According to *Crimesolutions.gov*, MST is considered an evidence-based intervention for youth, as it has been shown in multiple studies to reduce arrests and the seriousness of crime. It is currently being evaluated to determine if it can be effective with gang members in reducing arrests and violent

behavior. However, preliminary results from earlier evaluations suggest that youth involved in delinquent peer groups or gangs might not be amenable to the intervention (Boxer 2011). In fact, a recent study by Boxer and colleagues (2015) finds that gang involvement moderates the effectiveness of MST in a negative way. Indeed, only 33% of active gang members, compared to 80% of non-gang members, maintain successful short-term case outcomes, even though they received similar treatment (e.g., length of treatment days, number of contacts) as non-gang involved youth.

Becoming a Man (B.A.M.©) is a school-based intervention targeted to middle and high school students that focuses on building 'social cognitive skills' that include, but are not limited to emotional regulation, interpersonal problem solving, and conflict management. B.A.M. is comprised of 30 voluntary one-hour in-school group counseling and mentoring sessions that teach a skill each session. The program can be combined with an afterschool sports component that reinforces conflict resolution and the skills developed in the in-school sessions. An evaluation using a randomized control design found that the program (which included the sports component) was successful in reducing arrests for both violent and nonviolent crimes (Cook et al. 2014). Although B.A.M. might be categorized as secondary prevention because it targets high-risk youth and does not have defined eligibility criteria related to gang membership, it appears to be reaching youth embedded in gangs, and as such, we suggest the intervention could be a promising one for direct gang intervention and disengagement from gangs if one were developed explicitly for gang youth.

Reflection on interventions with regard to pushes and pulls

Based on the findings from Table 1 and our review of interventions in Table 2, we conclude that programs would have the highest likelihood of success if they: (1) address disillusionment and simultaneously leverage pulls; (2) have a long duration and high intensity of services; and (3) work with both individuals and the group. Programs that have a long duration and high intensity would be more likely to capture the changing images of the self at the appropriate time to tilt the individual past first doubts and into a role where disengagement is possible. Furthermore, even recognizing that some longitudinal studies indicate that the trajectories of gang membership are relatively brief, many of these youth who indicate leaving a gang have not necessarily cut ties with all or even most of their gang friends, which can hinder the development of new prosocial relationships.

At the first doubts stage and when one is trying on new roles, gang members would need support from prosocial others or opportunities that fit into one's newly developed identity. This dovetails with recent theoretical insight on gang desistance processes (Decker, Pyrooz, and Moule 2014; Healy 2013) where individuals evaluate the self in terms of possible social roles, seeking out opportunities for personal development and positive reinforcement about these new roles. Programs that have resources to provide these opportunities for development, opportunities that include both tangible resources such as jobs, job training, assistance with moving out of neighborhood, and relational aspects of social networks are important, but so are programs that introduce new friends or mentors who act as role models. These efforts provide a sound theory of change to presume a targeted outcome of gang disengagement. These role models can model new, acceptable behavior and reinforce positive behaviors over time. This is possible with programs based on street outreach, as street outreach has been identified as the primary mechanism to keeping hard-to-reach youth and gang members engaged (Varano and Wolff 2012). Outreach workers can help identify strategies that reinforce prosocial roles and prosocial contacts – new friends, new jobs, or support to move out of the neighborhood or to a different school. Outreach workers also can provide a stable, high quality relationship (Shute 2013).

These are all roles that are consistent with the Cure Violence model, as well as the focused deterrence model, if services in the latter are well-funded or solid referral systems have been put in place. Hospital-based interventions may also prove promising because they can capitalize on a very vulnerable period and link individuals to services, provide additional services to the family unit, and follow up in a holistic framework, while introducing and reinforcing prosocial roles. This is similar to what Decker and Lauritsen (1996, 66) concluded when they remarked on the importance of paying attention to triggering events like victimization, which frequently occur in gang members' lives. They emphasized that interventions in hospital emergency rooms are: 'likely to be successful to the extent that it (a) occurs very shortly after the victimization, and (b) occurs separate from the influence of the gang.' They added that follow-up services may be necessary so the violent event is not used as a method by fellow gang members to reinforce the need for the collective.

Hospital-based interventions with a long follow-up period (i.e., more than three months) that integrates community reintegration with street-based outreach workers have a sound theory of change and should also produce positive results. Research that evaluates these interventions should take care to examine the multiple components of the intervention so as to appropriately address the levels of care. More specifically, clearly identifying inputs and outputs of the intervention would be key to understanding and appropriately evaluating outcomes related to group membership and behavior. Indeed, as others have noted (Klein and Maxson 2006; Spergel 1995), identifying and addressing the micro-level interactions among individuals with reference to group interactions and influences can be the most difficult part of gang interventions. Implementation and outcome failures of gang interventions may simply reflect the lack of understanding of these processes. We reiterate that, in general, looking across the body of anti-gang programs, failure to find positive impacts of promising programs may be partly due to the limited number of high quality, rigorous evaluations of these programs and not due to failure in program designs (Esbensen and Matsuda 2013).

The fact that few programs directly attempt to change one's gang member status raises an important question: Is there utility in developing programs that have an express goal of changing gang identity and/or one's status as a gang member? A key consideration should be the focus of the intervention. Some interventions are focused on changing behavior (involvement in crime), others on status (gang membership). At this point it is not clear which of these is the most likely to produce positive changes, although some evidence suggests that curtailing levels of embeddedness in gangs matters as much for reducing criminal behavior as de-identifying as a gang member (Sweeten, Pyrooz, and Piquero 2013). Results from the second evaluation of the Gang Resistance Education and Training program indicated a statistically and substantively significant reduction in gang membership, but not parallel reduction in criminal activity, even violence (Esbensen et al. 2013), which led some to speculate about the value of emphasizing gang status over gang behavior (Maxson 2013; Pyrooz 2013). Indeed, others (Shute 2013) have argued for behavior as the most appropriate focus of interventions. We believe that a focus on behavior does not preclude a focus on status and as such, interventions that have a dual focus could be effective. An intervention need not directly articulate to a participant that it is important to leave the gang or gang peers, but could model prosocial behavior in a way that elicits that same prosocial behavior from the participant. Essentially, these potentially new, prosocial behaviors are an act of participatory socialization that are part of stages of gang exit (Decker, Pyrooz, and Moule 2014). More specifically, many of the pulls (e.g., jobs, family, new friendship groups) reflect behaviors that may lead to changes in status.

It is appropriate to leverage naturally occurring transitions in the life course when they occur. Those transitions produce hooks for change, but hooks that need to be engaged and sustained. Those hooks can be leveraged to incentivize gang leaving once those transitions are in place. Thus, urging individuals to leave their gang is not in itself a strategy to reduce gang membership but becomes more effective once other changes are in place. Many individuals who have left their gang talk about filling the void left by leaving the gang (Decker, Pyrooz, and Moule 2014). That void includes relationships as well as activities. Filling voids and reinforcing positive behavior should be an important priority in creating intervention plans for individuals contemplating leaving their gang or in the process of doing so. After all, the disengagement process has been described as 'teeter-tottering' to and from the gang (Decker, Pyrooz, and Moule 2014), which is why filling the void associated with such transitions with positive and sustained influences is critical.

Programs that utilize a focused deterrence approach do not necessarily provide a sustained prosocial demonstration of role change. Although these group- and community-level interventions have shown success in reducing violence in the short-term, we suggest that if communities desire long-term changes that reflect community-centered normative values, interventions should be based on building informal social control in communities through resident interaction and the development of prosocial networks among residents and community-based institutions. Such strategies could include MST, Cure Violence and related hospital response programs, and Homeboy Industries. Of course, it is important to note that these programs lack sound evidence with respect to promoting disengagement from gangs.

Conclusion

We agree with Sampson and Laub (2016, 330) that 'offender-given reasons for committing crime (or stopping crime) are not in themselves dispositive.' However, the reasons gang members give for leaving their gangs have salience for developing strong theory-of-change-based programs that can encourage and support gang exit, and in turn desistance from crime. Work in behavioral economics suggests, and Sampson and Laub (2016) seem to agree, that with regard to general behavior change, small interventions can have large effects and individuals can be 'nudged' to make better decisions (Thaler and Sunstein 2008). Although Sampson and Laub (2016) made their comments with regard to the structure versus agency debate in desistance, it is not the intent of this paper to argue for a set of causal mechanisms that falls on either side of this debate in gang disengagement or crime desistance, but to reiterate that if behavior does indeed change identity or that the conception of self does not necessarily need to change before improvements or changes in behavior occur, then perhaps gang intervention programs that re-structure behavior in prosocial directions can be successful. Going one step further, our review suggests that, with gang members, the nudge should be sustained.

In many ways, it is up to the research community (and funders) to construct and invest in sound evaluation designs that reflect the complexity of multi-component programs, and specifically those programs that have a theory of change that addresses the individual, the group, and the community. Similarly, practitioners and government agencies should be willing, within the limits of the law, to overcome hurdles to share client information, or else all the best efforts of researchers may be for naught. As Barlow and Decker commented in 2010 (124), 'Building an iterative process whereby theory and policy inform each other in an ongoing interaction is crucial.'

This review argues that developmental and life course theory – with its emphasis on transitions – has implications for disengaging from gangs and desisting from crime. These processes involve changes in behavior as well as status. Our review of three large studies of gang disengagement leads us to conclude that behaviors (i.e., trying out new prosocial roles) are likely the initial area of change, but can be used to leverage further changes in status as a gang member.

It also appears that this process differs across developmental and life course periods, as evidenced by the marked differences in the frequency and prevalence of pulls and pushes between samples employing younger and older research subjects. Although we recognize the limitations of our conclusions given the differences among the three survey samples with regard to age, survey administration and time elapsed between membership and survey response, we believe the findings still have implications for policy intervention because they intuitively align with life course theory. As gang members move into their late teens and early twenties, the disengagement process appears to become more complex, requiring simultaneous pushes and pulls. This makes sense because gang membership becomes ingrained in one's identity both as one ages and as membership length increases, which makes it more challenging to turn away from relationships with friends, family, and neighborhood – the criminal capital of the gang – that have taken years to cultivate. While identity change is certainly part of the disengagement process, there are other behavioral markers as well. These include reducing gang ties and gang involvement. Being engaged in activities with non-gang members is certainly one way to accomplish this goal. Practitioners should look to enhance opportunities and programs for such interactions, recognizing that leveraging these opportunities and interactions may be dependent on developmental and life course periods.

Notes

1. The Eurogang definition of gang membership has been widely endorsed and to be identified as a 'Eurogang member' a respondent must indicate that they have a group of friends, and that this group (1) is between ages 12 and 25 years, (2) spends time together in public places, (3) has been in existence for at least three months, (4) defines illegal activities as socially permissible, and (5) engages in illegal activities together.
2. We thank Dena Carson and her colleagues for providing us with supplemental analyses to populate the summary findings of Table 1. It should be noted that they examined whether motivations for leaving a gang differed by operational definitions of former gang membership, and found that although there were some differences, the overall patterns of findings with regard to frequency of responses were similar. We only draw on 'operational definition 3' because it most closely approaches the definitions used in the other data sets.
3. Although applicable to interventions with gang members, we do not include a review of comprehensive models that are designed to simultaneously address multiple 'levels of practice' (e.g., prevention, intervention, reentry, and suppression). Comprehensive interventions are highly context-specific, adapted differently across neighborhoods and cities. For instance, models such as Little Village/the Comprehensive Anti-Gang Model allow for variations in focus and balance across the prongs, specifically depending on context. Although when implemented with fidelity, evaluations of the Comprehensive Anti-Gang Model have shown positive impacts (Howell 2015; Spergel, Wa, and Sosa 2006), the multiple prongs make it difficult for us to associate specific mechanisms that could be leveraged for gang exit relative to motivations for leaving. However, undoubtedly, the Comprehensive Anti-Gang Model has components (e.g., street outreach) that could be highlighted relative to our findings.

Acknowledgments

The authors would like to thank Dena Carson for her assistance in providing the relevant statistics for the G.R.E.A.T. II dataset. Data collection for the Connect Survey was supported by Award No. 2011-JV-FX-0105, from the Office of Juvenile Justice and Delinquency Prevention, Office of Justice Programs, U.S. Department of Justice. Funding from Google Ideas supported the data collection for the Google Ideas study. The content of this paper, however, is solely the responsibility of the authors and does not necessarily represent the official views of the U.S. Department of Justice or Google.

Disclosure statement

No potential conflict of interest was reported by the authors.

Funding

As stated above, data collection for the Connect Survey was supported by the Office of Juvenile Justice and Delinquency Prevention, Office of Justice Programs, U.S. Department of Justice [grant number 2011-JV-FX-0105]. Funding from Google Ideas supported data collection for the Google Ideas study.

References

Barber, Bonnie L., Jacquelynne S. Eccles, and Margaret R. Stone. 2001. "Whatever Happened to the Jock, the Brain, and the Princess? Young Adult Pathways Linked to Adolescent Activity Involvement and Social Identity." *Journal of Adolescent Research* 16: 429–455.

Barlow, Hugh D. 1995. *Crime and Public Policy: Putting Theory to Work*. Boulder, CO: Westview Press.

Barlow, Hugh D., and Scott H. Decker. 2010. "Introduction to Part I: Putting Criminological Theory into Practice." In *Criminology and Public Policy: Putting Theory to Work*, edited by Hugh Barlow and Scott Decker, 3–5. Philadelphia, PA: Temple University Press.

Becker, Marla G., Jeffery S. Hall, Caesar M. Ursic, Sonia Jain, and Deane Calhoun. 2004. "Caught in the Crossfire: The Effects of a Peer-based Intervention Program for Violently Injured." *Youth Journal of Adolescent Health* 34: 177–183.

Bjorgo, Tore. 1999, "How Gangs Fall Apart: Processes of Transformation and Disintegration of Gangs." Paper Presented at the Annual Meeting for the American Society of Criminology, Toronto, November, 17–20.

Bjorgo, Tore. 2013. *Strategies for Preventing Terrorism*. New York: Palgrave MacMillan.

Block, Steven, Christopher A. Brown, Louis Barretti, Erin Walker, Michael Yudt, and Ralph Fretz. 2014. "A Mixed-method Assessment of a Parenting Program for Incarcerated Fathers." *Journal of Correctional Education* 65: 50–67.

Bolden, Christian. 2013. "Tales from the Hood: An Emic Perspective on Gang Joining and Gang Desistance." *Criminal Justice Review* 38 (4): 473–490. 0734016813509267.

Bottoms, Anthony. 2004. "Towards Desistance: Theoretical Underpinnings for an Empirical Study." *The Howard Journal of Criminal Justice* 43 (4): 368–389.

Boxer, Paul. 2011. "Negative Peer Involvement in Multisystemic Therapy for the Treatment of Youth Problem Behavior: Exploring Outcomes and Process Variables in 'Real-world' Practice." *Journal of Clinical Child Adolescent Psychology* 40: 848–854.

Boxer, Paul, Joanna Kubik, Michael Ostermann, and Bonita Veysey. 2015. "Gang Involvement Moderates the Effectiveness of Evidence-based Intervention for Justice-involved Youth." *Children and Youth Services Review* 52 (May): 26–33. doi:10.1016/j.childyouth.2015.02.012

Braga, Anthony A., and David Weisburd. 2012. "The Effects of Focused Deterrence Strategies on Crime: A Systematic Review and Meta-Analysis of the Empirical Evidence." *Journal of Research in Crime and Delinquency* 49 (3): 323–358.

Bubolz, Bryan F., and Pete Simi. 2015. "Disillusionment and Change: A Cognitive-emotional Theory of Gang Desistance." *Deviant Behavior* 36 (4): 330–345.

Bursik, Robert J., and Harold Grasmick. 1993. *Neighborhoods and Crime*. New York: Lexington Books.

Bushway, Shawn D., and Raymond Paternoster. 2013. "Desistance from Crime: A Review and Ideas for Moving Forward." In *Handbook of Life-course Criminology*, edited by Chris L. Gibson and Marvin D. Krohn, 213–231. New York: Springer.

Butts, Jeffrey A., and Caterina Gouvis Roman. 2010. "A Community Youth Development Approach to Gang Control Programs." In *Youth Gangs and Community Intervention: Research, Practice, and Evidence*, edited by Robert Chaskin, 175–205. New York: Columbia University Press.

Butts, Jeffrey, Caterina G. Roman, Lindsay Bostwick, and Jeremy R. Porter. 2015. "Cure Violence: A Public Health Model to Reduce Violence." *Annual Review of Public Health* 36 (1): 39–53.

Carson, Dena C., Dana Peterson, and Finn-Age Esbensen. 2013. "Youth Gang Desistance: An Examination of the Effect of Different Operational Definitions of Desistance on the Motivations, Methods, and Consequences Associated with Leaving the Gang." *Criminal Justice Review* 38: 510–534.

Carson, Dena C., and J. Michael Vecchio. 2015. "Leaving the Gang: A Review and Thoughts on Future Research." In *Handbook of Gangs*, edited by Scott H. Decker and David C. Pyrooz, 139–155. Hoboken, NJ: Wiley-Blackwell.

Clarke, Ronald V., and Derek B. Cornish. 1985. "Modeling Offenders' Decisions: A Framework for Research and Policy." In *Crime and Justice: A Review of Research*. 6 vol., edited by Michael Tonry and Norval Morris, 147–185. Chicago, IL: University of Chicago Press.

Cook, Philip J., Kenneth Dodge, George Farkas, Ronald G. Fryer Jr., Jonathan Guryan, Jens Ludwig, Susan Mayer, Harold Pollack, and Laurence Steinberg. 2014. *The (Surprising) Efficacy of Academic and Behavioral Intervention with Disadvantaged Youth: Results from a Randomized Experiment in Chicago*. Cambridge, MA: National Bureau of Economic Research, Working Paper No. 19862.

Curry, David G., Scott H. Decker, and David C. Pyrooz. 2014. *Confronting Gangs: Crime and Community*. 3rd ed. New York: Oxford University Press.

Decker, Scott H. 2003. "Policing Gangs and Youth Violence: Where Do We Stand, Where Do We Go from Here?" In *Policing Gangs and Youth Violence*, edited by Scott H. Decker, 287–293. Belmont, CA: Wadsworth Publishing Company.

Decker, Scott H., and Janet L. Lauritsen. 1996. "Breaking the Bonds of Membership: Leaving the Gang." In *Gangs in America*. 2nd ed., edited by C. Ronald Huff, 103–122. Newbury Park, CA: Sage.

Decker, Scott H., and David C. Pyrooz. 2011. "Gangs, Terrorism, and Radicalization." *Journal of Strategic Security* 4 (4): 151–166.

Decker, Scott H., and Barrik Van Winkle. 1996. *Life in the Gang: Family, Friends and Violence*. New York: Cambridge University Press.

Decker, Scott H., David C. Pyrooz, and Richard K. Moule Jr. 2014. "Disengagement from Gangs as Role Transitions." *Journal of Research on Adolescence* 24: 268–283.

Densley, James. 2015. "Joining the Gang: A Process of Supply and Demand." In *Handbook of Gangs*, edited by Scott H. Decker and David C. Pyrooz, 235–256. Hoboken, NJ: Wiley-Blackwell.

Ebaugh, Helen Rose Fuchs. 1988. *Becoming an Ex: The Process of Role Exit*. Chicago, IL: University of Chicago Press.

Eck, John, and William Spelman. 1987. *Problem-solving: Problem-Oriented Policing in Newport News*. Washington, DC: U.S. Department of Justice, National Institute of Justice.

Eidson, Jillian, Caterina G. Roman, and Meagan Cahill. 2016. "Successes and Challenges in Recruiting and Retaining Gang Members in Longitudinal Research: Lessons Learned from a Multi-Site Social Network Study." *Youth Violence and Juvenile Justice*. ePub July, 2016: Online first. doi:10.1177/1541204016657395

Elder Jr, Glen H. 1985. *Life Course Dynamics: Trajectories and Transitions, 1968–1980*. New York: Cornell University Press.

Esbensen, Finn-Age, and Kristy N. Matsuda. 2013. "Program Evaluation: How Do We Know if we are Preventing Gang Membership?" Chap. 11 in *Changing Course: Preventing Gang Membership*, edited by Thomas R. Simon, Nancy M. Ritter, and Reshma R. Mahendra, 151–162. Washington, DC: U.S. Department of Justice, Office of Justice Programs, and the Centers for Disease Control and Prevention.

Esbensen, Finn-Aage, D. Wayne Osgood, Dana Peterson, Terrance J. Taylor, and Dena C. Carson. 2013. "Short-and Long-term Outcome Results from a Multisite Evaluation of the GREAT Program." *Criminology & Public Policy* 12 (3): 375–411.

Farrall, Stephen. 2002. *Rethinking What Works with Offenders*. Cullompton: Willan Publishing.

Farrall, Stephen, Ben Hunter, Gilly Sharpe, and Adam Calverley. 2014. *Criminal Careers in Transition: The Social Context of Desistance from Crime*. Oxford: Oxford University Press.

Flores, Edward Orozco. 2013. *God's Gangs: Barrio Ministry, Masculinity, and Gang Recovery*. New York: New York University Press.

Gilman, Amanda B., Karl G. Hill, and David J. Hawkins. 2014. "Long-term Consequences of Adolescent Gang Membership for Adult Functioning." *American Journal of Public Health* 104 (5): 938–945.

Giordano, Peggy C., Stephen A. Cernkovich, and Jennifer L. Rudolph. 2002. "Gender, Crime, and Desistance: Toward a Theory of Cognitive Transformation." *American Journal of Sociology* 107: 990–1064.

Giordano, Peggy C., Ryan D. Schroeder, and Stephen A. Cernkovich. 2007. "Emotions and Crime over the Life Course: A Neo-meadian Perspective on Criminal Continuity and Change." *American Journal of Sociology* 112 (6): 1603–1661.

Goldstein, Herman. 1990. *Problem-oriented Policing*. Philadelphia, PA: Temple University Press.

Gordon, R. A., B. B. Lahey, E. Kawai, R. Loeber, M. Stouthamer-Loeber, and David P. Farrington. 2004. "Antisocial Behavior and Youth Gang Membership: Selection and Socialization." *Criminology* 42: 55–88.

Healy, Deirdre. 2013. "Changing Fate? Agency and the Desistance Process." *Theoretical Criminology* 17 (4): 557–574.

Henggeler, Scott W., Sonja K. Schoenwald, and Susan G. Pickrel. 1995. "Multisystemic Therapy: Bridging the Gap between University- and Community-Based Treatment." *Journal of Consulting and Clinical Psychology* 63 (5): 709–717.

Howell, J. C. 2015. "The Legacy of Irving A. Spergel." In *The Wiley Handbook of Gangs*, edited by S. Decker and D. C. Pyrooz, 424–439. Hoboken, NJ: Wiley.

Howell, James C., and Arlen Egley Jr. 2005. "Moving Risk Factors into Developmental Theories of Gang Membership." *Youth Violence and Juvenile Justice* 3: 334–354.

Jennings-Bey, Timothy, Sandra D. Lane, Robert A. Rubinstein, Dessa Bergen-Cico, Arnett Haygood-El, Helen Hudson, Shaundel Sanchez, and Frank L. Fowler. 2015. "The Trauma Response Team: A Community Intervention for Gang Violence." *Journal of Urban Health* 92 (5): 947–954. doi:10.1007/s11524-015-9978-8

Kennedy, David. 2011. *Don't Shoot: One Man, a Street Fellowship, and the End of Violence in Inner-City America*. New York: Bloomsbury.

Klein, Malcolm W., and Cheryl L. Maxson. 2006. *Street Gang Patterns and Policies*. New York: Oxford University Press.

Krohn, Marvin, Jeffrey T. Ward, Terence Thornberry, Alan J. Lizotte, and Rebekah Chu. 2011. "The Cascading Effects of Adolescent Gang Involvement across the Life Course." *Criminology* 49 (4): 991–1028.

Laub, John H., and Leana C. Allen. 1999. "Life Course Criminology and Community Corrections." *Executive Exchange* (Spring): 2–11.

Laub, John H., and Robert J. Sampson. 2001. "Understanding Desistance from Crime." *Crime and Justice* 28: 1–69.

Laub, John H., and Robert J. Sampson. 2003. *Shared Beginnings, Divergent Lives: Delinquent Boys to Age 70*. Cambridge, MA: Harvard University Press.

Laub, John H., Robert J. Sampson, R. P. Corbett Jr, and J. S. Smith. 1995. "Public Policy Implications of a Life-course Perspective on Crime." In *Crime and Public Policy: Putting Theory to Work*, edited by Hugh D. Barlow, 91–106. Boulder: Westview.

Laub, John H., Robert J. Sampson, and Gary A. Sweeten. 2006. "Assessing Sampson and Laub's Life-course Theory of Crime." In *Taking Stock: The Status of Criminological Theory*, edited by Francis T. Cullen, 313–333. New Brunswick, NJ: Transaction.

Leap, Jorja, Todd M. Franke, Christina A. Christie, and Susana Bonis. 2011. "Nothing Stops a Bullet like a Job: Homeboy Industries Gang Prevention and Intervention in Los Angeles." In *Beyond Suppression: Global Perspectives on Youth Violence*, edited by Joan Serra Hoffman, Lyndee M. Knox, and Robert Cohen, 127–137. Santa Barbara, CA: ABC-CLIO.

Loeber, Rolf, and Marc Le Blanc. 1990. "Toward a Developmental Criminology." In *Crime and Justice*. 12 vols., edited by Michael Tonry and Norval Morris, 375–437. Chicago, IL: University of Chicago Press.

Lurigio, Arthur, Gad Bensinger, S. Rae Thompson, Kristin Elling, Donna Poucis, Jill Selvaggio, and Melissa Spooner. 2000. *A Process and Outcome Evaluation of Project BUILD: Years 5 and 6*. Unpublished Report. Chicago, IL: Loyola University.

Maruna, Shadd. 2001. *Making Good: How Ex-Convicts Reform and Rebuild Their Lives*. Washington, DC: American Psychological Association.

Maruna, Shadd, Russ Immarigeon, and T. LeBel. 2004. "Ex-Offender Reintegration: Theory and Practice." In *After Crime and Punishment: Pathways to Ex-offender Reintegration*, edited by Shadd Maruna and Russ Immarigeon, 3–26. Cullompton: Willan Publishing.

Maxson, Cheryl L. 2013. "Do Not Shoot the Messenger: The Utility of Gang Risk Research in Program Targeting and Content." *Criminology & Public Policy* 12 (3): 421–426. doi:10.1111/1745-9133.12052

McClelland, David C., Richard Koestner, and Joel Weinberger. 1992. "How Do Self-attributed and Implicit Motives Differ?" In *Motivation and Personality: Handbook of Thematic Content Analysis* edited by Charles P. Smith, 49–72. New York, NY: Cambridge University Press.

McLean, Kate C., Andrea V. Breen, and Marc A. Fournier. 2010. "Constructing the Self in Early, Middle, and Late Adolescent Boys: Narrative Identity, Individuation, and Well-Being." *Journal of Research on Well Being* 20 (1): 166–187.

McVey, Erin, Juan C. Duchesne, Siavash Sarlati, Michael O'Neal, Kelly Johnson, and Jennifer Avegno. 2014. "Operation CeaseFire New Orleans: An Infectious Disease Model for Addressing Community Recidivism from Penetrating Trauma." *Journal of Trauma and Acute Care Surgery* 77 (1): 123–128.

Melde, Chris, and Finn-Aage Esbensen. 2011. "Gang Membership as a Turning Point in the Life Course." *Criminology* 49 (2): 513–552.

Melde, Chris, and Finn-Age Esbensen. 2013. "Gangs and Violence: Disentangling the Impact of Gang Membership on the Level and Nature of Offending." *Journal of Quantitative Criminology* 29: 143–166. doi:10.1007/s10940-012-9164-z

Merton, Robert K. 1957. *Social Theory and Social Structure*. New York: Free Press.

Moloney, Molly, Kathleen MacKenzie, Geoffrey Hunt, and Karen Joe-Laidler. 2009. *British Journal of Criminology* 49 (3): 305–325.

O'Neil, Eryn N., Scott H. Decker, Richard K. Moule, and David C. Pyrooz. 2016. "Girls, Gangs and Getting Out: Gender Differences and Similarities in Leaving the Gang." *Youth Violence and Juvenile Justice* 14: 43–60.

Paternoster, Raymond, and Shawn Bushway. 2009. "Desistance and the 'Feared Self': Toward an Identity Theory of Criminal Desistance." *The Journal of Criminal Law and Criminology* 99 (4): 1103–1156.

Peterson, Dana, Terrance J. Taylor, and Fin-Age Esbensen. 2004. "Gang Membership and Violent Victimization." *Justice Quarterly* 21: 793–815.

Piquero, Alex R., David P. Farrington, and Alfred Blumstein. 2003. "The Criminal Career Paradigm." *Crime and Justice* 30: 359–506.

Pyrooz, David C. 2013. "Gangs, Criminal Offending, and an Inconvenient Truth: Considerations for Gang Prevention and Intervention in the Lives of Youth." *Criminology & Public Policy* 12 (3): 427–436.

Pyrooz, David C. 2014a. "'From Your First Cigarette to Your Last Dyin' Day': The Patterning of Gang Membership in the Life-course." *Journal of Quantitative Criminology* 30 (2): 349–372. doi:10.1007/s10940-013-9206-1

Pyrooz, David C. 2014b. "From Colors and Guns to Caps and Gowns? The Effects of Gang Membership on Educational Attainment." *Journal of Research in Crime and Delinquency* 51 (1): 56–87. doi:10.1177/0022427813484316

Pyrooz, David C., and Scott H. Decker. 2011. "Motives and Methods for Leaving the Gang: Understanding the Process of Gang Desistance." *Journal of Criminal Justice* 39 (5): 417–425.

Pyrooz, David C., and Scott H. Decker. 2014. "Recent Research on Disengaging from Gangs: Implications for Practice." In *Effective Interventions in the Lives of Criminal Offenders*, edited by John A. Humphrey and Peter Cordella, 81–98. New York: Springer.

Pyrooz, David C., Scott H. Decker, and Vincent J. Webb. 2014. "The Ties That Bind: Desistance from Gangs." *Crime and Delinquency* 60: 491–516.

Roman, Caterina G., Meagan Cahill, and Jillian Eidson. 2016. "Street Gang Definitions across Two US Cities: Eurogang Criteria, Group Identity Characteristics, and Peer Group Involvement in Crime." In *Gang Transitions and Transformations in an International Context*, edited by Cheryl Maxson and Finn-Aage Esbensen, 15–32. Switzerland: Springer.

Roman, Caterina G., Hannah Klein, Kevin T. Wolff, Marla Davis Bellamy, and Kathleen Reeves. 2017. *Philadelphia CeaseFire: Findings from the Impact Evaluation*. Final Report to the Office of Juvenile Justice and Delinquency Prevention, US Department of Justice. Philadelphia, PA: Temple University.

Sampson, Robert J., and John H. Laub. 1990. "Crime and Deviance over the Life Course: The Salience of Adult Social Bonds." *American Sociological Review* 55: 609–627.

Sampson, Robert J., and John H. Laub. 1993. *Crime in the Making: Pathways and Turning Points through Life*. Cambridge, MA: Harvard University Press.

Sampson, Robert J., and John H. Laub. 2003. "Life-course Desisters? Trajectories of Crime Among Delinquent Boys Followed to Age 70." *Criminology* 41: 555–592.

Sampson, Robert J., and John Laub. 2005. "A Life-course View of the Development of Crime." *The ANNALS of the American Academy of Political and Social Science* 602 (1): 12–45.

Sampson, Robert J., and John Laub. 2016. "Turning Points and the Future of Life Course Criminology: Reflections on the 1986 Criminal Careers Report." *Journal of Research in Crime and Delinquency* 53 (3): 321–335.

Schochet, Peter Z., John Burghardt, and Sheena McConnell. 2006. *National Job Corps Study and Longer-term Follow-up Study: Impact and Benefit-cost Findings Using Survey and Summary Earnings Records Data*. Final Report submitted to the US Department of Labor. Princeton, NJ: Mathematica Policy Research, Inc.

Sharkey, Jill D., Skye W. F. Stifel, and Ashley Mayworm. 2015. "How to Help Me Get out of a Gang: Youth Recommendations to Family, School, Community, and Law Enforcement Systems." *Journal of Juvenile Justice* 4 (1): 64–83.

Sherman, Lawrence W. 2003. "Reason for Emotion: Reinventing Justice with Theories, Innovations, and Research. The American Society of Criminology 2002 Presidential Address." *Criminology* 41: 1–38.

Shute, Jon. 2013. "Family Support as a Gang Reduction Measure." *Children & Society* 27 (1): 48–59.

Soyer, Michaela. 2014. "The Imagination of Desistance: A Juxtaposition of the Construction of Incarceration as a Turning Point and the Reality of Recidivism." *British Journal of Criminology* 54: 91–108.

Spergel, Irving A. 1995. *The Youth Gang Problem: A Community Approach*. New York: Oxford University Press.

Spergel, I. A., K. M. Wa, and R. V. Sosa. 2006. "The Comprehensive, Community-wide, Gang Program Model: Success and Failure." In *Studying Youth Gangs*, edited by J. F. Short and L. A. Hughes, 203–224. Lanham, MD: AltaMira Press.

Sweeten, Gary, David C. Pyrooz, and Alex R. Piquero. 2013. "Disengaging from Gangs and Desistance from Crime." *Justice Quarterly* 30 (3): 469–500.

Teruya, Cheryl, and Yih-Ing Hser. 2010. "Turning Points in the Life Course: Current Findings and Future Directions in Drug Use Research." *Current Drug Abuse Review* 3 (3): 189–195.

Thaler, R., and Cass Sunstein. 2008. *Nudge: Improving Decisions about Health, Wealth, and Happiness*. New Haven, CT: Yale University Press.

Thornberry, Terence P., Marvin D. Krohn, Alan J. Lizotte, Carolyn A. Smith, and Kimberly Tobin. 2003. *Gangs and Delinquency in Developmental Perspective*. Cambridge: Cambridge University Press.

Trotti, Taylor, Jamie Dougherty, and John Klofas. 2014. *Overview of Hospital-based Violence Intervention Programs*. Working Paper #2014-15. Rochester, NY: Center for Public Safety Initiatives.

Varano, Sean, and Russell Wolff. 2012. "Street Outreach as an Intervention Modality for at-Risk and Gang-Involved Youth." In *Looking beyond Suppression: Community Strategies to Reduce Gang Violence*, edited by E. Gebo and B. Bond, 83–104. New York: Lexington Books.

Weaver, Beth. 2012. "The Relational Context of Desistance: Some Implications and Opportunities for Social Policy." *Social Policy and Administration* 46 (4): 395–412.

Weaver, Beth. 2016. *Offending and Desistance: The Role of Social Relations*. New York: Routledge.

Toward a multiracial feminist framework for understanding females' gang involvement

Dana Peterson and Vanessa R. Panfil

ABSTRACT
Despite growing interest in the gang involvement of girls and young women, tools with which to understand the experiences leading them to gangs remain fragmented. This article draws from existing gang theories and research on gendered pathways to illustrate the utility of a unified conceptual framework, particularly, one grounded in multiracial feminism. We explain what the primary components of such an integrated, life-course framework should be. Specifically, our framework attempts to account for multi-level influences: macro-level interlocking systems of inequality such as racialization and heteronormativity; interpersonal interactions in meso-level proximal spheres such as neighborhoods, families, schools, and peer groups; and micro-level processes of situated action, such as identity negotiation and agency within the context of constrained choice. We argue that our proposed conceptual framework will allow for more nuanced and complex understandings of females' gang involvement.

Introduction

Despite increasingly varied representations of females' gang involvement, the field of criminology lacks a unifying framework through which we may gain a more holistic and nuanced understanding. The goal in this paper is to propose a framework to understand females' gang involvement, synthesizing across multiple literatures and taking inequality at structural and individual levels into account. Our conceptual framework acknowledges interlocking oppressions and intersectional identities as producing gendered experiences, and affirms females' agency, identity, and resilience. We do not propose a generalizable 'theory' as such – though theories and testable hypotheses could certainly be derived from this framework – but instead a conceptualization of females' gang involvement that is informed by existing theories, literature on gangs, and multiracial feminism.

We first argue that a conceptual framework on females' gang involvement is warranted, then identify what the primary components should be, and finally, advance a normative argument for a multiracial feminist framework. Our framework accounts for macro-level inequalities; interactions in meso-level proximal spheres such as neighborhoods, families, schools, and peer networks; and micro-level processes of situated action, such as identity negotiation. Throughout, we illustrate the importance of mechanisms, processes, and the meanings people assign to events and identities, which we call attributed meanings, to better understand the 'how and why' of young women's gang involvement.

Is such a framework necessary?

Since females are less prevalent than males in gangs, and therefore potentially of less societal concern, one might ask, is it worthwhile to theorize and research their involvement? Most works about females as gang members commence with the refrain that they have long been overlooked and, thus, not much is known about them, except that when they are recognized, they are relegated to such essentialist roles as tomboys or, more frequently, sex objects. By contrast, we argue that we have amassed a large body of knowledge about females in gangs and can no longer claim that they are overlooked or cast solely in support roles: females are (and always have been) 'real' gang members,[1] they engage in many 'real' (licit and illicit) gang-related activities, and they experience 'real' consequences of involvement. Given these facts, it is time to emphasize females' lived experiences that bring them to gangs, and acknowledge their involvement, not in relation or juxtaposed to males, but as their *own* site of resistance, resources, and identity.

Doing so is not without risk. Prior works highlight the tensions in bringing females' gang involvement to the forefront. Some might argue it could: take away from those who 'need services the most' (e.g., young men, whose prevalence is higher); further pathologize and stigmatize young women (especially sensationalist media depictions[2]); or draw undesirable attention to them in the form of increased control and punishments rather than compassion and supports (Peterson 2009, 412; also Burgess-Proctor 2006; Chesney-Lind and Shelden 1998; Miller 2001; Schaffner 2006). While these are reasonable arguments, we assert that politically challenging issues of gender and sexuality in criminology are *not* 'better left unsaid' (Panfil 2014, 107): having honest conversations about females' gang involvement acknowledges those experiences, recognizes their agency, and affirms their humanity. However, we must proceed with caution, as we wish to contribute to neither 'the massive textual violence wreaked against inner-city youth in the name of social science research on "gangs"' (Conquergood 1994, 216), nor the 'academic-correctional-industrial complex' (Brotherton and Barrios 2004, 6).[3] We believe it is possible to write academically, even to *theorize*, about others in ways that do not exploit them or engender harm *if* such endeavors actively recognize and bring to the forefront hierarchical power relations. Accordingly, we argue that any useful framework for understanding gangs must consider gang involvement not necessarily as a deviant adaptation, but as an agentic situated choice that can be a site of empowerment, resiliency, and resistance.

Another contentious question is whether explanations proffered over the last century for males' involvement can explain females' involvement (i.e., the 'generalizability problem'; Daly and Chesney-Lind 1988, 508). Feminist scholars have critiqued 'general' explanations as dismissing or minimizing the importance of gender, not considering factors that may contribute to unique pathways for females, and essentially 'erasing' gender in favor of the 'dominant male norm' (Burgess-Proctor 2006; Cook 2016; Miller 2001; Steffensmeier 1983). To reduce essentialism, a framework must be interactional and multiplicative (not additive). Gender is important, but should be considered as it interacts with other statuses and shapes experiences.

Multiracial feminism seeks to avoid essentialism by taking into account gender relations conditioned by multiple inequalities (race, ethnicity, nationality, immigration status, class, sexuality, ability, etc.) that play out in both social structure, at the macro-level, and social interactions, at the micro-level (Collins 2000), thus recognizing that intersectional inequalities are 'dynamic, historically grounded, socially constructed power relationships' (Burgess-Proctor 2006, 37). Multiracial feminism guides our literature synthesis in constructing a lens through which to view females' gang involvement.

In sum, we assert that a 'female-centric' framework of gang involvement is warranted. Despite research supporting applicability of 'traditional' theories to females' delinquency and gang membership and despite commonalities in risk factors, developmental pathways, and trajectories for females and males, these examinations, for the most part, (1) started with males *at the center*, (2) operated under hegemonic assumptions about gender and sexual orientation, and (3) did not take intersectionality into account. By contrast, our proposed conceptual framework starts with females[4] at the center instead of using males as the referent, troubles hegemonic assumptions, and considers intersections as an important structuring element. Thus, we seek to rectify several important omissions in prior work, such as a relative lack of attention to intersectional identity, especially as it informs the meanings individuals attach to their experiences, and frequent descriptions of female gang membership *in relation to* males, based on the heteronormative primacy of male–female relationships. This last point is perhaps especially salient in light of long-standing assumptions within criminology and the study of gangs more specifically regarding gender, gender identity, and sexual orientation. Chesney-Lind (2015), in her application of feminist pathways and critical race feminism to female gang involvement, mentions sexual orientation and homophobia as potentially important, but does not investigate them. We illustrate why these are important, and provide examples as to how these issues can be meaningfully incorporated into analyses.

Contemporary understandings of adolescent gang involvement

Contemporary theories of adolescent gang involvement are integrated,[5] blending macro- and micro-influences and propositions drawn largely from 'traditional' criminological theories (e.g., social disorganization, underclass, subcultural, strain, labeling, social and self control, social learning). Common to them (although specific factors and mechanisms differ) are social structural factors that constrain communities and individuals. For example, Howell (2012; Howell, Braun, and Bellatty this issue; Howell and Egley 2005; Howell and Griffiths 2016), Klein (1995), Pauwels and Hardyns (2016), Thornberry (e.g., Thornberry et al. 2003), Vigil (1988 and later), and Wood and Alleyne (2010) begin with macro- or community-level factors such as racism, segregation, and structural disadvantage. Each author also theorizes the (interconnected) roles of various family, community, school, peer, and individual factors. However, these theories do not take into account additional gendered constraints that intersect and interact with race, class, and other hierarchical aspects to create unique social positions. Therefore, we and others argue, drawing on these more 'traditional' criminological theories of gang membership may be insufficient to fully account for females' involvement (Chesney-Lind 1989; Wing and Willis 1997).

Few theories give explicit or lengthy treatments of females' gang involvement. Most are regarded as 'general,' though require additional testing with regard to explanatory power for females and for subgroups based on multiplicative identities. Pauwels and Hardyns' (2016) model was supported for all 'sex X immigrant' subgroups, but other integrated theories await more detailed tests. Analyses of Thornberry's Interactional Theory uphold the model to explain males' involvement, but females numbered too few in their sample to support a full analysis (Thornberry et al. 2003); and, Vigil's model has been applied successfully to explain membership across race/ethnicity (Freng and Esbensen 2007; Krohn et al. 2011), but has not yet been tested with regard to gender. In addition, Howell and Egley's (2005) life-course developmental model of gang involvement has been generally validated in Raby and Jones' (2016) systematic review of risk factors for males' gang involvement and using Oregon Youth Authority data, though not separately for females (see Howell et al. in this issue). It thus remains to be seen whether there are different pathways or trajectories[6] for females' vs. males' gang involvement and whether there are specific gendered explanatory factors.

The theoretical and empirical literature on developmental or life-course pathways to delinquency and violence can also be consulted, with the caveat that the specific application of delinquency or violence explanations to gang involvement is in question (e.g., Klein and Maxson 2006). Huizinga and colleagues' (2013) analyses of females in two separate samples found no single common first offense, pathway, or trajectory, and diverse offense patterns, revealing important intra-gender variation. Howell's (2009, 2012) proposed gendered pathway (i.e., a greater impact for females than for males) to serious, chronic, and/or violent offending hypothesizes physical and sexual abuse leading to mental health problems; drug abuse; running or being thrown away (increasing exposure to dangerous people and places); gang involvement, increasing criminal activity; and detention/incarceration, resulting from arrests for running away, substance use, etc. While this pathway was proposed based on findings from an assortment of studies, it awaits adequate analysis with prospective longitudinal data, as one explicit test relied on juvenile court records from a single jurisdiction (Johansson and Kempf-Leonard 2009).

Comparing females to males, reviews or meta-analyses indicate quite similar pathways and trajectories. Russell, Robins, and Odgers (2014) reviewed 47 group-based trajectory model studies of antisocial behavior and determined that both females and males (though greater numbers of males) appear to follow several common trajectories, and that childhood risk profiles and antisocial outcomes associated with each trajectory do not differ significantly by sex (see too the review by Huizinga, Miller, and the Conduct Problems Prevention Research Group 2013). Further, they concluded that females' lower levels of antisocial behavior appear to be due to their faster cognitive and emotional development, lower neurodevelopmental vulnerability, and stronger monitoring from parents, teachers, and peers. Similarly, in their review of life-course studies, Macmillan and McCarthy (2014, 350) concluded that gender variation does not occur in temporal patterns of offending; however, the factors associated with likelihood and extent of offending are 'highly gendered.' They further argued that we lack enough empirical investigation about life-course dimensions of females' offending, gender comparisons of trajectories, factors that produce meaningful change, and full accounting of race, class, nativity, and other structural positions (see also Kruttschnitt 2016). Thus, we assert that a multiracial feminist framework is essential for understanding the developmental context of females' gang identities, intra- and inter-individual differences, and situational and temporal enactments of gang identity. Girls' gang enactments may also affect their identity construction later in life.

Interestingly, some insights from the gang literature would also suggest more similarity than difference. For example, females and males give similar reasons for joining gangs, such as for fun, protection, respect, and because a friend was in the gang (Huizinga et al. 2005; Peterson, Taylor, and Esbensen 2004; Thornberry et al. 2003; but see Maxson and Whitlock 2002). They also share many risk factors for gang involvement, such as holding delinquent beliefs, being committed to deviant peers, and perceiving their schools as disordered (Klein and Maxson 2006; Peterson and Morgan 2014). However, where differences do appear, they seem to be gendered. Summarizing potential gendered patterns, scholars have suggested, for example, that females may view their gangs in more emotional than instrumental terms and that school risk factors may be more important for females' gang involvement (Bjerregaard and Smith 1993; Campbell 1984; Esbensen and Deschenes 1998; Esbensen et al. 2010; Joe and Chesney-Lind 1995; Miller 2001).

We argue that these findings from research on reasons, risk factors, and theories indicating substantial sex-similarity are not 'incorrect,' but fail to take into account gendered processes and mechanisms by which females come to gangs. For example, what is behind joining for 'protection' or 'fun,' and how are those attributed meanings different from those of males? What aspects of 'conditions, controls, or exposure' vary by multiplicative intersections structured by such inequalities as patriarchy? Findings of sex-similarity are likely also due in part to methodological issues precluding nuanced consideration: our methods, samples, or measures (e.g., questions with pre-selected response options) reduce complexity, and thus impede our ability to explore context and meaning. In advancing our conceptual framework, we use specific examples to illustrate these tensions and address issues of incomplete or decontextualized understandings.

Toward an integrated developmental multiracial feminist framework

Although the gang literature (particularly cross-sectional studies) suggests similarity between females and males in explanations, reasons, or risk factors for gang involvement, we argue that the underlying mechanisms may differ, and that additional factors must be taken into account. Identifying these mechanisms, including the importance of attributed meanings, provides an understanding of the 'how' and 'why' behind gang membership, including differentiating 'the cause' from 'causes of causes' (Pauwels and Hardyns 2016) to explain how people come to hold views that influence behavior. Although structural forces like racism, sexism, and heterosexism permeate individuals' lives, people have varying levels of acceptance and response to these in interactions with others, and in their identity constructions. That is, it is not just personal characteristics, but also the *meaning* of those characteristics for that person, such as gender schemas, that affect interpersonal and person–institution interactions. For instance, gendered expectations have very different implications for young women who do not 'buy into' them. We argue that going deeper into attributed meanings in our theorizing will move us toward better practice: simply acknowledging that 'gender is important' does not go far enough to elucidate mechanisms that can provide effective guidance, whereas a multiracial feminist framework to uncover processes does.

The conceptual framework (see Figure 1) we propose for understanding females' gang involvement includes the following organizing elements or principles: (1) societal power inequalities forming (2) interlocking systems of oppression that are (3) produced and reproduced in more proximal spheres, and in (4) interpersonal interactions conditioned by intersectional identities, all of which in turn create (5) constrained or situated choices for young women. As seen in other developmental theories, we organize this framework as having intersecting and interacting macro-, meso-, and micro-level aspects that unfold/interact over time (i.e., developmentally over the life-course), offering entry- and exit-points to gangs. Below, we elaborate these elements by offering examples of how consideration and application of this multiracial feminist perspective can achieve a deeper understanding of females' gang involvement not as maladaptive, but resilient.

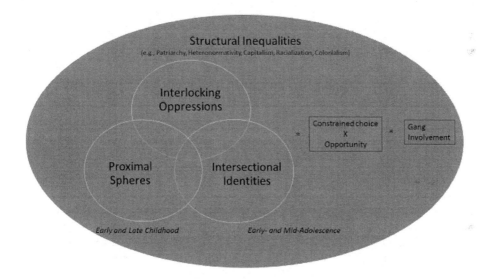

Figure 1. Multiracial feminist framework.

Macro-level: interlocking inequalities and oppressions

Setting the stage for potential gang formation and membership are interlocking inequalities and resulting oppressions created by macro-structural factors such as capitalism, colonialism, racialization, and isolation (e.g., Brotherton 2015; Vigil 1988 and later). As Vigil's (2002) application of his multiple marginality theory indicates, macro-historical and -structural forces create economic and social inequalities and dislocations, fragmented institutions, stress, and strain. Institutions such as families, schools, and law enforcement each fail young people, and their *joint* failure compounds the strains.

Missing from these discussions of interlocking inequalities that form young people's developmental contexts are the additional layers that constrain females as a result of societal sexism, patriarchy, and heteronormativity. A multiracial feminist approach urges us to consider how sexism, patriarchy, heterosexism, classism, racism, ethnocentrism, and other systems of inequality create and recreate hierarchical social positioning, define values (including devaluing feminine gender), and identify females' behaviors as normatively 'acceptable' or not (Collins 2000). This approach has been applied for crime and deviance more generally (e.g., Belknap and Holsinger 2006; Burgess-Proctor 2006; Cook 2016; Jones and Flores

2013; Miller 2002; Potter 2015), but less often specifically for gang involvement, and these latter works (e.g., Chesney-Lind 2015; Miller 2001; Vigil 2008; Wing and Willis 1997) tend to focus on intersections of gender, race or ethnicity, and sometimes class, to the exclusion of other salient identities.

Hegemonic laws and conceptions of 'deviance' (including gendered expectations) are also produced and influenced by interlocking inequalities and oppressions. For reasons of social control, 'gangs' are defined as inherently deviant and maladaptive, rather than available social groupings and/or 'modes of resistance' (Brotherton and Barrios 2004, 26; also Alonso 2004; Durán 2009; Vigil 2002; Zatz and Portillos 2000). Likewise, gender role stereotypes borne out of sexism and patriarchy mean that females' gang involvement is hegemonically defined as inherently and especially problematic. Patriarchy structures inequality for young women, defining and imposing ideals of femininity expected to guide and constrain females' attitudes, values, expressions, and behaviors, as well as societal perceptions of females' attributes and roles. Attempting to understand females' gang involvement without attending to hegemonic structures is to locate the explanation solely at the individual level (and often pathologically), devoid of context and meaning.

Meso-level: intersectional experiences in proximal spheres

Experiences in more proximal spheres, such as neighborhoods, families, schools, and peer networks, are structured by and interactional with macro-level influences and with each other, and vary by intersectional identities. As described, societal power inequalities and resulting interlocking systems of oppression are produced and reproduced in these more proximal spheres and in interpersonal interactions. For females, gendered and heteronormative social interactions (conditioned by race, culture, class, and other intersections) occur and recur within these overlapping contexts, from birth (or even prior) throughout the life-course, and experiences in adolescence are particularly salient in the formation of gang identities.

Neighborhoods

The above-described interlocking inequalities create 'structural factors' that place varying levels of stress on families, schools, and other institutions; affect community connections (or lack thereof); foster formation of gangs; and push or pull youth toward them. Factors including neighborhood disorder, concentrated disadvantage, industrial shifts and inadequate employment, educational system failure, housing insecurity, and out-migration of the upwardly mobile are commonly acknowledged in theorizing about the conditions giving rise to gangs and gang membership (Howell 2012; Howell and Egley 2005; Klein 1995; Pauwels and Hardyns 2016; Thornberry et al. 2003; Wood and Alleyne 2010).[7] These too are often regarded as 'general' in extant theorizing, and variously supported in research as predictors of both females' and males' gang involvement (e.g., Gilman et al. 2014; Joe and Chesney-Lind 1995; Thornberry et al. 2003). Taking a multiracial feminist perspective, we argue that neighborhood experiences are further structured by gendered and heteronormative organization and expectations, causing females to experience neighborhoods differently, both directly and indirectly, through families (especially in childhood), schools, and peers. This is manifested in a variety of ways that produce inter- and intra-gender variation (once aspects such as race, class, sexuality, gender schemas, etc. are taken into account, as detailed in some later examples), from the amount of time they spend in public spaces (which are tied to familial aspects such as supervision, abuse, and gender ideals), the neighborhood activities to which they are exposed and in which they engage (which can be structured by gendered exclusions or expectations), the persons to whom they are exposed (the effects of which interact with gendered moral values and intimate commitments, e.g., Mears, Ploeger, and Warr 1998; Zimmerman and Messner 2010), and the treatment they experience. All of these shape their activities and behavior. This means that neighborhood variations in cultural ideals about femininity will produce variations in the gender prevalence of gang membership, and the intervening mechanisms may be gender-moderated or gender-differentiated.

Neighborhood gendered violence, for instance,[8] provides important context. Many females tell of sexual harassment as they move through their neighborhoods: unwanted words and touching that sometimes escalate to physical and/or sexual assault, for which young women often feel they have little or no recourse (Harris 1994; Logan 2011; Miller 2008). The extent to which young women have interpersonal support and empowering contexts influences their internal and external responses to neighborhood conditions such as gendered structure and violence. Logan (2011) relays that while unsettling street harassment by males was universal among Asian, black, Latina, and white women, the form differed depending on race, sexuality, and gender expression, and females' reactions to harassment were similarly variable, with females of color expressing more concern than white females for their safety in public, in part coupled with their perceptions that those who victimize females of color face few consequences. As well, norms in disadvantaged communities can stifle intervention and reporting to authorities (Miller 2008). Specifically, a body of literature explains an additional conundrum faced by black females: given the over-policing and over-incarceration faced by black communities, many black females feel that to report harassment or victimization will only further demonize their communities and, especially, black men (e.g., Alexander 2010; Collins 2004). They must find ways to protect themselves. Miller (1998, 440) notes, 'the gendered nature of the streets may make the empowerment available through gang involvement an appealing alternative to the individualized vulnerability they otherwise would face.' Young women in gangs with males also reported a specifically gendered sense of protection, which represents a bit of a paradox, but explains why young women might seek out male-dominated gangs in order to help avoid harassment by males. Gang membership provides a space for young women to project outward displays of toughness and impenetrability (Miranda 2003), not necessarily to enact masculinity or cast off femininity, but to stand up for themselves and perhaps achieve equality with males (Mendoza-Denton 2008).

Families

Extant theorizing and research suggest that experiences in families of origin, sometimes reflective of stresses associated with structural inequalities, lead youths to seek surrogate or complementary families such as gangs. Below, we focus on experiences and effects of gendered socialization and various traumas, which can be compounded by intersectional identities.

In addition to being structured by race and class, familial socialization and expectations are gendered and heteronormative (Chesney-Lind 1989, 2015; Miller 2001; Moore 1991; Moore and Hagedorn 1999; Portillos 1999; Vigil 2008), originating from societal gender typescripts that place expectations on behavior, emotions and their expression, and parental controls. In many families, females are socialized differently than males in terms of appearance, demeanor, and behavior, but specific expectations vary by race, culture, and class. For example, power-control theory suggests different messages are relayed by mothers and fathers to daughters and sons depending on class, and these create variations in gender schemas (Hagan, Simpson, and Gillis 1987; Hagan, Boehnke, and Merkens 2004; Heimer and De Coster 1999). Childrearing styles in turn influence affective bonds, and females' displays of non-normative behavior can create contentious relationships at home, beginning even in early childhood. Hipwell et al. (2008), for instance, demonstrate reciprocal relationships between parents' (mostly mothers') harsh punishment practices and low warmth and girls' conduct problems. Further, rebelling against gender role expectations has resulted in young women being rejected and abused by parents (while males are punished for delinquency) (Brotherton and Barrios 2004; Joe and Chesney-Lind 1995). It is important, therefore, to understand parents' attributed meanings regarding parenting practices and young women's meanings in interpreting them, in order to know how they can lead to gender differences. Findings about differential effects of direct controls (i.e., through supervision for boys) and indirect controls (i.e., through affective bonds for girls) on learning of definitions about both gender and crime comprise one indicator of how the *meaning* of experiences is gendered and can differentiate pathways for females and males (Heimer and De Coster 1999; also Heimer 1996).

Aspects such as culture and religion shape transmission of gender ideals and can create both intra- and inter-gender variation. Hegemonic and localized femininities and masculinities prescribe different values, and have implications for female and male children's and adolescents' responses, beliefs, and behaviors, according to their gender schemas (Hagan et al. 2004; Rosenfield, Phillips, and White 2006). Rosenfield and Mouzon's (2013) review suggests that (1) white (hegemonic) conceptualizations of femininity emphasize the collective (i.e., valuing connectedness at the expense of autonomy), (2) black femininities embrace the collective while also valuing achievement (autonomy and assertiveness), and (3) masculinities are similar by race. These differences manifest, for example, in white female adolescents' schemas contributing to high internalizing as compared to black females, whose collective and autonomous schemas resulted in low internalizing (Rosenfield et al. 2006; also Holsinger and Holsinger 2005). Halim et al. (2016) found stricter gender roles in traditional Mexican, Dominican, and East Asian households, and more gender equity in African-American families in which girls are brought up to be strong, though parents from all backgrounds expressed belief in gender differences and needing to treat girls and boys differently. In Heimer's (1996) study, endorsement of traditional gender definitions was less likely among higher- than lower-income girls, and black females and younger females were less likely than nonblack and older girls to be delinquent, in part through gender definitions. Further, girls from female-headed households were more delinquent (less likely to endorse gender definitions). Importantly, the greater their endorsement of traditional gender ideals, the more strongly girls feel that males are valued more than females (Halim et al. 2016).

For adolescent females in the midst of identity formation, issues of culture as they relate to gender identity (and sexual orientation) can be challenging and even treacherous in households operating under hegemonic ideals about appropriately feminine roles, relationships, behaviors, and appearance. Although young men must avoid performing femininity because it is devalued (lest they face harassment), young women must perform it successfully, often in particular and sometimes rigid ways. Thus, some young women push back against societally- and culturally-prescribed roles, simultaneously 'doing' and 'undoing' gender (Connell 2005; West and Zimmerman 1987). Females of Mexican, Puerto Rican, and Dominican heritage have described their gang membership as a way to rebuff aspects of their cultures that represent tensions between 'traditional' family values and 'American ideals,' while simultaneously creating their own self-made identities that may incorporate some (e.g., value of family) but not other (e.g., female passivity) aspects of their cultures (Brotherton and Salazar-Atias 2003; Campbell 1984; Harris 1994; Moore 1991; Portillos 1999; Vigil 2008). Conversely, because of the male-dominated and heteronormative qualities of many gangs, males' gang involvement can be a way to accept and perform localized masculine expectations.[9] These experiences are exacerbated for young women whose sexual and gender identities and expressions contrast with hegemonic, cultural, and/or religious norms: if their sexual orientation and/or gender identity are hidden, females who identify as LGBT can feel isolated, unsupported, and/or ashamed, and if these identities are suspected or known, young women can be neglected, rejected, and/or maltreated by family members and kicked out of or leave their homes due to conflicts with parents (especially mothers) and psychological distress (Belknap and Holsinger 2006; Frederick 2014; Grossman et al. 2009; Savin-Williams 1994). Because the meaning of relationships (attachments) is often greater for females due to their gendered socialization, disruptions in familial relationships (e.g., parental rejection, neglect, and/or abuse) may have greater effects for females than males (Broidy and Agnew 1997).

Compounding issues related to culture, sexual orientation, and gender identity are gendered familial experiences that complicate young women's identity development. For example, cross-sectional and retrospective studies indicate that the following experiences are far more common for gang-involved young women compared to non-involved females and gang-involved males: childhood physical, emotional, or sexual trauma; parental or sibling drug/alcohol abuse, crime, and gang activity; needing to act as parent to parents and siblings; and running away (Brotherton and Salazar-Atias 2003; Fishman 1999; Fleisher 1998; Harris 1994; Hunt and Joe-Laidler 2001; Marshall et al. 2015; Miller 2001; Moore and Hagedorn 1999; Nurge 2003; Valdez 2007; Vigil 2008; Zatz and Portillos 2000). Studies of seriously disruptive, delinquent, justice- and/or gang-involved girls routinely illustrate more severe background challenges compared to similarly situated boys (e.g., Chesney-Lind and Shelden 1998; Loeber et al. 2013); Moore (1991), for example, reveals males more often came from 'conventional' working class families, while females came from lower class, chaotic homes characterized by unemployment, addiction, arrests, gang member siblings (often brothers), abuse, physical handicap, chronic illness, and/or death. Thus, one apparent gender difference is simply the greater accumulation of risk in the backgrounds of young women for which gangs provide resiliency and resistance. Yet, we argue, it is not simply a matter of magnitude differences, but also different factors that might set gendered pathways.

Some scholars have theorized a child abuse/childhood trauma pathway to gang involvement for females. Indeed, sexual abuse as a contributing factor to gang involvement figures in many studies of female gang members. For example, Moore's (1991) study found that nearly one-third of gang-involved females had been sexually abused by a family member, while Miller's (2001) study of female gang members in Columbus and St. Louis found that over one-half had been sexually assaulted, with two-thirds of assaults occurring in family contexts. As a result of these harms, and in combination with other family problems and dangers, girls started spending time away from home, even running away, attempting to avoid victimization and meet their needs elsewhere. Gilman and colleagues (2016) also substantiate childhood sexual abuse and harsh punishment as correlated with females' later gang involvement.

Research indicates that while females and males experience physical and emotional abuse and neglect at similar rates, females are much more likely to be sexually abused; abuse often occurs in broader contexts of troubled home environments that include issues such as parental conflict and alcohol/drug use, making it difficult to isolate the specific effects of abuse (Ireland, Smith, and Walter 2015; Widom 2014). A possible pathway may be through relationships between childhood sexual abuse, conduct disorder, and PTSD (Bernhard et al. 2016; Maniglio 2015).[10] Specifically, in tumultuous households, girls who are sexually abused (in itself devaluing of female identity) may be likely to engage in disruptive behavior (contrasting with gender ideals) which can lead to coercive, harsh, and/or rejecting parental reactions that, coupled with lack of trauma supports, can have cascading consequences. Consequences depend upon interactions between appraisals (by self and others), developmental tasks to which appraisals are applied, coping strategies, and environmental buffers (Finkelhor and Kendall-Tackett 1997; see too Agnew 2001).

Determining whether sexual abuse provides a gender-specific pathway for females requires prospective, comparative analyses, as other studies show that male gang members' pasts can include such experiences (e.g., Brotherton and Barrios 2004; Decker and Van Winkle 1996; Hagedorn 1998; Joe and Chesney-Lind 1995). Victimization is part of the picture in explaining females' gang involvement, but caution is warranted to avoid assumptions that sexual abuse leads directly and definitively to girls' gang joining. Such a linear path fails to account for structural or intersectional constraints, females' agency, variations in resources, and the facts that most females who experience childhood trauma do *not* engage in later deviance, that it is not the *only* contributor to later deviance, and that it is an influencing factor for males as well (Belknap and Holsinger 2006; Chesney-Lind 2015; Kruttschnitt 2016; Widom 2014). Females' resources in response to maltreatment vary, sometimes in ways that are raced and classed[11]; Schaffner (2006) argues that while risks and rates of gendered victimization are high among all females, middle-class females may be more likely than lower class females to have access to friends' homes, therapy, and medications for safety and healing. In cases such as these, social class can inhibit gang joining when girls' needs can be met utilizing other resources. Hawkins et al.'s (2009) study of protective factors found that for girls who had been physically abused in childhood, the presence of a caring adult decreased rates of gang membership to a greater extent than for girls not physically abused. And, differential responses to abuse, such as depression and/or anger's interactions with gender to produce delinquency[12] or other forms of coping (De Coster and Zito 2010; Posick, Farrell, and Swatt 2013), are affected by race and class and can influence a trajectory or pathway to gang membership.

We also argue that conceptions of gang involvement as a *maladaptive* response to childhood traumas may be misguided: while females in Nurge and Shively's (2008) study had PTSD and flashbacks from the abuse they experienced, their gang involvement was therapeutic, as they were able to share their experiences with other girls and gain empathy and support. (Such adaptations are likely less common among young men, who are not socialized to share emotion or to disclose abuse.) Further, young women described their gangs as empowering: providing excitement, diversionary activities, and importantly, feelings of being in control, power, respect, and status. Similarly, home-leaving and gang life, while simultaneously offering subsistence challenges, can be freeing and empowering for bisexual and transgender young women who feel they can finally live their lives free from their families' prejudices and abuses (Totten 2012).

Schools

The extent to which schools provide a safe environment and meaningful education varies tremendously, and for many, school is a 'bourgeois institution' that reinforces dominant values and fails to recognize and appreciate youths' raced, classed, and cultural histories (Brotherton and Barrios 2004; Garot 2010; Miranda 2003; Vigil 1999; Zatz and Portillos 2000). From a multiracial feminist perspective, we need also consider that schools are gendered and heteronormative in organization and expectations (Chesney-Lind 2015; Fleisher 2009; Johnson 2008; Jones 2009; Vigil 2002, 2008; Zatz and Portillos 2000), resulting in microaggressions and overt aggressions based on gender, race, sexuality, and other multiplicative characteristics.

For instance, young women of color can be subject to stereotyping by teachers, who dismiss them based on gendered/racial/ethnic typescripts (such as 'not likely to succeed/lacks ability'; 'will end up pregnant'), and subsequent educational neglect can result in poorer academic performance and commitment[13] (Brotherton and Barrios 2004; Chesney-Lind 2015; Fleisher 2009; Jones 2009; Mendoza-Denton 2008). As well, gender typescripts in their home lives can conflict with females' school life and create additional challenges: in addition to difficulty completing homework in crowded, noisy, and chaotic households and getting enough sleep and sustenance to function well, females often have additional caregiving responsibilities in the home (such as looking after parents, younger siblings, or other family members) that reduce available time for school endeavors (Brotherton and Barrios 2004; Miranda 2003; Vigil 2008). Regarding gendered or sexualized harassment in underfunded and struggling schools, urban African-American young women 'described most teachers as ineffectual or unconcerned' with it, and they were pessimistic about the abilities of school personnel and programs to make lasting impacts in preventing such violence (Miller 2008, 104). Degrading, isolating, and/or neglectful treatment from others, such as school officials and peers, affects perspectives of self, values, goals, and identities, and this is especially the case when such treatment is based on ascribed characteristics (Agnew 2001). As illustrated in other sections, females' cognitive, emotional, and behavioral strategies in response to these experiences can differ from males' (and also according to intersectional identities that structure various coping resources).

Females who identify as LGBT can be alienated or worse at school, as at home, feeling a lack of 'goodness of fit', safety, and support (Grossman et al. 2009). Feeling unsafe and unprotected (related to gang membership in studies by Dukes, Martinez, and Stein 1997; Lenzi et al. 2014; Stretesky and Pogrebin 2007) can lead to defensive weapon-carrying and/or school avoidance, bringing girls up against school 'zero tolerance' and attendance policies that further marginalize them (Chesney-Lind and Shelden 1998; Fleisher 2009; Miranda 2003; Steffensmeier et al. 2005). For females who are devalued and lack supports by school personnel, who experience unchecked bullying and sexual harassment, and for LGBT youth for whom school is an unsafe environment, leaving school (normally a 'risk factor') can be a resilient strategy to keep themselves safe (DiFulvio 2015). Joining together with similarly marginalized others can be conceptualized as a resilient resistance strategy, as highlighted by Johnson (2008) who traces the multiplicative intersections of gender, race, class, and sexual orientation in shaping the formation of 'Dykes Taking Over'. DTO was a gang formed by black lesbian students in response to their experiences of sexual-orientation-based harassment in an inner city Philadelphia school. Enactment of resistance identities by young women can entail additional stigmatization, even before joining their gangs, resulting in rejection by peers (which can have greater effects for females than males) and disdain from adults that can push them closer to gang involvement.

Peers

Friendship networks become an increasingly important aspect of life as youth reach adolescence, and friends' involvement in or support of gang life is influential in their exposure, opportunities, and decisions (Huizinga et al. 2005; Peterson, Taylor, and Esbensen 2004; Thornberry et al. 2003). The extent to which the gang is an actual and perceived available option varies by the interplay of structural inequalities, proximal spheres, and intersectional identities that constrain choice. Young people may join other types of groups they believe can provide them with identity and resources and to which they have access. Yet, it is sometimes an issue of opportunity, including the role of reciprocity by which both individuals and groups have agency to choose their associations (Densley 2015; Garot 2015); 'We don't take everybody,' one female gang member exclaimed in Harris' study (1994, 292). From a multiracial feminist perspective, 'gang member' is not necessarily a master status or necessarily consistent or constant for young people, and enactment of gang identity is situational and even performative (Brotherton and Barrios 2004; Garot 2010, 2015; Katz and Jackson-Jacobs 2004). Youth may only identify as a 'gang' in the absence of another suitable cultural referent (Panfil 2017), and gangs are not the only peer groups they may value. A multiracial feminist perspective, we argue, can also help us understand variation in when, why, and under what circumstances gang identity matters and is 'invoked' (Garot 2015).

For instance, there is some evidence of gendered patterns that replicate gendered socialization, such as females attaching more importance to social or relational aspects of their gangs as providing 'sisterhood,' 'belonging,' and/or 'family,' and males viewing gangs in more instrumental terms as a context for acquisition of material goods or respect/status (Campbell 1984; Esbensen, Deschenes, and Winfree 1999; Joe and Chesney-Lind 1995; Miller 2001). In addition to providing pulls to gangs, interactions with peers can also provide gender-specific pushes. Relational problems with peers can be particularly distressing for females – an issue of moderating factors, not necessarily differential exposure (Vigil 2008; Warr 2002). Experiencing rejection by school-based peers, repeated indirect bullying, or peer victimization can lead young women, even more than young men, to seek or form alternative peer groups, including gangs such as DTO, for support, protection, and identity construction (Carbone-Lopez, Esbensen, and Brick 2010; Dishion, Nelson, and Yasui 2005; Farmer and Hairston 2013; Gilman et al. 2016; Johnson 2008). Gendered mechanisms linking the effects of peers on gang involvement may also be at work: while attachments to alternative (deviant) peers can increase both females' and males' deviance, Heimer (1996) found this was through more deviant attitudes for males, but through endorsement of fewer gender definitions for females. The examples we evaluate here suggest that cultural or gendered resistance is especially salient for young women who join gangs, vs. young men who may be resisting middle-class values.

In addressing McGloin and DiPietro's (2012, 300, emphases in original) exhortation to determine '*which* peers are influential, *why*, and *under what circumstances*,' and drawing from our multiracial feminist framework, we must avoid heteronormative assumptions about romantic and sexual interests and recognize that societal gendered expectations are reproduced in peer groups and interactions (Panfil and Peterson 2015). Much of the literature around females' behavior links their deviance to associations with and influence of males, in many cases as romantic and/or sexual partners, and ignores females' agency and identities. And, indeed, even heterosexual young women have varying opinions about the relative necessity of young men and/or sexual autonomy in their lives; such attitudes are also shaped by race/ethnicity and culture, and have implications for the types of gangs young women join (Moore and Hagedorn 1999). Acknowledging females' own perspectives is essential, as these examples illustrate.

Micro-level: identity, constrained choice, and situated action

Micro-level considerations are structured by and interactional with each of the macro- and meso-level factors and intersections described above. As demonstrated throughout, within our multiracial feminist framework, we assert how interlocking inequalities and intersectional identities produce constrained choice and situated action (De Coster and Heimer 2017; Messerschmidt 1997; Pauwels and Hardyns 2016; Wood and Alleyne 2010). However, multiplicative identities also allow for agency. These overarching elements of intersectional identity are inseparable from and thus have been woven through our discussions of macro- and meso-level elements. Gangs can be sites for identity construction of various forms.

Identity development is a salient process in adolescence, as young people negotiate neighborhood, family, school, and peer group expectations. As we have argued, females must also sift through societal and cultural scripts regarding femininity, female gender roles, sexual orientation, and gender identity in shaping identities that represent their authentic selves. Social identity theories, and particularly uncertainty-identity theory (Hogg 2000, 2016), argue that individuals seek group membership to reduce feelings of uncertainty, anxiety, and lack of control regarding their place in the social world (such as when individuals' feelings, attitudes, beliefs, and behaviors are incongruent with those around them) and that greater uncertainty is associated with greater likelihood of associating with groups that are more 'distinctive,' offering clear and strongly identifiable group norms, values, and behaviors.

While some social psychological concepts and propositions have been included in gang theorizing, a few scholars (e.g., Goldman, Giles, and Hogg 2014; Vasquez, Lickel, and Hennigan 2010; Wood 2014) have made explicit applications of social identity theory to gang affiliation and violence. Hennigan and Spanovic (2012) theorized and found that stronger social (gang) identity is related to positive self-esteem, uncertainty reduction, and needs fulfillment, as well as adoption of in-group expectations of attitudes and behaviors (ideas also captured to an extent in Wood and Alleyne's [2010] inclusion of social cognitions and their influence on peer selection). As demonstrated through examples in prior sections, females may feel uncertainty about their identities and their place in contextual realms offering devaluing messages about femininity and females' roles in society; males' roles are conversely more culturally valued.

Applying a multiracial feminist perspective, females' intersectional identities further complicate messages about 'appropriate' ways of being, placing their feelings, attitudes, and behaviors in direct contrast; for these young women, self-categorization as part of a 'gang' can provide positive self- and social-identity, self-enhancement, a space for resistance against gendered expectations, and a resilient site of empowerment (Fishman 1999; Garot 2015; Lauderback, Hansen, and Waldorf 1992; Mendoza-Denton 2008; Miller 2002; Moore and Hagedorn 1999; Taylor 1993; Venkatesh 1998; Young and Brotherton 2014). A multiracial feminist framework incorporating social identity theory helps illustrate contrasts between young women and young men, who arguably have other social and cultural routes to status and empowerment, and also helps us understand variations among seemingly similarly situated young women. Miller (2001) interviewed young women who experienced seeing gangs in their communities and/or homes, conflict and chaos within their home lives, and/or abuse and neglect, yet who were not self-identified gang members. These young women, for a variety of reasons (including self-reliance, freedom, and individuality), viewed themselves as not the 'kind of person' to join a gang. Hogg (2000) argues that contextual uncertainty plays a role in which groups become salient, in line with Densley's (2015, 243) observation that 'not all young people covet the services gangs supposedly provide.' Young women may also choose gangs knowing that gangs cannot cure the other problems they face. One constrained choice observed for females of Puerto Rican and Dominican heritage was to 'remain outside the group and face ethnic discrimination or join the group and face gender discrimination' (Salazar, in Brotherton and Barrios 2004, 194).

Patriarchy prescribes hegemonic and heteronormative femininity for females, and intersections such as culture, race/ethnicity, and class produce constraining local femininities; however, for some, hegemonic femininity is immaterial in their worldviews or conceptions of self, and we should recognize such variations to avoid making unwarranted assumptions. The effects of culture, religion, and associated gendered traditions and expectations are all partially dependent on young women's acceptance and 'buy-in.' For example, females in Schaffner's (2006) study did not see their aggressive behavior or gang involvement as 'out of the norm,' and self-described *cholas* displayed to Mendoza-Denton (1996) that they had no desire to engage in hegemonic feminine beauty ideals, and instead contradicted them. For these young women, hegemonic femininity was unimportant and inconsequential. This alone may help explain why females might become gang involved, while young men who do not buy into hegemonic masculinity would avoid gang membership. Finally, we should remain aware that some individuals (or cultures) do not identify with binary gender constructs, such as social identities like 'girl/boy' or gendered pronouns (she/he), and instead incorporate various elements into an agender or gender fluid identity and presentation of self (Ford 2015). This further complicates our understandings of how a lack of gender or the performance of multiple genders may influence behavior, but can still be explored through a multiracial feminist framework.

Thinking about pathways

To summarize and illustrate potential pathways that could be extrapolated from and explored with our conceptual model, we include Figure 2, which exemplifies a meso-level pathway derived from examples presented in the previous sections. Societal and cultural contexts, such as patriarchy and heteronormativity, devalue femininity and being female. Experiences in homes and schools illustrate this devaluing of identity. For example, adherence to rigid gender ideals can manifest in acts such as coercive discipline or child abuse. Similar structural contexts, such as racism and capitalism, inhibit the ability of young women to regain 'value' through formal means. Specifically, they are prevented from gaining status in normative ways, even when cultural standards provide some flexibility for gender performance. Gangs, when available, become an avenue to empowerment (especially if other peer groups are unavailable), as a way to respond to and/or resist these forces. Gang membership may appear the most attractive option even when it mirrors the above processes.

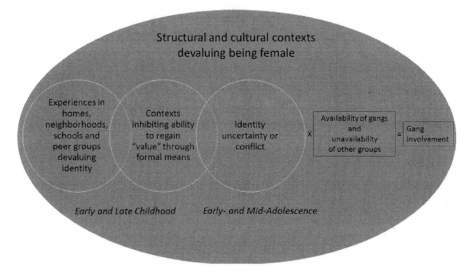

Figure 2. Potential general pathway.

This meso-level pathway provides insight into the many potential micro-level pathways illustrated above. One pathway especially suited to a multiracial feminist framework relates to gender schemas and gender socialization (Figure 3). Socialization plays a large part in conveying gender norms and expectations in infancy and early childhood, when children develop the cognitive capacity to understand gender and act and react accordingly, including categorization of self and others. Aspects such as race/ethnicity, culture, and religion shape transmission of gender ideals, creating both intra- and inter-gender variation. Family factors such as poor affective bonds, harsh (or permissive) parenting practices, and conflict are associated with children's disruptive and problematic behavior, and may be differentially influential (gendered) in terms of how children react. Young people then must also navigate gendered expectations in schools, neighborhoods, and with peers. For young women, more

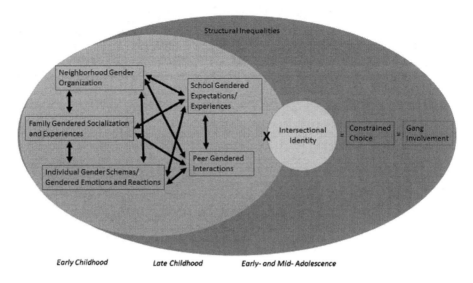

Figure 3. Potential specific pathway.

than young men, gendered school experiences and emotional intimacy to gang-involved or delinquent peers in neighborhoods can propel them toward gangs, which must be both an available outlet and perceived as attractive in light of the gendered meanings a young woman attaches to it and to her prior experiences.

Reflection and discussion

Building on prior feminist scholarship and gang research, we have endeavored to assemble the components necessary for a unified conceptual framework to understand females' gang involvement. We brought together several theoretical frameworks, such as integrated theories of gang membership across the life-course and social identity theories, and combined these with conceptions of gang involvement as sites for resistance and identity construction rather than maladaptive response, as well as attention to situated choice or choice within constraint. Throughout, we have been guided by a multiracial feminist perspective, which focuses on interlocking inequalities and intersectional identities. We are especially committed to challenging damaging assumptions and exploring experiences directly related to gender and sexuality, particularly within the structural contexts of patriarchy and heteronormativity. Because our framework utilizes existing theories and research, we admittedly have not presented something brand new, but instead packaged useful tools in such a way that they can be deployed for nuanced, contextualized, and ethical understandings of females' gang involvement.

While we focus herein on females, this conceptual framework could very well be utilized more broadly, as it is an intersectional framework that would be a useful starting point to bring humane understanding of the experiences and subsequent behaviors of *all* persons. However, *applying* the framework we describe will likely bring about understanding of female-specific or gendered pathways to gangs. We propose it with females at the forefront and urge that future theorizing and research that intends to understand their gang involvement do so as well. In addition, though not explicitly discussed, this framework can also be applied to better understand when, why, and under what circumstances 'gang member' identities matter or are invoked; experiences and behaviors during gang affiliation; processes of gang desistance and identity change; and consequences of gang affiliation for developmental/life-course trajectories.

A multiracial feminist framework that embeds interlocking structural inequalities and intersectional identities fits well with other life-course or developmental frameworks, since the latter emphasize: historical context; transitions and trajectories; linked lives (networks, interactions, expectations, reinforcers, inhibitors); and agency. Clearly, these share similarities with our conceptual framework. We have illustrated how early childhood experiences, such as differential gendered socialization, help to structure experiences that can point young women in the direction of gang involvement. For future researchers' consideration, important factors in early childhood could include how gender expectations, racial/cultural differences in parenting practices, and family and community cultural ideals about individualism and communalism all play a role in the socialization of children, setting and resetting trajectories in reciprocal interactions.

We acknowledge that our conceptual framework is not yet a testable theory, and any theories stemming from it would call for the ability to test: developmental/life-course issues, which often entail time-consuming methodological procedures; intersectional experiences, which require consideration at micro, meso, and macro levels; and fluid/performative identities, the richness and nuance of which can sometimes be blunted in the variable construction and data collection processes. Nevertheless, taking these theoretical and methodological components into account is essential to utilize this framework to its maximum potential. Although it is a challenging undertaking, pursuing contexts, mechanisms, and attributed meanings on the various dimensions specified herein is necessary to achieve the equally complex goal of better understanding females' gang involvement.

Notes

1. While the ratio of female-to-male prevalence is 1:2 in general adolescent samples (3–4% of females and 6–8% of males) and 1:1.5 in high-risk samples (11% of females, 16% of males), the proportion of members that is female ranges from about one-fifth to one half, averaging one-third (Esbensen and Carson 2012; Esbensen, Deschenes, and Winfree 1999; Esbensen and Huizinga 1993; Klein and Crawford 1967; Moore 1991; Thornberry et al. 2003).
2. See, for example, Chesney-Lind and Irwin (2013); Mendoza-Denton (1996).
3. So named by Santo, Spiritual Advisor of the Almighty Latin King and Queen Nation.
4. The contradiction of centering the framework on 'females' yet attempting to avoid hegemonic and binary assumptions about gender is readily conceded. Though we understand that this approach places this work in contrast to some critical queer criminological scholarship (Ball 2014), we maintain this focus to provide a bridge to 'orthodox criminology' and to 'complicate criminological theorizing' (Panfil and Miller 2014, 3).
5. See Howell and Griffiths (2016) for an excellent review.
6. Though, a recent study found that of six trajectories identified based on age at onset, stability, and persistence, females were present mostly (though not exclusively) in the Early Adolescence trajectory characterized by onset (mean age 11.6) and desistance in middle school years, with an average duration of 1.39 years (Pyrooz 2014).
7. Clearly not all females in neighborhoods where gangs exist will join those gangs. Gangs also do not solely exist in 'disorganized' neighborhoods (see e.g., Patillo 1998). Additional influences in other realms (families, schools, peers) can insulate, fail to protect, or actively promote gang membership.
8. Although we focus on gendered violence against females, such violence could also be targeted at transgender or gender nonconforming youth or at effeminate young men – anyone who falls outside of our society's strict expectations for gender presentation in public.
9. For an example of gang-involved young gay men who push back against expectations for their gender presentation and sexuality (and the consequences of doing so), see Panfil (2017).
10. Although Maniglio's (2015) meta-analysis did not show the sex abuse-conduct disorder relationship differed by sex, the relationship was stronger for repeated molestation and abuse involving penetration, both of which females experience at higher rates, in addition to higher sex abuse rates overall. And, the meta-analysis by Bernhard et al. (2016) linking trauma, conduct disorder, and PTSD showed females' trauma was more likely than males' to be sexual abuse, and that females compared to males with conduct disorder were at greater risk of developing PTSD.
11. Immigrant status provides another layer of complexity, inhibiting resource access, such as to authorities and institutions, for those without 'legal standing'.
12. In several places, we draw from the delinquency literature on nuanced gendered effects to help build our argument because such examinations are largely lacking in the gang literature. We reiterate our caveat that being gang-involved is not synonymous with being crime-involved (in fact, some gang members are involved in little or no delinquency), so drawing from delinquency or violence pathways literature should be done with caution until gang research can substantiate similar patterns.

13. Quantitative studies suggest differential effects of school factors by sex, such as low school commitment and educational expectations being associated only or more strongly with females' gang joining (Bjerregaard and Smith 1993; Esbensen and Deschenes 1998; Esbensen et al. 2010), effects we argue are produced by these underlying gendered processes. In future research, a multiracial feminist framework could help go beyond constructs such as school attachment or commitment by measuring experiences within school in ways that explicate the *meanings* of those experiences and *how they lead to* school attachment or commitment (or lack thereof).

Acknowledgments

The authors wish to express their gratitude to Buddy Howell, Marv Krohn, Mike Leiber, and the anonymous reviewers for their valuable feedback on prior versions.

Disclosure statement

No potential conflict of interest was reported by the authors.

References

Agnew, Robert. 2001. "Building on the Foundation of General Strain Theory: Specifying the Types of Strain Most Likely to Lead to Crime and Delinquency." *Journal of Research in Crime & Delinquency* 38: 319–361.
Alexander, Michelle. 2010. *The New Jim Crow: Mass Incarceration in the Age of Colorblindness*. New York: The New Press.
Alonso, Alex A. 2004. "Racialized Identities and the Formation of Black Gangs in Los Angeles." *Urban Geography* 25: 658–674.
Ball, Matthew. 2014. "What's Queer about Queer Criminology?" In *Handbook of LGBT Communities, Crime, and Justice*, edited by Dana Peterson and Vanessa R. Panfil, 531–555. New York: Springer.
Belknap, Joanne, and Kristi Holsinger. 2006. "The Gendered Nature of Risk Factors for Delinquency." *Feminist Criminology* 1: 48–71.
Bernhard, Anka, Anne Martinelli, Katharina Ackermann, Daniel Saure, and Christine M. Freitag. 2016. "Association of Trauma, Posttraumatic Stress Disorder and Conduct Disorder: A Systematic Review and Meta-analysis." *Neuroscience & Biobehavioral Reviews*. OnlineFirst.
Bjerregaard, Beth, and Carolyn Smith. 1993. "Gender Differences in Gang Participation, Delinquency, and Substance Abuse." *Journal of Quantitative Criminology* 9: 329–355.
Broidy, Lisa, and Robert Agnew. 1997. "Gender and Crime: A General Strain Theory Perspective." *Journal of Research in Crime and Delinquency* 34: 275–306.
Brotherton, David. 2015. *Youth Street Gangs: A Critical Appraisal*. New York: Routledge.
Brotherton, David, and Luis Barrios. 2004. *The Almighty Latin King and Queen Nation: Street Politics and the Transformation of a New York City Gang*. New York: Columbia University Press.
Brotherton, David, and Camila Salazar-Atias. 2003. "Amor De Reina! The Pushes and Pulls of Group Membership among the Latin Queens." In *Gangs and Society: Alternative Perspectives*, edited by Louis Kontos, David Brotherton and Luis Barrios, 183–209. New York: Columbia University Press.
Burgess-Proctor, Amanda. 2006. "Intersections of Race, Class, Gender, and Crime: Future Directions for Feminist Criminology." *Feminist Criminology* 1: 27–47.
Campbell, Anne. 1984. *The Girls in the Gang*. Cambridge, MA: Basil Blackwell.
Carbone-Lopez, Kristin, Finn-Aage Esbensen, and Bradley T. Brick. 2010. "The Correlates and Consequences of Peer Victimization: Gender Differences in Direct and Indirect Forms of Bullying." *Youth Violence and Juvenile Justice* 8: 332–350.
Chesney-Lind, Meda. 1989. "Girls' Crime and Woman's Place: Toward a Feminist Model of Female Delinquency." *Crime and Delinquency* 35: 5–29.

Chesney-Lind, Meda. 2015. "Girls and Gangs: Gendered Contexts Gendered Consequences." *Criminologie* 48: 209–236.
Chesney-Lind, Meda, and Katherine Irwin. 2013. *Beyond Bad Girls: Gender, Violence and Hype*. New York: Routledge.
Chesney-Lind, Meda, and Randall G. Shelden. 1998. *Girls, Delinquency, and Juvenile Justice*. 2nd ed. Belmont, CA: West/Wadsworth.
Collins, Patricia Hill. 2000. *Black Feminist Thought: Knowledge, Consciousness, and the Politics of Empowerment*. 2nd ed. New York: Routledge.
Collins, Patricia Hill. 2004. *Black Sexual Politics: African Americans, Gender, and the New Racism*. New York: Routledge.
Connell, R. W. 2005. *Masculinities*. 2nd ed. Berkeley: University of California Press.
Conquergood, Dwight. 1994. "For the Nation! How Street Gangs Problematize Patriotism." In *After Postmodernism: Reconstructing Ideology Critique*, edited by Herbert W. Simons and Michael Billig, 200–221. London: Sage.
Cook, Kimberly J. 2016. "Has Criminology Awakened from Its 'Androcentric Slumber'?" *Feminist Criminology* 11: 334–353.
Daly, Kathleen, and Meda Chesney-Lind. 1988. "Feminism and Criminology." *Justice Quarterly* 5: 497–538.
Decker, Scott H., and Barrik Van Winkle. 1996. *Life in the Gang: Family, Friends, and Violence*. New York: Cambridge University Press.
De Coster, Stacy, and Karen Heimer. 2017. "Choice within Constraint: An Explanation of Crime at the Intersections." *Theoretical Criminology* 21: 11–22.
De Coster, Stacy, and Rena Cornell Zito. 2010. "Gender and General Strain Theory: The Gendering of Emotional Experiences and Expressions." *Journal of Contemporary Criminal Justice* 26: 224–245.
Densley, James A. 2015. "Joining the Gang: A Process of Supply and Demand." In *The Handbook of Gangs*, edited by Scott H. Decker and David C. Pyrooz, 235–256. Oxford: Wiley.
DiFulvio, Gloria T. 2015. "Experiencing Violence and Enacting Resilience: The Case Story of a Transgender Youth." *Violence against Women* 21: 1385–1405.
Dishion, Thomas J., Sara E. Nelson, and Miwa. Yasui. 2005. "Predicting Early Adolescent Gang Involvement from Middle School Adaptation." *Journal of Clinical Child and Adolescent Psychology* 34: 62–73.
Dukes, Richard L., Ruben O. Martinez, and Judith A. Stein. 1997. "Precursors and Consequences of Membership in Youth Gangs." *Youth & Society* 29: 139–165.
Durán, Robert J. 2009. "Legitimated Oppression: Inner-city Mexican American Experiences with Police Gang Enforcement." *Journal of Contemporary Ethnography* 38: 143–168.
Esbensen, Finn-Aage, and Dena C. Carson. 2012. "Who Are the Gangsters? An Examination of Age, Race/Ethnicity, Sex, and Immigration Status of Self-reported Gang Members in a Seven-city Study of American Youth." *Journal of Contemporary Criminal Justice* 28: 465–481.
Esbensen, Finn-Aage, and Elizabeth P. Deschenes. 1998. "A Multisite Examination of Youth Gang Membership: Does Gender Matter?" *Criminology* 36: 799–828.
Esbensen, Finn-Aage, Elizabeth P. Deschenes, and L. Thomas Winfree, Jr. 1999. "Differences between Gang Girls and Gang Boys: Results from a Multi-site Survey." *Youth & Society* 31: 27–53.
Esbensen, Finn-Aage, and David Huizinga. 1993. "Gangs, Drugs, and Delinquency in a Survey of Urban Youth." *Criminology* 31: 565–589.
Esbensen, Finn-Aage, Dana Peterson, Terrance J. Taylor, and Adrienne Freng. 2010. *Youth Violence: Sex and Race Differences in Offending, Victimization, and Gang Membership*. Philadelphia, PA: Temple University Press.
Farmer, Antoinette Y., and Timothy Hairston, Jr. 2013. "Predictors of Gang Membership: Variations across Grade Levels." *Journal of Social Service Research* 39: 530–544.
Finkelhor, David, and Kathy Kendall-Tackett. 1997. "A Developmental Perspective on the Childhood Impact of Crime, Abuse, and Violent Victimization." In *Developmental Perspectives on Trauma: Theory, Research, and Intervention*, edited by Dante Cicchetti and Sheree L. Toth, 1–32. Rochester, NY: University of Rochester Press.
Fishman, Laura T. 1999. "Black Female Gang Behavior: An Historical and Ethnographic Perspective." In *Female Gangs in America: Essays on Girls, Gangs, and Gender*, edited by Meda Chesney-Lind and John M. Hagedorn, 64–84. Chicago, IL: Lake View Press.
Fleisher, Mark. 1998. *Dead End Kids: Gang Girls and the Boys They Know*. Madison: University of Wisconsin Press.
Fleisher, Mark. 2009. "Coping with Macro-structural Adversity: Chronic Poverty, Female Youth Gangs, and Cultural Resistance in a US African-American Urban Community." *Journal of Contingencies and Crisis Management* 17: 274–284.
Ford, Tyler. 2015. "My Life without Gender: 'Strangers Are Desperate to Know What Genitalia I Have'." *The Guardian*, August 7. https://www.theguardian.com/world/2015/aug/07/my-life-without-gender-strangers-are-desperate-to-know-what-genitalia-i-have.
Frederick, Tyler. 2014. "Diversity at the Margins: The Interconnections between Homelessness, Sex Work, Mental Health, and Substance Use in the Lives of Sexual Minority Young People." In *Handbook of LGBT Communities, Crime, and Justice*, edited by Dana Peterson and Vanessa R. Panfil, 473–501. New York, NY: Springer.
Freng, Adrienne, and Finn-Aage Esbensen. 2007. "Race and Gang Affiliation: An Examination of Multiple Marginality." *Justice Quarterly* 24: 600–628.
Garot, Robert. 2010. *Who You Claim: Performing Gang Identity in School and on the Streets*. New York: New York University Press.
Garot, Robert. 2015. "Gang-banging as Edgework." *Dialectical Anthropology* 39: 151–163.

Gilman, Amanda B., Karl G. Hill, J. David Hawkins, James C. Howell, and Rick Kosterman. 2014. "The Developmental Dynamics of Joining a Gang in Adolescence: Patterns and Predictors of Gang Membership." *Journal of Research on Adolescence* 24: 204–219.

Gilman, Amanda B., James C. Howell, Alison E. Hipwell, and Stephanie D. Stepp. 2016. "The Reciprocal Relationship between Gang Involvement and Victimization by Peers: Finding from the Pittsburgh Girls Study." *Journal of Developmental and Life-Course Criminology*, Online. doi:10.1007/s40865-016-0046-1.

Goldman, Liran, Howard Giles, and Michael A. Hogg. 2014. "Going to Extremes: Social Identity and Communication Processes Associated with Gang Membership." *Group Processes & Intergroup Relations* 17: 813–832.

Grossman, Arnold H., Adam P. Haney, Perry Edwards, Edward J. Alessi, Maya Ardon, and Tamika Jarrett Howell. 2009. "Lesbian, Gay, Bisexual and Transgender Youth Talk about Experiencing and Coping with School Violence: A Qualitative Study." *Journal of LGBT Youth* 6 (1): 24–46.

Hagan, John, Klaus Boehnke, and Hans Merkens. 2004. "Gender Differences in Capitalization Processes and the Delinquency of Siblings in Toronto and Berlin." *British Journal of Criminology* 44: 659–676.

Hagan, John, John Simpson, and A. R. Gillis. 1987. "Class in the Household: A Power-control Theory of Gender and Delinquency." *American Journal of Sociology* 92: 788–816.

Hagedorn, John M. 1998. *People and Folks: Gangs, Crime, and the Underclass in a Rustbelt City*. 2nd ed. Chicago, IL: Lake View Press.

Halim, May Ling, Kristina M. Zosuls, Diane N. Ruble, Catherine S. Tamis-LeMonda, Seunghee Amy Baeg, Abigail S. Walsh, and Keith H. Moy. 2016. "Children's Dynamic Gender Identities: Cognition, Context, and Culture." In *Child Psychology: A Handbook of Contemporary Issues*. 3rd ed, edited by Lawrence Balter and Catherine S. Tamis-LeMonda, 193–218. New York: Psychology Press/Taylor & Francis.

Harris, Mary G. 1994. "Cholas, Mexican-American Girls, and Gangs." *Sex Roles* 30: 289–301.

Hawkins, Stephanie R., Phillip W. Graham, Jason Williams, and Margaret A. Zahn. 2009. *Resilient Girls – Factors That Protect against Delinquency*. Washington, DC: Office of Juvenile Justice and Delinquency Prevention.

Heimer, Karen. 1996. "Gender, Interaction, and Delinquency: Testing a Theory of Differential Social Control." *Social Psychology Quarterly* 59: 39–61.

Heimer, Karen, and Stacy De Coster. 1999. ""The Gendering of Violent Delinquency." *Criminology* 37: 277–318.

Hennigan, Karen, and Marija Spanovic. 2012. "Gang Dynamics through the Lens of Social Identity Theory." In *Youth Gangs in International Perspective: Findings from the Eurogang Program*, edited by Finn-Aage Esbensen and Cheryl L. Maxson, 127–149. New York: Springer.

Hipwell, Alison, Kate Keenan, Kristen Kasza, Rolf Loeber, Magda Stouthamer-Loeber, and Tammy Bean. 2008. "Reciprocal Influences between Girls' Conduct Problems and Depression, and Parental Punishment and Warmth: A Six Year Prospective Analysis." *Journal of Abnormal Child Psychology* 36: 663–677.

Hogg, Michael A. 2000. "Subjective Uncertainty Reduction through Self-categorization: A Motivational Theory of Social Identity Processes." *European Review of Social Psychology* 11: 223–255.

Hogg, Michael A. 2016. "Social Identity Theory." In *Understanding Peace and Conflict through Social Identity Theory: Contemporary Global Perspectives*, edited by Shelley McKeown, Reeshma Haji and Neil Ferguson, 3–17. New York: Springer.

Holsinger, Kristi, and Alexander M. Holsinger. 2005. "Differential Pathways to Violence and Self-injurious Behavior: African American and White Girls in the Juvenile Justice System." *Crime & Delinquency* 42: 211–242.

Howell, James C. 2009. *Preventing and Reducing Juvenile Delinquency: A Comprehsive Framework*. 2nd ed. Thousand Oaks, CA: Sage.

Howell, James C. 2012. *Gangs in America's Communities*. Thousand Oaks, CA: Sage.

Howell, James C., and Arlen Egley, Jr. 2005. "Moving Risk Factors into Developmental Theories of Gang Membership." *Youth Violence and Juvenile Justice* 3: 334–354.

Howell, James C., and Elizabeth Griffiths. 2016. *Gangs in America's Communities*. 2nd ed. Thousand Oaks, CA: Sage.

Huizinga, David, Linda Cunningham, Amanda Elliott, Kimberly Henry, and Kate Johnson. 2005. "How Do I Get in? What Have I Joined? And, How Do I Get out? Joining, Leaving, and the Structure of Gangs." Paper presented at the annual meeting of the American Society of Criminology, Toronto, Canada, November.

Huizinga, David, Shari Miller, and the Conduct Problems Prevention Research Group. 2013. *Developmental Sequences of Girls' Delinquent Behavior*. Washington, DC: Girls Study Group, OJJDP.

Hunt, Geoffrey, and Karen Joe-Laidler. 2001. "Situations of Violence in the Lives of Girl Gang Members." *Health Care for Women International* 22: 363–384.

Ireland, Timothy O., Carolyn A. Smith, and Jamie E. Walter. 2015. "Maltreatment and Damaging Outcomes in Adolescence: Longitudinal Research and Policy." In *The Handbook of Juvenile Delinquency and Juvenile Justice*, edited by Marvin D. Krohn and Jodi Lane, 581–600. Malden, MA: Wiley.

Joe, Karen A., and Meda Chesney-Lind. 1995. "Just Every Mother's Angel: An Analysis of Gender and Ethnic Variations in Youth Gang Membership." *Gender & Society* 9: 408–431.

Johansson, Pernilla, and Kimberly Kempf-Leonard. 2009. "A Gender-specific Pathway to Serious, Violent, and Chronic Offending? Exploring Howell's Risk Factors for Serious Delinquency." *Crime and Delinquency* 55: 216–240.

Johnson, Dominique. 2008. "Taking over the School: Student Gangs as a Strategy for Dealing with Homophobic Bullying in an Urban Public School District." *Journal of Gay & Lesbian Social Services* 19: 87–104.

Jones, Nikki. 2009. *Between Good and Ghetto: African American Girls and Inner City Violence*. New Brunswick, NJ: Rutgers University Press.

Jones, Nikki, and Jerry Flores. 2013. "At the Intersections: Race, Gender and Violence." In *Routledge International Handbook of Crime and Gender Studies*, edited by Claire M. Renzetti, Susan L. Miller and Angela R. Gover, 73–84. New York: Routledge.

Katz, Jack, and Curtis Jackson-Jacobs. 2004. "The Criminologists' Gang." In *The Blackwell Companion to Criminology*, edited by Colin Sumner, 91–124. London: Blackwell.

Klein, Malcolm W. 1995. *The American Street Gang: Its Nature, Prevalence, and Control*. New York: Oxford University Press.

Klein, Malcolm W., and Lois Y. Crawford. 1967. "Groups, Gangs, and Cohesiveness." *Journal of Research in Crime and Delinquency* 4: 63–75.

Klein, Malcolm W., and Cheryl L. Maxson. 2006. *Street Gang Patterns and Policies*. New York: Oxford University Press.

Krohn, Marvin D., Nicole M. Schmidt, Alan J. Lizotte, and Julie M. Baldwin. 2011. "The Impact of Multiple Marginality on Gang Membership and Delinquent Behavior for Hispanic, African American, and White Male Adolescents." *Journal of Contemporary Criminal Justice* 27: 18–42.

Kruttschnitt, Candace. 2016. "2015 Presidential Address to the American Society of Criminology: The Politics, and Place, of Gender in Research on Crime." *Criminology* 54: 8–29.

Lauderback, David, Joy Hansen, and Dan Waldorf. 1992. "'Sisters Are Doin' It for Themselves': A Black Female Gang in San Francisco." *The Gang Journal* 1: 57–72.

Lenzi, Michela, Jill Sharkey, Alessio Vieno, Ashley Mayworm, Danielle Dougherty, and Karen Nylund-Gibson. 2014. "Adolescent Gang Involvement: The Role of Individual, Family, Peer, and School Factors in a Multilevel Perspective." *Aggressive Behavior* 41: 386–397.

Loeber, Rolf, Deborah M. Capaldi, and Elizabeth Costello. 2013. "Gender and the Development of Aggression, Disruptive Behavior, and Delinquency from Childhood to Early Adulthood." In *Disruptive Behavior Disorders*, edited by Patrick H. Tolan and Bennett L. Leventhal, 137–160. New York, NY: Springer.

Logan, Laura. 2011. "Violence and Resistance: An Intersectional Study of Lesbians and Queer Women and Street Harassment." Paper presented at the annual meeting of the American Society of Criminology, November.

Macmillan, Ross, and Bill McCarthy. 2014. "Gender and Offending in a Lifecourse Context." In *The Oxford Handbook of Gender, Sex, and Crime*, edited by Rosemary Gartner and Bill McCarthy, 343–361. New York: Oxford University Press.

Maniglio, Roberto. 2015. "Significance, Nature, and Direction of the Association between Child Sexual Abuse and Conduct Disorder: A Systematic Review." *Trauma, Violence, & Abuse* 16: 241–257.

Marshall, Brandon D. L., Kora DeBeck, Annick Simo, Thomas Kerr, and Evan Wood. 2015. "Gang Involvement among Street-Involved Youth in a Canadian Setting: A Gender-Based Analysis." *Public Health* 129 (1): 74–77.

Maxson, Cheryl L., and Monica L. Whitlock. 2002. "Joining the Gang: Gender Differences in Risk Factors for Gang Membership." In *Gangs in America*, 3rd ed., edited by C. Ronald Huff, 19–35. Thousand Oaks, CA: Sage.

McGloin, Jean Marie, and Stephanie DiPietro. 2012. "Girls, Friends and Delinquency." In *The Oxford Handbook of Criminological Theory*, edited by Francis T. Cullen and Pamela Wilcox, 294–312. New York: Oxford University Press.

Mears, Daniel P., Matthew Ploeger, and Mark Warr. 1998. "Explaining the Gender Gap in Delinquency: Peer Influence and Moral Evaluations of Behavior." *Journal of Research in Crime and Delinquency* 35: 251–266.

Mendoza-Denton, Norma. 1996. "'Muy Macha': Gender and Ideology in Gang-girls' Discourse about Makeup." *Ethnos* 61 (1/2): 47–63.

Mendoza-Denton, Norma. 2008. *Homegirls: Language and Cultural Practice among Latina Youth Gangs*. Oxford: Wiley-Blackwell.

Messerschmidt, James. 1997. *Crime as Structured Action: Gender, Race, Class, and Crime in the Making*. Thousand Oaks, CA: Sage.

Miller, Jody. 1998. "Gender and Victimization Risk among Young Women in Gangs." *Journal of Research in Crime and Delinquency* 35: 429–453.

Miller, Jody. 2001. *One of the Guys: Girls, Gangs, and Gender*. New York: Oxford University Press.

Miller, Jody. 2002. "The Strengths and Limits of 'Doing Gender' for Understanding Street Crime." *Theoretical Criminology* 6: 433–460.

Miller, Jody. 2008. *Getting Played: African American Girls, Urban Inequality, and Gendered Violence*. New York: New York University Press.

Miranda, Marie "Keta". 2003. *Homegirls in the Public Sphere*. Austin: University of Texas Press.

Moore, Joan W. 1991. *Going down to the Barrio: Homeboys and Homegirls in Change*. Philadelphia, PA: Temple University Press.

Moore, Joan W., and John M. Hagedorn. 1999. "What Happens to Girls in the Gang?" In *Female Gangs in America: Essays on Girls, Gangs, and Gender*, edited by Meda Chesney-Lind and John M. Hagedorn, 177–186. Chicago, IL: Lake View Press.

Nurge, Dana. 2003. "Liberating Yet Limiting: The Paradox of Female Gang Membership." In *Gangs and Society: Alternative Perspectives*, edited by Louis Kontos, David Brotherton and Luis Barrios, 161–182. New York: Columbia University Press.

Nurge, Dana, and Michael Shively. 2008. "Victimization, Resistance, and Violence: Exploring the Links between Girls in Gangs." In *Globalizing the Streets: Cross-cultural Perspectives on Youth, Social Control, and Empowerment*, edited by Michael Flynn and David C. Brotherton, 147–166. New York: Columbia University Press.

Panfil, Vanessa R. 2014. "Better Left Unsaid? The Role of Agency in Queer Criminological Research." *Critical Criminology* 22: 99–111.

Panfil, Vanessa R. 2017. *The Gang's All Queer: The Lives of Gay Gang Members*. New York: New York University Press.

Panfil, Vanessa R., and Jody Miller. 2014. "Beyond the Straight and Narrow: The Import of Queer Criminology for Criminology and Criminal Justice." *The Criminologist* 39 (4): 1–8.

Panfil, Vanessa R., and Dana Peterson. 2015. "Gender, Sexuality, and Gangs: Re-envisioning Diversity." In *The Handbook of Gangs*, edited by Scott H. Decker and David C. Pyrooz, 208–234. Oxford: Wiley.

Patillo, Mary E. 1998. "Sweet Mothers and Gang-bangers: Managing Crime in a Black Middle-class Neighborhood." *Social Forces* 76: 747–774.

Pauwels, Lieven, and Wim Hardyns. 2016. *Problematic Youth Group Involvement as Situated Choice: Testing an Integrated Condition-Controls-Exposure Model*. The Hague: Eleven International Publishing.

Peterson, Dana. 2009. "The Many Ways of Knowing: Multi-method Comparative Research to Enhance Our Understanding of and Responses to Youth Street Gangs." In *Handbook on Crime and Deviance*, edited by Marvin D. Krohn, Alan J. Lizotte, and Gina Penly Hall, 405–432. New York: Springer.

Peterson, Dana, and Kirstin A. Morgan. 2014. "Sex Differences and the Overlap in Risk Factors for Gang Membership and Violence." *Journal of Crime and Justice* 37: 129–154.

Peterson, Dana, Terrance J. Taylor, and Finn-Aage Esbensen. 2004. "Gang Membership and Violent Victimization." *Justice Quarterly* 21: 793–815.

Portillos, Edwardo Luis. 1999. "Women, Men, and Gangs: The Social Construction of Gender in the Barrio." In *Female Gangs in America: Essays on Girls, Gangs, and Gender*, edited by Meda Chesney-Lind and John M. Hagedorn, 232–244. Chicago, IL: Lakeview Press.

Potter, Hillary. 2015. *Intersectionality and Criminology: Disrupting and Revolutionizing Studies of Crime*. New York: Routledge.

Posick, Chad, Amy Farrell, and Marc L. Swatt. 2013. "Do Boys Fight and Girls Cut? A General Strain Theory Approach to Gender and Deviance." *Deviant Behavior* 34: 685–705.

Pyrooz, David C. 2014. "'From Your First Cigarette to Your Last Dyin' Day': The Patterning of Gang Membership in the Life-Course." *Journal of Quantitative Criminology* 30: 349–372.

Raby, Carlotta, and Fergal Jones. 2016. "Identifying Risks for Male Street Gang Affiliation: A Systematic Review and Narrative Synthesis." *The Journal of Forensic Psychiatry and Psychology* 27: 601–644.

Rosenfield, Sarah, and Dawne Mouzon. 2013. "Gender and Mental Health." In *Handbook of the Sociology of Mental Health*, edited by Carol S. Aneshensel, Jo C. Phelan, and Alex Bierman, 277–296. Dordrecht: Springer.

Rosenfield, Sarah, Julie Phillips, and Helene Raskin White. 2006. "Gender, Race, and the Self in Mental Health and Crime." *Social Problems* 53: 161–185.

Russell, Michael A., Summer J. Robins, and Candice L. Odgers. 2014. "Developmental Perspectives: Sex Differences in Antisocial Behavior from Childhood to Adulthood." In *The Oxford Handbook of Gender, Sex, and Crime*, edited by Rosemary Gartner and Bill McCarthy, 286–315. New York: Oxford University Press.

Savin-Williams, Ritch. 1994. "Verbal and Physical Abuse as Stressors in the Lives of Lesbian, Gay Male, and Bisexual Youths: Associations with School Problems, Running Away, Substance Abuse, Prostitution, and Suicide." *Journal of Consulting and Clinical Psychology* 62: 261–269.

Schaffner, Laurie. 2006. *Girls in Trouble with the Law*. New Brunswick, NJ: Rutgers University Press.

Steffensmeier, Darrell J. 1983. "Organization Properties and Sex-segregation in the Underworld: Building a Sociological Theory of Sex Differences in Crime." *Social Forces* 61: 1010–1032.

Steffensmeier, Darrell, Jennifer Schwartz, Hua Zhong, and Jeff Ackerman. 2005. "An Assessment of Recent Trends in Girls' Violence Using Diverse Longitudinal Sources: Is the Gender Gap Closing?" *Criminology* 43: 355–406.

Stretesky, Paul B., and Mark R. Pogrebin. 2007. "Gang-related Gun Violence: Socialization, Identity, and Self." *Journal of Contemporary Ethnography* 36: 85–114.

Taylor, Carl S. 1993. *Girls, Gangs, Women, and Drugs*. East Lansing: Michigan State University Press.

Thornberry, Terence P., Marvin D. Krohn, Alan J. Lizotte, Carolyn A. Smith, and Kimberly Tobin. 2003. *Gangs and Delinquency in Developmental Perspective*. New York: Cambridge University Press.

Totten, Mark. 2012. "Gays in the Gang." *Journal of Gang Research* 19 (2): 1–24.

Valdez, Avelardo. 2007. *Mexican American Girls and Gang Violence: Beyond Risk*. New York, NY: Palgrave Macmillan.

Vasquez, Eduardo A., Brian Lickel, and Karen Hennigan. 2010. "Gangs, Displaced, and Group-based Aggression." *Aggression and Violent Behavior* 15: 130–140.

Venkatesh, Sudhir A. 1998. "Gender and Outlaw Capitalism: A Historical Account of the Black Sisters United 'Girl Gang.'" *Signs: Journal of Women in Culture and Society* 23: 683–709.

Vigil, James Diego. 1988. *Barrio Gangs: Street Life and Identity in Southern California*. Austin: University of Texas Press.

Vigil, James Diego. 1999. "Streets and Schools." *Harvard Educational Review* 69: 270–289.

Vigil, James Diego. 2002. *A Rainbow of Gangs: Street Cultures in the Mega-city*. Austin: University of Texas Press.

Vigil, James Diego. 2008. "Female Gang Members from East Los Angeles." *International Journal of Social Inquiry* 1 (1): 47–74.

Warr, Mark. 2002. *Companions in Crime: The Social Aspects of Criminal Conduct*. Cambridge: Cambridge University Press.

West, Candace, and Don H. Zimmerman. 1987. "Doing Gender." *Gender & Society* 1: 125–151.

Widom, Cathy Spatz. 2014. "Longterm Consequences of Child Maltreatment." In *Handbook of Child Maltreatment*, edited by Jill E. Korbin and Richard D. Krugman, 225–247. Dordrecht: Springer.

Wing, Adrien Katherine, and Christine A. Willis. 1997. "Critical Race Feminism: Black Women and Gangs." *Journal of Gender, Race & Justice* 1: 141–175.

Wood, Jane L. 2014. "Understanding Gang Membership: The Significance of Group Processes." *Group Process & Intergroup Relations* 17: 710–729.

Wood, Jane L., and Emma Alleyne. 2010. "Street Gang Theory and Research: Where Are We Now and Where Do We Go from Here?" *Aggression and Violent Behavior* 15: 100–111.

Young, Jock, and David C. Brotherton. 2014. "Cultural Criminology and Its Practices: A Dialog between the Theorist and the Street Researcher." *Dialectical Anthropology* 38: 117–132.

Zatz, Marjorie S., and Edwardo L. Portillos. 2000. "Voices from the Barrio: Chicano/A Gangs, Families, and Communities." *Criminology* 38: 369–402.

Zimmerman, Gregory M., and Steven F. Messner. 2010. "Neighborhood Context and the Gender Gap in Adolescent Violent Crime." *American Sociological Review* 75: 958–980.

The practical utility of a life-course gang theory for intervention*

James C. (Buddy) Howell, Margaret J. F. Braun and Paul Bellatty

ABSTRACT

This article presents findings from an exploration of the prospects of applying an empirically supported developmental life-course model of gang involvement to a juvenile justice setting. Our research strategy utilizes risk data from systems that precede or 'feed' criminal justice involvement (e.g., child welfare, family welfare, alcohol and drug treatment, mental health treatment, medical assistance programs, and education) to predict gang joining among 3072 youth placed on probation or committed to incarceration in Oregon. The research process entailed mining proximal indicators of risk factors for gang joining that research has identified in the individual, family, school, peer group, and community sectors of young offenders' lives. A multivariate analysis was carried out to isolate the strongest predictors of gang joining. The analysis explores the practical utility of the Howell and Egley life-course model of gang involvement (from preschool to mid-adolescence), in everyday juvenile justice system practice in a statewide setting. Given our findings, this research could be used to help target delinquency prevention and intervention programs and services, with encouraging prospects for preventing and reducing gang involvement.

Introduction

The immediate purpose of the current study is to investigate empirically based risk factors for gang involvement among juvenile delinquents brought to the attention of juvenile justice system authorities. Our long-term aim is to establish an empirical foundation for the practical purpose of targeting potential and current gang members with prevention and intervention strategies and programs by drawing upon existing Oregon data associated with gang involved juvenile delinquents. We analyzed statewide data that were recorded on juvenile offenders who either were on probation or confined in the Oregon Youth Authority. We also extracted data on this offender group and their families in 'feeder' systems (i.e., welfare, medical assistance programs, mental health treatment, alcohol and drug treatment, foster care, Child Protective Services, and education). Juvenile justice system involvement is a common stage in the life-course of adolescent gang members, as demonstrated statewide in Florida (Baglivio et al. 2014), North Carolina (M. Howell and Lassiter 2011), and among serious juvenile offenders in Phoenix, AZ and Philadelphia, PA (Pyrooz, Sweeten, and Piquero 2013).

---

*The opinions, findings, and conclusions or recommendations expressed in this publication are those of the author(s) and do not necessarily reflect the views of the US Department of Justice nor the Institute for Intergovernmental Research.
This article was originally published with errors. This version has been corrected. Please see Corrigendum (https://doi.org/10.1080/0735648X.2017.1343783).

The present study was guided by research-supported risk factors for gang joining drawn exclusively from rigorous longitudinal studies of representative samples in multiple large cities. Prospective longitudinal studies of gang involvement conducted in the mid-1990s with random samples of children and adolescents in four large US cities – Denver, Colorado (Denver Youth Survey), Rochester, New York (Rochester Youth Development Study), Pittsburgh, Pennsylvania (Pittsburgh Youth Study), and Seattle, Washington (Seattle Social Development Project) – first provided a generalizable set of risk factors for gang joining (Howell and Egley 2005). Risk factors compiled from these and other high quality studies over the ensuing decade recently yielded an up-to-date listing of research-supported predictors of gang involvement (Raby and Jones 2016). Like other adolescent problem behaviors, gang involvement commences gradually over time, owing mainly to accumulating risk exposure in the absence of buffering strengths (commonly called protective or promotive factors) (Howell and Egley 2005) – and gang life is often a chosen pathway because of the perceived benefits of gang joining (Esbensen, Deschenes, and Winfree 1999). Vigil (2002) explains that what established gangs in the neighborhood can offer is nurturing or emotional support, protection, friendship, and other ministrations for unattended resident youths.

Risk factors for gang involvement

It is well-established in research that risk factors for juvenile delinquency, gang involvement, and other adolescent problem behaviors typically operate in four distinctive ways over the life-course. First, these have a cumulative impact; that is, the greater the number of risk factors the youth experiences, the greater the likelihood of gang involvement. In the first life-course gang study, undertaken in Seattle (Hill et al. 1999), children under the age of 12 who evidenced as many as 7 of 19 measured risk factors were 13 times more likely to join a gang than children with none or only one risk factor. In this study, risk factors measured at ages 10–12 predicted gang joining at ages 13–18. The multi-site G.R.E.A.T. survey (Esbensen et al. 2009) revealed a similar dynamic relationship beyond the accumulation of six of the particular risk factors identified in that study.

Second, the presence of risk factors in multiple developmental domains and the interaction of these further enhance the likelihood of gang membership. Consistent with developmental criminology research on children and adolescents, risk factors for gang membership are found in several interacting domains, including individual, family, peer, school, and neighborhood, and considerable gang research shows that certain domains are more influential in various developmental stages in childhood and adolescence (Howell and Egley 2005). In the Rochester study, the *interaction* of risk factors across domains produced the greatest risk of gang membership. A majority (61%) of the boys and 40% of the girls who had elevated scores in all measured risk factor domains eventually joined gangs (Thornberry et al. 2003). Recent research on the Seattle sample demonstrated that neighborhood and peer antisocial environments along with gang exposure (living with a gang member) most strongly predicted gang joining (Gilman, Hill, Hawkins, Howell et al. 2014).

Third, risk factors can have life-course effects, extending from early childhood onward into the adult stage of life. Gilman, Hill, and Hawkins (2014) found that the effects of gang membership extended well into adulthood (age 33). Compared to their non-gang peers, gang membership in childhood and early adolescence predicted lower rates of high school graduation, poor general health, depression, drug abuse or dependence, self-reported crime, official felony conviction, and incarceration in adulthood.

Fourth, up to a given threshold, risk factors for general delinquency and gang involvement are similar. As youth accumulate more risk factors, they are more likely to become involved with gangs as opposed to less violent delinquent groups. For example, in the G.R.E.A.T. multi-city study of middle school students, Esbensen and colleagues (2009) demonstrate that, as youth accumulated additional risk factors, they were more likely to become involved with gangs as opposed to violence (52% of gang members experienced 11 or more risk factors, compared with 36% of violent offenders); 'that is, it takes a greater push for youths to become gang-involved than violence-involved' (327). As further evidence of this observation, sizeable proportions of youth joined gangs in Seattle (15%), Denver (17%), Pittsburgh (24%), and Rochester, NY (32%) in the 1990s (Esbensen and Huizinga 1993; Hill et al. 1999; Lahey et al. 1999; Thornberry et al. 2003), in comparison with the national average, just 8% (Pyrooz 2014).

A life-course developmental model of gang involvement

A substantial body of research shows that gang joining is a life-course social developmental process (Howell and Egley 2005; Krohn and Thornberry 2008; Raby and Jones 2016).

Moreover, considerable evidence suggests that the progression toward gang joining typically begins very early in life (Howell and Egley 2005). The continuous influence of risk and protective factors at certain developmental stages is illustrated in Figure 1, the top section of which shows the developmental stages in which clusters of risk factors influence gang joining – beginning with community, family, and child characteristics in the preschool period.[1] At birth – or beginning in the prenatal period for some infants who experience birthing complications – the biological family is the central influence and remains so throughout infancy and early childhood. Family, school, and peer influences continue from childhood to young adulthood, although family influences gradually fade as friends become more important. In addition, individual characteristics and community factors can come into play at any point during childhood and adolescence.[2]

A lack of buffering strengths or 'protective' factors also contributes to a young person's risk of gang involvement. Protective factors have been described as having dual functions, both insulating persons from risk and reducing the negative impacts of risk factors (Howell, Lipsey, and Wilson 2014). Considerable research shows that in extremely high-risk conditions, youth need more than a simple majority of protective or promotive factors to overcome multiple sources of risk. Just two rigorous studies to date have examined the long-term effects of protective factors against gang involvement. The first such study found research support for protective factors in the major developmental domains from the 5th to 12th grades: prosocial family, school, neighborhood, peer environments, and individual

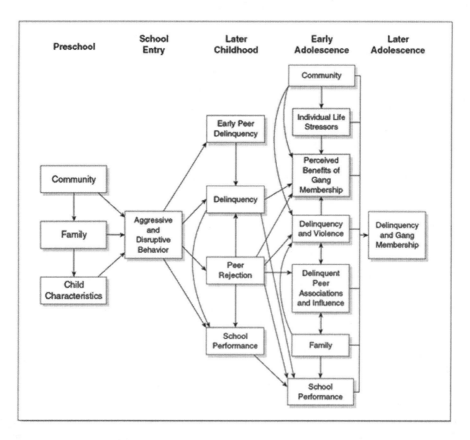

Figure 1. A developmental model of gang involvement. Source: Howell and Griffiths 2016, 105. Copyrighted by Sage Publications, Inc. Used with permission.

characteristics (Gilman Hill, Hawkins, Howell et al. 2014). Not living with a gang member was a key protective factor. Research in the Rochester Youth Developmental study (Krohn et al. 2014) finds that, from mid-adolescence onward, six protective factors reduced violent events (i.e., gang fighting) and weapon use (i.e., gun carrying) including: (1) cumulative protection across domains, (2) cumulative protection in the family domain, (3) educational aspirations and (4) self-esteem in the individual domain, and (5) parental supervision and (6) parent partner status in the family domain.

Howell and Egley (2005) initially identified 46 risk factors for gang joining that were drawn exclusively from longitudinal studies.[3] A decade later, a systematic review (Raby and Jones 2016) of 102 longitudinal and cross-sectional studies (that met certain restrictive criteria for inclusion) substantiated Howell and Egley's compilation of risk factors for gang joining, encompassing the family, individual, school, peer, and community domains of children and adolescent's lives; also across developmental domains in the life-course from preschool to adolescence. Although the developmental domains apply to girls as well as boys, there is far less empirical support for female-specific risk factors, and there is the prospect of a reciprocal relationship between girls' gang involvement and peer victimization across adolescence (Gilman et al. 2016).

Howell and Egley's (2005) life-course developmental model of gang involvement spans four stages: preschool, school entry, childhood, and adolescence (Figure 1). Succinctly stated, preschool factors predict early child conduct problems such as aggressive and disruptive behavior upon school entry, and these problem behaviors, in turn, predict childhood delinquency that – combined with risk factors in other developmental domains – increases the probability of delinquent activity and gang involvement during late childhood and adolescence. The influence of risk factors for delinquency varies with age, and by the time youths enter high school, most of the risk factors affecting gang involvement will have been established. Raby and Jones (2016) systematic review of risk factors for gang joining drawn from longitudinal studies generally substantiates Howell and Egley's four developmental age periods as well as their compilation of associated risk factors, while also identifying several other predictors that have received some research support, including developmental trauma. The distinct developmental stages of influence for gang joining specified by Howell and Egley (2005) follow.

Preschool period

Immediately prior to school entry (at ages 3–5), children who later join gangs are often living in a single parent household, with low parental education and poor child supervision – perhaps growing up in foster care – and frequently victims of abuse and neglect (Hamoudi et al. 2015); and these forms of victimization are linked with gang joining (Raby and Jones 2016). Developmental trauma exposure related to family violence is not an uncommon condition in high-risk communities, and this also is associated with gang joining (Raby and Jones 2016). Vaughn and colleagues (2009) describe a 'severely impaired subgroup' (9.3%) of children (meaning cognitively deficient, and displaying impulsive and externalizing behaviors) in a nationally representative cohort of more than 17,000 kindergartners. Preschool factors predict early child conduct problems such as aggressive and disruptive behavior during school entry, and these problem behaviors predict childhood delinquency, which, coupled with other risk factors in all developmental domains, increases the probability of gang involvement during adolescence (Howell and Egley 2005). Research on the life histories of gang members has consistently revealed family conditions characterized by alcohol and drug abuse, domestic violence, sexual assault and incest, neglect, and broken homes (Fleisher 2000; Moore 1991; Pogarsky, Lizotte, and Thornberry 2003). Again, children who grow up in a single-parent household or foster care and with low parental supervision are vulnerable to gang influences (Hill et al. 1999; Raby and Jones 2016).

School entry

During the elementary school period and onward, the array of risk factors expands, as some children are exposed to negative peer influences outside the home. Growing up in foster care or a single parent household are predictors (Raby and Jones 2016). By the point of school entry (age 6), a host of indicators of unstable families may have come into play as risk factors for gang joining, including multiple changes in caretaker, family poverty or low family socioeconomic status, limited parental education, living with a gang member (siblings or parents), and parents with pro-violent attitudes (Howell and Egley 2005).

Later childhood

In later childhood, notably by ages 10–12, other risk factors that contribute to gang membership begin to emerge, including minor delinquent acts and displays of aggression, which may lead to pro-social peer rejection (Howell and Egley 2005). A school-based study identified current or future gang members among a small subgroup of 'highly rebellious' students (ages 12 and older) who attended the most 'difficult' of 16 French schools – those characterized by greater levels of student victimization, self-reported violence, poor student–teacher relations, and systems of punishment that were not well-accepted by students (Debarbieux and Baya 2008). This core group (4–5% of all students) was responsible for most of the disorder and violence in 16 schools that were studied. The dysfunctional schools contained a significant proportion of gang members – up to 11% of students in the most 'difficult' schools.

Early adolescence

It is in early adolescence (ages 12–17) that future gang members become particularly mobile and participate in more risky behaviors and experience increased exposure to dangerous environments; including general delinquency involvement, alcohol/drug use, illegal gun ownership/carrying, physical violence/aggression, and perhaps violent victimization (Howell and Egley 2005). A youth typically begins hanging out with gang members at age 11 or 12 and joins the gang between ages 12 and 15 (Craig et al. 2002; Esbensen and Huizinga 1993; Hill et al. 1999; Huff 1996, 1998; Pyrooz 2014). Children who are on a trajectory of worsening antisocial behavior are more likely to join gangs during adolescence, and they tend to have more problems than non-gang members (Esbensen et al. 2010; Howell and Egley 2005). Lacourse and colleagues (2006) find associations with delinquent peers increase delinquency and the likelihood and frequency of physical aggression and violence, which in turn increases the likelihood of gang membership in early adolescence. 'For protection' is a major reason that youth give for having joined a gang (Esbensen, Deschenes, and Winfree 1999; Melde, Taylor, and Esbensen 2009).

The present research: applying the developmental life-course model of gang joining in everyday practice

The present analysis explores the practical utility of the Howell–Egley life-course developmental model in everyday juvenile justice system practice. With this goal in mind, statewide administrative data were pulled from Oregon systems that precede or 'criminal justice involvement (e.g., child welfare, welfare, medical assistance programs, alcohol and drug treatment, mental health treatment, and education) to predict gang joining among a large sample ($n = 3072$) of youth committed to juvenile probation or incarceration in the state. The state data provided proximal indicators of risk factors for gang joining that research has identified in the individual, family, school, peer, and community sectors of young offenders' lives. A multivariate analysis was carried out with these indicators to isolate the strongest predictors of gang involvement among young offenders in Oregon. The principal aim of this research is to explore the utility of addressing gang involvement among juvenile justice system clients utilizing readily-available multi-system data. Should this prove useful, and then it may be feasible to tailor prevention and intervention programs that could buffer youth's risk and negative behaviors associated with gang involvement on an ongoing basis, and possibly produce worthwhile benefits in reducing gang-related crime.

Method

Data related to historical individual-level involvement with major human service agencies and education (i.e., 'feeder' systems) were linked together with juvenile justice records for Oregon youth who were committed to state level probation or incarceration between January 2008 and July 2013. Human services data included records dating back to 2000 for out-of-home foster care placements, Child Protective Services, mental health treatment, alcohol and drug treatment, and various subprograms pertaining to welfare (e.g., Supplemental Nutrition Assistance Program, assistance programs for domestic violence survivors and their children, and Temporary Assistance for Needy Families) and medical care assistance (e.g., Medicaid and Children's Health Insurance Program). Data from education covered many aspects of youths' school experiences, such as attendance, test scores, disciplinary incidents, family economic circumstances, participation in special education programs, and limited English proficiency services since the 2004–2005 academic year. Juvenile justice records included history of delinquency referrals to local juvenile departments and type(s) of offense(s) committed since 2000, actuarial estimates of recidivism risk, and dynamic factors influencing delinquent behavior (e.g., attitudes, behaviors, relationships, and use of free time) at the time of commitment.

The extracted data were linked by a third party in order to maintain the privacy of participant identities. Specifically, data were linked by an interagency group, Integrated Client Services (ICS), which builds and maintains linked data systems to support the forecasting units of Oregon's state human services and health departments. ICS relies on software with advanced capabilities to match individual records using identifiers – including first, last, and middle name, date of birth, and social security number where available. A social security number was available for some data-sets. Records are matched using a combination of deterministic (i.e., exact), probabilistic, and manual matching. All data-sets were sent to ICS for matching, after which identifiers were removed and replaced with random participant identification numbers and returned to the researchers for analysis.

Sample

The sample included 3072 youth who were committed to state-level juvenile probation or incarceration between January 2008 and July 2013. The majority ($n = 1766$, 57%) were committed to probation while a substantial proportion were committed to incarceration in a youth correctional facility ($n = 1306$, 33%). Of those committed to incarceration, most were adjudicated in juvenile court ($n = 2597$, 84%) while the remainder were convicted in adult criminal court ($n = 475$, 16%) despite their young age, and mandated to the custody of youth correctional facilities until their 25th birthday. Most subjects were male ($n = 2579$, 84%). The racial/ethnic composition of the sample was 61% Caucasian ($n = 1864$), 22% Hispanic/Latino ($n = 681$), 9% African-American ($n = 283$), 3% Native American ($n = 103$), and 1% Asian or Pacific Islander ($n = 34$). The remaining 4% identified as Multiracial/Multiethnic and 'Other' race/ethnicity. Age at the time of commitment to state custody ranged from 12 to 19 years old with an average of 15.8 years old (SD = 1.4).

Variables, measures, and analytical approach

Data sources and descriptive information for variables tested in the overall model predicting gang membership are displayed in Table 1.

The dependent variable – gang involvement – was measured via youth self-report on the Risk/Needs Assessment (RNA; Barnoski 2004). The RNA is administered via a staff-youth interview at the time of commitment, and covers 18 risk/need domains that are known to influence delinquent behavior. Youth who reported that they had been or were a 'gang member/associate' at the time of commitment were categorized as gang-involved ($n = 596$, 19%); all other youth in the sample were considered non-gang ($n = 2476$, 81%).

Table 1. Data sources and descriptive information for variables tested in overall model predicting gang membership (n = 3072).

	Data source	n (%)	Mean (SD)	Range
Self-reported history of and/or current gang membership/association (Yes)	RNA	596 (19)		
Foster care placement (Yes)	HS	610 (20)		
Child Protective Services experience (Yes)	HS	918 (30)		
Alcohol and drug treatment involvement (Yes)	HS	1495 (49)		
Welfare involvement (Yes)	HS	2504 (82)		
Medical care assistance involvement (Yes)	HS	2770 (90)		
Cumulative years enrolled in mental health treatment prior to commitment	HS		1.3 (2.4)	0–19
Count of mental health treatment episodes prior to commitment	HS		2.4 (3.5)	0–30
Count of mental health treatment episodes where youth was referred by personal support system	HS		0.5 (1.0)	0–13
Prior psychiatric day treatment (Yes)	HS	157 (5)		
Prior crisis treatment (Yes)	HS	586 (19)		
Number of days absent from school most recent academic year (out of 170)	EDU		33 (30)	0–158
History of truancy discipline events prior to commitment (Count)	EDU		0.9 (1.9)	0–17
History of out-of-school suspensions prior to commitment (Count)	EDU		2.6 (3.6)	0–29
History of expulsions prior to commitment (Count)	EDU		0.2 (0.5)	0–4
History of qualifying for free/reduced lunch (Yes)	EDU	2585 (84)		
Sixth grade math test score below standard (Yes)	EDU	886 (29)		
Tenth grade math test score below standard (Yes)	EDU	241 (8)		
Count of prior delinquency referrals with a weapons offense	JJ		0.3 (0.5)	0–4
Count of prior delinquency referrals for runaway	JJ		1.4 (2.9)	0–30
Count of prior delinquency referrals for misdemeanor criminal mischief	JJ		0.4 (1.1)	0–19
Risk score of felony readjudication	JJ		23.8 (0.3)	2–87
Intensity level for most severe offense to date (Larger number = More severe)	JJ		14.4 (2.9)	1–19
Prior delinquency referral for a sex offense (Yes)	JJ	745 (24)		
Peer status is main purpose for criminal behavior (Yes)	RNA	469 (15)		
Revenge is main purpose for criminal behavior (Yes)	RNA	121 (4)		
Excitement is main purpose for criminal behavior (Yes)	RNA	362 (12)		
Money is main purpose for criminal behavior (Yes)	RNA	741 (24)		
Anger is main purpose for criminal behavior (Yes)	RNA	377 (12)		
Sexual desire is main purpose for criminal behavior (Yes)	RNA	489 (16)		
Impulse is main purpose for criminal behavior (Yes)	RNA	513 (17)		
Believes physical aggression and fighting to resolve a disagreement is often appropriate (Yes)	RNA	361 (12)		
Household member with jail/imprisonment history (Yes)	RNA	313 (10)		
Currently has no health insurance	RNA	496 (16)		
History of deliberately inflicting pain on others (Yes)	RNA	627 (20)		
Youth leads other peers in antisocial behavior (Yes)	RNA	340 (10)		
History of using or threatening others with weapons (Yes)	RNA	451 (15)		

Notes: Data sources: RNA = Risk/Needs assessment; HS = Human services; EDU = Education; JJ = Juvenile justice.

Given the extent of data from multiple human service programs and education (i.e., the 'feeder' systems), a substantial number and variety of independent (i.e., predictor) variables were available for consideration and testing during statistical model development. From welfare and medical assistance programs, predictors were age at first enrollment, type(s) and count of program(s) accessed, and length of service. From foster care, predictors included age at first removal from home, number of removal episodes and total time spent in foster care to date, type of maltreatment (if any) at removal, reason(s) for removal, and family/caregiver issues at removal (e.g., caregiver alcohol and drug use, inability to cope, and inadequate housing). Child Protective Services variables were age at first substantiated maltreatment claim, type of maltreatment, number of maltreatment claims (both substantiated and unsubstantiated) for the family, and family characteristics (e.g., child behavior problem, domestic violence). From mental health and alcohol and drug treatment data, predictors included age at first enrollment, type(s) and count of program(s) accessed, number of treatment episodes, length of service, referral source, indicators of treatment completion and termination, and reason(s) for termination. Within alcohol and drug treatment data, primary drug of choice, frequency of use, and route of use (i.e., intravenous or other) were also considered. Variables from education data included student mobility (i.e., mid-year change in school attended), days absent, number of disciplinary incidents, disciplinary outcomes (e.g., expulsion and suspension), discipline days, standardized test scores for reading and math by grade level, special education enrollment, limited English proficiency enrollment, and student eligibility for free and reduced lunch. A number of independent variables from juvenile justice data-sets were also considered, including age at first delinquency referral, number of delinquency referrals, number of referrals for specific offenses (e.g., runaway, felony, weapons, criminal mischief, assault, and sex offenses), risk of felony readjudication at the time of commitment, intensity level of most severe offense to date, and 18 risk/need domains measured by the RNA that are known to influence delinquent behavior (e.g., attitudes and behaviors, aggression, peer influence, relationships, use of free time).[4]

Although the quantity and variety of predictors available for testing is impressive, one difficulty in the analysis was the handling of missing data. Specifically, while all youth in the sample had juvenile justice and education records, not all youth were involved with each of the remaining feeder systems prior to being committed to probation or incarceration. Youth contact with feeder systems ranged from a single program to all seven (i.e., welfare, medical assistance programs, mental health treatment, alcohol and drug treatment, foster care, Child Protective Services, and education) that preceded juvenile justice involvement. Therefore, each youth observation had patterns of existing and missing data, which reflected their individual path through the feeder systems. In other words, not all predictors were available to test with all youth in the sample.

As a solution, the authors employed a systematic model selection strategy to minimize the impact of missing data and maximize our ability to select relevant variables for testing in the final model predicting gang involvement. Specifically, data were examined within each system data-set independent of the others, and the likelihood of gang involvement was estimated using the predictors available within that system data-set alone. To illustrate, a forward stepwise logistic regression model predicting gang involvement was estimated among youth in the foster care subsample using only foster care data. Another forward stepwise logistic regression model was estimated among youth in the mental health treatment subsample using only mental health treatment data, and so on until we had a series of models predicting gang involvement within each feeder system data-set, the education data-set, and the juvenile justice data.

The results of this process revealed that statistically significant predictors of gang involvement emerged only out of mental health treatment, education, and juvenile justice data. No variables within foster care, Child Protective Services, alcohol and drug treatment, welfare, and medical assistance programs could reliably differentiate between gang and non-gang youth; therefore, issues related to missing data were eliminated. In other words, by doing separate analyzes within agency data-sets, it was discovered that variables from those agencies (i.e., foster care, Child Protective Services, alcohol and drug treatment, welfare, and medical assistance programs) were not significantly related to gang membership. Hence, those variables were not considered for further testing in the overall model predicting gang membership. The only difference between gang and non-gang youth in these systems was that overall, more gang than non-gang youth were involved with foster care, Child Protective Services, alcohol and drug treatment, welfare, and medical assistance programs prior to being committed to the state juvenile justice system. To account for gang youths' overrepresentation in these systems, dichotomous indicators of involvement/no involvement were created and advanced for testing along with the significant predictors of gang membership that emerged from mental health treatment,[5] education, and juvenile justice data.

Results

The predictors selected for testing were entered into a forward stepwise logistic regression model predicting gang involvement. Results of the final step of the model are presented in Table 2. The 17 variables that remained in the model at the final step represented four of the five social development domains of gang joining (i.e., individual, peers, family, and school experiences) and included 12 predictors from juvenile justice data, three from education, one from mental health treatment, and the dichotomous (i.e., yes/no) indicator of foster care involvement. Together, these variables significantly predicted gang involvement (−2LL = 2094.01; $\chi^2[25] = 928.75$, $p < .0001$) and correctly classified 77% of the sample as either gang or non-gang (with a logistic regression cutoff value of .20 to maximize sensitivity and specificity).

Odds ratio values provide the odds that a youth is gang-involved given a one-unit change in the associated predictor variable, all other variables being equal. Positive Beta coefficients (β) indicate the predictor increases the odds while negative Beta coefficients indicate the predictor decreases the odds that the youth is a gang member. Results indicate that among the individual-level factors, significant predictors of gang involvement include certain youth attitudes and beliefs, tendencies toward violence and aggression, general delinquency involvement, and mental health treatment need. Specifically, youth who believe that physical aggression is *often* appropriate were nearly 14 times more likely to be gang members than youth who believe physical aggression is never appropriate. Evidence of violent tendencies also significantly predicted gang membership, such that the odds were 2.2 times higher for youth who have a history of deliberately inflicting physical pain on others and over two times higher for youth with a history of using or threatening others with weapons. Similarly, the total number of delinquency referrals for weapons offenses was also significant in that each additional weapons referral increased the odds of gang membership by 1.8 times. Significantly larger odds of gang involvement also corresponded with having committed a more severe offense, as did the number of delinquency

Table 2. Logistic regression coefficients for predictors of gang involvement among youth committed to state probation or incarceration ($n = 3072$).

	B	Std. err.	Odds ratio
Individual-level risk factors			
Belief that physical aggression is often appropriate	2.6***	0.4	13.59
Belief that physical aggression is sometimes appropriate	1.7***	0.4	5.67
Belief that physical aggression is rarely appropriate	1.0*	0.4	2.70
Belief that physical aggression is never appropriate (Indicator)			
History of deliberately inflicting pain (Yes)	0.8***	0.1	2.22
History of using or threatening others with weapons (Yes)	0.7***	0.1	2.06
Number of referrals for weapons offenses	0.6***	0.1	1.81
Intensity level of most severe offense	0.1***	0.0	1.09
Number of referrals for misdemeanor criminal mischief	0.2***	0.0	1.21
Risk score of felony readjudication	0.0***	0.0	1.02
Prior referral for sex offense (Yes)	−0.9***	0.2	0.40
Number of mental health treatment episodes	−0.1***	0.0	0.88
Peer-related risk factors			
Peer status is primary purpose for criminal behavior	1.2***	0.2	3.28
Revenge is primary purpose for criminal behavior	1.2***	0.3	3.37
Excitement is primary purpose for criminal behavior	0.5*	0.2	1.68
Money is primary purpose for criminal behavior	0.4*	0.2	1.50
Anger is primary purpose for criminal behavior (Indicator)			
Youth leads other peers in antisocial behavior (Yes)	0.4***	0.1	1.43
Family risk factors			
Currently has private health insurance	−1.0***	0.2	0.38
Currently has public health insurance	−0.7***	0.1	0.52
Currently has no health insurance (Indicator)			
Household member with jail/imprisonment history (Yes)	0.6***	0.2	1.85
One or more out-of-home foster care placements (Yes)	0.5**	0.2	1.70
School-related risk factors			
Sixth grade math test score below standard (Yes)	0.7***	0.1	2.09
Tenth grade math test score below standard (Yes)	0.8**	0.3	2.18
Days absent from school most recent academic year	0.0**	0.0	1.01

*$p < .05$; **$p < .01$; ***$p < .0001$.

referrals for misdemeanor criminal mischief – each additional referral increased the odds of gang membership by 1.2 times. Youth with higher risk scores for felony readjudication were also more likely to be gang affiliated, with each 1% increase in risk corresponding to a 1.02 increase in the odds of gang involvement. Having any prior referral for a sex offense was associated with significantly decreased odds of gang membership, indicating that gang members are not likely to have sex offenses in their criminal histories. Finally, at the individual level, evidence of having received treatment for an assessed mental health need was related to lower odds of gang involvement, such that each time a youth participated in a mental health treatment episode the odds of gang membership decreased 0.88 times.

Findings show that several peer-related factors were also significantly related to the odds of gang involvement. Youth who reported engaging in criminal behavior for the main purpose of achieving status among their peers were over three times more likely to be gang affiliated relative to youth who reported anger as their main purpose for committing crime. Similarly, youth who indicated their criminal behavior was motivated by enacting revenge upon others were also over three times more likely to be gang involved compared to youth who committed crime out of anger. Excitement and money as motivators for criminal behavior were also significantly associated with the odds of gang membership. Lastly, at the peer level, youth who reported that they lead other peers in antisocial behavior were 1.4 times more likely to be gang involved than youth who reported that they usually resist going along with antisocial peers.

At the family level, results indicate that health insurance coverage,[6] household members' incarceration history, and foster care involvement were all statistically related to gang involvement among the youth in our sample. Youth who reported having some kind of health insurance – either public or private – were significantly less likely to be gang affiliated compared to youth who had no health insurance at all. Youth with private health insurance were 0.38 times as likely to be gang involved, and those with public health insurance were 0.52 times as likely. The criminal history of individuals living with the youth was also significantly related to gang involvement, such that youth who reported having a household member (other than immediate family) with a history of jail/imprisonment were 1.8 times more likely to be gang members. Finally, at the family level, youth involvement with foster care was also associated with gang membership. Specifically, youth who were placed in out-of-home foster care one or more times prior to their commitment to state custody were 1.7 times more likely to be gang affiliated compared to youth with no foster care history.

Among youths' school experiences, significant predictors of gang membership included standardized test scores and attendance indicators. Specifically, performance on standardized math tests was associated with gang membership in that youth who did not meet proficiency standards in either 6th or 10th grade were over two times more likely to be gang involved relative to youth who either met or exceeded proficiency standards in math. Regarding attendance, the number of days a youth was absent from school during the academic year immediately preceding commitment to state custody was also associated with gang involvement. Each additional day absent from school corresponded with a statistically significant increase in the odds of gang membership.

Discussion

The Howell–Egley life-course gang model suggests that risk factors within multiple domains of young people's lives influence their gravitation toward gang involvement from early childhood across developmental periods extending into adulthood, and this process has been substantiated in longitudinal research in multiple cities, also in a systematic review of predictive gang studies (Raby and Jones 2016). However, the specific interactive relationships among the developmental domains of influence (suggested in Figure 1) remain to be specified. Because of the nature of the systems data analyzed herein, it cannot be determined with certainty whether those risk factors emerged before gang involvement (and therefore shaped youths' trajectories toward the gang) or evolved from gang involvement. Even though the current analysis does not fully recognize the gradual migration toward gang involvement suggested by the life-course developmental gang model, the findings reflect the relative influence of risk factors for gang involvement within four out of the five social development domains (i.e., individual, peers, family, and school). Results indicate that the strongest predictors of gang involvement are at the individual level (i.e., individual attitudes, such as the belief in physical aggression to resolve disagreements and violent tendencies, such as deliberately inflicting pain and weapons use) and within the peer domain (i.e., leading peers in antisocial behavior and committing crimes for peer status or revenge). Certain family circumstances also significantly predicted gang involvement, including a lack of health insurance, the jailing or imprisonment of a household member, and foster care placement. At the school level, performance on standardized math assessments in the 6th and 10th grades and attendance were significantly associated with gang involvement. Interestingly, many factors supported by prior research (i.e., Howell and Egley 2005; Raby and Jones 2016) and tested in the current analysis were not found to be significantly associated with gang involvement relative to other variables in the model. Of note, school disciplinary actions, family violence, family poverty (i.e., eligibility for free and reduced lunch), and participation in treatment for drug and alcohol abuse did not remain in the final step of the statistical model predicting gang membership. This finding likely reflects less than ideal school and family data on these particular variables linked with juvenile offenders in system files.

The strength of the associations between individual characteristics and peer influence variables and gang involvement are not surprising; i.e., belief in the use of physical aggression, peer status and revenge as motivators for committing crimes, use of weapons, history of deliberately inflicting pain, crime severity, and leading other peers in antisocial behavior are common among known gang associates (Howell & Griffiths, forthcoming). The relative influence of individual characteristics and peers might be explained by the data itself, which is weighted toward criminal history information and dynamic factors collected by the juvenile justice system for youth who are already heavily involved with delinquency and, in some cases, established gang members. If the same analysis were performed on youth during the period of migration toward gang involvement (i.e., instead of after they have already become involved with the juvenile justice system), it is likely that some community and even more family factors would be significantly related to the probability of being a gang member. To that effect, the current findings may reflect more about the individual characteristics and peer factors that are common among known gang affiliates and less about the community and family circumstances that influence youth decisions to become gang affiliated. On an important note, the current analysis suggests that many of the predictors of gang involvement are *dynamic* factors – indicating that changing these characteristics is possible. Knowledge regarding where the youth is positioned in his migration toward gang involvement is critical to juvenile justice system managers' ability to identify higher risk youth and provide services that reduce the likelihood of gang involvement.

The current model identifies only the main effects of considered variables on gang involvement, i.e., the possibility of interactions between variables and the relative influences of race, ethnicity, and gender were not tested. Although the main effects are dominated by individual characteristics and peer influences, all domains save one (i.e., community) are represented. This is owing to the reality that juvenile justice system managers do not have immediate access to data on this sector of offender's lives. In general, taking into account experiential factors that influence youth to move toward gang involvement will likely provide more nuanced view of the association between a wider variety of social dynamics and gang involvement.

Study implications: the case for prevention and early intervention

This research suggests that risk factors in various developmental domains that influence gang involvement can be tagged in certain feeder systems. Juvenile justice system programs are much more likely to be effective in preventing/reducing gang involvement if they address the pertinent predictor variables identified as significant in this research, ideally in a comprehensive continuum of program services that extend across the developmental domains. The programs noted below exhibit this potential and could possibly be effective with future or current gang members. Prevention measures and targeted early intervention programs have the best chance of succeeding because gang involvement increases with age in childhood and early adolescence (Howell and Griffiths, in press; Pyrooz 2014). Community-level variables, combined with family structural variables (e.g., low parental education, broken homes, and family violence), generally exert influence on the risk of gang membership indirectly through the inhibition and/or attenuation of prosocial bonds (Thornberry et al. 2003). This influence is particularly strong in severely distressed communities. In particular, those persons who experience 'toxic' stress 'are the children who grow up in poverty, live in dangerous neighborhoods, are exposed to violence both inside and outside the home, and face personal and familial substance abuse and a peer group of similarly associated individuals' (Rivera 2012, 160). Understandably, the environment or context in which a child lives appears to have a profound influence on that child's ability to self-regulate (Hamoudi et al. 2015; Murray et al. 2015, 17).

Traumatic experiences are very common among children in the United States. The nationwide Adverse Childhood Experiences Study of approximately 17,000 adults asked questions about seven categories of adverse experience in childhood: psychological, physical, or sexual abuse; witnessing violence against a mother; and household dysfunction, including living with household members who were substance abusers, mentally ill or suicidal, or who had been imprisoned (Centers for Disease Control[7]). Such 'adverse childhood experiences' led to a broad range of undesirable outcomes later in life. It is estimated that between 75 and 93% of youth entering the juvenile justice system have experienced some type of trauma, in comparison to 25–34% of the general population (Baglivio et al. 2015). In sum, those who suffer most from toxic stress are the children who grow up in poverty, live in dangerous neighborhoods, and are exposed to violence both inside and outside the home – each of which is a risk factor for gang joining.

Preschool children

Those preschool-aged children (3–4 years) who live in adversity or are at-risk can benefit from cognitive, emotional, and behavioral self-regulation via direct skills instruction, typically provided in implemented in daycare/preschools (Murray, Rosanbalm, and Christopoulous 2016). Effective programs include Triple P, Incredible Years, PATHS, Parent Corps, Tools of the Mind, and Head Start REDI; although Incredible Years likely has the best track record for delinquency prevention purposes.

School entry

For at risk elementary-aged children, effective social, emotional, and learning (SEL) programs (typically implemented in schools) include FAST Track, Strengthening Families, Making Choices, I can Problem-Solve, Strong Start, and Second Step (Murray, Rosanbalm, and Christopoulous 2016). These SEL programs hold great promise, even in socially toxic communities. In addition, 'when teachers are taught positive behavior management skills and ways to build relationships with students, classroom climate improves measurably' (Murray, Rosanbalm, and Christopoulous 2016, 51).

Later childhood

For middle-school-aged children (implemented in schools with few exceptions), effective programs (particularly for cognitive and behavioral regulation, mental health, delinquency prevention, and health/self-care) include Coping Power, Multisite Violence Prevention, SEAL (Going for GOAL), Family Check-Up and a variety of other coping, life skills, problem-solving, conflict-resolution, and youth development programs (Murray, Rosanbalm, and Christopoulous 2016). Botivn's LifeSkills Training is recognized as one of the most effective school-based programs for youths ages 10–18, including delayed early use of alcohol, tobacco, and other substances and reduced rates of use of all substances up to 5 years after the intervention ended (US Department of Health and Human Services 2016).

The Gang Resistance Education and Training (G.R.E.A.T.) program is a school-based gang and violence prevention program mainly for children in the year immediately before the prime ages for introduction into gang and delinquent behavior. The curriculum is taught mainly in entire classrooms of middle school students by uniformed law enforcement officers in a 13-week course of one day per week and less than 1 hour each. In addition to educating students about the dangers of gang involvement, the lesson content places considerable emphasis on cognitive-behavioral training, social skills development, refusal skills training, and conflict resolution. Thus, the curriculum aims to reduce risk factors and increase protective factors. A rigorous, long-term, multisite evaluation of the middle school program conducted in seven geographically and demographically diverse cities found that the G.R.E.A.T. program has the intended program effects on youth gang membership and on a number of risk factors and social skills thought to be associated with gang joining. Results one year post-program showed a 39% reduction in odds of gang joining among students who received the program compared to those who did not and an average of 24% reduction in odds of gang joining across the four years, post-program (Esbensen et al. 2013; Esbensen, Peterson, Taylor et al. 2012). These outcomes are remarkable for such a short-term program, producing large cost-benefits because schools are not required to remunerate law enforcement agencies or school resource officers who typically would be on school premises in the absence of G.R.E.A.T. (Howell 2013a).[8]

For high-risk children age 12, Stop Now and Plan (SNAP®) program is a cognitive-behavioral program that helps children and parents to gain more emotion regulation, self-control and problem-solving skills so they are better able to stop, think, and plan positive alternatives before acting impulsively. SNAP is internationally recognized as the leading evidence-based program for aggressive, high-risk children (Howell, Lipsey, and Wilson 2014). This program is designed specifically for aggressive, bullying, and delinquent behaviors in children (ages 6–11) of both genders – the Stop Now And Plan (SNAP®) for boys, and the corresponding SNAP Girls Connection (Augimeri, Walsh, and Slater 2011). Providing parent skills training in SNAP Parent Group and/or family counseling in tandem with the child's services (e.g., SNAP Child Group; Individual Counseling/Mentoring) is essential to the success of the program in reducing risk factors and increasing protective factors among children. Tailored for adolescents ages 12–18 and their families, the Youth Justice (SNAP YJ) Model can serve as the cornerstone program for high-risk youth – including gang members – even when housed in juvenile justice correctional facilities.

Brief Strategic Family Therapy (BSFT) was designed to strengthen Hispanic families and thereby eliminate or reduce behavior problems, including drug use. It targets children and adolescents aged 6 – 18 years. An adapted version of BSFT targeted an extremely high-risk adolescent Mexican-American population in an historic gang-ridden city, San Antonio. The experiment included only gang-affiliated (i.e., self-identified or having a friend or family member in a gang) Mexican-American adolescents 12–17 years of age, who reported current (past month) use of alcohol or illicit drugs and use of these substances on at least six occasions in the past year. This BSFT-adapted version took into account cultural values of Mexican-American families as well as contextual factors, including frequent gang involvement in high crime neighborhoods characterized by low levels of education, multigenerational use of drugs, extensive criminality, and high incarceration rates. Three behavioral problems were addressed (delinquency, impulsivity, and hyperactivity) along with drug/alcohol use. In addition to the adapted BSFT family therapy, gang diversion training for the adolescents and gang awareness for the parent were provided by outreach workers. This BSFT adapted version proved effective with a sample of gang-involved boys and girls (Valdez et al. 2013). The program reduced gang membership by 22% in the near term (six months), and there were significant differences between the BFST and control groups on adolescent alcohol use at six months and parents' reports of their children's delinquency. These are excellent choices among intervention programs.

A comprehensive approach

A broad strategy is required to interrupt life-course pathways to gang participation, accelerated involvement in serious and violent delinquency, and sustained criminal activity in adulthood with ongoing gang involvement. The Comprehensive Gang Program Model (CGPM) provides an administrative framework that can support a coordinated initiative that improves a community's capacity to respond to youth gangs, whether emerging or entrenched. The ideal strategy is a community-wide balanced and integrated approach employing multiple-level intervention and services, and research supports the effectiveness of this approach. When the CGPM has been implemented with high fidelity, statistically significant reductions in gang violence were seen in controlled studies in three sites, and in overall crime reduction in other sites (Howell 2013b; Office of Juvenile Justice and Delinquency Prevention 2010; Spergel 2007; Spergel, Wa, and Sosa 2006).

Among several sites in which implementation of the CGPM is currently underway in the U.S, Multnomah County, Oregon, stands out as a blueprint for other jurisdictions to follow. The Multnomah County Local Public Safety Coordinating Council (LPSCC) provides effective coordination and oversight in the implementation of the CGPM. In 2014, the LPSCC Executive Committee conducted a countywide assessment to identify areas with the highest risk of youth marginalization and gang-related violence in Multnomah County. The product is the most comprehensive urban gang problem assessment to date.[9] Three target areas were identified within the county, as having both high levels of gang violence and concentration of youth marginalization risk.

Based on the Multnomah County Comprehensive Gang Assessment, the CGPM Steering Committee developed an Implementation Plan (a living document that is open to ongoing revision of goals and objectives) that facilitates the development of primary prevention, secondary prevention, intervention, suppression, and re-entry activities while utilizing effective services (e.g., noted above). The plan revision process will allow for the re-evaluation of priorities, the selection of new strategies or realigning existing ones, and for alternative resource allocations in a process that will be led by the Youth and Gang Violence Steering Committee in collaboration with community partners.

As a unique feature, Multnomah County has supplemented the CGPM with several social development frameworks, including a public health perspective, trauma informed practices, and an equity and empowerment lens. As an important benefit of this multi-faceted model, the Multnomah County Implementation Plan identifies strategies that involve not only gang youth but also their families and the various community institutions that play a role in young people's transition from adolescence to productive members of society. This extension of the Implementation Plan outward to communities, families, and early child and family 'feeder systems' – from which data were drawn in the present statewide Oregon study – holds considerable progress for successful CGPM implementation, also for reducing gang incubation and growth in Multnomah County communities and elsewhere.

Conclusion

This research contributes to the growing body of knowledge on risk factors that characterize gang involved youth in juvenile justice systems, and has potentially important implications for reducing gang involvement among young offenders referred to juvenile justice systems. In the present study, 19% of the juvenile offenders were gang affiliated. This prevalence figure is comparable to North Carolina, where 24% of juveniles placed on probation, in detention, or in a secure correctional facility statewide were gang members) (Howell and Lassiter 2011), and 15% among samples of serious juvenile offenders in Phoenix and Philadelphia (Pyrooz, Sweeten, and Piquero 2013). Thus, juvenile justice system involvement is a common stage in the life-course of adolescent gang members, and this should be addressed in efforts to reduce the total volume of serious, violent, and chronic juvenile delinquency (Howell, Lipsey, and Wilson 2014).

As a final caveat, it is important to emphasize that the data analyzed in this study are weighted toward criminal and dynamic factors collected by the juvenile justice system for adjudicated delinquent offenders age 12 and older. Given this limitation and others, a complete test of the practical application of the Howell–Egley model was not feasible under the circumstances of the research setting. If the same analysis were performed on children under age 12, more factors would predict movement into gang participation; particularly more community conditions (as discussed earlier) and family variables. In the family domain, family structure and management; child maltreatment, low attachment to parents or family, and low parent supervision, control, or monitoring are strong predictors of early onset of gang involvement in multiple rigorous longitudinal studies (Howell and Egley 2005). For example, in the multi-year statewide North Carolina sample (M. Howell and Lassiter 2011), gang members were assessed as generally functioning below grade level or have un-served 'Exceptional Children' needs, mental health issues, marital/domestic discord in the home, parents/ guardians with marginal or inadequate parenting skills, and household members who use or abuse drugs. Moreover, gang-identified youth had parents/guardians involved with the criminal justice system and/or gang members themselves, nearly twice as often as non-gang-identified youth.

Gang membership in childhood and early adolescence is a pathway to serious and violent delinquency, and if this life-course is not interrupted, many gang members are likely to continue active involvement into adulthood. In two other statewide gang member studies, these youths were about three times more likely than other offenders to be chronic serious property and violent juvenile delinquents (Baglivio et al. 2014; Howell and Lassiter 2011). Our findings suggest that, as a matter of public policy, it is important to mount individual-, peer-, family-, and school-based gang prevention and intervention programs that can reduce the likelihood of gang joining in late childhood and early adolescence (Howell 2010; Wyrick 2006). This approach also is supported by other developmental criminology research (Dong, Gibson, and Krohn 2015; Krohn and Thornberry 2008).

Notes

1. However, the research to date on protective factors that buffer gang involvement is very thin.
2. The age range for childhood is approximately ages 4–12 (which overlaps with the preschool and school-entry periods), and the range for adolescence is ages 13–25.
3. Cross-sectional studies were excluded because these measure both risk factors and outcomes at the same time, hence the causal ordering cannot be determined with certainty; what appears to be a predictor could well be an outcome of gang involvement.
4. For a more thorough list of all independent variables that were tested along with their operational definitions, please contact the second author.
5. Statistically significant predictors of gang involvement within the mental health treatment subsample included the number of years in treatment, number of treatment episodes, number of treatment referrals made by the youth's support system (e.g., parents, friends, and attorney), a dichotomous indicator of participation in psychiatric day treatment, and a dichotomous indicator of participation in crisis services. Youth in the overall sample who did not experience mental health treatment and are missing these data points received scores of zero for these variables in the overall model. Imputing scores of zero was appropriate in this case given that each mental health predictor is either a count or a 0/1 (i.e., yes/no) indicator. Scores zero accurately reflect these youths' participation in mental health treatment (i.e., no participation).
6. Health insurance is an indicator of family stability and resources such as an employed caregiver whose job provides group coverage, income to pay for insurance premiums, and/or knowledge about eligibility criteria and available services within public programs (Institute of Medicine (US) Committee on the Consequences of Uninsurance 2002).
7. Adverse Childhood Experiences (ACE) Study. Available online: http://www.cdc.gov/violenceprevention/acestudy/ (accessed October 31, 2016).
8. It is misleading to suggest that G.R.E.A.T. has yielded 'mixed findings' (as stated by Huey, Lewine, and Rubenson 2016; also in a less than systematic literature review by Klein and Maxson 2006). The initial curriculum that failed to reduce gang joining was modified significantly. The substitute G.R.E.A.T. curriculum that incorporated program elements of the evidence-based LifeSkills Training program (Dusenbury and Botvin 1992) then proved remarkably effective using gold-standard research methods (Esbensen et al. 2012, 2013).
9. Available at https://multco.us/lpscc/multnomah-county-comprehensive-gang-assessment.

Disclosure statement

No potential conflict of interest was reported by the authors.

Funding

This work was supported by Cooperative Agreement No. 2014-MU-MU-K011, awarded by the Office of Juvenile Justice and Delinquency Prevention, Office of Justice Programs.

References

Augimeri, L. K., M. Walsh, and N. Slater. 2011. ""Rolling out SNAP", an Evidence-based Intervention: A Summary of Implementation, Evaluation, and Research." *International Journal of Child, Youth, and Family Studies* 2: 330–352.

Baglivio, M. T., K. Jackowski, M. A. Greenwald, and J. C. Howell. 2014. "Serious, Violent, and Chronic Juvenile Offenders: A Statewide Analysis of Prevalence and Prediction of Subsequent Recidivism Using Risk and Protective Factors." *Criminology and Public Policy* 13: 83–116.

Baglivio, M. T., K. T. Wolff, A. R. Piquero, and N. Epps. 2015. "The Relationship between Adverse Childhood Experiences (ACE) and Juvenile Offending Trajectories in a Juvenile Offender Sample." *Journal of Criminal Justice* 43: 229–241.

Barnoski, R. 2004. *Assessing Risk for Re-offense: Validating the Washington State Juvenile Court Assessment*. Olympia, WA: Washington State Institute for Public Policy.

Craig, W. M., F. Vitaro, C. Gagnon, and R. E. Tremblay. 2002. "The Road to Gang Membership: Characteristics of Male Gang and Non-gang Members from Ages 10 to 14." *Social Development* 11: 53–68.

Debarbieux, E., and C. Baya. 2008. An Interactive Construction of Gangs and Ethnicity: The Role of School Segregation in France. In *Street Gangs, Migration and Ethnicity*, edited by F. Van Gemert, D. Peterson, and I. L. Lien, 211–226. Portland, OR: Willan Publishing.

Dong, B., C. L. Gibson, and M. D. Krohn. 2015. "Gang Membership in a Developmental and Life-course Perspective." In *The Wiley Handbook of Gangs*, edited by S. Decker and D. C. Pyrooz, 78–97. Hoboken, NJ: Wiley.

Dusenbury, L., and G. J. Botvin. 1992. "Competence Enhancement and the Development of Positive Life Options." *Journal of Addictive Diseases* 11: 29–45.

Esbensen, F., and D. Huizinga. 1993. "Gangs, Drugs, and Delinquency in a Survey of Urban Youth." *Criminology* 31: 565–589.

Esbensen, F., E. P. Deschenes, and L. T. Winfree. 1999. "Differences Between Gang Girls and Gang Boys: Results from a Multi-site Survey." *Youth and Society* 31: 27–53.

Esbensen, F., D. Peterson, T. J. Taylor, and A. Freng. 2009. "Similarities and Differences in Risk Factors for Violent Offending and Gang Membership." *The Australian and New Zealand Journal of Criminology* 42: 1–26.

Esbensen, F., D. Peterson, T. J. Taylor, and A. Freng. 2010. *Youth Violence: Sex and Race Differences in Offending, Victimization, and Gang Membership*. Philadelphia, PA: Temple University Press.

Esbensen, F., D. Peterson, T. J. Taylor, and D. W/ Osgood. 2012. "Results from a multi-site evaluation of the G.R.E.A.T. Program." *Justice Quarterly* 29, 125–151.

Esbensen, F., D. W. Osgood, D. Peterson, T. J. Taylor, and D. C. Carson. 2013. "Short and Long Term Outcome Results from a Multi-site Evaluation of the G.R.E.A.T. Program." *Criminology and Public Policy* 12: 375–411.

Fleisher, M. S. 2000. *Dead End Kids: Gang Girls and the Boys They Know*. Madison, WI: The University of Wisconsin Press.

Gilman, A. B., K. G. Hill, and J. D. Hawkins. 2014. "The Long-term Consequences of Adolescent Gang Membership on Adult Functioning." *American Journal of Public Health* 104: 938–945.

Gilman, A. B., K. G. Hill, J. D. Hawkins, J. C. Howell, and R. Kosterman. 2014. "The Developmental Dynamics of Joining a Gang in Adolescence: Patterns and Predictors of Gang Membership." *Journal of Research on Adolescence* 24: 204–219.

Gilman, A. B., J. C. Howell, A. E. Hipwell, and S. D. Stepp. 2016. "The Reciprocal Relationship between Gang Involvement and Victimization by Peers: Findings from the Pittsburgh Girls Study." *Journal of Developmental and Life-course Criminology*: 1–17 doi: 10.1007/s40865-016-0046-1.

Hamoudi, A., D. W. Murray, L. Sorensen, and A. Fontaine. 2015. *Self-regulation and Toxic Stress: A Review of Ecological, Biological, and Developmental Studies of Self-regulation and Stress*. Durham, NC: Center for Child and Family Policy, Duke University.

Hill, K. G., J. C. Howell, J. D. Hawkins, and S. R. Battin-Pearson. 1999. "Childhood Risk Factors for Adolescent Gang Membership: Results from the Seattle Social Development Project." *Journal of Research in Crime and Delinquency* 36: 300–322.

Howell, J. C. 2010. "Gang Prevention: An Overview of Current Research and Programs." *Juvenile Justice Bulletin*. Washington, DC: U.S. Department of Justice, Office of Juvenile Justice and Delinquency Prevention.

Howell, J. C. 2013a. "GREAT Results: Implications for PBIS in Schools." *Criminology and Public Policy* 12: 413–420.

Howell, J. C. 2013b. "Why is Gang Membership Prevention Important?" In *Changing Course: Preventing Gang Membership*, edited by T. R. Simon, N. M. Ritter, & R. R. Mahendra, 7–18. Washington, DC: U.S. Department of Justice, U.S. Department of Health and Human Services, National Center for Injury Prevention and Control.

Howell, J. C., and A. Egley Jr. 2005. "Moving Risk Factors into Developmental Theories of Gang Membership." *Youth Violence and Juvenile Justice* 3: 334–354.

Howell, J. C., and E. Griffiths. 2016. *Gangs in America's Communities*. 2nd ed. Thousand Oaks, CA: Sage Publications.

Howell, J. C., and E. Griffiths. forthcoming. *Gangs in America's Communities*. 3rd ed. Thousand Oaks, CA: Sage.

Howell, M. Q., and W. Lassiter. 2011. *Prevalence of Gang-involved Youth in NC*. Raleigh, NC: North Carolina Department of Juvenile Justice and Delinquency Prevention.

Howell, J. C., M. W. Lipsey, and J. J. Wilson. 2014. *A Handbook for Evidence-based Juvenile Justice Systems*. Lanham, MD: Lexington Books.

Huey, S. J., G. Lewine, and M. Rubenson. 2016. "A Brief Review and Meta-analysis of Gang Intervention Trials in North America." In *Gang Transitions and Transformations in an International Context*, edited by C. L. Maxson and F. Esbensen, 217–233. Cham, Switzerland: Springer.

Huff, C. R. 1996. "The Criminal Behavior of Gang Members and Non-gang At-risk Youth." In *Gangs in America*. 2nd ed, edited by C. R. Huff, 75–102. Thousand Oaks, CA: Sage.

Huff, C. R. 1998. *Comparing the Criminal Behavior of Youth Gangs and at-risk Youth. Research in Brief*. Washington, DC: U.S. Department of Justice, Office of Justice Programs, National Institute of Justice.

Institute of Medicine (US) Committee on the Consequences of Uninsurance. 2002. *Health Insurance is a Family Matter*. Washington, DC: National Academies Press (US).

Klein, M. W., and C. L. Maxson. 2006. *Street Gang Patterns and Policies*. New York: Oxford University Press.

Krohn, M. D., and T. P. Thornberry. 2008. "Longitudinal Perspectives on Adolescent Street Gangs." In *The Long View of Crime: A Synthesis of Longitudinal Research*, edited by A. Liberman, 128–160. New York: Springer.

Krohn, M. D., A. J. Lizotte, S. D. Bushway, N. M. Schmidt, and M. D. Phillips. 2014. "Shelter during the Storm: A Search for Factors That Protect at-risk Adolescents from Violence." *Crime and Delinquency* 60: 379–401.

Lacourse, E., D. S. Nagin, F. Vitaro, S. Cote, L. Arseneault, and R. E. Tremblay. 2006. "Prediction of Early-onset Deviant Peer Group Involvement." *Archives of General Psychiatry* 63: 562–568.

Lahey, B. B., R. A. Gordon, R. Loeber, M. Stouthamer-Loeber, and D. P. Farrington. 1999. "Boys Who Join Gangs: A Prospective Study of Predictors of First Gang Entry." *Journal of Abnormal Child Psychology* 27: 261–276.

Melde, C., T. J. Taylor, and F. Esbensen. 2009. ""I Got Your Back": An Examination of the Protective Function of Gang Membership in Adolescence." *Criminology* 47: 565–594.

Moore, Joan W. 1991. *Going down to the Neighborhood: Homeboys and Homegirls in Change*. Philadelphia, PA: Temple University Press.

Murray, D. W., K. Rosanbalm, C. Christopoulos, and A. Hamoudi. 2015. *Self-regulation and Toxic Stress: Foundations for Understanding Self-regulation from an Applied Developmental Perspective*. Durham, NC: Center for Child and Family Policy, Duke University.

Murray, D. W., K. Rosanbalm, and C. Christopoulous 2016. *Self-regulation and Toxic Stress Report 3: A Comprehensive Review of Self-regulation Interventions from Birth through Young Adulthood*. OPRE Report # 2016-34. Washington, DC: Office of Planning, Research and Evaluation, Administration for Children and Families, U.S. Department of Health and Human Services.

Office of Juvenile Justice and Delinquency Prevention. 2010. *Best Practices to Address Community Gang Problems: OJJDP's Comprehensive Gang Model*. Washington, DC: Author.

Pogarsky, G., A. J. Lizotte, and T. P. Thornberry. 2003. "The Delinquency of Children Born to Young Mothers: Results from the Rochester Youth Development Study." *Criminology* 41: 1249–1286.

Pyrooz, D. C. 2014. ""From Your First Cigarette to Your Last Dying Day": The Patterning of Gang Membership in the Life-course." *Journal of Quantitative Criminology* 30: 349–372.

Pyrooz, D. C., G. Sweeten, and A. R. Piquero. 2013. "Continuity and Change in Gang Membership and Gang Embeddedness." *Journal of Research in Crime and Delinquency* 50: 239–271.

Raby, C., and F. Jones. 2016. "Identifying Risks for Male Street Gang Involvement: A Systematic Review and Narrative Synthesis." *The Journal of Forensic Psychiatry and Psychology* 1–44. doi:10.1080/14789949.2016.1195005.

Rivera, F. P. 2012. "The Future of Preventive Public Health: Implications of Brain Violence Research." In *The Future of Criminology*, edited by R. Loeber and B. C. Welsh, 159–165. Oxford, NY: Oxford University Press.

Spergel, I. A. 2007. *Reducing Youth Gang Violence: The Little Village Gang Project in Chicago*. Lanham, MD: AltaMira Press.

Spergel, I. A., K. M. Wa, and R. V. Sosa. 2006. "The Comprehensive, Community-wide, Gang Program Model: Success and Failure." In *Studying Youth Gangs*, edited by J. F. Short and L. A. Hughes, 203–224. Lanham, MD: AltaMira Press.

Thornberry, T. P., M. D. Krohn, A. J. Lizotte, C. A. Smith, and K. Tobin. 2003. *Gangs and Delinquency in Developmental Perspective*. New York: Cambridge University Press.

U.S. Department of Health and Human Services. 2016. *Facing Addiction in America: The Surgeon General's Report on Alcohol, Drugs, and Health*. Washington, DC: U.S. Department of Health and Human Services.

Valdez, A., A. Cepeda, D. Parrish, R. Horowitz, and C. Kaplan. 2013. "An Adapted Brief Strategic Family Therapy for Gang-affiliated Mexican American Adolescents." *Research on Social Work Practice* 23: 383–396.

Vaughn, M. G., M. DeLisi, K. M. Beaver, and J. P. Wright. 2009. "Identification of Latent Classes of Behavioral Risk Based on Early Childhood Manifestations of Self-control." *Youth Violence and Juvenile Justice* 7: 16–31.

Vigil, J. D. 2002. *A Rainbow of Gangs: Street Cultures in the Mega-city*. Austin: University of Texas Press.

Wyrick, P. A. 2006. "Gang Prevention: How to Make the "Front End" of Your Anti-gang Effort Work." *United States Attorneys' Bulletin* 54: 52–60.

The labor market and gang membership in adulthood: is the availability, quality, and nature of legal work associated with adult gang involvement?

Adam M. Watkins

ABSTRACT
Gang scholars generally contend that adult gang membership has grown more common in US cities since the 1970s. The greater presence of adult members is often attributed to conditions in the local labor market, an explanation that has been rarely tested. This research tests whether measures of the availability, quality, and nature of legal work are associated with the rate of adult gang membership among large US cities ($N = 133$). The current findings offer mixed support for the tested hypotheses and, in general, indicate that labor market conditions account for a small share of the variation in the rate of adult membership. Nonetheless, the current findings provide some support for measuring labor market conditions beyond simply the availability of work (e.g., rate of unemployment), for measures of the quality (e.g., extent of full-time employment) and the nature of work (e.g., degree of employment in service occupations) were no less important in explaining the rate of adult membership. The implications of the current findings for social responses to gang membership (opportunities provision) and for future research are discussed.

Introduction

Panel studies generally find that youth join a gang by 14 or 15 and leave the gang within two years, indicating that most adolescents who become gang involved do not extend membership into adulthood (Howell 2007; Maxson 2011). Some adolescents, however, prolong membership into adulthood or initiate membership for the first time at an adult age (18 or older). Pyrooz (2014) identified a sizeable percentage of such youth with panel data from the National Longitudinal Survey of Youth 1997 (NLSY97), finding that 40% of gang-involved youth reported active membership at an adult age, and one-half (20%) of these gang youth did not become active members until adulthood. National Youth Gang Survey data gathered from law enforcement personnel also indicate that adult members account for a sizeable share of active gang members. These survey data reveal that from 1996 to 2011, police personnel overall reported that at least 50% of gang members were aged 18 or older (NGC, n.d.).

The literature suggests that the presence of adult members affects gang structure and dynamics. For instance, most research finds that gangs are loosely structured (Howell and Griffiths 2016), but there is some contention that gangs become more organized as members age (e.g., Decker, Katz, and Webb 2008). The evidence suggests that as gangs or criminal groups grow more structured, their members are more likely to perpetrate especially serious violence (Sheley et al. 1995). Research also suggests that older-adolescent and young-adult gang members adversely affect gang-related behaviors by way of greater gun ownership. Watkins and Moule (2014) found, for instance, that while gun ownership was common among active gang members, it was particularly common among active adult members. Greater structure and gun ownership may explain why, in part, research consistently finds that the median age of victims and offenders in gang homicide incidents (usually 18–24 years of age or young adults) is 'older than might be expected of "youth gang" members' (Maxson, Gordon, and Klein 1985, 220).

These findings call attention to the importance of understanding the circumstances that give rise to adult membership. Theoretical explanations of adult membership are discussed in the gang literature, and they primarily focus on circumstances in the local labor market. For instance, gang scholars such as Hagedorn (1998), Huff (1993), Moore (1998), and Spergel (1990) attribute adult gang membership to 'demand-side' dynamics in the 'post-industrial' labor market. The foundation of their arguments is that street gang members have always lacked job and educational skills, but the modern 'service'- and 'information'-driven economy found in many urban communities has made it increasingly difficult for such youth to secure employment, especially low-skilled, entry-level jobs that 'offer a modicum of social respect and income' (Spergel 1990, 219). As discussed in greater detail below, the implication is that the availability, quality, and nature of legal work affect to what extent adult gang members are present in a community. This research directly tests whether these labor market factors are related to the rate of adult gang membership in large US cities ($N = 133$). Despite the generally accepted position that labor market circumstances are important drivers of prolonged or adult membership, this position has been subject to little empirical testing.

Literature review

Labor market factors

Availability of work

There is general agreement in the gang literature that adult gang membership has grown more prevalent in US cities since the 1970s (e.g., Hagedorn 1988; Huff 1993; Moore 1998; Spergel 1990; Vigil 1988). The greater prevalence of adult membership in core urban areas is mainly attributed to circumstances in the local labor market, especially the availability of jobs for low-skilled workers. The evidence suggests that European immigrant groups studied by gang scholars such as Thrasher ([1927] 1963) and Miller ([1966] 2011) benefited from the expansion of manufacturing in the US, particularly in Midwest and Northeast states after World War II (Hagedorn 1988). This growth in manufacturing generated demand for low-skilled workers and greatly expanded employment opportunities for young males in particular (Bluestone 1988; Ousey 2000).

Thrasher's ([1927] 1963) seminal research on Chicago gangs in the 1920s only sparingly addressed employment circumstances in the local labor market, but the extent of out-migration in the neighborhoods studied by Thrasher is consistent with the position that immigrants benefited from increased employment opportunities. Thrasher's study mostly focused on second-generation immigrant youth of Polish, Italian, or Irish descent who resided in 'interstitial' areas located between the city's industrial core and more stable residential neighborhoods. Thrasher described these interstitial areas as disorganized slums that experienced high rates of poverty, physical decay, and residential mobility. These areas were also adversely affected by unemployment, low wages, and 'monotony in occupational activities' (37). While these structural conditions now serve as explanations for the greater presence of adult gang members, Thrasher indicated that it was uncommon for a gang to survive beyond the 'embryonic' phase in interstitial areas, making gang membership a largely 'adolescent phenomenon' (36). Some gangs persisted, however, and became 'conventionalized' (e.g., athletic clubs) or criminal gangs with adult members.

Explaining why most gangs ended rather quickly, while considerably fewer gangs endured, was not a central focus of Thrasher's research, which was more concerned with gang formation, but Thrasher did offer some discussion on the longevity of gangs. Thrasher noted that an intense pattern of in- and out-migration, or 'immigrant succession,' meant that many immigrant families in interstitial areas eventually moved to nearby neighborhoods that were more stable and lacked a gang presence (Thrasher [1927] 1963), suggesting that these families economically advanced and, in the process, severed any gang ties maintained by younger family members who followed. Therefore, the immigrant youth studied by Thrasher may not have benefited from the availability of work directly, but there is a clear suggestion that many of their parents did benefit by moving to more economically advantaged neighborhoods (Moore 1998).

Miller's ([1966] 2011) gang research in Boston during the early 1950s also focused in part on immigrant (primarily Irish) youth. Relative to Thrasher, however, Miller discussed more extensively the work and labor conditions experienced by gang youth in his study. In particular, many of the gang youth studied by Miller, although not all, struggled academically, generally considered school boring and useless, and consequently were only qualified for low-skilled, typically manual, jobs. Miller indicated that such work was available, but periods of unemployment were still prevalent among gang youth. Miller ([1966] 2011, 518) described these periods as a form of 'voluntary unemployment' because gang members elected not to work despite the relative demand for low-skilled labor. When gang youth were employed, many worked for a short time and moved from job to job. Miller ([1966] 2011, 519) characterized this employment behavior as a 'pattern of sporadic work.' Long-term employment was generally avoided because it made regular gang involvement difficult, and it was often not pursued by gang youth until they married or entered a serious relationship. The degree to which a youth's work history adhered to this episodic pattern was generally conditioned by the social status of the gang. Lower class or status gangs were typically more disapproving of members working than were gangs with higher status members (Miller [1966] 2011, 527). Nonetheless, Miller's discussion of work suggests that most gang youth in his study were never far removed from the labor force and the possibility of semi-stable employment, further suggesting that the availability of work provided an accessible pathway for youth in his study to weaken or sever ties to the gang (although see Whyte 1981).

Miller's ([1966] 2011) description of the role of work in the lives of Boston gang youth in the 1950s departs from more recent commentary on gang members' involvement (or lack thereof) in legal work. For instance, Miller's ([1966] 2011) research clearly suggests the first rung of the job ladder was repeatedly grabbed by gang-involved youth, but Hagedorn (1988) and Moore's (1991) research suggests that reaching the lowest rung of the employment ladder has grown more difficult for current or former gang members since Miller's study. Moore's (1991) research focused on the evolution (1940s–50s to 1960s–70s) of select Chicano gangs in East Los Angeles, whereas Hagedorn (1988) focused on black gangs in Milwaukee during the 1980s. Despite differences in the location, timing, and gang racial/ethnic composition of these studies, both scholars attributed adult gang involvement to a process of 'deindustrialization' (in Milwaukee) or 'economic restructuring' (in Los Angeles) that further distanced gang and low-skilled youth, in general, from the workforce (see also Hagedorn 1998; Moore 1998; Padilla 1992). This process created a 'structural' form of unemployment (e.g., jobs moved to periphery or suburban areas not easily accessible without a vehicle) that made it even more difficult for gang-involved youth 'to find the kind of work that would encourage them to cut loose their adolescent ties' (Moore 1991, 23). Decker and Van Winkle (1996, 220) spoke of similar circumstances in St. Louis, finding that only 17 of 99 active gang members they interviewed were employed at the time of their study.

The availability of work may be of greater importance for 'post-industrial' gang-involved youth, such as those members studied by Hagedorn (1988) because Thrasher ([1927] 1963) and Miller ([1966] 2011) both indicated that among youth who remained active gang members into or near adulthood, their ties to the gang were often severed, or considerably weakened, after they married. As Thrasher ([1927] 1963, 36) put it, 'marriage is one of the most potent causes for the disintegration of the older [gang] groups.' Miller ([1966] 2011, 627) indicated in similar terms that 'it was necessary for the boys to seek out external levers to help them break away from the gang,' and 'marriage was one such lever.' Whyte's

(1981) research on Italian 'corner boys' during the late 1930s suggests that marriage did not always disrupt gang involvement among immigrant youth, but it did take at least some time away from the gang given 'the married man regularly sets aside one evening a week to take out his wife' (255). More recently, of course, marriage is a 'lever' sparingly pulled by young persons in general (see Cohn et al. 2014), giving strong reason to assume that it is no longer a 'potent cause' for older youth to leave the gang. The declining role of marriage in the lives of young persons may mean that the availability of work is more relevant for understanding prolonged or adult membership among post-industrial youth.

Quality of work
Arguments surrounding economic restructuring and its effects on the growth and age profile of gangs also call attention to the quality of work, not just job availability, in urban labor markets (Shelden, Tracy, and Brown 2013). Average wages among the local workforce are often used as proxy for employment quality and therefore most conceptual arguments on work quality address wages. For instance, both economists and criminologists have taken an interest in the relationship between wages and crime more generally (e.g., Allan and Steffensmeier 1989; Fagan and Freeman 1999). From the perspective of economists, 'the chance to earn higher wages raises the "opportunity costs" of not working' (Bernstein and Houston 2000, 3). The basic argument is that higher wages make legal work more attractive and, in turn, make behaviors that threaten these better earnings (e.g., crime or drug use) more costly to consider or commit. Criminologists contend that higher wages strengthen the 'bond' to conventional society by intensifying the level of social control that the labor market exercises over employed persons (Crutchfield and Wadsworth 2013; Lee and Slack 2008).

These arguments have been increasingly raised as the wages of lower skilled workers have declined in the US. As Blackburn, Bloom, and Freeman (1990, 31) indicated, 'from 1900 through the 1960s the real earnings of less skilled American workers grew substantially.' In the 1970s and 1980s, however, the wages of these workers began to stagnate and decline (Bushway 2011). In fact, for male workers at the 20th percentile of the wage distribution, their earnings fell 'from almost $12 per hour in 1973 to $10 per hour in 2009' (Kalleberg 2011, 106; see also Autor 2010). This downward trend in wages is often attributed to the 'dual' or 'segmented' nature of the post-industrial labor market that financially rewards highly skilled workers but offers limited economic opportunity for low-skilled workers (Crutchfield 1989, 2014).

Hagedorn (1988, 2002) and Moore (1991, 1998) indicated that economic restructuring or deindustrialization had an adverse effect on the wages of low-skilled youth in Milwaukee and East Los Angeles. Hagedorn (1988, 42) noted the development of a labor market in Milwaukee that increasingly restricted black workers, more generally, to low-wage jobs. Hagedorn (1988, 44) argued that at least one consequence of this segmented job and wage trend was 'the structural narrowing of the opportunity to mature out of delinquent and deviant ways of life.' Moore (1991, 22) described a similar pattern among Chicanos in East Los Angeles, where 'good jobs had largely vanished' and were 'replaced by jobs that had low wages' and 'no future.' She further argued that such jobs offered little incentive for youth in Chicano gangs to 'cut loose their adolescent ties' (Moore 1991, 23). Hagedorn and Moore's observations from Milwaukee and East Los Angeles suggest that, in addition to the availability of work, the quality of work may also have an effect on the age profile of gangs.

Nature of work
The broader literature also provides some suggestion that, independent of the availability and quality of work, the type or nature of accessible work may affect the presence of adult gang members in core urban communities. Wilson (1996) has argued that recent changes in the US labor market have particularly affected young minority males, a demographic that is at greater risk for gang involvement (Freng and Taylor 2013; NGC, n.d.). Wilson (1996, 143) specifically noted that employers now 'have a greater need for workers who can effectively serve and relate to the consumer [a soft skill]. Inner-city black men are not perceived as having these qualities.' Consequently, employers in search of low-skilled workers who generally interact with the public are less willing to employ minority males (see also Moss and Tilly 2001; Pager, Bonikowski, and Western 2009).

Apart from such discriminatory practices on the part of employers, there is also some indication that the nature of low-skilled work in the service-driven economy is unattractive to youth, such as current gang members, who especially value an image of toughness and who command respect (e.g., Anderson 1999; Bourgois 1995). Because many low-skilled jobs, such as employment at a fast food or retail chain, are more visible to the public than are jobs in manufacturing, production, or construction, persons employed in these service-related occupations are more likely to encounter family, peers, or neighbors in the workplace. Such encounters may undermine a youth's image or reputation because low-skilled jobs in service, retail, and food occupations, sometimes referred to unfavorably in the past as 'McJobs' (Newman 1999), do not personify an image of toughness or respectability (Bourgois 1989; Crutchfield 2014).

There are undoubtedly features of *any* legal work, whether it is a job in manufacturing or retail, that do not suit most gang-involved youth (e.g., working structured hours or respecting authority figures; Decker and Van Winkle [1996]; Short and Strodtbeck [1965]). The argument raised here is that the greater concentration of jobs in service-related occupations makes legal work even less attractive to gang-involved youth because such employment is generally more visible, viewed less as 'man's' work, and thus more socially degrading than employment in other occupations such as manufacturing. Couple these features with an employer resistance to hire minority male youth for jobs requiring customer interaction (Wilson 1996), and it suggests that adult gang membership may be more prevalent in communities where service-related occupations make up a larger share of the local labor market.

Empirical research

A growing body of 'macro-level' research has addressed the effects of social and economic factors on gang-related behaviors or outcomes across neighborhoods and cities. These studies often combine work availability measures (e.g., unemployment) with indicators of economic (e.g., household poverty) and social (e.g., female-headed households) disadvantage to assess the joint (SES) effect of these variables on neighborhood or city levels of gang membership or violence (e.g., Mares 2010; Pyrooz 2012a; see Decker, Melde, and Pyrooz 2013 for a review). However, some macro-level studies have examined the unique or separate effects of workforce dynamics on gang-related outcomes, including Jackson's (1991) assessment of the type of work (i.e., employment in manufacturing and retail/wholesaled trade) on the presence of gangs among large US cities. Another example includes Howell and Griffiths' (2016) examination of the bivariate relationship between work availability measures (i.e., unemployment and labor force participation) and a stable gang presence among US cities as well (see 158).

Macro-level studies have not explicitly addressed whether labor market factors are related to the age composition of gangs or the presence of adult members at the neighborhood or city level. The closest examples include a multilevel study that assessed the effect of county-level unemployment on gang participation among adolescents and young adults, and a single-level study that examined the relationship between parental job and educational status and the age of active gang members. The latter study was conducted by Lasley (1992), who assessed the relationship between socioeconomic status (SES) and the age of black and white gang members ($N = 435$) located in Los Angeles and Orange counties. SES was a standardized scale that captured the education level and occupational prestige of a gang member's parent(s), a measure that was strongly correlated with household incomes or wages in a youth's census tract (440). Lasley found no relationship between this parental or individual measure of SES and the general ages of gang members in his sample, leading him to conclude that 'adult gang membership is as statistically rare in neighborhoods where opportunities are few as it is in neighborhoods where opportunities are many' (445). Although Lasley referred to adult membership as statistically rare, he still found that 35% of the 'low' SES gang members and 29% of the 'middle/upper' SES gang members in his sample were aged 18 or older (see 444).

Seals (2009) completed a multilevel study that examined the relationship between the rate of unemployment in a youth's county of residence and self-reported gang membership with data from the National Longitudinal Survey of Youth 1997 (NLSY97). He found that the likelihood of a youth reporting gang involvement increased as the level of unemployment went up in a county, specifically for youth nearing (aged 16 to 17) and in adulthood (aged 18 or older) and not for youth aged 15 or younger (see Table 4, 420). From these findings, Seals (2009, 419) concluded that gang members are sensitive to economic incentives in the labor market, for his findings suggested that older adolescents and young adults (or those youth 'most eligible for legitimate employment') were less receptive to gang involvement when legal work was more accessible.

Current study

The theoretical position that conditions in the local labor market contribute the rate of adult gang membership is tested in the current study with data from large US cities ($N = 133$). This research expands on prior macro-level studies and the works of Lasley (1992) and Seals (2009) by accounting for *multiple* indicators of labor market conditions (i.e., availability, quality, and nature of work), rather than testing a combined measure of disadvantage or only a single workforce measure such as unemployment. As discussed above, the theoretical arguments raised by gang scholars such as Hagedorn (1988) and Moore (1991) address multiple dimensions of the labor market. This research also adds to the literature by focusing on gang membership in adulthood. In general, adult gang membership has not been a central focus of empirical gang research, even though national data from police and youth suggest that a sizeable share of active gang members are of adult age and that serious violence is especially pronounced among young-adult members.

Three general hypotheses are tested in this study. These hypotheses concern the anticipated effects of the availability, quality, and nature of legal work on the rate of adult gang membership.

Availability hypothesis: Cities where a greater share of residents are unemployed and not in the labor force will have higher rates of adult gang membership.

Quality hypothesis: Cities where a greater share of employed residents are working full-time and earn better wages will have lower rates of adult gang membership.

Nature hypothesis: Cities where a greater share of employed residents are working in service occupations or the retail industry will have higher rates of adult gang membership.

Methods

Data

Multiple data sources were used in this research, including data (2002 and 2004–2006) from the National Youth Gang Survey (NYGS). Since 1996, the NYGS has been administered annually to a nationally representative sample of law enforcement agencies by the National Youth Gang Center and, more recently, by the National Gang Center (n.d.). The NYGS gathers information from police personnel on such factors as the number and demographic characteristics of gang members in a jurisdiction. NYGS data are increasingly used in empirical gang studies (e.g., Jensen and Thibodeaux 2012), and these data have demonstrated strong measurement properties, especially for larger jurisdictions. For instance, Decker and Pyrooz (2010) found that for the 100 largest cities in the US, NYGS data on reported gang homicides from 2002 to 2006 met accepted standards of validity and reliability, leading them to conclude that criminologists can use the NYGS data with confidence. Katz et al. (2012) also assessed the reliability of NYGS data from a similar time period (2005 to 2009), but they focused on the number of reported gangs and gang members along with the number of gang homicides. In addition, Katz et al. examined the reliability of these measures among jurisdictions as small as 25,000 persons to those in excess of 200,000 persons. Similar to Decker and Pyrooz (2010), Katz et al. (2012, 121) concluded that 'NYGS data on the number of gangs, gang members, and gang homicides…are generally reliable enough to be used by policymakers and academics alike.' NYGS data were supplemented here with demographic and socioeconomic data from the 2000 census, as well violent crime data from the 2000 Uniform Crime Report, and police agency data from the 2000 Law Enforcement Management and Administrative Services survey.

The current sample is composed of 133 US cities that had a population of 150,000 or more persons based on the 2000 census. The smallest city in the sample (Tallahassee, FL) had slightly more than 150,000 residents, and the largest city in the sample (New York, NY) had a population of more than 8 million residents. These cities were identified after an initial examination of NYGS data (2002 and 2004–2006) from jurisdictions of 100,000 or more persons in 2000. Prior studies with NYGS data have generally involved cities of more than 200,000 persons, including Pyrooz's (2012a) aforementioned analysis of gang homicides in the 88 largest US cities, as well as Pyrooz, Fox, and Decker's (2010) assessment of the number of gang members in the 100 most populous US cities. An initial effort was made to determine if smaller US cities with a population of less than 200,000 had more missing data on the NYGS adult membership variables than US cities with a population exceeding 200,000. The level of missing data on these variables, which were used to generate the dependent variable, was not all that different for larger and smaller cities (see Katz et al. 2012), although missing data were more prevalent as a city's population neared 100,000, which were the least populous cities initially considered for inclusion in the current study. In general, it was more common for smaller cities to have multiple years of missing data on the NYGS adult membership variables. Smaller cities also expectedly reported fewer gang members. From 2002 to 2006, a sizeable percentage (33% to 50%) of cities with a population of 100,000–150,000 reported fewer than 100 gang members, whereas larger cities overwhelmingly reported more than 100 gang members. For these reasons, greater missing data and fewer reported gang members, smaller cities of less than 150,000 were excluded from the study.[1]

Variables

Dependent

NYGS data were used to construct the dependent variable, which is the average *rate of adult gang members* per 10,000 population over four years (2002 and 2004–2006) in a city. In the NYGS, police agencies were asked to indicate the number of active gang members in their jurisdiction, and these agencies were also asked to indicate how many (or the percentage) of these active members were of a certain age (e.g., under 15, 15–17), providing the opportunity to identify active gang members who were adults (i.e., 18 or older). Data from 2002 onward were used in the calculation of the adult gang member rate because the NYGS underwent a sample redesign after the 2001 survey (see NGC, n.d.). In addition, 2003 data were not available because information on gang member age was not collected that year on the NYGS, so the averaged adult rate was calculated using four years of data (2002 and 2004–2006). Similar to Pyrooz (2012a) and Pyrooz, Fox, and Decker (2010), an averaged rate was used to account for variation in reported (adult) gang members from year to year.

Missing data on the adult gang member variables were addressed before calculating this averaged rate for each city. The use of four years of NYGS adult membership data meant there were 532 city-year observations (133 cities × 4 years) among cities in the current study, and roughly 48% of these city-year observations were missing data. However, 70% of the cities (*n* = 94) had at least two years of adult membership data. Missing data on the yearly (e.g., 2002) rate of adult membership variables were first imputed (procedure discussed in greater detail below) and then averaged to create the dependent variable. Prior to imputation, however, a constant of one was added to each annual rate variable and then a natural log transformation was performed.[2] This log transformation was beneficial for three reasons. First, compared to imputing the untransformed (original metric) adult membership variables, the imputation of the transformed variables produced fewer values that were substantially out-of-range (e.g., especially large rates). Second, the imputation of transformed variables improved model convergence during the imputation procedure. Third, the multiple regression analysis of a transformed dependent variable produced greater normality in the residual errors. After imputation, the average inter-item correlation among the logged adult membership variables was 0.58, with a Chronbach's alpha reliability score of 0.84.[3]

Independent

Data from the 2000 census were used to create seven measures that collectively address the availability, quality, and nature of legal work in the local labor market. Two of these measures capture the availability of work. *Unemployment* is the percentage of civilians aged 16 or older who were unemployed. The second measure, *not in labor force (NILF)*, captures the percentage of civilians aged 16 or older who were not employed and who were not seeking a job. This measure includes persons who have become frustrated with their job search and have given up on locating employment. As Allan and Steffensmeier (1989, 109) indicated, 'the official measure of unemployment does not actually tap joblessness per se, but job-seeking.'

Two variables account for the quality of work in the local labor market. *Full-time work* measures the percentage of employed persons aged 16 or older who typically worked 35 or more hours for at least 50 weeks in 1999. The second measure of work quality, *wages*, indicates the percentage of full-time workers aged 16 or older who earned at least $25,000 in 1999. This value was a categorical cut-off for individual income in the 2000 census, and this value was 150% of the federal poverty line for a family of four ($16,700) in 1999.[4] These measures closely parallel the work quality measures used by Lee and Slack (2008) to examine the relationship between labor market conditions and violent crime in metro and non-metro counties.

The final set of labor market variables account for the nature of work. These measures capture the percentage of workers employed in certain sectors of the economy. *Manufacturing* represents the percentage of civilians aged 16 or older employed in manufacturing. *Service* measures the percentage of persons employed in the service industries of art, entertainment, recreation, accommodation, and food services. The last labor market variable is *retail*, which captures the percentage of persons employed in retail.

Control

A number of control variables were also accounted for in this research. Four of these measures include socioeconomic status, racial and ethnic composition, and residential mobility. *Socioeconomic (SE) disadvantage* is a standardized factor score that was generated from four items: the percentage of households headed by females with children, the percentage of households receiving public assistance, the percentage of persons without a high school diploma or GED, and the percentage of persons living below the poverty line. Racial/ethnic *heterogeneity* is a variable that ranges from 0 to 1, with scores closer to one indicating a city has greater racial/ethnic diversity. This measure was generated from seven racial/ethnic categories: white, black, Hispanic, Asian, Pacific Islander, Native American, and other.[5] A measure of *residential mobility* is also accounted for in the analyses, which is measured as the percentage of residents aged 5 or older who resided in a different house in 1995. Similar economic, racial, and mobility indicators have been used to explain variation in the presence of gangs or gang violence across cities (e.g., Pyrooz 2012a). These structural characteristics have been considered important for understanding gang formation and involvement since the work of Thrasher ([1927] 1963).

The *youth population* and *population density* were also measured. Youth population represents the percentage of persons aged 15 to 24. Research indicates that gang involvement typically occurs during adolescence or young adulthood (e.g., Pyrooz 2014), and research also indicates that gang-related activity and violence is spatially concentrated, especially at the boundaries that separate one gang's territory from another gang's territory (Brantingham et al. 2012). These spatial patterns, and gang formation and persistence more generally, may be shaped by urban dynamics such as population density, which is measured here as the number of persons per square mile.

Another control variable addresses the level of crime in a city. *Violent crime rate* represents the number of violent crimes per 100,000 population in 2000. One reason youth may join and remain gang involved is the threat of violence in the broader community (Felson 2006; Shelden, Tracy, and Brown

2013). While the evidence indicates that gang membership does not reduce the risk of victimization (Peterson, Taylor, and Esbensen 2004), gang membership may reduce the fear of victimization (Melde, Taylor, and Esbensen 2009). Therefore, there may be greater perceived utility in remaining gang involved in higher crime communities.

The final two control variables serve as indicators of the level of gang establishment in a city. *Gang unit* is coded one if a local police agency indicated it had a gang unit in the 2000 Law Enforcement Management and Administrative Services (LEMAS) survey and coded zero otherwise. *Year of gang problem* is a continuous variable that indicates the approximate year that the most recent gang problem in a jurisdiction originated. This question was asked on the NYGS, and values in the current sample range from 1920 to 2005. Jurisdictions that report a gang unit or an earlier onset of gang problems may have more established gangs that give rise to adult membership. More established gang cities presumably had more time for members to age in the gang relative to cities with less established or more recently 'emergent' gang problems. In addition, the gang unit measure may account for 'any potential bias associated with the reporting techniques' of police agencies with or without a specialized gang unit (Pyrooz, Fox, and Decker 2010, 877).

Analytic strategy

This research first examines the distribution (i.e., means and standard deviations) of the independent and control variables by rate of adult membership (i.e., low-, mid-, and high-rate cities; Table 1). This initial analysis involves (bivariate) tests of association between each labor market and control variable and the rate of adult membership. The next set of analyses regresses the adult membership rate on the labor market and control variables (Table 2). In general, these multiple regression analyses assess model performance after the introduction of the labor market variables. Separate regression models are estimated for the availability, quality, and nature of work measures.

These descriptive and multiple regression analyses are performed on imputed data. All missing data were imputed using the *mi impute chained* command in Stata, a sequential regression approach to filling in missing data (see Enders 2010). In total, 50 imputed (complete) data-sets ($m = 50$) were generated using this approach. The sizable number of imputations generated here was driven by the extent of missing data on the adult membership variables. As mentioned, 48% of the city-year observations in the current data were missing information on adult membership. Graham, Olchowski, and Gilreath (2007) recommend at least 40 imputations given this rate of missing data. The missing data were imputed using the labor market and control variables described above, as well as 'auxiliary' variables (or variables used *only* for imputation) from the NYGS, specifically the number of reported gangs (2002–2006) and the overall rate (2002–2006) of gang membership for a city. These auxiliary variables from the NYGS had less missing data than the adult membership measures.

Results

Descriptive statistics

Table 1 displays descriptive statistics for all cities ($N = 133$), as well as for cities grouped by their rate of adult membership: lower one-third (low-rate city), middle one-third (mid-rate city), or upper one-third (high-rate city) of the adult rate distribution. The average rate of membership among all cities was roughly 29 adult gang members per 10,000 population, with a standard deviation of 41. The size of the standard deviation is a reflection of a small number of cities (e.g., Phoenix and Chicago) reporting much higher rates (>100) of adult membership than the overall average, resulting a right-skewed distribution. As mentioned, a natural log transformation of this variable was performed before conducting any statistical tests. This transformation improved the distributional form of the adult membership variable and improved model performance in the regression analyses. The same transformation was performed on the population density and crime rate variables. These variables also had a small number of cities with especially large values that produced a skewed distribution.

Table 1. Descriptive statistics for all cities and for cities by rate (low, mid, and high) of adult membership.

	All cities		Low-rate cities		Mid-rate cities		High-rate cities		Bivariate test	
	N=133		N=45		N=44		N=44		N=133	
Variable	Mean	SD	Mean	SD	Mean	SD	Mean	SD	r/d	p
Adult gang member rate[a]	28.97	41.45	4.75	2.14	15.29	4.28	67.43	53.9	–	–
Unemployed	4.51	1.32	4.37	1.44	4.59	1.20	4.57	1.30	0.062	0.456
Not in labor force	35.63	5.20	34.56	6.18	36.17	5.17	36.17	3.90	0.106	0.160
Full-time work	56.31	4.55	57.64	4.74	55.62	3.71	55.64	4.88	−0.131	0.132
Wages	64.14	8.19	64.58	9.98	63.75	7.73	64.08	6.56	−0.037	0.626
Service	16.49	2.90	15.92	3.17	16.84	2.66	16.73	2.80	0.123	0.151
Manufacturing	11.47	5.02	11.38	5.23	11.16	4.29	11.87	5.53	0.009	0.929
Retail	11.42	1.34	11.59	1.44	11.33	1.38	11.34	1.18	−0.085	0.370
SE disadvantage	0.000	0.974	−0.194	1.03	0.163	1.01	0.036	0.83	0.078	0.334
Heterogeneity	0.505	0.125	0.471	0.123	0.505	0.143	0.541	0.098	0.181	0.009
Youth population	22.54	2.90	22.21	3.71	22.91	2.62	22.51	2.12	0.012	0.891
Population density[a]	4399.3	3683.8	4011.6	3240.7	4343.8	3631.0	4851.3	4119.7	0.143	0.143
Residential mobility	48.30	5.95	48.77	6.05	47.73	6.17	48.40	5.66	−0.014	0.879
Violent crime rate[a]	915.5	506.1	814.2	532.5	1005.5	470.1	929.19	501.0	0.047	0.521
Gang unit	0.768	–	0.678	–	0.792	–	0.837	–	0.572	0.002
Year of gang problem	1983.1	12.54	1985.3	11.21	1983.6	14.28	1980.3	11.57	−0.154	0.131

Note: Imputed data (m = 50); means and standard deviations (SD) are displayed in original metric; bivariate tests (r = Pearson's r and d = Cohen's d) performed on all cities (N = 133).
[a]Natural log transformation of variable used in bivariate statistical (r) test.

The means for the labor market variables in Table 1 reveal that, on average, 4.5% of persons aged 16 or older were unemployed and roughly one in three persons (35%) were not in the labor force.[6] Most employed persons were working full-time (56%) and earned more than $25,000 annually for this full-time work (64%). In addition, roughly 16% of workers on average had a service occupation, and roughly the same percentage (11%) of workers were employed in the manufacturing and retail industries. The size of the standard deviations for the labor market variables indicates there is much less variability in these measures than in the rate of adult gang membership. Therefore, labor market conditions may indeed contribute to the rate of adult membership, but the greater variation in adult membership clearly suggests that other factors play a role.

Table 1 also displays descriptive statistics for cities grouped by their rate of adult membership. For instance, cities with a low rate of adult membership (or cities in the bottom one-third of the adult rate distribution) had an average unemployment rate of 4.4%, whereas cities with a comparatively high rate of adult membership (or cities in the top one-third of the adult rate distribution) had an average unemployment rate of 4.6%. In general, there are some labor market differences between low-, mid-, and high-rate cities, more so for low-rate cities, but these distributional differences, such as with unemployment, are quite modest.

Results from statistical tests of association between each of the labor market and control variables and the rate of adult membership are also indicated in Table 1. These bivariate tests were performed after the adult rate, population density, and violent crime variables were log-transformed, for these modified variables were used in the multiple regression analyses. The bivariate tests, equivalent to a Pearson's r for the continuous independent variables (e.g., unemployment) and a Cohen's d for the gang unit (bivariate) variable, confirm a generally null to slight relationship between labor market conditions and the rate of adult gang membership.[7] Using 0.1 as a minimum threshold, which Cohen

(1988) described as a 'small' effect for a Pearson's r, three labor market variables in Table 1 have Pearson values that exceed this benchmark: NILF (+0.106), full-time work (−0.131), and service occupations (+0.123). These effects or relationships are in the theoretically expected direction. Among the control variables, racial/ethnic heterogeneity, population density, gang unit, and year of gang onset each have at least a 'small' effect (r or d) on the rate of adult membership. The effects for these latter two variables suggest that cities with a more prolonged history of gang problems and cities with a specialized gang unit, perhaps established as a response to a lengthier gang problem, generally reported higher rates of adult membership.

Regression models

The next set of analyses was completed in two general stages. In the first stage, a *base model* was estimated that regressed the rate of adult membership on *just* the control variables. Each control variable was used in the estimation of the base model, for Bushway, Sweeten, and Wilson (2006, 9) consider it 'bad practice' to exclude 'control variables because of a lack of statistical significance.' In the second stage, labor market variables were added to the base model, but this was done separately for the availability, quality, and nature of work measures, resulting in the estimation of three labor market models.

The results from these regression models are presented in Table 2. Some data and modeling issues need to be mentioned before these results are discussed. First, the regression findings in Table 2 were generated once again from imputed data ($m = 50$), and the dependent variable (adult rate) was log-transformed beforehand. Second, the descriptive findings in Table 1 suggested that some variables may share a nonlinear relationship with adult membership (e.g., violent crime and full-time work). Among these variables, further analyses (not shown) indicated a nonlinear relationship between disadvantage and the rate of adult membership in particular, a relationship that is accounted for by the inclusion of a squared disadvantage variable in the regression models. Third, each of the regression models estimated in Table 2 include all of the control variables, but the coefficients for these control measures are only displayed for the 'base model,' which excludes any labor market variables (e.g., unemployment). Multicollinearity was present in the current data given the strong correlations between disadvantage and the measures of work availability ($r > 0.80$) and between disadvantage and the measures of work quality ($r > 0.60$). In general, the effects of the labor market variables on adult membership were *not* affected by these strong collinear relationships, but the effect of disadvantage on adult membership was affected (e.g., change in coefficient sign). Aside from disadvantage, however, the effects of the remaining control variables on adult membership were stable (i.e., magnitude and direction) across the various regression models.[8] Therefore, the displayed coefficients for the control variables in Table 2 provide an accurate assessment of the effect of disadvantage on adult membership absent any issues with multicollearity, and these 'base' findings also provide an accurate assessment of the effects of the other control variables on adult membership across each of the labor market regression models.

Turning to the findings in Table 2, the estimates from the *base model*, which excludes any labor market variables, indicate that heterogeneity and gang unit have sizeable effects on the rate of adult membership. The coefficient for heterogeneity ($b = 0.870$), however, represents the improbable case of moving from no to complete heterogeneity (from 0 to 1 or a one unit increase). The effect for gang unit indicates that the predicted rate of adult membership is 54% higher $[(\exp(0.434) - 1) \times 100]$ for cities with a gang unit. In addition, the estimates for disadvantage indicate a curvilinear relationship, with disadvantage initially associated with a greater rate of adult membership ($b = 0.217$), but this relationship turns negative ($b = -0.161$) among the most disadvantaged cities (see Pyrooz 2012a). In general, these estimates are not 'significant' based on conventional p-value cut-offs (e.g., $p < 0.05$), but Bushway, Sweeten, and Wilson (2006) caution researchers not to claim an insignificant relationship when the confidence interval of an estimate includes a particularly 'meaningful effect.'

Table 2 also includes results from models that regress adult membership on the control and labor market variables. As mentioned, these models were estimated separately for measures of work availability, quality, and type. In addition, for the work availability model, unemployment and NILF were not

Table 2. Imputed models that regress adult membership rate (ln) on control and labor market variables (N = 133).

Model	b	SE	p	95% CI	β
Base model					
Youth population	−0.017	0.045	0.698	[−0.108, 0.073]	−0.044
SE disadvantage	0.216	0.160	0.179	[−0.101, 0.534]	0.182
SE disadvantage²	−0.161	0.088	0.074	[−0.338, 0.016]	−0.187
Heterogeneity	0.870	0.762	0.257	[−0.642, 0.383]	0.094
Residential mobility	0.020	0.024	0.405	[−0.028, 0.068]	0.105
Population density (ln)	0.139	0.176	0.433	[−0.213, 0.491]	0.089
Violent crime rate (ln)	0.204	0.241	0.399	[−0.274, 0.682]	0.095
Gang unit	0.434	0.272	0.115	[−0.108, 0.977]	0.158
Year of gang problem	−0.013	0.009	0.160	[−0.032, 0.005]	−0.146
R^2	0.181				
Base model + availability					
Not in labor force	0.046	0.039	0.242	[−0.031, 0.125]	0.209
R^2	0.191				
ΔR^2 from base model	0.010				
Base model + quality					
Full-time work	−0.058	0.035	0.103	[−0.128, 0.011]	−0.229
Wages	−0.021	0.020	0.296	[−0.060, 0.018]	−0.148
R^2	0.207				
ΔR^2 from base model	0.026				
Base model + nature					
Manufacturing	0.017	0.024	0.458	[−0.029, 0.065]	0.078
Retail	−0.002	0.098	0.978	[−0.197, 0.192]	−0.003
Service	0.074	0.051	0.150	[−0.027, 0.176]	0.187
R^2	0.203				
ΔR^2 from base model	0.022				

Notes: Imputed data (m = 50); N = 133 cities; standard error (SE) represents robust or Huber/White estimators; beta represents standardized regression coefficients; and (ln) indicates a natural log-transformed variable. The values indicated in the p column provide the exact significance of the estimates, although none are significant at the conventional threshold of .05.

modeled together due to the strong correlation between these two variables (r = 0.64), which resulted in unstable estimates for these variables when modeled jointly. Supplemental analyses (not shown) revealed that the estimates for NILF were more stable and robust. Therefore, the *work availability* model only estimated and displays the regression coefficient for NILF. This estimate (b = 0.046) indicates that a one unit (1%) increase in NILF is associated with roughly a 5% increase [(exp(0.046) − 1) × 100] in the expected rate of adult membership. The labor market estimates from the *work quality* model are comparable, for a unit (1%) increase in persons working full-time (b = −0.058) and earning at least $25,000 annually (b = −0.021) is associated with roughly a 6 and 2% decline in the rate of adult membership. The only *nature of work* variable that has an effect on adult membership of a similar magnitude is service work. More specifically, cities where a greater percentage of workers are employed in service occupations have a higher expected rate of adult membership.

Overall, the labor market findings in Table 2 are generally consistent with the directional hypotheses, although there are exceptions (e.g., manufacturing), but these estimates are not significant at traditional p-value cut-offs, even though some of the effects sizes are nontrivial. Nonetheless, the change in R^2 (ΔR^2) values in Table 2 suggests that the addition of labor market variables only marginally improves model fit, and the absence of especially 'significant' labor market coefficients (p < 0.05) may be attributable to a lack of precision in the model estimates (i.e., size of standard errors), suggesting that a 'resampling' (e.g., analyzing different years or cities) may generate disparate findings.

Supplemental regression models

To explore this possibility, supplemental analyses were performed to reassess the stability of the regression estimates displayed in Table 2. To be included in the supplemental analyses, a city had to have at least two years of observed adult membership data and no missing data on the remaining variables.

These criteria reduced the number of cities included in the analyses from 133 to 91. As with the initial analyses using imputed data, the rate of adult membership was log-transformed prior to estimation, and separate models were generated for the control and labor market variables.

The results from these *listwise* analyses are displayed in Table 3. In general, relative to the imputed data, the base (control variable) model fits the listwise data better due to the continued effects of gang unit and year of gang problem onset. In addition, the rate of violent crime ($b = 0.437$) proves more relevant in the listwise data, whereas the effect of heterogeneity on the rate of adult membership is substantially reduced. As for the labor market variables, the effects of the availability and quality of work measures were mitigated in the listwise analyses. The effects of the nature of work variables were also affected in the listwide model, for employment in the retail industry increases in magnitude and is negative ($b = -0.178$) and the effect of service employment is mitigated. Finally, as with the imputed data, the addition of the labor market variables only marginally improved model fit.

Table 3. Supplemental listwise models that regress adult membership rate (ln) on control and labor market variables ($N = 91$).

Model	b	SE	p	95% CI	β
Base model					
Youth population	−0.009	0.047	0.838	[−0.104, 0.085]	−0.026
SE disadvantage	0.306	0.159	0.058	[−0.011, 0.625]	0.254
SE disadvantage^2	−0.151	0.071	0.038	[−0.294, −0.008]	−0.162
Heterogeneity	0.127	0.762	0.868	[−1.38, 1.64]	0.014
Residential mobility	0.008	0.027	0.743	[−0.045, 0.063]	0.046
Population density (ln)	−0.078	0.195	0.691	[−0.468, 0.311]	−0.047
Violent crime rate (ln)	0.437	0.279	0.122	[−0.119, 0.993]	0.206
Gang unit	0.498	0.311	0.114	[−0.121, 1.11]	0.175
Year of gang problem	−0.019	0.011	0.106	[−0.042, 0.004]	−0.213
R^2	0.239				
Base model + availability					
Not in labor force	0.033	0.040	0.415	[−0.047, 0.113]	0.155
R^2	0.245				
ΔR^2 from base model	0.006				
Base model + quality					
Full-time work	−0.035	0.037	0.339	[−0.109, 0.038]	−0.150
Wages	−0.010	0.021	0.646	[−0.053, 0.033]	−0.074
R^2	0.248				
ΔR^2 from base model	0.009				
Base model + nature					
Manufacturing	0.018	0.023	0.454	[−0.029, 0.065]	0.079
Retail	−0.178	0.113	0.121	[−0.405, 0.048]	−0.189
Service	0.048	0.053	0.374	[−0.058, 0.155]	0.124
R^2	0.275				
ΔR^2 from base model	0.036				

Notes: Listwise data; $N = 91$ cities; standard error (SE) represents robust or Huber/White estimators; beta represents standardized regression coefficients; and (ln) indicates a natural log-transformed variable. The values indicated in the *p* column provide the exact significance of the estimates, although none are significant at the conventional threshold of .05.

Discussion

This research tested whether the availability, quality, and nature of work were related to the rate of adult gang membership among large US cities. Adult membership has not been a vibrant area of study in the gang literature. This inattention is surprising given that gang scholars generally agree that adult membership has grown more common in US cities since the 1970s, a position supported in part by the sizeable share of gang members considered of adult age by police personnel. In addition, evidence suggests that adult membership can negatively affect communities by making gang activity more structured (Decker, Katz, and Webb 2008), by increasing the lethality of interpersonal conflicts due to a greater tendency to possess firearms (Spergel 1995; Watkins and Moule 2014), and by serving as problematic role models for younger youth (Hagedorn 1988). Each of these adverse dynamics offers a compelling reason to better understand the drivers of adult membership (Jankowski 1991). In the literature, a leading explanation for the presence of adult gang members centers on circumstances in the local labor market, an explanation that has received little empirical testing.

The current findings generally indicated that:

- The proposed (inverse) effects of work availability and quality on the rate of adult membership were consistent with theoretical expectations, whereas the effects of the nature of work were not always consistent with the proposed hypotheses.
- The effects of the labor market variables on adult membership were modest and, for some of the variables (e.g., employment in retail), not altogether insensitive or robust to the modeling strategy employed.
- The effects of certain control variables, such as disadvantage and violent crime, suggest that other factors may be more relevant than labor market circumstances in understanding the rate of adult membership in a community, especially measures that account for how entrenched gang membership may be in a community (e.g., length of gang problem and establishment of a specialized gang unit).

The remaining discussion will mainly focus on the labor market findings, and the implications of these findings, and suggestions for future research. Regarding the *availability of work*, namely labor force participation, the current findings were consistent with the theoretical prediction that less labor force participation would be associated with a higher rate of adult membership, but the magnitude of this work availability effect was mitigated in the supplemental (listwise) analyses, suggesting that the relationship was not especially robust. However, isolating the separate effect of work availability on adult membership was a challenge given unemployment and labor force participation were strongly correlated with each other and with the measure of disadvantage. Of course, this empirical overlap is why researchers typically combine these measures into a multi-item index of economic disadvantage, even though the presence of work is conceptually distinct from poverty or deprivation (Wilson 1996). When modeled separately, though, the findings here provide some additional reason to take notice of the recent drop in labor force participation in the US, declining from an historical high of 67% in 2000 to 63% in 2014 (Aaronson et al. 2014).

The current findings also provide some validation of the utility of accounting for more than simply the availability of work in the labor market. Measures of the quality and nature of work proved no less relevant in explaining the rate of adult membership. In the case of *work quality*, full-time employment and better wages were, as hypothesized, associated with a lower rate of adult membership, but the effect of these measures was mitigated in supplemental analyses and thus was not especially robust. Nonetheless, the quality of work findings offers some support for the position that better quality work, particularly in the form of full-time employment, generally strengthens the bond to the labor market and increases the opportunity costs of gang involvement.

The final set of labor market findings dealt with the *nature of work*. In general, the findings concerning such dynamics provided evidence both supportive and not supportive of the initial hypotheses. There was no evidence that cities where more workers were employed in manufacturing, an industry that is presumably more open and attractive to current or former gang members, had a lower rate of adult membership. A primary reason for this anticipated effect is the traditional belief that manufacturing pays entry-level workers, in particular, better than other industries (see Huff 1993; Spergel 1990). However, wages in US manufacturing have generally stagnated (in inflation-adjusted dollars) the last two decades, and new hires in the industry often make very modest incomes (Ruckelshaus and Leberstein 2014), suggesting that relative to employment in other industries or occupations, employment in manufacturing may not offer the same economic benefits it once did for workers. In addition, Cherlin (2014, 164) noted that a potential benefit of a general movement away from 'disciplined, industrial wage labor [is it] may have fortuitously freed men from the emotional constraints of conventional masculinity,' perhaps forcing men to become more skillful communicators in the workplace and, by extension, in the home.

These wage and communication arguments, along with the current findings, suggest that even if work in manufacturing could be substantially increased on a broad scale, it is doubtful that such change would generate in a sizeable reduction in the rate of adult gang membership.

Another nature-of-work hypothesis that was not supported here was the expectation that retail work would be associated with an increased rate of adult membership. The listwise results provided evidence to the contrary, finding that greater retail work was linked to a lower rate of adult membership. Further analysis revealed that retail work was inversely related to socioeconomic disadvantage ($r = -0.32$) and positively related to full-time work ($r = +0.21$), suggesting that cities with a greater retail presence were more economically vibrant in 2000, although employment in the retail industry was associated with lower wages for full-time workers ($r = -0.21$).

This retail finding should be considered with the results for service occupations, which indicated that cities where a larger share of workers were employed in service occupations had a higher rate of adult membership, although as with other labor market variables, this effect was not significant at common *p*-value cut-offs. Nonetheless, the effect for service occupations indicated that a 2% increase in this type of work (e.g., from 8% to 10%) was associated with roughly a 10% increase [(exp(0.048 × 2) − 1 × 100] in the predicated rate of adult membership in the listwise analyses. These conflicting results for the retail and service measures offer a cautionary note on lumping together industries or occupations that, in general, may be considered 'service-related' work. Perhaps work in retail is not viewed as negatively as, say, work in food service (e.g., 'McJobs'), or perhaps employer discriminatory practices are less prevalent in the retail industry. Unfortunately, this research is unable to address these possibilities, but, once more, the current findings suggest that work of a similar nature may have divergent effects.

Collectively, these findings speak to the broader context that gives rise to adult gang involvement. Hagedorn (1988) considers the regular presence of adult members in a community as an indicator that gangs are 'institutionalized,' a circumstance that likely makes it even more difficult to effectively reduce gang activity in a community. The arguments of Hagedorn (1988) and others (e.g., Moore 1998) clearly suggest that undoing this institutionalized state requires the development of external 'levers' or 'pulls' that are not exclusive to the criminal justice system or entirely suppression-based (e.g., incarceration). Some responses to gang activity are 'comprehensive' initiatives that include 'opportunities provision,' such as job training and placement, which seek to pull youth from gang involvement (see Curry, Decker, and Pyrooz 2014; Howell and Griffiths 2016). These comprehensive initiatives generally target youth in neighborhoods especially affected by gang violence, or undertaken on a smaller geographic scale than the city-level focus of this research. However, the current findings may offer some insight on challenges that such neighborhood-based initiatives may face if employment services, in particular, are considered an integral component. For instance, cities where full-time work is less plentiful and work opportunities are more concentrated in service occupations may need to make a greater investment (increase the dosage) in employment services compared to cities where full-time work is more accessible and work is less often service-related. In other words, it is perhaps likely that employment services for gang-involved youth will prove ineffective if careful consideration is not given to the broader labor market dynamics in a city.

These findings and implications should be considered with certain weaknesses in mind. First, the adult membership variable was generated with NYGS data from the police. As Pyrooz, Fox, and Decker (2010, 875, footnote 4) indicated, 'it would be difficult for any study to undertake a macro-level study of gangs/gang membership without the extensive assistance of law enforcement.' However, a concern with data from the police is that these data may overestimate the extent of adult gang involvement if the 'gang databases' maintained by law enforcement are not regularly cleared of inactive members (see Barrows and Huff 2009). Therefore, future research should consider alternative sources of information on adult membership that substitute for or complement police data. In addition, Decker, Melde, and Pyrooz (2013, 393) indicated that macro-level gang research is 'overwhelmingly cross-sectional,' and this study was no different in this regard. While the independent and control variables were measured before adult membership in time, a more optimal or rigorous test of the proposed hypotheses would use panel data to assess whether *change* in the availability, quality, or nature of work is associated with *change* in the rate of adult gang membership. Ideally, change in these labor market factors would be assessed for less-educated residents (e.g., those with a high school diploma/GED or less) in particular, for gang-involved youth are often behind academically (Pyrooz 2012b).

Another weakness of this study that should be considered deals with possible omitted variable bias. Most theoretical discussion on the labor market and gang involvement also mentions opportunities for illicit work or earnings (e.g., drugs or stolen property; see Hagedorn 1988; Fagan and Freeman 1999). Such earning opportunities may be more abundant or lucrative in some communities. For instance, a recent study on the underground sex market in eight U.S cities found that this market was much more lucrative in some cities compared to others (Dank et al. 2014). The effects of legal work on gang involvement may be less salient or mitigated by the strength of illicit markets for earning money in a community. Measuring the strength of such markets is difficult, but accounting for illegal means of generating income may provide a better understanding of the relationship between legal work and adult gang involvement.

This research nonetheless added to the literature by empirically testing whether the availability, quality, and nature of work were related to the rate of adult membership in large US cities. Labor market dynamics have long been considered important in understanding prolonged or adult membership, yet these macro-level factors have seldom been the central focus of empirical gang research. The current findings suggest a need for gang scholars to conceptually rethink how certain industries or occupations likely affect adult gang involvement, especially manufacturing, for greater work in this industry was unrelated to the rate of adult membership, even though this industry in the past has been considered an important pathway for formerly gang-involved youth to enter the workforce. In addition, the current findings also suggest that the quality and nature of work are no less important than the availability of work for understanding adult gang involvement. Work availability has been the only feature of the labor market regularly accounted for in prior gang research, often included in a disadvantage index, but the evidence here suggests that work availability may insufficiently capture the full influence of the labor market on gang involvement. Finally, the findings here suggest that factors not specific to the labor market, such as the rate of violent crime and duration of the gang problem in a city, are important for understanding the rate of adult membership. Such dynamics are often not considered as causes of prolonged or adult gang membership in the literature, something future research should address, along with some of the weaknesses mentioned above concerning this research.

Notes

1. After imputation, the average inter-item correlation among the annual adult gang member variables was also examined for cities of more than 200,000 persons in 2000 ($N = 88$). This correlation (0.59) is only slightly better than the average correlation (0.58) among cities of more than 150,000 persons ($N = 133$), indicating that the inclusion of smaller jurisdictions had no marked effect on the reliability of the outcome variable.
2. Police personnel in some jurisdictions reported that only a small percentage of gang members were adult age, resulting in an adult membership rate of less than one ($n < 10$ cities in any given year) per 10,000 population. The addition of a constant allowed these less-than-one values to be transformed.
3. As Katz et al. (2012, 116, footnote 6) indicated in their assessment of the reliability of NYGS data, 'attaching labels or categorizing correlation coefficients is to be avoided,' although they make reference to a correlation threshold of 0.61 or higher as 'substantial' (116, endnote 6). The average inter-item correlation here (0.58) nears this threshold, and the reliability coefficient (0.84) exceeds the generally accepted cut-off (0.70) for internal consistency (Nunnally 1978).
4. An annual salary of $25,000 in 1999 would equate to an annual salary of roughly $35,000 in 2016.
5. Each racial/ethnic category was initially measured as a proportion. These proportions were squared, then summed, and finally subtracted from one to generate a heterogeneity score for each city. The same measure was used by Pyrooz, Fox, and Decker (2010) in their city-level analysis of gang homicide, although they accounted for more racial or ethnic groups (see also Pyrooz 2012a).
6. The Stata command *misum* was used to generate the descriptive statistics (i.e., means and standard deviations) in Table 1. This command combined the summary statistics across multiply imputed data-sets ($m = 50$) using 'Rubin's rules' (see Rubin 1987).

7. In Table 1, the bivariate relationship between the continuous independent variables and the rate of adult membership was examined by first standardizing these variables for each imputed data-set ($m = 50$) and then regressing the standardized score of adult membership on each standardized score of the labor market and control variables. The generated bivariate regression coefficients (b) are equivalent to a Pearson's correlation coefficient (r) that has been combined across imputed data-sets using Rubin's combination rules.
8. A number of additional models were estimated that excluded disadvantage and its squared term from the regression analyses. These findings indicated that the effects of the labor market variables (e.g., not in labor force) on adult membership were comparable across models that excluded and included the disadvantage variables. As Allison (1999, 149) indicated, 'multicollinearity does not violate any assumptions of the standard regression model,' but its presence is a problem when it affects the performance of the main explanatory variables of interest. In the current data, multicollinearity only affected the performance of the measure of disadvantage.

Disclosure statement

No potential conflict of interest was reported by the author.

References

Aaronson, S., T. Cajner, B. Fallick, F. Galbis-Reig, C. Smith, and W. Wascher. 2014. *Labor Force Participation: Recent Developments and Future Prospects*. Finance and Economics Discussion Series, Divisions of Research & Statistics and Monetary Affairs. 2014-64. Washington, DC: Federal Reserve Board. https://www.federalreserve.gov/pubs/feds/2014/201464/201464pap.pdf.

Allan, E. A., and D. J. Steffensmeier. 1989. "Youth, Underemployment, and Property Crime: Differential Effects of Job Availability and Job Quality on Juvenile and Young Adult Arrest Rates." *American Sociological Review* 54 (1): 107–123.

Allison, P. D. 1999. *Multiple Regression: A Primer*. Thousand Oaks, CA: Pine Forge Press.

Anderson, E. 1999. *Code of the Street: Decency, Violence, and the Moral Life of the Inner City*. New York: W.W. Norton & Company.

Autor, D. 2010. *The Polarization of Job Opportunities in the U.S. Labor Market: Implications for Employment and Earnings*. Washington, DC: Center for American Progress.

Barrows, J., and C. Ronald Huff. 2009. "Gangs and Public Policy: Constructing and Deconstructing Gang Databases." *Criminology and Public Policy* 8 (4): 675–703. doi:10.1111/j.1745-9133.2009.00585.x.

Bernstein, J., and E. Houston. 2000. *Crime and Work: What We Learn from the Low-wage Labor Market*. Washington, DC: Economic Policy Institute.

Blackburn, M. L., D. E. Bloom, and R. B. Freeman. 1990. "The Declining Economic Position of Less Skilled American Men." In *A Future of Lousy Jobs? The Changing Structure of U.S. Wages*, edited by G. Burtless, 31–67. Washington, DC: The Brookings Institute.

Bluestone, B. 1988. "Deindustrialization and Unemployment in America." *The Review of Black Political Economy* 17 (2): 29–44.

Bourgois, P. 1989. "In Search of Heratio Alger: Culture and Ideology in the Crack Economy." *Contemporary Drug Problems* 16 (4): 619–649.

Bourgois, P. 1995. *In Search of Respect: Selling Crack in El Barrio*. New York: Cambridge University Press.

Brantingham, P. J., G. E. Tita, M. B. Short, and S. E. Reid. 2012. "The Ecology of Gang Territorial Boundaries." *Criminology* 50 (3): 851–885. doi:10.1111/j.1745-9125.2012.00281.x.

Bushway, S. D. 2011. "Labor Markets and Crime." In *Crime and Public Policy*, edited by J. Q. Wilson and J. Petersilia, 183–209. New York: Oxford University Press.

Bushway, S. D., G. Sweeten, and D. B. Wilson. 2006. "Size Matters: Standard Errors in the Application of Null Hypothesis Significance Testing in Criminology and Criminal Justice." *Journal of Experimental Criminology* 2 (1): 1–22.

Cherlin, A. J. 2014. *Labor's Love Lost: The Rise and Fall of the Working-class Family in America*. New York: Russell Sage Foundation.

Cohen, J. 1988. *Statistical Power Analysis for the Behavioral Sciences*. 2nd ed. Hillsdale, NJ: Lawrence Erlbaum Associates.

Cohn, D., J. S. Passel, W. Wang, and G. Livingston. 2014. *Barely Half of U.S. Adults Are Married—A Record Low*. Washington, DC: Pew Research Center. http://www.pewsocialtrends.org/2011/12/14/barely-half-of-u-s-adults-are-married-a-record-low/.

Crutchfield, R. D. 1989. "Labor Stratification and Violent Crime." *Social Forces* 68 (2): 489–512. doi:10.1093/sf/68.2.489.

Crutchfield, R. D. 2014. *Get a Job: Labor Markets, Economic Opportunity, and Crime*. New York: New York University Press.

Crutchfield, R. D., and T. Wadsworth. 2013. "Aggravated Inequality: Neighborhood Economics, Schools, and Juvenile Delinquency." In *Economics and Youth Violence: Crime, Disadvantage, and Community*, edited by R. Rosenfeld, M. Edberg, X. Fang, and C. S. Florence, 152–180. New York: New York University Press.

Curry, G. D., S. H. Decker, and D. C. Pyrooz. 2014. *Confronting Gangs: Crime and Community*. 3rd ed. New York: Oxford University Press.

Dank, M., B. Khan, P. M. Downey, C. Kotonias, D. Mayer, C. Owens, and L. Yu. 2014. *Estimating the Size and Structure of the Underground Commercial Sex Economy in Eight Major U.S. Cities*. Washington, DC: Urban Institute.

Decker, S. H., C. M. Katz, and V. J. Webb. 2008. "Understanding the Black Box of Gang Organization: Implications for Involvement in Violent Crime, Drug Sales, and Violent Victimization." *Crime & Delinquency* 54 (1): 153–172. doi:10.1177/0011128706296664.

Decker, S. H., C. Melde, and D. C. Pyrooz. 2013. "What Do We Know about Gangs and Gang Members and Where Do We Go from Here?" *Justice Quarterly* 30 (3): 369–402. doi:10.1080/07418825.2012.732101.

Decker, S. H., and D. C. Pyrooz. 2010. "On the Validity and Reliability of Gang Homicide: A Comparison of Disparate Sources." *Homicide Studies* 14 (4): 359–376. doi:10.1177/1088767910385400.

Decker, S. H., and B. Van Winkle. 1996. *Life in the Gang: Family, Friends, and Violence*. New York: Cambridge University Press.

Enders, C. K. 2010. *Applied Missing Data Analysis*. New York: Guilford Press.

Fagan, J., and R. B. Freeman. 1999. "Crime and Work." *Crime and Justice* 25: 225–290.

Felson, M. 2006. *Crime and Nature*. Thousand Oaks, CA: Sage.

Freng, A., and T. J. Taylor. 2013. "Race and Ethnicity: What Are Their Roles in Gang Membership?" In *Changing Course: Preventing Gang Membership*, edited by T. R. Simon, N. M. Ritter, and R. R. Mahendra, 135–169. Washington, DC: National Institute of Justice.

Graham, J. W., A. E. Olchowski, and T. D. Gilreath. 2007. "How Many Imputations Are Really Needed? Some Practical Clarifications of Multiple Imputation Theory." *Prevention Science* 8: 206–213. doi:10.1007/s11121-007-0070-9.

Hagedorn, J. M. 1988. *People and Folks: Gangs, Crime and the Underclass in a Rustbelt City*. Chicago, IL: Lake View Press.

Hagedorn, J. M. 1998. "Gang Violence in the Postindustrial Era." *Crime and Justice* 24: 365–419.

Hagedorn, J. M. 2002. "Gangs and the Informal Economy." In *Gangs in America III*, edited by C. R. Huff, 101–120. Thousand Oaks, CA: Sage.

Howell, J. C. 2007. "Menacing or Mimicking? Realities of Youth Gangs." *Juvenile and Family Court Journal* 58 (2): 39–50. doi:10.1111/j.1755-6988.2007.tb00137.x.

Howell, J. C., and E. Griffiths. 2016. *Gangs in America's Coummunities*. 2nd ed. Thousand Oaks, CA: Sage.

Huff, C. R. 1993. "Gangs and Public Policy: Macrolevel Interventions." In *The Gang Intervention Handbook*, edited by A. P. Goldstein and C. R. Huff, 463–475. Champaign, IL: Research Press.

Jackson, P. I. 1991. "Crime, Youth Gangs, and Urban Transition: The Social Dislocations of Postindustrial Economic Development." *Justice Quarterly* 8 (3): 379–397.

Jankowski, M. S. 1991. *Islands in the Street: Gangs and American Urban Society*. Berkeley: University of California Press.

Jensen, G. F., and J. Thibodeaux. 2012. "The Gang Problem: Fabricated Panics or Real Temporal Patterns?" *Homicide Studies* 17 (3): 275–290. doi:10.1177/1088767912460664.

Kalleberg, A. L. 2011. *Good Jobs, Bad Jobs: The Rise of Polarized and Precarious Employment Systems in the United States, 1970s to 2000s*. New York: Russell Sage Foundation.

Katz, C. M., A. M. Fox, C. L. Britt, and P. Stevenson. 2012. "Understanding Police Gang Data at the Aggregate Level: An Examination of the Reliability of National Youth Gang Survey Data." *Justice Research and Policy* 14 (2): 103–128.

Lasley, J. S. 1992. "Age, Social Context, and Street Gang Membership: Are 'Youth' Gangs Becoming 'Adult' Gangs?" *Youth & Society* 23 (4): 434–451. doi:10.1177/0044118X92023004003.

Lee, M. R., and T. Slack. 2008. *Labor Market Conditions and Violent Crime across the Metro–Nonmetro Divide* 37 (3): 753–768. doi:10.1016/j.ssresearch.2007.09.001.

Mares, D. 2010. "Social Disorganization and Gang Homicides in Chicago: A Neighborhood Level Comparison of Disaggregated Homicides." *Youth Violence and Juvenile Justice* 8 (1): 38–57.

Maxson, C. 2011. "Street Gangs." In *Crime and Public Policy*, edited by J. Q. Wilson and J. Petersilia, 158–182. New York: Oxford University Press.

Maxson, C. L., M. A. Gordon, and M. W. Klein. 1985. "Differences Between Gang and Nongang Homicides." *Criminology* 23 (2): 209–222. doi:10.1111/j.1745-9125.1985.tb00334.x.

Melde, C., T. J. Taylor, and F.-A. Esbensen. 2009. "'I got your back': An Examination of the Protective Function of Gang Membership in Adolescence." *Criminology* 47 (2): 565–594. doi:10.1111/j.1745-9125.2009.00148.x.

Miller, W. B. [1966] 2011. *City Gangs*. Phoenix, AZ: Arizona State University.

Moore, J. W. 1991. *Going down to the Barrio: Homeboys and Homegirls in Change*. Philadelphia, PA: Temple University Press.

Moore, J. W. 1998. "Understanding Youth Street Gangs: Economic Restructuring and the Urban Underclass." In *Cross-cultural Perspectives on Youth and Violence*, edited by M. W. Watts, 65–78. Stamford, CT: Jail.

Moss, P., and C. Tilly. 2001. *Stories Employers Tell: Race, Skill, and Hiring in America*. New York: Russell Sage Foundation.

NGC (National Gang Center). n.d. *National Youth Gang Survey Analysis*. http://www.nationalgangcenter.gov/Survey-Analysis.

Newman, K. S. 1999. *No Shame in My Game: The Working Poor in the Inner*. New York: Russell Sage Foundation.

Nunnally, C. 1978. *Psychometric Theory*. New York: McGraw-Hill.

Ousey, G. C. 2000. "Deindustrialization, Female-headed Families, and Black and White Juvenile Homicide Rates, 1970–1990." *Sociological Inquiry* 70 (4): 391–419. doi:10.1111/j.1475-682X.2000.tb00917.x.

Padilla, F. M. 1992. *The Gang as an American Enterprise*. New Brunswick, NJ: Rutgers University Press.

Pager, D., B. Bonikowski, and B. Western. 2009. "Discrimination in a Low-wage Labor Market." *American Sociological Review* 74 (5): 777–799. doi:10.1177/000312240907400505.

Peterson, D., T. J. Taylor, and F.-A. Esbensen. 2004. "Gang Membership and Violent Victimization." *Justice Quarterly* 21 (4): 793–815.

Pyrooz, D. C. 2012a. "Structural Covariates of Gang Homicide in Large U.S. Cities." *Journal of Research in Crime and Delinquency* 49 (4): 489–518. doi:10.1177/0022427811415535.

Pyrooz, D. C. 2012b. *The Non-criminal Consequences of Gang Membership: Impacts on Education and Employment in the Life-course (Doctoral Dissertation)*. Tempe: Arizona State University.

Pyrooz, D. C. 2014. "'From Your First Cigarette to Your Last Dyin' Day': The Patterning of Gang Membership in the Life-course." *Journal of Quantitative Criminology* 30 (2): 349–372. doi:10.1007/s10940-013-9206-1.

Pyrooz, D. C., A. M. Fox, and S. H. Decker. 2010. "Racial and Ethnic Heterogeneity, Economic Disadvantage, and Gangs: A Macro-level Study of Gang Membership in Urban America." *Justice Quarterly* 27 (6): 867–892. doi:10.1080/07418820903473264.

Rubin, D. B. 1987. *Multiple Imputation for Nonresponse in Surveys*. New York: Wiley.

Ruckelshaus, C., and S. Leberstein. 2014. *Manufacturing Low Pay: Declining Wages in the Jobs That Built America's Middle Class*. New York: National Employment Law Project.

Seals, A. 2009. "Are Gangs a Substitute for Legitimate Employment? Investigating the Impact of Labor Market Effects on Gang Affiliation." *Kyklos* 62 (3): 407–425.

Shelden, R. G., S. K. Tracy, and W. B. Brown. 2013. *Youth Gangs in American Society*. 4th ed. Belmont, CA: Wadsworth.

Sheley, J. F., J. Zhang, C. J. Brody, and J. D. Wright. 1995. "Gang Organization, Gang Criminal Activity, and Individual Gang Members' Criminal Behavior." *Social Science Quarterly* 76 (1): 53–68.

Short, J. F., and F. L. Strodtbeck. 1965. *Group Process and Gang Delinquency*. Chicago, IL: University of Chicago Press.

Spergel, I. A. 1990. "Youth Gangs: Continuity and Change." *Crime and Justice* 12: 171–275.

Spergel, I. A. 1995. *The Youth Gang Problem: A Community Approach*. New York: Oxford University Press.

Thrasher, F. M. [1927] 1963. *The Gang: A Study of 1,313 Gangs in Chicago* (Abridged). Chicago, IL: University of Chicago Press.

Vigil, J. D. 1988. *Barrio Gangs: Street Life and Identity in Southern California*. Austin: University of Texas Press.

Watkins, A. M., and R. K. Moule Jr. 2014. "Older, Wiser, and a Bit More Badass? Exploring Differences in Juvenile and Adult Gang Members' Gang-related Attitudes and Behaviors." *Youth Violence and Juvenile Justice* 12 (2): 121–136. doi:10.1177/1541204013485607.

Whyte, W. F. 1981. *Street Corner Society: The Social Structure of an Italian Slum*. 3rd ed. Chicago, IL: University of Chicago Press.

Wilson, W. J. 1996. *When Work Disappears: The World of the New Urban Poor*. New York: Vintage Books.

Index

Note: Page numbers followed by bold, italics and 'n' refers to table, figures and endnotes respectively.

ACE Study *see* Adverse Childhood Experiences (ACE) Study
Administration for Children and Families (ACF) 103
adult gang membership: analytic strategy 160; availability of work 153–5, 165, 167; control variable 159–60; data sources 157–8; dependent variable 158–9; descriptive statistics 160–2, **161**; independent variable 159; local labor market 157; macro-level research 156–7; nature of work 155–6, 165, 166; overview of 152–3; quality of work 155, 165; regression models 162–3, **163**; supplemental listwise models 163–4, **164**
Adverse Childhood Experiences (ACE) Study 145, 148n7
age-graded theory 94–5
Allan, E. A. 159
Alleyne, Emma 124
Allison, P. D. 168n8
anticipated guilt 57
antisocial socialization 43, 46
Auty, K. M. 12
availability hypothesis 157

B.A.M.© *see* Becoming a Man (B.A.M.©)
Bandura, A. 3, 54, 55, 64; *see also* social cognitive theory (SCT)
Barlow, Hugh D. 107
Becoming a Man (B.A.M.©) 105
Bellatty, Paul 4
Bjerk, D. 59
Blackburn, M. L. 155
Bloom, D. E. 155
Bouchard, M. 55, 56
Boyle, Greg 4
Braun, Margaret J. F. 4
Brief Strategic Family Therapy (BSFT) 146
Broader Urban Involvement and Leadership Development (BUILD) program 103

BUILD Violence Intervention Curriculum 103
Bushway, S. D. 162

Carson, Dena C. 97, 108n2
Cernkovich, S. A. 75, 79
CFA *see* confirmatory factor analysis (CFA)
CGPM *see* Comprehensive Gang Program Model (CGPM)
CGPM Steering Committee 147
Chesney-Lind, Meda 115
Chicago schools, African American youth in 67n2, 88n3
Child Protective Services (CPS) 14, 140, 141
Cohen, A. K. 55
Cohen, J. 161–2
Coid, J. W. 12
Comprehensive Anti-Gang Model 108n3
Comprehensive Gang Program Model (CGPM) 3, 146–7
confirmatory factor analysis (CFA) 37
Connect Survey 98–100
contemporary theories, of adolescent gang involvement 115–16
counseling intervention 104–5
CPS *see* Child Protective Services (CPS)
Crimesolutions.gov 104
criminal behavior: impact on 1; implications for 2; intergenerational transmission of 11; involvement in 10; justice interventions 93
Cullen, F. T. 1
Cure Violence model 103–5

Decker, S. H. 3, 97, 105, 107, 154, 158, 166
delinquent peer groups 3, 52–3, 64–5, 67n3
Densley, James A. 124
deterrence-based law enforcement programs 101–2
differential association theory 32
DiPietro, Stephanie 123
Dong, B. 11

INDEX

Dykes Taking Over (DTO) 122, 123
dynamic selection bias 59

Egley, A. 2, 4, 11, 93, 115, 137
Elder, G. H. 1
empathy, definition of 57
Esbensen, F. -A. 72, 76
Eurogang Program of Research 88n4
European immigrant groups 153

Farrington, D. P. 12
female-centric framework 114
females' gang involvement 4, 113; contemporary theories 115–16; multiracial feminism *see* multiracial feminist framework; violence against females 127n8
fixed-effects models 53, 59, 66, 67n7
focused deterrence strategies 101, 106
Fox, A. M. 158, 166
Freeman, R. B. 155
Functional Family Therapy 5

gang disengagement, pushes and pulls of: data sources 98–100; deterrence-based law enforcement programs 101–2; developmental framework 93–4; hospital-based and trauma-focused interventions 102; human agency and identity reformation 95; interventions 100; life course framework 93–5; motivations in 96; motives and factors in 97–8; overview of 92–3; programs and policies 102–5; pushes and pulls of 96–7, **99, 101**, 105–7
Gang Resistance Education and Training (G.R.E.A.T.) 3, 45, 56, 64, 76, 87, 88n5, 97, 98–100, 106, 135, 145–6, 148n8
Gilman, A. B. 135
Giordano, P. C. 25n1, 75, 79
Google Ideas study 98, 100
G.R.E.A.T. *see* Gang Resistance Education and Training (G.R.E.A.T.)
grounded theory approach 79

Hagedorn, J. M. 154, 155, 166
Hardyns, Wim 115
Harris, Mary G. 123
Hawkins, J. D. 135
hegemonic laws 118
Heimer, Karen 120, 123
Hennigan, Karen 124
Hill, K. G. 135
Hogg, Michael A. 124
Holm, A. 17
Homeboy Industries 4, 103
Horowitz, R. 8
hospital-based interventions 102, 106
Houston Independent School 11

Howell–Egley life-course gang model 138, 143, 147
Howell, J. C. 2, 4, 11, 93, 115, 137
Huff, C. R. 8
hybrid model 67n11

Integrated Client Services (ICS) 139
Interactional Model 3
interactional theory 8–10, 23, 25, 115
Intergenerational gang membership 5; analytic plan 15, *17*, 17–18; consequences of 10; control variables 15; data and methods 13; dependent variable 13–14; descriptive statistics **16**; father's gang participation 23–4; independent variable 14; interactional theory 11; life course and development theories 25; linking parent to child *12*; mediation analyses 19–22, **20–2**; naïve direct effects 18–19; overview of 7–8; parent–child dyads 25n6; parenting practices 10–11; potential mediators 14–15; proposed moderators 14; sample analysis 13; theoretical foundations for 9–10

Jackson, P. I. 156
JobCorps program 103
Johnson, Dominique 122
Jones, F. 4, 115, 137
juvenile justice system 134, 144

Kaplan, H. B. 11
Karlson, K. B. 17
Kennedy, David 102
KHB method 17
Kohler, U. 17
Krohn, M. D. 11; interactional theory 1

Lasley, J. S. 156
Laub, J. H. 71–3, 76, 94, 107
Lauritsen, Janet L. 105
Law Enforcement Management and Administrative Services (LEMAS) survey 160
life-course gang theory 3, 4, 93–5; cross-sectional studies 148n3; developmental model *136*, 136–8, 143–4; human service agencies and education 139; overview of 134–5; peer-related factors 143; prevention and early intervention programs 144–7; risk factors 135; sample analysis 139; variables, measures and analytical approach 139–41, **140**
LifeSkills Training program 145, 148n8
Little Village Project 4
Liu, X. 11
Local Public Safety Coordinating Council (LPSCC) 147
Logan, Laura 119
LPSCC *see* Local Public Safety Coordinating Council (LPSCC)

INDEX

McCarthy, Bill 116
McGloin, Jean Marie 123
Macmillan, Ross 116
Maniglio, Roberto 127n10
Matza, D. 78
Melde, C. 72, 76, 166
Mendoza-Denton, Norma 124
Miller, Jody. 121, 124
Miller, W. B. 153, 154
mixed-methods approach 3
Moore, J. W. 52, 120, 121, 154, 155
moral disengagement strategies 55
Moule, R. K. 97, 153
Mouzon, Dawne 120
MST *see* Multisystemic Therapy (MST)
multiple marginality theory 117
multiracial feminist framework 114–15, **117**; integrated developmental 116–17; interlocking inequalities and oppressions 117–18, 126–7; micro-level considerations 123–5; potential pathways *125*, 125–6, *126*; proximal spheres, intersectional experiences in 118–23; quantitative studies 128n13
Multisystemic Therapy (MST) 104, 105
Multnomah County Comprehensive Gang Assessment 147

National Fatherhood Initiative InsideOut Dad® program 103
National Longitudinal Survey of Youth 1997 (NLSY97) 152, 156
National Network of Hospital-based Violence Intervention Programs 102
National Youth Gang Survey (NYGS) 4, 152, 158, 160, 166, 167n3
nature hypothesis 157
negative binomial hybrid model 67n10
negative peer commitment 58
neutralization techniques, for violence 55
NILF *see* not in labor force (NILF)
NLSY97 *see* National Longitudinal Survey of Youth 1997 (NLSY97)
Nongang Delinquent Group 61
nonviolent delinquency frequency index 58
not in labor force (NILF) 159
Nurge, Dana 121
NYGS *see* National Youth Gang Survey (NYGS)

OCFS *see* Office of Child and Family Services (OCFS)
Odgers, Candice L. 116
Office of Child and Family Services (OCFS) 13, 14
Operation CeaseFire 101
Oregon Youth Authority (OYA) 4, 115, 134, 138, 139
orthodox criminology 127n4

Panfil, Vanessa R. 4
Pauwels, Lieven 115
Peterson, Dana 4
power-control theory 119
prosocial peers 58
Pyrooz, D. C. 3, 13, 97, 152, 158, 166

quality hypothesis 157

Raby, C. 4, 115, 137
RIGS *see* Rochester Intergenerational Study (RIGS)
Risk/Needs Assessment (RNA) 139
Robins, Summer J. 116
Rochester Intergenerational Study (RIGS) 2, 8, 11, 13, 23
Rochester Youth Development Study (RYDS) 2, 8, 11, 13, 23, 137
Roman, Caterina G. 3
Rosenfield, Sarah 120
Russell, Michael A. 116
RYDS *see* Rochester Youth Development Study (RYDS)

Sampson, R. J. 71–3, 76, 94, 107
Schaffner, Laurie 121, 124
school commitment 58
school mobility 73
school transitions 3; control variables 76–7; descriptive statistics **82**; effect of **82–4**; gang membership 77–8, 81, 85, 87; goals 85; guilt and anger identity 79; mixed-methods approach 76; multivariate analyses 81; negative peer commitment 79; normative and non-normative 78; operationalizing turning point **77**; overview of 71–2; parental monitoring 79; peer group size and delinquency 78; potential impact of 73–5, 86; prosocial peers 78; qualitative and quantitative analytic plan 79–80, 86; school commitment 78; turning point, for gang desistance 80–1; unstructured socializing 79; violence neutralization 78–9
Schroeder, R. D. 75, 79
SCT *see* social cognitive theory (SCT)
Seals, A. 156
Seattle Social Development Project (SSDP) 2, 35
self-centeredness 57–8
SEL programs *see* social, emotional, and learning (SEL) programs
SEM *see* structural equation modeling (SEM)
Shively, Michael 121
SNAP® program *see* Stop Now and Plan (SNAP®) program
social cognitive theory (SCT): analytic plan 59; dependent variable 57–8; fixed-effects analysis 61–3, **62, 63**; and gang membership 53–5, 59–61, **60**, *60*; gangs *vs.* delinquent peer groups 55–6; independent variable 57;

methods 56–7; overview of 52–3; time-varying control variables 58
social control theory 32; age-graded 102
social, emotional, and learning (SEL) programs 145
social learning theory 32
socioeconomic status (SES) 156
Spanovic, Marija 124
Spergel, I. A. 4
Spindler, A. 55, 56
SSDP *see* Seattle Social Development Project (SSDP)
Steffensmeier, D. J. 159
Stop Now and Plan (SNAP®) program 146
structural equation modeling (SEM) 37
supplemental listwise models 163–4, **164**
Sweeten, G. 162
Sykes, G. M. 78

therapeutic intervention 104–5
Thornberry, T. P. 9, 11; interactional theory 1
Thrasher, F. M. 153–4
time-stable characteristics 59
trauma-focused interventions 102
Trauma Response Team 102

uncertainty-identity theory 124
U.S. Department of Labor 103

Van Winkle, B. 154
Vecchio, J. Michael 97
Vigil, J. D. 8, 54, 74, 87, 117, 135
violent delinquency frequency index 58
violent neutralizations 58

Warr, M. 66
Watkins, A. M. 4, 153
Whyte, W. F. 154–5
Wilson, D. B. 162
Wilson, W. J. 155
Wood, Jane L. 124

YouthBuild program 103
youth gang membership: analytic procedures 37; factor intercorrelations 38, **39**, 40, **40**; first-order factor model 40–1, *41*; gender, ethnicity and socioeconomic status 36–7; limitations 46–7; missing data 38; overview of 30–1; potential model modifications 44–5; preventive-intervention efforts 45–6; risk and protective factors 31; sample analysis 35; second-order factor model 41–4, *42*, **43**; self-report measures 35; social development model 31–4, *33*, 36; structural models 37–8
Youth Justice (YJ) Model 146
youth's support system 148n5